TRI-AXIUM WRITINGS 1

TRI-AXIUM WRITINGS 1

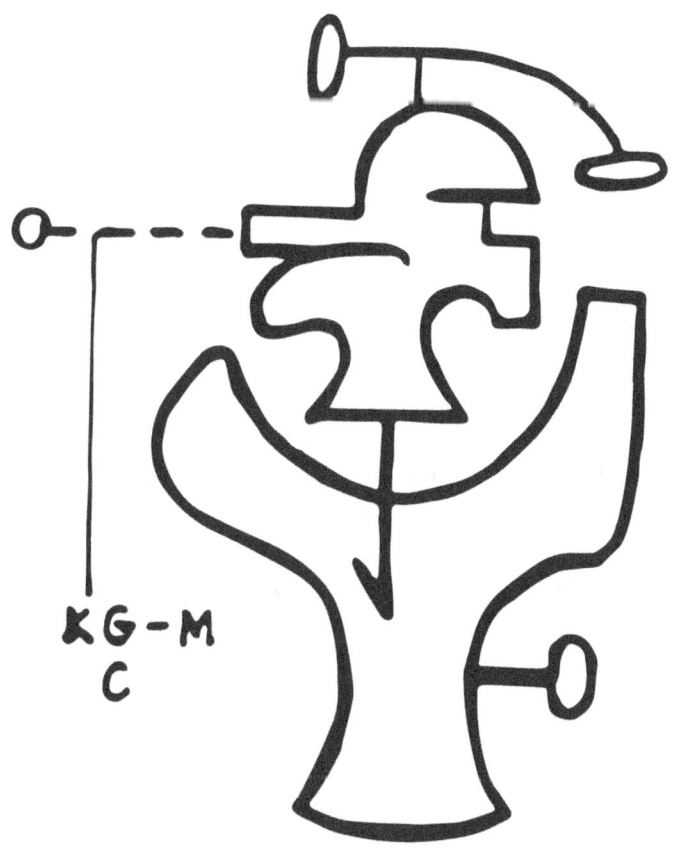

ANTHONY BRAXTON

TRI-AXIUM WRITINGS 1

1985 first edition: Synthesis Music

1985–2023 distributed by Frog Peak Music

2024 second edition: Frog Peak Music

Paperback ISBN 978-0-945996-23-1

FROG PEAK MUSIC
(a composers' collective)

Tri-Axium Writings 1

Contents

1	Preface & Acknowledgements (second edition)	
3	Introduction	
15	Glossary Integration	

chapter prefix

I. Underlying Philosophical Bases — UPB
    A. Level One
- 25 — 1. World Music — *WM*
- 59 — 2. Western Art Music — *WAM*
- 97 — 3. Trans-African Music — *T(AF)M*
- 139 — B. Level Two — *UPB (II)*
- 185 — C. Level Three: Questions & Answers — *UPB (III)*

II. Transition — *TR*
    A. Level One
- 203 — 1. Western Art Continuance — *WAC*
- 245 — 2. Creative Music From the Black Aesthetic — *CMBA*
- 285 — 3. The White Improvisor — *WI*
- 317 — 4. The Post-Cage Continuum — *PCC*
    B. Level Two (no Level Two)
- 347 — C. Level Three: Questions & Answers — *TR(III)*

III. Extended Functionalism — *EXT.F*
    A. Level One
- 367 — 1. The New York Movement — *NYM*
- 407 — 2. The Midwest (and West Coast) Continuum — *MID-W*
- 439 — B. Level Two — *EXT.F(II)*
- 471 — C. Level Three: Questions & Answers — *EXT.F (III)*

489   Glossary

PREFACE & ACKNOWLEDGEMENTS

The *Tri-Axium Writings* were approached as the beginning of a re-philosophic system that could map out fresh options and choices for the friendly experiencer on the tri-plane. This is not a system of thought that tells the individual what to think or do, but rather a set of choices that can be interpreted by a friendly experiencer based on one's individual experiences and individual value systems. This system is not a forming religion, but rather an attempt to create a model that is trans-idiomatic with flex options to suit the needs of the individual in real time. The word here is "agency."

I thank the creator of the universe that the Tri-Centric community has come into my life. What we have here is a movement of positive spirits who believe in the power of creativity and the wonder of radiant hope—and these artists are activists who are not simply waiting for public acknowledgment and/or faux celebrity status. The key word here is "action," with old-time serious groundwork and planning. The men and women of the Tri-Centric Foundation are foot soldiers for third millennial evolution and reconstruction—based on a love of composite humanity and world unification. I have no doubt that the good work of the Tri-Centric Foundation will inspire the creation of new artistic models all over the country and will continue the tradition of exposing our citizens to the challenge of composite creativity as a separate subject from marketplace focus and/or popular music—which I also love, but there's no lack of support for this community and we do not have to worry about its survival. Even so, let it be said that there is creativity all over: in America—from sea to shining sea—and in the world beyond. We have the people and the energy to evolve fresh visions to explore every focused discipline and strata.

I want to thank the Tri-Centric Foundation for the profound help this organization has given me—both in initiating the re-publication of

Tri-Axium Writings, and for the effort to literally save my creative work from the last sixty years and some. Because of their dedication I can now hope to have my music and writings documented safely into the future so that anyone interested in my effort can assess the material in the classic sense of research and discovery. In thanking my colleagues I am referring to Taylor Ho Bynum, James Fei, Kyoko Kitamura, Carl Testa, Zach Rowden, Jean Cook, Jonathan Piper, Jeanette Vuocolo, Rachael Bernsen, Tyler Rai, Chris Jonas, Chris McIntyre, and Andrew Raffo Dewar.

I would also like to thank Frog Peak Music (a composers' collective) for the support they have given me since the first publication of the Tri-Axium Writings in 1985. A special thank you to Jody Diamond and Larry Polansky for the great courage and dedication they have shown in the nearly forty years since Frog Peak Music began.

For this new edition, I am especially grateful to John McGhee for copyediting and proofreading all three books, to Carl Testa for making new schematics, and to Jody Diamond for designing both the print and digital versions. Proofreaders for Book One included Scott Campbell, Andrew Dewar, Michael Heller, Forrest Larson, and Carl Testa.

There is a difference between talk and action. All of these people can be viewed as real champions of global values and free expression—they are all artists in their own right and deserve more support as we move forward through the vibrational challenges of the recent time period.

We seem to be coming to a new era of vibrational realignment and sub-specialization. There is now a struggle to redefine reality and fantasy from a two-dimensional perspective that might not be in our best interest. More than ever, we need the input of the artist community to balance the spectrum of possibilities in a given political moment. This is a challenge that must be defended. Together, we have the creativity and the talent to succeed in every vibrational space.

Anthony Braxton
Hamden, Connecticut
2021

INTRODUCTION

WRITINGS ONE IS THE FIRST BOOK IN A SET OF THREE on creative music and its related information continuum. Hopefully, this series of books will be viewed as a positive contribution to the reality of information surrounding creativity. More than ever before, there is a need for alternative viewpoints on this most important subject, and unless efforts are made to restore a more practical—and positive—basis for viewing creativity in this time period, serious repercussions will await us in the near future. The release of this book is the end result of seven years of struggling—and involved more than four complete rewrites (and more on given sections). Needless to say, I am extremely grateful to have completed this project, and I hope that the thrust of this work will be viewed as worth the effort. I believe the future will see more musicians become involved in writing about creative music, for the present reality of this subject—and especially creative music from the black aesthetic—has never been more in disarray. We have now entered what can only be called a very serious period in the progressional continuum of world creativity, and the challenge of redefinitions can no longer only be left to the so-called experts. I have written this book—and this series of books—as a response to the present state of things, with the hope that my viewpoint will inspire other efforts—this is what is needed. The writings which have helped motivate my interest in this area have all come from people who were (and are) involved in the dynamics of creativity, and I feel the special insight that creative people must have—by virtue of their involvement with creativity—can be beneficial to restoring a more correct and just viewpoint about this most important subject. I believe if more people were exposed to the writings of creative people, many of the present distortions surrounding creative music would not have materialized. To read the works of thinking musicians like Rex Stewart, Harry Partch, and Leo Smith is to gain a viewpoint from people whose lives are not separate from what they wrote about. The inspiration I have received from their work gave me the strength to complete this project, and hopefully this work will serve as a positive source to others.

I originally began this series of writings in response to the reality of information surrounding creative music in the early seventies—especially the misinformation that characterized creative music writings in monthly periodicals and newspapers. It seemed to me at the time that the level of accurate commentary had gone from bad to worse, and it also seemed as if the smearing of post-Ayler creativity was more than a series of unrelated coincidences, but instead a co-ordinated attack. My first efforts on this book took place in Paris in September 1973, as a means to challenge what I felt to be deliberate misinformation about black creativity and black creative dynamics, and the thrust of this first effort would take over a year before completion. For if my original efforts had been directed towards combating the manipulation of post-Ayler creativity, by the end of 1974 the act of writing and researching had totally changed my own perspective of the music as well as the reality of information that supported my understanding of music. For the most basic assumption that dictated my early attempts to respond to creative music commentary was the mistaken belief that western journalists had some fundamental understanding of black creativity—or even western creativity—but this assumption was seriously in error. Rather, I now believe that the reality of African and trans-African continuance is being undermined by interpretations that seek to destroy both the dynamic implications of its information nature and the particulars of its affinity dictates. As such, the whole of my first draft had nothing to do with the real reality of western commentary, because the actualness of this phenomenon is much greater than the focus on a given argument—or opinion.

It is important to understand that the reality of a given interpretation cannot be outside of the affinity nature it purports to comment on. As such, one cannot comment on the reality specifics of non-western focuses without making serious adjustments in the vibrational nature of one's use of language, as well as the particulars underlying how a given conceptual focus is viewed. In actual fact, many of the distortions that have come to permeate black music journalism are directly related to the use of western inquiry terms that have no relevance to the reality nature of black creativity, or not in the way presently understood. Nor have I meant to imply that only black creativity has suffered from the misuse of western definitions, because the whole of world creativity has been profoundly misdocumented in this same manner. The challenge of erecting a positive basis for understanding creative music must necessarily involve a complete examination of every area of creative music—regardless of form or style. We must move to seek out a more human understanding of this subject that is free of petty accusations or racist doctrine, and the time to do it is now—not later. The act of writing this book has helped me to see how deeply I disagree with the present reality of commentary about creativity—and its related information continuum. Because the dynamic misinformation that has been generated in music commentary is not separate from what has transpired in the composite quilt of our society; that is, the misinformation presently attempting to solidify our relationship with creative invention also affects our composite relationship with fundamental information (or as this period of time would have it, "alternative fundamental information")—and this is what worries me.

By 1976—and after two more drafts—the essence of the book began to form, and I have attempted in this series of works to develop another approach for writing about creative music. That being: an approach that attempts to vibrationally and systematically view the whole of earth creativity and its related information continuums as a basis to resolidify a transformational viewpoint about this subject. Yet by no means does this book accomplish the whole of this challenge, nor have I meant to imply that my understanding of the universe is such that I have the necessary insight for such a task—because this is not what I mean. Instead the realness of this challenge will involve every sector of humanity. For to really attempt understanding of the reality of creativity is to transcend the particulars of a given focus, and instead reinvestigate the dynamics of composite earth information.

As such, the thrust of these writings is as concerned about the vibrational and philosophical implications of a given information focus (interpretation) as the particulars of its related music. Because the reality of creativity is not limited to only how a given phenomenon works but also involves the meta-reality context from which that phenomenon takes its laws. This is what concerns me, and this is what my writing is directed towards examining.

I believe the thrust of the eighties and nineties will see many more individual efforts of this sort—involving attempts to redefine every area of information and information dynamics. Nothing less than this will do—because the composite realness of present-day information is profoundly distorted—and I do not view this distortion as the result of a grand accident, but instead the end product of deliberate policies and intentions. The spectrum of this misinformation seems to encompass every area of dynamic focus—our understanding of science, music, spiritualism and functionalism. No area has been untouched—and if we are to ever shape the future then we must first correct the present: that is, we must first correct the reality of information that influences how we have come to either approach living, or approach understanding information about living. Certainly I have not meant to imply my writings will clarify all of these dynamic questions—because to imply such would be nonsense. But I do feel that the challenge of attempting to change a given state begins with the first step, and I also feel that the success of a given change indirectly relates to how many people are involved. In this series of books I have tried to the best of my ability to contribute a viewpoint that could be of relevance towards re-examining the realness of creativity. The dynamic implications of this book should hopefully stimulate the commentary scan of creative music if nothing else. This is my hope anyway. I have also deliberately not included scholastic-type footnotes in this series of books because (1) the thrust of this book is only an affirmation of what I have been learning and feeling—which is to say a snapshot of what I have been thinking from a period of September 1973 to March 1980, and (2) the thrust of this book is also conceived with respect to what I believe—which is to say I offer nothing in this book as definitively "true" (because for too long we have been deluged by so-called experts with interpretations that are presented as fact—but aren't—and this misuse of interpretation has moved to damage the whole of this time period). I have also tried in this series of books to refrain from attacking any individuals—even when I felt a given attack would clarify the nature of a particular viewpoint—because there can be no room for petty accusations if the basic focus of this book is concerned about what is really true (not to mention, the present state of things is not about any one or two given individuals).

Finally, it is important to state that none of the viewpoints written in this book are viewed as complete in any real sense. Instead I have made the decision to release this material because the completion of the entire project is dependent on what I am able to totally realize in my life—and hopefully I will have another ten, twenty, or thirty years (and some) on this planet to continue my learning, and work. After rewriting these sections for seven years, I felt this material was good enough to publish and, moreover, holding it any longer actually made no sense. But it is important to emphasize that all of these concepts are only one aspect of a much greater viewpoint—and this is really what is important. I believe the reality of commentary about creativity should give insight on more than just the surface specifics of the music but also its conceptual and philosophical implications—and this is what I have attempted in this series of writings. There are so many aspects of creative music that have been ignored in the last three hundred years that something must be done to review our present reality and vibrational position with composite information and composite information dynamics. Like most musicians, I have always thought the job of attempting to secure cultural awareness about creativity was the responsibility of so-called music journalism—and to some extent the music journalist has functioned as a positive generator for real understanding. But for the most part few, if any, of these functioning journalists have worked in the area of creative music or black creativity. As such, the thrust of journalism in the past fifty years has developed much dynamic information about western art music but very little on black creativity—or improvised music. I believe the present reality of black creativity is directly related to what information has not been developed—as opposed to what has—and this is indeed a tragedy for anyone concerned about world creativity. Rather than wait for a change of attitude by jazz journalists, I have instead made the decision to become involved in writing—and now I understand that this decision should have been made fifteen years ago. We can no longer wait for black music journalism to rise to the challenge of what it implies nor can we afford to wait on the so-called liberal white documentalists to straighten out the present state of things—for that matter, we can no longer hope for the emergence of black writers who are not afraid to speak out. We can no longer wait, because time is running out. The challenge is to solidify the correct and positive definitions that are needed now—in this time period. At present, the reality of creative music commentary has very little to do with supplying transformational viewpoints—let alone transformational solutions. As such—if you want something done—you must do it yourself. I offer this book—and this series of books—as an attempt to begin re-examining the composite reality of creative music. These writings are offered as only the beginning of what I hope will be a massive body of alternative literature on creative music.

Construction

Each of the books in this series of writings is constructed so as to insure maximum idea interchange. This has been done in accordance with my belief that given viewpoints must now be examined not only on more than one level or focus—but on as many levels as possible. Moreover, the thrust of this effort is conceived as a composite attempt to examine the whole of earth creativity—and as such, the reality of a given definition must necessarily "be presented in its broadest terms," because I am not concerned with only some aspect of what seems to be true—I am interested in what seems to be really true. Since the complexity of creative music commentary involves so many different areas of inquiry, I believe the challenge of transformational journalism is to find creative ways to interpret information. It is because of this belief that I have solidified this approach to my writings. For the great thrust of creative music writings in this time period is in extremely uncreative attempts at journalism, and this is especially interesting when one considers the position jazz critics have put themselves in—that being attempting to evaluate the worth of other people's creativity. As such, the basic construction of these books contains several approaches for both reading and interconnecting concepts. I have tried to construct a systematic approach that gives the greatest focus reference possible, because the seriousness of creativity demands something more than a one-dimensional viewpoint.

The dictates of these books are constructed so that the reader must read through the material in at least six different ways, and the interconnections of concepts are set up so as to give maximum diversity. In other words, the reader will be able to view a given concept from as many different standpoints as possible. The thrust of these writings is not about any one concept but instead involves the reality of cross-information, as a means to solidify the broadest possible inquiry terms. It is my hope that an approach of this nature might prove useful for establishing a more realistic look at creative music, for much of the literature I have seen on this subject seems either too simplistic or too academic. Yet, by the same token, I have not solidified this approach as a joke, nor have I included anything in these books which was not necessary. I have tried, in this effort, to view a given concept to the farthest point of my ability with the hope that either real understanding can come from an approach of this type, or that real intellectual stimulation about world creativity can be developed. I view either objective as positive.

The construction of this book is as follows:

Within each principal section or chapter (which is designated by the use of capital letters) there are what I call levels of inquiry—or simply levels. The whole of these series of writings is constructed around the dynamics of this approach. There are three inquiry sections that can be used in a given chapter, and every idea is expressed throughout each aspect of what this division means. The explanation of each level designation is as follows:

1. Level One has to do with focusing on some particular aspect of its principal chapter, and this region of inquiry can number from one to four approaches (depending on how many "particulars" are focused on in a given section). Each of these areas of focus is separated into different colors for convenience.

The code is as follows:
>   brown for approach one;
>   green for approach two;
>   orange for approach three;
>   purple for approach four.

2. Level Two investigation is a summary of the given approaches focused on in Level One. In other words, this area of inquiry can only be utilized if there are two or more approaches examined in Level One. The thrust of a given focus in this context is geared towards the composite context of what a given viewpoint might mean in a broader context (or with respect to the whole of this book and this series of books). The color of this section is blue.

3. Level Three investigation involves the use of questions and answers in a one-dimensional context as a means to include shorter viewpoints that can be integrated throughout the whole of this book. This is necessary because the basic structure of the book is systematic to the degree that "grounded definitions" can provide a healthy pivotal factor for clarification. By including this section, the range of a given focus is all-encompassing—that is, the dynamics of this total approach run from open interpretation possibilities (i.e., understanding something in your own way—with respect to one's own affinity dynamics) to closed exact definitions. The color for this section is red.

I have tried to accent many of the important concepts in bold type as a means for the reader to have easy referral to a given viewpoint more readily.

Thus, to really utilize this book in the way I have intended, the reader is expected to read this book:

(1) completely from the beginning to the end;

(2) with respect to the arguments of only one level region at a time (i.e., read only Level One sections in each chapter, later read only Level Two chapters, etc.);

(3) read the whole book interconnected with the other books in this series through what I call the integration code—which is in every section of every focus;

(4) read only the isolated concepts that have been marked by bold type;

(5) study the isolated terminology chart—or glossary of terms (at the back of the book)—to understand the systemic interconnection (as well as application) of these concepts throughout the total integration complex of all three books, as a means to better understand both my extended viewpoint as well as the logic dynamics of its total application; and

(6) the reader is asked to translate my terminology—from the glossary and throughout the whole book—as a means to view each focus in one's own terms: in other words, I am saying, "this is my viewpoint in this content, and these are my terms, but what do you think?" with respect to your own personal viewpoint and/or perception dynamics (in the context of my terminology—as well as your own terminology) about this same information. Only after all of the approaches have been tried can the reader have some idea as to what I am trying to communicate—yet on this comment it is important to explain my intentions. I have not meant to imply that my understanding of phenomena is such that one must necessarily reach for my so-called level, because to believe this has nothing to do with reality. Instead, I have constructed these writings in this manner because the realness of what I am really trying to communicate is not about "only one point of view"—or one level of transference. I believe the traditional use of so-called deductive logic has been greatly violated in this time period. What we now need is the use of every kind of information transference affinity position—whether or not it corresponds to what is now called logic. It is for this reason that *Tri-Axium Writings* is constructed in the manner you have before you. I have also included a code for all of the signs and symbols used in this book—and series of books.

CODE

1. A straight line under a paragraph means that the focus of that particular subject has been completed; after which the next paragraph will move to another area of relevant focus.

2. A dotted line under a paragraph means that the next paragraph is an insert that is separate from the basic flow of what is being written on. As such, the end of the insert is also marked with a dotted line—and

the reader is back on the same subject material. It is possible to simply skip the material that is presented between the dotted line sections and come back to it later.

3. All of the concepts are abbreviated as a means to trace an information line in the integration charts.

The bracketed abbreviations are:

(R) = the reality of
(C) = the concept of
(IN)DE = inquiry degree
(CT) = the criterion of
(P) = point of idea completion for a given interpretation (or schematic)
(PFC) = point for future calibration
(PO) = point of
(L) = level
(P-AT) = point of activation (a physical universe term to point out where a given idea or the effects of a given idea—can take shape or become real)
(D) = the dynamics of = when viewed in the context of
    = can be viewed
    = as it involves
    = viewed with respect to
    = particulars of a given
    = (dotted line) amplifies some aspect of the main concept it is connected to
    = is connected to on the physical universe level
(P-IN) = its position in
(D-T) = determines the _____ of its _____

The name of this system of thought is "TRI-AXIUM," which is my term for gathering axiom tenets from the past and present—to get to the future. The reality of this inquiry is perceived and offered as a bridge for re-information designation (for possible transformational observation—tenets—and/or use). For the most part, this series of writings is based on present-time affinity postulation (or affinity observation). But the whole of the completed effort—in the next ten, twenty years—or whatever time I have to work on this project—will deal with:

1. Affinity postulation:
(a) establishing basis (through physical universe observation—and research);
(b) challenging present time definitions;
(c) establishing affinity redesignation systems (that also allow for individual interpretation)

2. Axiom correlation:
(a) researching world culture information tenets for resolidification;
(b) re-establishing transformational functionalism particulars;
(c) establishing a platform for alternative investigation.

3. Reality imposition:
(a) isolating particulars with respect for respiritual participation;
(b) resecuring the significance of ritualism and symbolic participation;
(c) re-investigating spiritual dynamics as a basis to establish transformational spiritualism.

To use the integration schematics one must first become familiar with the abbreviation of terms. The basic idea of this system is that all of the concepts in this book—and this series of books—must be viewed in more than one context. The reality of a given schematic is not isolated to only what it poses for a given focus; rather, I have designed this approach as a means to keep an extended information platform—which is to say each given schematic should be viewed as axiom tenets. To read a given schematic the reader must first view it in terms of its basic designation—which has an arrow to denote its starting point. In actual fact the term (or abbreviation) with the arrow pointing to it is the subject of the schematic. In the figure below this paragraph the subject then is "vibrational dynamics" (and since there is also an [R] in brackets, the subject is "the reality of vibrational dynamics" as this concept relates to the concept of "postulation"). Whenever there is no prefix or bracket before a given abbreviation it means to view the terms as a concept—or as the concept (in this case) of "postulation."

This is then the schematic:

(R)VT. DY. ------ POST.

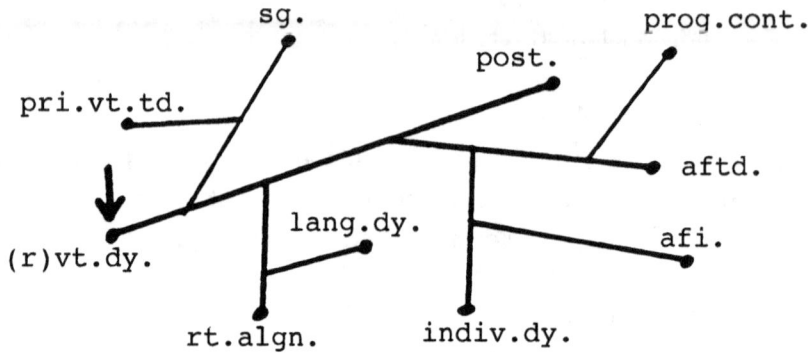

To read (or see) this schematic in words would go like this:

The reality of vibrational dynamics as this term relates to the concept of "postulation"—in three different contexts, those being: in the context of (1) SG, source initiation (involving PRI-VT-TD, primary vibrational tendencies); or in the context of (2) RT-ALGN, reality alignment (involving LANG-DY, language dynamics); or in the context of (3) AFTD, affinity tendencies (involving INDIV-DY, individual dynamics as related to AFI, affinity insight—or involving PROG-CONT, progressional continuance).

The reader is expected to probe the dynamics of this axiom as a means to better understand these terms (i.e., what is being posed in a given information complex), as well as what all of this information means when calibrated into a composite philosophy (my philosophy at first, after which the reader is expected to view this same material—and terms—[with substitutions when needed] for his or her own philosophy).

All of the various symbols that are attached to particular schematics can be found in this CODE section.

GLOSSARY INTEGRATION

See the Glossary at the back of the book for definitions of terms.

A-PR	all-purpose
ACC-DY	accelerated dynamics
ACC-FT	accelerated functionalism
ACT	activism
ACT-T	actual terms
ACT-TR	actual transformation
AF-COMP	affinity compression
AF-CON	affinity convergence
AF-NT	affinity nature
AF-POST	affinity postulation
AFI	affinity insight
AFI(1)	affinity insight—first degree
AFI(2)	affinity insight—second degree
AFL	affinity alignment
AFL-DT	affinity dictates
AFL-DY	affinity dynamics
AFN	affinity negation
AFTD	affinity tendencies
AFTF	affinity transfer
AGT	agreement
ALT-ACT	alternative activism
ALT-C-PG	alternative composite progressionalism
ALT-D	alternative definitions
ALT-F	alternative functionalism
APL-DT	application dictates
APP-RDEF	applied redefinitions
ASP-ES	aspect essence
ATT	attitude
ATTC	attachment
ATTN	attraction

BIA	bi-aitional (or bi-aitionalism)
BSCF	basic science (or basic scientific functionalism)
C-ACT	composite activism
C-AF-ALGN	composite affinity alignment
C-CONT	composite continuance
C-CULT-AT	composite culture attitude
C-FO-ACT	composite focused activism
C-HM	composite humanity
C-INFO	composite information
C-RH	composite research
CN-INFO	controlled information
COLC-FR-WC	collected forces of western culture
COS-AGN	cosmic assignment
COS-D	cosmic dictates
COS-P	cosmic particulars
CR-INFO-DY	circular information dynamics
CRT	criticism
CRTF-D	cross-transfer definitions
CRTF-PROG	cross-transfer progressionalism
CUL-TF-S	cultural transfer shift(s)
CULT-AF-BS	culture affinity basis
CULT-INFO-B	culture information basis
CULT-INFO-DY	culture information dynamics
CULT-INFO-F	culture information focus
CULT-O	culture order
CULT-SOLD	culture solidification
DE-SPTL	despiritualization (or despiritualism)
DEC	decentralization
DEF	definition
DIS-C-CT	disintegration of a culture's center
DOC	documentation
DYM-F	dynamic functionalism

DYM-SEP	dynamic separation
DYM-SPT	dynamic spiritualism
ECO-DYM	economic dynamics
EXB-H-OR	establishing high order
EXP-CONT	expansion condition (the concept of)
EXP-CONT(1)	expansion condition (composite focus)
EXP-CONT(2)	expansion condition (isolated focus)
EXP-DT	expansion dictates
EXP-DYM	expansion dynamics
EXP-INFO-B	expansion information basis
EXPM	expansionism
EXT-DYM	extended dynamics
EXT-FT	extended functionalism
EXTN	existentialism
EXTN-D	existential definition
EXTN-OB	existential observation
EXTS	extension (or nature of extension)
F	form
FUND-DYN	fundamental dynamics
FUND-P	fundamental particulars
GRAD	gradualism
HI-P	high purpose
IF-SPT	infra-spirituality
IF-ST-DY	infra-structure dynamics
IMPOV	improvisation (the concept of)
INDIV-DY	individual dynamics
INDIV-DY-RT	individual dynamic reality
INDIV-TD (or INDIV-DY-TD)	individual tendencies (the reality of or concept of)

INFO-AF-B	information affinity basis
INFO-ALGN	information alignment
INFO-COMP	information compression
INFO-CON	information convergence
INFO-DE(B)	information degrees (or information degree basis)
INFO-DOC	information documentation
INFO-DS	information dissemination
INFO-F	information focus
INFO-F-D	information focus distortion
INFO-FM (or FR)	information forum
INFO-INTG	information integration
INFO-INTR	information interpretation
INFO-OR	information order
INFO-PROJ	information projection
INFO-RT	information reality
INFO-SOLD	information solidification
INFO-TRNS	information transference
INT	intention (the reality of)
INTL	intellectualism
INTR	interpretation
INVT-DT	investigation dictates
IST-ACT	isolated activism
IST-F	isolated focus
IST-F-AT	isolated focus activism
IST-F-DT	isolated focus dictates
IST-PT	isolated particulars
IST-S-ALGN	isolated systematic alignment
JR-DYM	journalism dynamics
LANG	language
LANG-DY	language dynamics
LG-DISA	logical dissolution
LG-DY	logical dynamics

LG-EXT	logical extension
LK-IMP	linkage implications
MD-DY	media dynamics
MDT-DY	motivation dynamics
MN-DI	mono-dimensional
MPT	manipulation (the reality of)
MT-DEVF	multiple diversification
MT DI	multi dimensional (or ISM)
MT-IF-DB	multi-informational degree basis
MT-IMP	multi-implications
MT-INFO	multi-information
MT-INTR	multiple interpretation
MT-TFS-AT	multi-transfer shift activity
MTA-IMP	meta-implications
MTA-RT	meta-reality
MTA-RT-SIGN	meta-reality significance
MTH	methodology
OBS	observation (or reality of)
OP-SPD	option spread
P-FC	particular focus
P-PROG	particular progressionalism
PART	participation
PER-DY	perception dynamics
PER-PHY-U-FUND	perceived physical universe fundamental
PER-TR	perceived transformation
PER-TRS	perceived transition
PER-VT-U-FUND	perceived vibrational universe fundamental
PHY-U-C	physical universe context
PHY-U-FUND	physical universe fundamental
PHY-U-P	physical universe particular
POL-CON	political consciousness

POL-DYM	political dynamics
POL-OR	political order
POL-P	political policies (or execution of)
POL-SIGN	political significance
POL-ST	political state
POST	postulation
PR-INT	primary intention
PRI-AF-TO	primary affinity tendencies
PRI-INFO	principle information
PRI-VT-TD	principle vibrational tendencies
PROG-CONT	progressional continuance
PROG-EXT-FT	progressional extended functionalism
PROG-SIGN	progressional significance
PROG-TF-C	progressional transfer cycles
PROJ	projection
PROJ-CONT	projectional continuance
PROJ-DY	projectional dynamics
RC	race
RE-CONT	recontinuance
RE-DIF	redefinitions
RE-DOC	redocumentation
RE-ST	restructuralism
REL-APC	relevant application
REL-TECH	relevant technology
RES-RT	responsibility ratio
RET-AF-TD	retrograde affinity tendencies
RIT-DY	ritual dynamics
ROTP	responsibility of the position (the concept of)
RT-ALGN	reality alignment
RT-DY	reality dynamics
RT-IMP	reality implications
RT-INT-TR	reality initiative traits

RT-OP	reality options
RTD-PRD	related procedure
S-PROJ	source projection
S-ST	source shift (progressionalism) manipulation
SCI-DYM	scientific dynamics
SF-RZ	self-realization
SI	source initiation
SOC-PR	social programs
SOC-RT	social reality
SOC-RT-DEVF	social reality diversification
SOC-RT-DT	social reality dictates
SOC-RT-DY	social reality dynamics
SOC-RT-INT	social reality interpretation
SOC-RT-P	social reality particular(s)
SPT-AW	spiritual awareness
SPT-DY	spiritual dynamics
SPT-GH	spiritual growth
SPT-UNF	spiritual unification
SPTC-D	spectacle diversion
STF	source transfer
STY	style (or the concept of)
T-C-IMP	time continuum implications
T-L	time lag
T-P	time presence
T-SC	theoretical science
TECH-DY	technological (or technology) dynamics
TF-SH	transfer shift(s)
TH-AF-ALGN	thrust affinity alignment
TH-CONT	thrust continuance
TH-CONT-DY	thrust continuance dynamics
TM	terminology—or terms of a definition

TR	transformation
TR-DEF	trans-definition
TR-INFO	trans-information
TRS	transition
UNF-PI	unification (positively intended)/world unification
UPB	underlying philosophical basis
UTZ	utilization
V-SY	value system
VT-AF/ATT	vibrational affinity and/or attitude
VT-ATT	vibrational attitude
VT-DY	vibrational dynamics
VT-IMP	vibrational implications
VT-PLT	vibrational platform
VT-POST	vibrational postulation
VT-S	vibrational science
VT-TD	vibrational tendencies
VT-U-PT	vibrational universe particulars
WO-CH	world change
WO-EXP-PRI	world expansion principle
WO-MTH	world methodology
WO-UNF	world unification

UNDERLYING PHILOSOPHICAL BASIS

(Level One) WORLD MUSIC

IF WE ARE EVER TO AWAKEN TO THE REALNESS OF CREATIVITY as a life-giving factor, then the seriousness of this subject must be re-examined from every viewpoint and context. For the most basic understanding of creativity perpetuated in this time zone seeks to accent the entertainment or spectacle value of a given projection, rather than what that same projection might mean in its cosmic vibrational sense (as pertaining to either its mystical, spiritual, or positive functional value). In other words, the present reality of western information dynamics is geared to focus more on the surface of a given focus, as opposed to "what is most true" about that focus, and this phenomenon has come to profoundly distort our perception of everything—including creativity. The end result of this cultural attitude sheds light on the times we now live in, for, to many people, the meta-reality of a given creative projection is a subject not worthy of serious thought. And, as the progressional expansion of technology continues to reshape every aspect of our lives, this gradual unconcern about composite information (and/or philosophical content) that is now taking place in our culture will pose even greater complexities for generations to come. Every day the realness of creativity becomes less and less clear—and this is true on many different levels.

On the physical universe level this phenomenon could be understood by dealing with the rapidity surrounding the progressional shifting of information by the controlling forces dictating western culture. Every week there is a new spectacle on display, and all of us are constantly bombarded with what music to buy, what art is "in"—what fashions are correct—what music is the best, etc., etc. In the time zone of a given year, many of us would be shocked to discover how many spectacles we have gone through—with regards to either creativity or, more important, how the controlling forces of American culture would have us perceive creativity. We are constantly forced to keep up with both the changing social jargon related to how given creative thrusts are perceived as well as the effect of what that jargon helps create in vibrationaltory terms—with regards to actual physical universe life. It does not matter whether the spectacle involves "op-art" or the emergence of what is now called "funky" music, because in the final analysis the thrust continuum of creativity is constantly changing, and it would be to our advantage to have some understanding of what this means.

The realness of the changes taking place in creativity must be viewed from many different viewpoints, because in this subject we are not discussing a mono-dimensional thrust projection, but rather a multi-dynamic continuance that touches on every aspect of life on this planet—regardless of culture. Moreover, it would not be correct to simply imply that all of the changes reshaping creativity in this time zone are based on manipulation from big business, because while this is true for some areas of creativity, it certainly does not apply to the composite thrust of world culture. Instead, we are talking of a subject much too complex to generalize, and much too diverse to lump together. The composite actualness of creativity transcends any single category. This is a subject related to the realness of life itself, for the seeds underlying what a given creative projection really is touch on more areas than many of us might imagine. The scope of creativity is not limited to either the doing or experiencing of a given creative thrust, rather the totalness of a given thrust sheds light on the culture itself—both in terms of what that culture is and also in terms of what that culture could be (with the implications having to do with "what that culture was and what is what"). The dynamic realness of creativity is a subject too important to ignore any longer, for our ability to participate in the next time cycle is directly related to what knowledge we secure in this cycle—and nothing is more important than the vibrational and cosmic forces surrounding the creativity that permeates this planet (for now). Nor have I meant to imply that only certain creative thrusts are significant, as opposed to the composite actualness of creativity, because this is not what I believe. Many of the separations we have made between various strains of creativity are alien to the real actualness of this subject. In other words, there is no real separation between what we have come to call dance, music, sculpture or art, in the real sense of what these projections are. Nor, in the cosmic sense of the word, is there any separation between any of the various cultural and racial thrust projections that exist on this planet—having to do with either creativity or any other consideration. All of these categories have to do with many other factors, and it is the purpose of this book to begin laying a basis to deal with the composite actualness of earth creativity.

To investigate the realness of earth creativity is to recognize the dynamic realness of culture on this planet. For the implications of this subject cannot be restricted to any one area—in other words, every cultural thrust is related to a cross-section of creative thrusts. From Alpine Mountain music in Switzerland to Salsa music from Cuba, what we see is the spectrum of how creativity is manifested on this planet, and what we also see is the ingenuity and imagination of the composite whole of humanity. I am not writing of a consideration relevant to only one time zone but rather a subject manifested in every cycle of recorded history. The progressional thrust of earth creativity parallels progressional continuity of earth culture, and this is important to remember. So many forms have been developed and lost that it would be practically impossible to trace every projection to its original beginning. To understand and view the composite actualness of earth creativity is to transcend both the consideration of time, as well as the superficial boundaries that all of us at some point have erected. For the dynamic continuum of earth creativity is not dependent on one area of the planet, or one racial or cultural group—but rather, everyone and every culture group has helped bring us to the junction we are in at present. Thus, to experience the realness of earth creativity is to be open to the dynamic implications of what this subject means—both in actual terms as well as cosmic terms. It is important to understand that creativity represents a vibrational picture of what a given culture thrust means in cosmic terms. That is, it is no more possible to change a person's (or culture's) basic creative vibrational thrust than it is to change one's fingerprints. In other words, the thrust continuum of creativity can tell us much about the progressional actualness of earth culture as well as the vibrational implications of principle thrust alignments. This information is essential if we are to establish some basis for transformation, for it is my belief that the challenge of the next cycle is directly related to what we are able to understand about the composite realness of earth knowledge—regardless of time zone. The investigation of world creativity is also related to what this means, for the seeds underlying how given cultures move—in physical universe or vibrational terms—shed light on every aspect of that culture (whether we are referring to a culture's vibration or spiritual reality).

It is necessary to examine the total vibrational arena that underlines how we have come to view creativity if we are to arrive at some basis for dealing with the uniqueness of this subject. For the creativity happening in this time zone did not simply come from nowhere, but rather is the progressional extension of what happened before it. To examine the essence implications of creativity would imply that some effort is put forth to establish the widest possible context for examination. For to deal with the realness of this subject would imply some awareness of the progressional expansion of given vibrational projections, as well as some understanding of the basis which solidified what those projections are. With a composite perspective we are able to view the dynamic implications surrounding how given creative thrusts expand as well as how that expansion has affected the present realness of earth culture. The information we gain from this viewpoint can better prepare us to deal with the underlying philosophical and vibrational factors that dictate the nature and actualness of this subject. For the philosophical consideration defines both the significance of what a given projection is, as well as what the inherent potential of that projection could be if extended. Thus, for the purpose of investigation—everything, in terms of meaning, is relative to its philosophical or vibrational basis, because this factor functions as "center."

For investigational purposes, I have found it necessary to dismantle many of the considerations related to how we have come to view creativity. This is so because there is a need to re-examine every aspect of this subject in a new light—both for what it could mean with regards to the present actualness of culture (what is happening at present) as well as for what this type of investigation could mean towards further expansion. The seriousness of creativity demands this type of investigation, if we are to truly have some awareness of our real position on the planet in this cycle. For if many of the problems we are dealing with in this time zone directly relate to the inability of western culture to provide the proper ethical and spiritual dictates necessary for culture, then the restoration of creativity can be viewed as the first step towards re-establishing positive change. Moreover, if the realness of the present time zone exceeds the limitations of any one given culture, then the actualness of creativity can also give us some insight into what this state means with regards to both functional change and vibrational change. Whatever, the dynamics of creativity is a subject that must be dealt with on some level, for there are many questions related to this subject that could directly shed light on the progressional expansion of earth culture as well as those vibrational factors that underline how physical universe change (i.e., transition and/or transformation) is actualized. The progressional actualness of a given creative thrust could give us insight into the question of spirituality as well as culture—and in its ultimate state this information should reveal something about the realness of existence (whatever level). The seriousness of the time period we are living in seems to imply that some of these questions be examined. And while I do not pretend my awareness is so advanced that I am qualified to deal with this subject, at the same time—a collective viewpoint concerning creativity and its related meta-reality implications must come from a dynamic spectrum of quarters: including both philosophers, scientists and, yes, creative people. My attempts to comment on the composite realness of creativity is offered in the same spirit of positive investigation that characterizes those who are trying to understand anything.

This section of the book is concerned with viewing the meta-reality of world creativity—both as a means to draw new light on this subject, and also as a necessary route for re-examining creativity in this time zone. However, the dynamic realness of this subject must be approached very sensitively, for the actualness of world creativity does not necessarily correspond to the thrust alignment of western language—that is, the vibrational significance of world creativity, in its most basic state, transcends the parameters of western language as an accurate descriptive tool. Thus if this section is to be of any value—and related to true information—I am forced to be as careful in my use of language as possible. Because the actualness of a given word might mean one thing in the west, but when applied universally mean something else entirely. In short, there are reasons why given languages can't comment on certain factors outside of their natural affinity projection, and this must be respected. I have chosen to write on the underlying philosophical and vibrational realness of world creativity only as a means to establish a basis for observation. Moreover, because of the nature of this subject, I am forced to also utilize separation as a tool for showing the distinguishing features of world creativity—as opposed to lumping this consideration with aesthetics that aren't compatible. For the multi-complexual implications of this subject necessitate some level of separation as a means to comment on (the dynamics of) given culture groups. This is true for unique particular subject matter as well as for the structure of this inquiry. By world music in this section of the book, I am referring to the creativity "ised" from all of the world's cultures with the exception of western art music and creative music from the black aesthetic—which was also "ised" in America (both of these thrusts are discussed separately in the next section of this book). It is not the purpose of this book to deal with any particular group as a means to totally understand what that group is about. That is the purpose of historians, anthropologists, or musicologists—I am interested in looking at world creativity as a means to draw light on certain inherent factors regarding the meta and functional realness of the creative process that has always been apparent to the world group. My reason for taking this approach is to establish a basis for understanding world creativity and how given culture groups function from this information.

    The limitations of western language as an accurate descriptive tool for inquiring into world creativity can become apparent by dealing with the essence foundation underlying how world creativity is perceived. For the nature of creativity in world terms is perceived quite differently from that of western culture—especially in this time period. Perhaps the most distinguishing factor manifested in world creativity is the unification of all aspects of postulation to the degree that the creative process and the very reality of the culture group are intertwined. In other words, not only is the creative process indistinguishable as a separate entity in the world group's viewpoint, but in many cases the creative process is not even looked at in terms of being a creative process. In other words, the idea of creativity is not even dealt with by many culture groups from the world community. It is difficult, then, to make systematic references or relationships on world creativity as a means to establish one criterion for investigation—because the study of world creativity is not only about creativity.

In 1968, I had an opportunity to meet a young African flutist whose musical ability impressed me enormously. The meeting I was to have with this musician helped me to view the uniqueness of world creativity as a factor perceived quite differently from western creativity, and as a consideration that reflected on the dynamic implications of culture in ways very new to me. The basis of our meeting had to do with me asking the African musician whether or not he was a professional musician, for I was quite impressed with his musical ability and would have liked to experience more of his work in performances if possible. His reply was that he was not a professional musician, and I was quite surprised to hear that this musician was not a professional (musician)—in the sense of how the word is used in the west—for I found his musical ability to be on the highest level with regards to both invention (creativity) and discipline (technique). Moreover, I do not mean to imply that his response to my question required an understanding of complicated concepts or advanced algebra, because in fact the simplicity of his viewpoint would really be the factor that accented my interest. For I was not prepared for this young musician's response (to my question), and the basis of our conversation would make a deep impression on my total understanding of creativity. His response was simply that when he was growing up he always wanted to play the flute—so he played the flute. The idea of becoming a professional musician had no meaning to him because in his country not only would there be no one to play for—and make a living from—as such, but also in his tribe everyone played the flute as well as he did—if not better. He went on to say that it was only in coming to Europe that he began to see other considerations concerning creativity—as a professional spectacle factor—and while he grew to understand this viewpoint, it was outside of his basic vibrational and historical alignment with creativity. For me, this meant in his tribe there was no such thing as creativity separated from the culture to the degree that it became an entity unto itself. Thus, to deal with world creativity is to understand what this alignment really means. For if creativity as an actualization is not dealt with by the world group, then what does this imply—and how is it perceived? To understand these questions is to deal with establishing some criteria for viewing the realness of this subject. I say this because whether or not the young African saw himself as potentially being a professional flutist is not the point. The fact that he played the flute is what I am focusing on.

To deal with the realness of world creativity is to be confronted with the dynamic scope of how it is manifested. And while the surface particulars of a given culture group differ—in terms of identity alignment—every culture utilizes in its own way the total dynamic spectrum of creativity. In other words, the projectional realness of music, dance, sculpture, theatre, etc., is an integral part of the basic creative arena of world creativity—but it goes even deeper than that. The fact is, all of these various projections (i.e., dance, music, etc.) were actualized in the progressional continuum of world culture and as such are not merely adaptations or recent developments, but factors conceived from the basic thrust expansion of world creativity. Moreover, the surface realness underlying how a given projection is viewed cannot be separated from the composite meta-reality of its culture group. That being, **to deal with world creativity is not to analyze the surface actualness of a given creative projection but rather to understand the vibrational and cultural base which actualized it.** The realness of this approach can help us understand both the uniqueness of a given culture group as well as the concept of "affinity alignment." Our attention must be directed to the essence foundation of world culture—not necessarily with regards to any particular function or group—as a means to observe the nature of this concept. For obviously the progressional development of Scottish bagpipe music is different from that of Pygmy music—yet the essence foundation of world creativity can be viewed as reflecting one essential attitude—or affinity alignment (and this is especially true for non-western cultures—because the underlying vibrational and philosophical realness of western creativity—and culture—in many ways represents its own separate affinity balance). The essence realness of a given projection in world culture terms must finally be viewed in its composite context. For the particulars of a given focus in this context share a common vibrational affinity denominator—and this is true for the whole of world culture—with the one exception being western culture, and in particular western art music. This difference can especially be understood if the concept of affinity alignment is viewed as related to the "reality of principle information" and/or affinity dynamics in world terms (i.e., the concept of race in particular)—yet I have not presented this concept as a means to proclaim any notions of superiority or inferiority because this is not my belief (nor does this route of investigation really interest me—not to mention, the basic vibrational categories I am referring to do not necessarily break down into our present concepts concerning "race" in any real sense, because this concept is only one criterion among many others of equal importance).

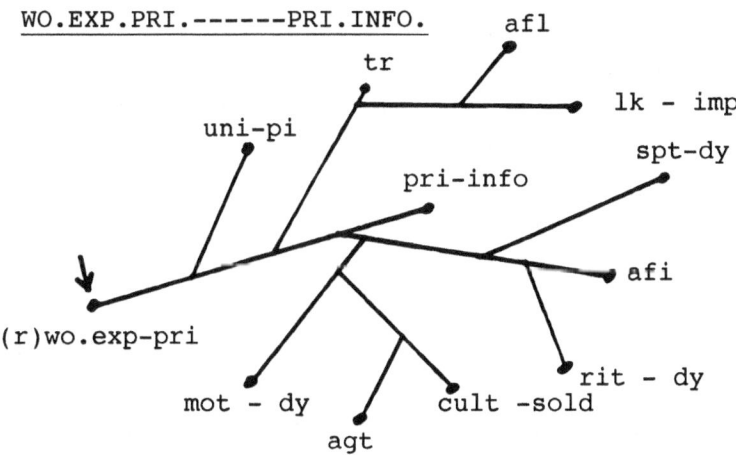

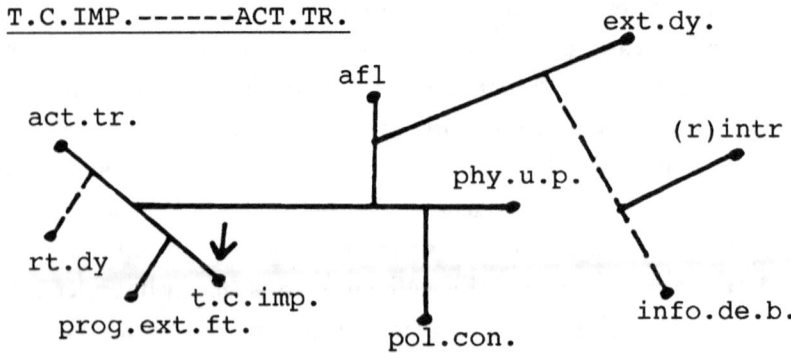

To examine the essence foundation of world creativity is to be made aware of the relationship of this subject to how given culture groups perceive of life. This relationship is the "stuff" that solidifies the realness of world creativity as a composite affinity thrust, for I am writing of an attitude that transcends both regional and tribal considerations—commenting instead on a particular way of perceiving things. To understand the affinity alignment of world culture is to observe the nature of this relationship, for there are many aspects of this question that can be commented on. The most basic of which is that creativity "ised" from the world consideration can be looked at as a ritualization of the total understanding of its given culture group (with regards to that group's affinity and vibrational alignment to either spiritual or cosmic matters). In other words, creativity in this context functions in the position of re-enforcing the essence foundation of its culture group's meta-reality position, and this is done by the nature of its relationship to essence—through ritualism. Moreover, in every case, creativity "ised" from the composite affinity alignment of world creativity can be viewed as functional as opposed to an aspect conceived only for viewing. By "functional" I mean "conceived to be about something," both affecting the actualness of particular situations (in the natural life thrust of a given community) as well as a factor attached to the vibrational lining—and thus secrets and science—of its culture as well. Thus I am writing of a consideration which means nothing in itself but is instead a manifestation (i.e., ritualization or affirmation) of the basic life force (essence foundation) of its culture group. The problem for this section, then, is to find a way to communicate about this basic life force without talking about "a given life force"—for in focusing on world creativity, we are touching on a subject much too complex for any one level of investigation. The realness of viewing totality as a fact can present many problems for the western analytical position, for this observation context is outside of the basic affinity alignment of western functionalism (i.e., science). Yet this is exactly what must happen if we are to deal with the realness of world creativity. Because any attempt to isolate a given aspect of world culture will invariably lead to some type of distortion—because the meta-reality underlying how this consideration (i.e., creativity) is viewed has nothing to do with separation as perceived in the annals of western thought. To deal with the actualness of a given creative projection from the world's community is to have some awareness of that projection's "real" purpose.

To examine the particulars underlining the composite realness of world culture is to take into account the spectrum of earth creativity in all of its various strains. For when I wrote that there is a difference in how given culture groups manifest their creativity, we should understand what this means with regards to an actual creative projection. Because in the final analysis, a given creative projection from world culture might relate to many factors not normally associated with creativity in the west—and this is important. The clearest example of the multi-implicational realness of creativity can be found in viewing the progressional realness of Indian creativity, where certain sounds imply a multitude of considerations—having to do with what we call music as well as the total life experience. In short, where the western interpretation of the Pythagorean junction had to do with the search for acoustically correct intervals as a means to view the universe in one-dimensional systematic terms, the Indian mantra on the other hand dealt not only with the science of a given sound in functional terms but also with the total meta-reality of that sound—with regards to both its physical and aesthetic position in Indian culture. Nor is this total understanding of sound by Indian culture unique in world culture terms, for this example corresponds directly to the nature of affinity alignment in world culture. My point is that the meta-reality of world culture must be viewed in dynamic terms, for a given creative manifestation is not limited to one stratum but rather has multi-complexual implications. This can be better understood by dealing with the consideration of functionalism, for the composite thrust of world culture—no matter what culture group—has long insisted that a given aspect has much wider implications than merely the empirical science which defined how it worked. To deal with the realness of creativity as a healing factor is but one example of the multi-complexual position of given creative strains in world culture. The use of certain creative projections for given parts of the day (or night) has long characterized the meta-reality of creativity from the world group—and the realness of what this use implies should not be taken lightly. To really understand the meta-reality implications of world creativity is to be aware that creativity is not separated from the realness of the culture itself. The nature of its affinity alignment can be viewed with regards to the realness of functionalism as well as aesthetics. We are thus viewing a relationship that transcends basic categories, for the progressional continuance of world creativity does not have a real separation between its creativity and science, or its creativity and religion—or its creativity and its community. To deal with the meta-reality of world creativity is then to examine the nature of this relationship as a means to better understand the multi-complexual implications of what creativity really is—or can be.

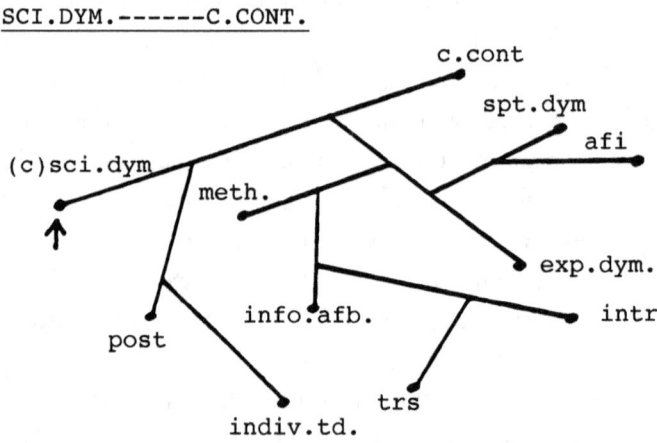

TH.CONT.------MF.IF.DF.

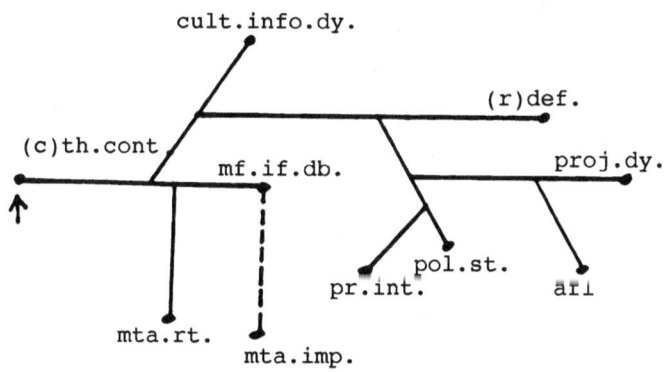

EXP.INFO.P.------MT.INFO.

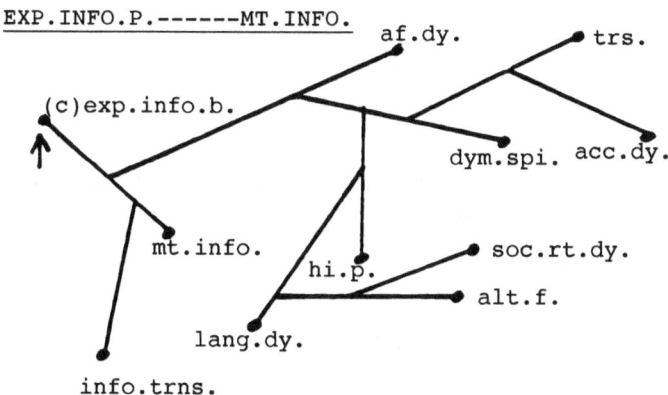

(R) EXT.F.------AF.DY.

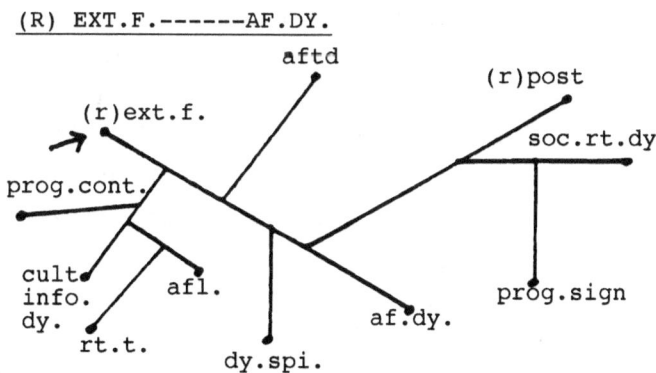

In actual terms, it is possible to view the solidification of dynastic Egypt as a basic point to begin examining the particulars of world methodology—and/or meta-reality high purpose. For to view the solidification of the Nile Valley Mystery System—that being, the emergence of a composite information and spiritual system for culture dynamics—is to begin understanding the reality nature and spiritual purpose of creativity—as viewed in world culture terms. Creativity in that context was viewed as a discipline not separate from composite spiritual dynamics—having to do with what forces it activated and/or participated in—and this information was dynamically intertwined throughout the whole of Egyptian culture. Hopefully the next cycle will see attempts to re-understand this phenomenon, for the African Nile Valley Mystery System information complex (and spiritual platform) remains one of the more amazing information blockages in this time cycle. Sooner or later this information must assume its rightful place in world information dynamics—especially since its tenets and focus spectrum have provided the foundation for present-day western culture dynamics. It is important that the reality particulars of creativity are viewed with respect to their greater implications.

One needs only to lightly examine the composite thrust of world culture, and immediately certain relationships are revealed concerning the multi-dynamic realness of world creativity. Moreover, I am not simply referring to one aspect of creativity, but rather the composite solidification of this subject—whether we are discussing painting, music, dance, etc.—for all of these areas functioned as one basic thrust alignment with regards to culture. In the consideration that we refer to as astrology, the very realness of a given sound (note) has definite implications engulfing the totalness of how existence is viewed—even to the point of how birth and death are viewed. The significance of this one area of composite aesthetic gives insight and awareness that western culture has not even begun to deal with. It cannot be lightly dismissed that a person, depending on his or her birthdate, is born into a vibrational realm that in the world position is not only understood but also prepared for. To understand this consideration is to have some idea of the multi-complexual realness of world creativity as a dynamic factor permeating the whole of its given culture group. We are thus dealing with a consideration that engulfs the total spectrum of perceived existence, as well as a consideration that has maintained both concern and awareness about composite life matters—even extending to one's entry into this planet. For the realness of what we call astrology is a multi-dynamic consideration in itself, having to do with the solidification of information that can be used in a positive way to deal with the actualness of life on a spectrum of levels. The dynamic realness of this consideration is most profound—but this is only the beginning. For however the science realness of astrology was arrived at, it was not the result of a mono-dimensional probe, but instead the natural result of a basic affinity thrust that relates to the whole of its given culture. I am commenting on a vibrational thrust projection that can be viewed as a synthesis between empirical flows—in terms of perception of events on the planet and the functional science that grew from that perception—and aesthetic vibrational flows—having to do with the realness of both affinity alignment (and the affinity insight principle) as well as spiritualism. To view the dynamic actualization of astrology and its utilization from world culture is to have some understanding of the multi-complexual factors that determine how given projections are conceived through world culture. Because if the actualness of world culture can be viewed with regards to the concept of affinity alignment, then a given culture's utilization of creativity can better be understood by viewing the linkage implications underlining its perception nature. This is so because the creative process is not viewed as a separate factor from the total life of the culture in world music terms. The linkage implications of a given actualization in world culture only outline the dynamic realness of what that actualization really is—in its total sense—and in doing so, gives the correct definition to both the creative process and the realness of its culture. Nor have I meant to over-emphasize the actualness of astrology as a multi-dynamic example of creative linkage, because this is only one example among many. The concept of music for meditation—where through sound a person is able to deal with certain realizations concerning his or her life—is an integral part of the multi-dynamic implications surrounding how the meta-reality of world creativity is perceived. This then is another example of what we are dealing with in trying to understand the underlying vibrational and philosophical realness of world creativity.

One of the most basic factors that serves to distort the actualness of this subject is present-day misinformation and prejudice. It is important to understand that the composite realness of world creativity is viewed as primitive by western culture (primitive in the sense that when measured against the western philosophical and creative position, world creativity is somehow lacking or even retarded). We have been led to believe that when compared to the music of Iannis Xenakis, for example—who purportedly has evolved structural techniques with architecture—Pygmy music is less advanced. Any attempt to deal with the realness of world creativity would necessitate that some effort is made to deal with this attitude. For if the dynamic realness of this subject can be checked in practically every library in the country then it must be assumed that the disregard for world creativity by western culture is based on something other than the actual music.

Without doubt, the strongest factor that has served to distort the subject of world creativity is the realness of cultural racism as well as misdocumentation. The disregard of world creativity can be directly linked to how Europeans have come to see themselves and what this viewpoint has necessitated in terms of functional position. The many notions concerning white superiority in this time zone are directly connected to how the expansion of western culture has come to be viewed by white people—that being: the rise of western civilization and the progressional decline of non-western civilization (as a controlling force) can be viewed as sufficient basis to proclaim an inherent superiority of the white race. Thus whether applied to creativity or anything else, western culture has come to view outside initiations in a somewhat distorted manner (and yet to write this without also commenting that the natural affinity make-up of every culture and racial group can be viewed in this same manner would be grossly unfair). The fact is, every cultural and racial group seems to have problems experiencing outside initiations. My reasons for focusing on western culture in this section has only to do with the dynamics of this time period—which is to say, no matter how prejudiced given culture groups are, or can be, only western culture is in the economic and political position to influence how the composite progressional continuance of information is to be perceived and transmitted—that is, on any real influential level, for even the realness of creativity is affected by the political realities of a given time zone. It is this semantical and vibrational subjugating of world creativity that is actually transmitted when most people speak of what they have come to call "primitive" music. However, we are slowly coming to a period when the realness of this subject must again be dealt with; for now, more than ever, there is a need for having a sound understanding of world creativity. This is because the actualness of the next cycle will necessitate that creativity play an important role—either with regards to particulars or real transformation. Before this can happen there are many factors that must be re-clarified, because the natural thrust progression of western culture has been detrimental to the realness of creativity—outside of its ability to function with regards to economics and spectacle. The study of world creativity can only help put the totalness of this subject in better focus—which is to say, a more realistic and accurate appraisal of world creativity could help everyone view the creative process in its purest sense (what it really is—or could be).

The study of world creativity is a necessary factor that must be dealt with because of a multitude of reasons. For I believe there are basic vibrational laws that dictate how creativity is to function in any culture—and the basic underlying "stuff" of these laws has nothing to do with the dynamic particulars concerning how a given form functions in itself (i.e., whether a form is more or less when compared to other forms). The distortions surrounding how world creativity is understood in this time zone are directly related to the flaws which permeate western culture—in its progressional and functional sense. I do not mean to imply there is a conscious attempt to manipulate how world creativity is understood from any given wing of western culture, nor have I meant to imply that there is a concerted conspiracy in the west to undermine world creativity, because this is not what I believe. Rather, the vibrational lack of respect for world creativity that exists in present-day western culture is related to what I call the collective forces of western culture—that is, the compilation of many different factors taking place in western culture seeks to promote a special type of affinity alignment (and this alignment is not conducive to experiencing world creativity among other things). Certainly I have not meant to imply that any particular form of creativity is better than any other form—because this has nothing to do with anything—my point instead is this: **if there are universal laws having to do with what creativity is actually about, then any attempt to negate those laws would risk establishing important flaws in the actual aesthetic lining of that given culture group.** It is not a question of one culture being more advanced than another culture as much as what is the end result of this deviation, if any. The study of world creativity can supply the proper basis to deal with the realness of what is happening in this time zone. By examining the thrust continuum of this subject, it is possible that we might better understand what creativity really is, for the realness of world creativity transcends any one time period. This subject corresponds to the progressional continuum of our total beingness on earth (yet I do not mean to imply that creativity is about earth). The study of world creativity can shed light on the whole of creativity with regards to the past, present, and future.

If cultural racism is the motivating factor that has provided impetus for the distortions surrounding how world creativity is presently perceived, then the effect of this phenomenon cannot be separated from the reinterpretations which have historically underlined what this subject really means. For many contributions from world culture have simply not been acknowledged or recognized—even though the science that supports western culture would not be possible without these contributions—and in most cases the composite actualness of this phenomenon is distorted only as a means to apply gradualism. Nor have I meant to imply that only certain aspects of world creativity are distorted, because this is not necessarily true. In actual fact, the misdocumentation that surrounds how world creativity is understood in this time period extends from both given particulars to the essence realness underlying the meta- and vibrational foundation of this subject (and without a proper understanding of the essence foundation of world culture, it is impossible to deal with the realness of its creativity). The extent of this misdocumentation cannot be separated from any real attempt to deal with world creativity—for the distortions that surround this subject permeate every level of available information in this period. Given this situation, it remains for our generation to initiate the reconstruction of both the history of world creativity and what the true nature of the vibrational and philosophical (and functional) implications of this subject really imply. Only by having a clear (and correct) idea of world creativity will we have basis for establishing what role creativity today can have for future generations.

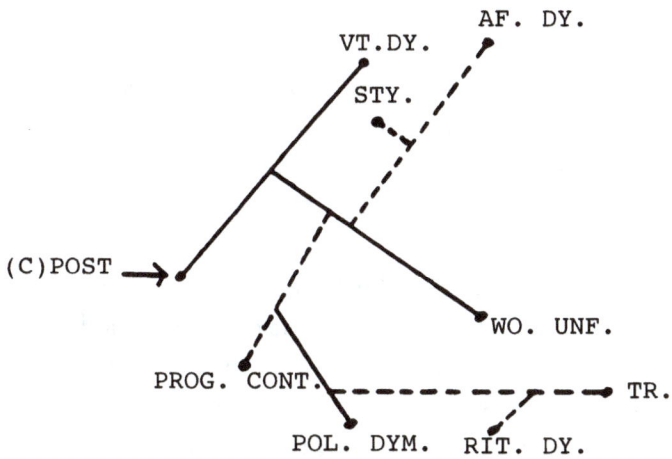

The study of world creativity must be approached in both its composite realness and its individual brilliance, because all of this information is essential if we are to have some real basis for perceiving the dynamic scope of this subject. With regards to investigation it is necessary to examine the actualness of this subject in both composite and separate terms. For the composite realness of world creativity can help us better see the dynamics of this subject in broad universal terms (while separate investigation of given focuses can give us some idea of the particulars related to how these universal considerations were actualized on the physical universe level). For example, the realness of African creativity has much to offer this period in time if it can be re-assessed with regards to what is happening with the music, rather than the people analyzing the music. A more accurate understanding of African creativity could give profound insight about the realness of composite creative music today in America, regardless of level, because of the position of black creativity in western culture. This is so because the vibrational realness of black creativity has not really changed in terms of affinity alignment and/or affinity dynamics. Any real attempt to understand the significance of American creativity would imply that the affinity-alignment implications of black creativity be dealt with on many different levels.

It is also clear that the study of world creativity cannot be undertaken in conventional terms, for the "particular reality" surrounding the state of various culture groups varies depending on what time zone is being examined (and it must be remembered that the time perimeter encasing this subject can be traced back thousands of years before the Christian era). Moreover, in the case of African creativity there are many other variables that must be dealt with as well, for the thrust continuum of African creativity cannot be separated from how the systematic destruction of black culture was achieved and maintained. For the time zone which saw the decline of black civilization was also the same period that saw the functional and meta-reality of African creativity subjected to "vibrational transfer" (another way of saying this is "stolen"). Given the present situation in Africa it will be extremely difficult to piece together the historical references related to how this dissolution was brought about in a complete sense—for in dealing with Africa, we are talking of a continent that has experienced a succession of wars on a time scale that boggles the mind. Historians—who are only too aware of the progression surrounding the decline of black civilization—have been able to use the succession of transitions in Africa as a means to redefine what actually happened (i.e., in the use of racially motivated speculation without basis). The end result of this situation is that the historical community would have us believe black Africa has never developed advanced cultures (or creativity)—and this position, while interesting, has nothing to do with the truth.

It is not the purpose of this book to detail the factors that dictated the historical progressions surrounding African civilization, because this is a task for more qualified writers (e.g., Chancellor Williams or Yosef Ben-

Jochannan). But as the real truth about this subject slowly emerges, it will be possible to gain some idea of the essence foundation that dictated how African creativity was to be understood and utilized. This information will better enable us to deal with the actualness of world creativity—regardless of culture. Because whatever we learn about the essence realness of African creativity should also shed light on the resultant physical universe state that world creativity is now in. For while the systematic distortion of African culture pertains to only one community of world culture, it would be a great mistake to assume that only Africa will suffer in the long run from distorted interpretations. The realness of world creativity is directly related to our ability to gain true information with regards to all of the various culture groups that make it up. For the basis of the distortions surrounding the realness of African creativity cannot be separated from the thrust expansion of composite world creativity—and this is important, because the reality of cultural documentation affects the composite implications of world creativity. In other words, **western historians would have us believe that the many different tribal groups in Africa today can be viewed as proof that (1) there was never a unified African aesthetic (center) and, as such, there was never an "advanced" African culture, (2) the creativity "ised" from these various tribal communities has never changed (and as such doesn't expand), and (3) the essence foundation underlying how given tribal groups see their activity has no relation to any kind of principal African viewpoint (or no value in the search for a unified aesthetic).** The seriousness of these charges cannot be lightly dismissed, for the net effect of this viewpoint seeks to undermine the progressional spread (and expansion) of world culture. Only in this time period have specialists begun to objectively examine the realness of African civilization (and for the most part this is because of the work of black historians who are dealing with the challenge of this most important area).

Rather than pointing out surface differences in world creativity as a means for dis-unification, historians and musicologists could better serve humanity by using these differences to trace back to the underlying source that "ised" the world aesthetic in its pure sense. For with the destruction of the historical records, and the natural limitations of oral history, it is possible that honest research in world creativity could prove most valuable in helping to recover information on particular culture groups. (This would not only pertain to the progressional continuance of African creativity, but to every projection that has experienced blockage regardless of level.) Whatever, the work being done in Africa and India towards tracing the historical and progressional development of given culture groups represents a new field of research—in many cases the solidification of this kind of research has been developing for the last fifty years and some—and there will be much relevant information for us to deal with in the coming cycles. We are now in a time period where there is a need for true information about world culture—regardless of racial or vibrational category. For example, only recently have we been able to learn about the realness of early Chinese creativity—or Dogon culture. Slowly, but surely, it is becoming increasingly clear that all notions of cultural superiority or national superiority must be re-examined, for the composite realness of world creativity has no room for prejudice. In this period, the notion of western creativity being superior to other cultures is finally shown to be only a cultural tool for suppression, and this must be understood, for not only is creativity not about being superior in that sense, but every culture is a superior example of its own natural thrust alignment. There are really no examples of developments in creativity, with the possible exception of the emergence of electronic music, that cannot be traced back to the composite dynamics of world culture. Everyone has had a hand in making earth creativity what it is in this period because the multitude of forms utilized on this planet are all interrelated. Whatever, **the realness of world creativity is included in this book because of several reasons—(1) to better establish groundwork for the expansion of this series of books; (2) to rectify one of the most suppressed areas of our present-day information scan—with regard to supplying motivation to help establish a total musical environment based on respect for all of the creativity on this planet; (3) to use what we are able to understand about world creativity as a factor to assist in decoding what options are available to the creative person today; and finally (4) to establish the realness that world creativity is related to the next transformation cycle.**

C.INFO.------INFO.AF.B.

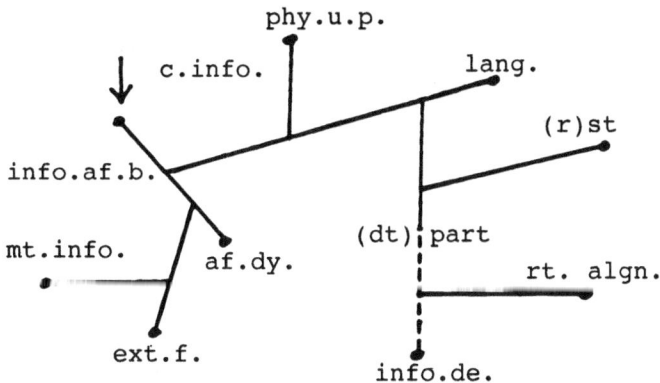

LK.IMP.------C.CONT.

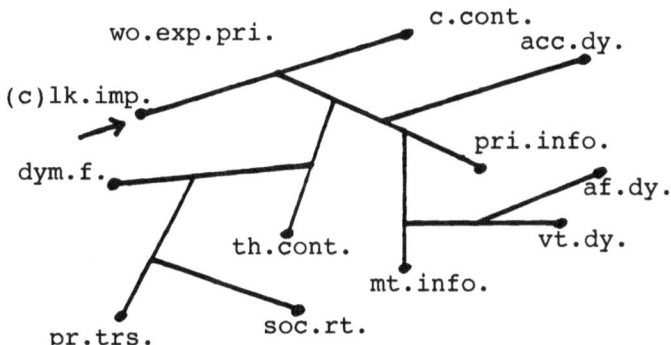

RT.ALGN.------WO.EXP.PRIN.

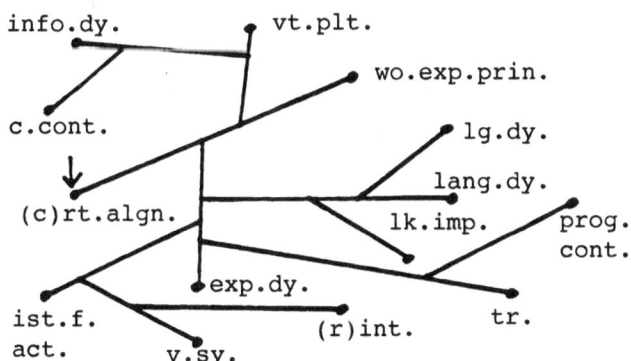

WM–24

To examine the realness of world creativity in positive terms is to approach this subject in a universal context. What is the point of examining the meta-reality of world creativity unless that examination relates to the total scheme of what creativity is about in both cosmic and functional terms? In itself this type of research means very little unless we are enlightened to move towards a universal love of all various forms of creativity. This is what I am interested in. For too long the study of world creativity has been used as a political or ethnic tool at the expense of the actual creativity. The end result of this mis-use of ethno-musicology (and history) has helped to make this period in time very interesting—for what we do not know, rather than what we know. The composite realness of world creativity has nothing to do with the attitude many people have brought to this subject, and as such we are all losing. For if the significance and realness of a given culture group is distorted, what is the end effect of that distortion? It must be understood that not only are we the effects of what we do not know, but our ignorance about multi-information also will determine how we flow (involving what options we will have in the future). In short, we are slowly coming to the junction where we cannot afford the luxury of not dealing with what we could know. For a better understanding of earth creativity can help us on many different levels. There is no aesthetic or vibrational flow happening on this planet that we can afford to not know about. Because if a given projection is indeed related to a multitude of factors, it would be to our advantage to understand what this means—both with regards to the multitude of information that corresponds to what each projection really signifies, as well as what information means with regards to the spiritual factor related to how it is approached. As we move towards the next transformation, we cannot afford to disregard the realness of world culture.

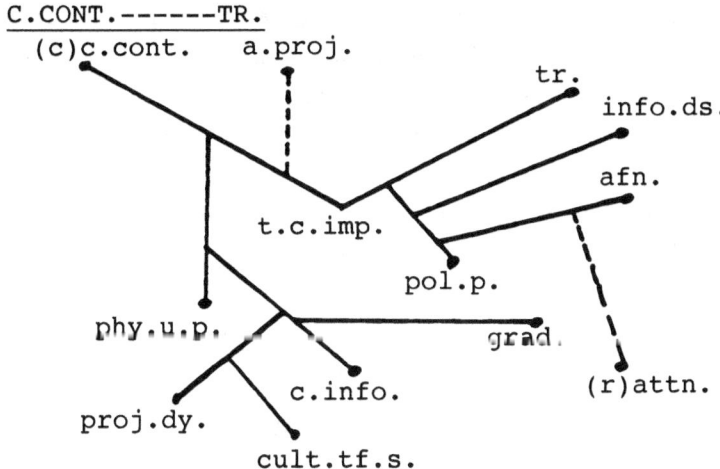

There are many reasons for writing about the underlying philosophical questions that determine how creativity is to be perceived. For the meta-reality of a given projection transcends any one aspect of creativity and, in fact, permeates the realness of existence. Moreover, the science of a given aesthetic is directly related to the meta-reality base of its aesthetic. Thus any attempt to deal with the functional actualness of a given projection would also reveal some aspect of what world creativity really is. In other words, the underlying philosophical arena of a given thrust alignment determines the aesthetic and functional realness of its given projections. It is important to understand what this means, for at present there is much misinformation surrounding how many avenues of world creativity are perceived. For example, the inability of the western methodological and vibrational alignment to properly deal with the meta-realness of world creativity can be clearly viewed in the many analyses which have been made on African music that are completely outside of the "base aesthetic" consideration of African culture. For example, the reducing of African music to scales without a clear understanding of what those scales mean on a vibrational-spiritual level; or the research practiced on African rhythm which ignored that rhythm's place on the vibrational-ritual level of African culture (where a given rhythm gets its significance) but instead focused only on how that rhythm works in one-dimensional terms in the music.

All of these factors might be of interest to western analysis, but this type of activity should not be confused with African music. Not to mention that because of the limitations of language it is probably impossible to write on what a given element really means in the actual sense of what is happening in a given creative functionalism—as it happens in that moment. For all of these meanings are connected to factors that are much more profound than a physical universe sound (or appearance) being executed in a given time zone.

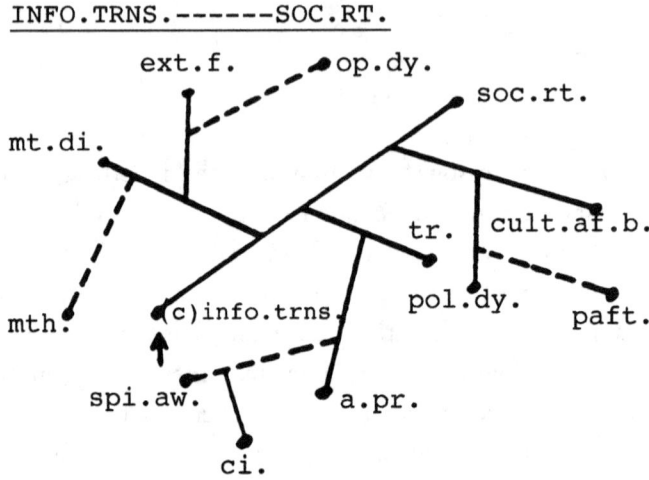

My point is this: the progressional actualness of a given creative manifestation transcends the particulars of any one empirical criterion, and as such the whole subject of musicology has to be dealt with very delicately. For while I do not mean to negate an entire area of research—certainly many important factors have emerged in musicology—it is essential to maintain an overview about the spectrum of extended creativity. For the base of any real inquiry into a given thrust alignment must respect the affinity alignment of that thrust if it is to be meaningful. With few exceptions (i.e., Alan Lomax) this is never done—especially if the form under scrutiny is of or related to black culture. Moreover, I am not saying that empirical investigation in itself is not useful—because this would not be a true statement either. Instead, I have focused on the spirit factor underlining how western culture deals with the study of world creativity, as a means to say that we know very little about this subject. We know very little about the realness of world creativity because the criterion that substantiates how western culture perceives phenomena is not universal.

It is understood that the concepts and tools of a given culture group are perceived in accordance with how that group sees itself. If this is true, then not only should certain allowances be made when a given culture group attempts to understand another culture group, but the vibrational implications of "affinity transfer" must also be dealt with. This is especially true if we are to understand the realness of world creativity. For the factors which underlie how the composite thrust of western culture sees itself are directly in accordance to its own alignment—with regards to what it views as rational. Yet this same alignment, when formulated into functional and intellectual concepts, can serve as a factor for misinformation when applied to certain sectors of the world's community—especially again, African music. This is so because the western affinity to what it would call "logical" can become a straitjacket for comprehending world creativity (or culture). Thus, it comes as no surprise that many western historians have little or no respect for many areas of world creativity. Concepts like "advanced" or "retarded" have nothing to do with world culture's basic vibrational thrust alignment (or at least these concepts are viewed in completely different terms from western observation)—yet it would be wrong to assume that the progressional realness of world creativity has no standards. Understanding world creativity involves dealing with projections whose ultimate actualness has nothing to do with many of our notions concerning either creativity or life. And as such these areas of information must be approached very sensitively.

To view the initiations of a given culture from world creativity is to deal with many factors, for the realness of a given projection is related to the time junction it is in (as well as the time junction it is perceived from). All of these factors are related to the position of a given culture in its own cycle (with regards to the aspect being examined)—and where that culture is at, in present time terms. In other words, a culture like India cannot be viewed in the same context as Africa—because the major differences would have to do with the destruction of practically all of the historical records related to the essence expansion of black creativity (in its most high state—the solidification of its empire-culture), while India—even in its decline from its former position—does have its historical records. Thus, it is possible to study the vibrational and conceptional identity of Indian culture—and how it relates to the creativity—and gain some understanding of the meta-realness of Indian culture (on the surface). Yet if the essence alignment of world creativity is based on the synthesis of concept and spiritualism, it would also imply that any attempt to understand the reality of a given projection would necessitate that same synthesis. Certainly this fact in itself is not profound, but what it implies is rarely dealt with. For while there has always been a need in every culture to examine and seek new realities—and of course this is as it should be (what else can I say?)—the realness of how outside initiations are viewed is rarely put in proper perspective. My point is that it is one thing to learn something—but quite another to realize that while you are learning, it has nothing to do with what is actually happening (or at least the relationship between what you learn and "what is" is wide enough so that one should not confuse the two).

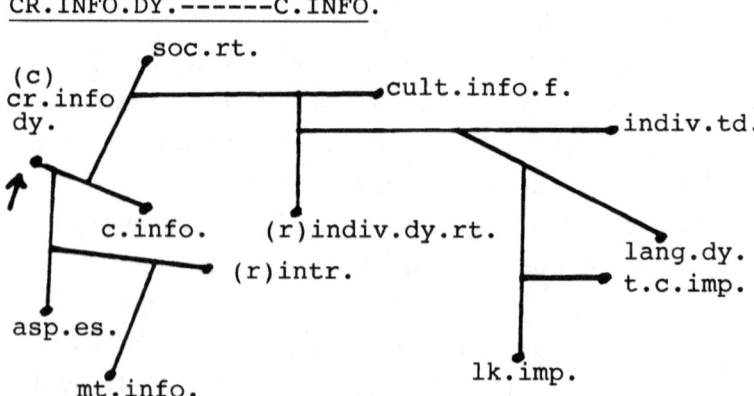

On the physical universe level, the actuality of a given performance of music and dance reveals the extent of how different the basic aesthetic of world creativity is from western culture. For while it is clear that the dynamics of world creativity function from another sensibility with regard to its meta- and vibrational presence, nowhere can the realness of what this means be better understood/experienced than by focusing on the actualness of a given performance in ceremony. Nowhere can the source presence that determines the meta-reality actualness of a given thrust projection be better viewed than by experiencing how music and dance function in actual context. In every way, a given performance underlines the realness of vibrational interaction (the particulars of which depend on the alignment nature of the culture itself) and in its natural state this phenomenon also reveals the realness of its own discipline—with regards to the particulars of the actual moment (through improvisation). Yet just as it is impossible to separate the music from a given projection in world creativity (as a means to understand what it really is), it is also impossible to view any component of world creativity in that manner.

For all of the different creative areas in world creativity must be viewed in terms of the composite hierarchy (culture) that determines what role a given individual can function in—with regards to the composite actualness of a given manifestation (or ceremony). It is not a question of musicians performing while the majority of people—after paying their tickets—experience the performance. The meta-realness of world creativity functions as an integral part of how life itself is understood/felt. In other words, the vibrational alignment that determines the nature of how given culture groups relate to the "is" also dictates the natural affinity reality that gives meaning as to how the total hierarchy of creative dynamics is to be utilized in a given ceremony. With this in mind, a given ceremonial occasion would have musicians functioning in accordance to the vibrational and physical universe principles which defined the nature of the occasion—the dancers would also function in relationship to these same coordinates, as well as the "moment-actualness" of the music being created—the scripters would have already created masks or other ornaments relevant to the occasion, in accordance to the ritual that underlines the ceremony, etc., etc. (In other words, a multitude of factors are at work in a given creative manifestation in world creativity.) Moreover, the composite lining of world creativity is manifested from a principle unification factor, embracing both ritual and symbolic meaning. The end result of creativity from this type of alignment can be viewed on many different levels. For the projectional thrust of world creativity moves towards the unification of culture, and the actualness of ceremony, as designed throughout the annals of world culture, moves towards "maintaining the community." The nature of this interrelationship is outside of anything present-day western culture has been able to come up with. Only by examining the essence realness of world creativity can western culture establish a basis for perceiving what is really happening with this subject.

Thus it is when the totalness of a given creative thrust is experienced that we are better able to have a basis for attempting to understand world culture. For the realness of creativity from the world group encompasses more factors than what we have come to realize. There are many other considerations in world creativity that must also be dealt with if we are to have even an elementary grasp of given creative flows. For while the realness of any particular creative manifestation in world music utilizes many different levels—either in terms of essence factor or what a given physical universe event is at any given moment—it should be remembered that the very arena which defined the events of a particular creative manifestation are also directly related to the meta-reality of the culture itself. In other words, the form of a particular creativity actuality is also part of the ritual of that creativity. But where this idea can be seen utilized later in contemporary German functional composition concepts (the technique of Klangfarbenmelodie can be looked at in relationship to this most basic African idea), the major differences in the use of this technique relate to the spiritual-essence factor in world creativity. The nature, then, of African creativity in its normal flow dictates a more profound understanding of the concept of form.

If improvisation is the most universal element to be found in world culture, it would also be to our advantage if this consideration were refocused on and better understood. I say this because, in this time zone, there seems to be some disagreement as to (1) the underlying essence factor which determines how we have come to view improvisation, and (2) the functional nature underlying how improvisation has to be utilized before it is valid. There are many factors in African music that must be understood if we are to have a more realistic view of what is implied in the concept of "composite aesthetic" creativity. The most basic of these factors would be the understanding of form and the underlying tools which have always been properties in a given creative actualization in world music. I have already stated that a given manifestation of African music utilizes a composite identity on a level I believe to be the most sophisticated that is documented in this period. But it is also necessary to reiterate that all of this activity (in a given creative manifestation)—that being, the use of particular elements (e.g., mask-headdress) and the use of certain rhythms for certain occasions—can be looked at in relation to the form of the creativity. (I do not mean, however, to imply that this is the only use of form.) If this is true, then what we have is an extended understanding of form—and this is only the first level.

My reasons for attempting to understand what constitutes form in African music (world music) is to hopefully gain a better understanding of what is really happening in world creativity. For, if my previous observations are meaningful on any level, there is another level of world creativity that is of even more importance. That level would be the significance of the concept of form in the world music aesthetic.

I have already stated that the basic underlying vibrational thrust in world music can be viewed as activity which moves towards ritual. But what does this mean? Well, it is my opinion that the consideration of form as ritual completes the total meta-reality cycle that dictates how a person participates in a composite creative manifestation (as far as what that participation really means). **Form viewed as ritual can be understood not only as functional unification in the creative act but also in regards to what it means for the society. Ritual, then, is the alignment which serves to keep the participating individuals in accord with the meta-reality of the culture as well as a factor that substantiates the essence factor of the culture itself.** Form as ritual is also the most important factor in the stabilizing of a given culture's relationship to its spiritual essence foundation. With this understood, the implications of a "composite aesthetic" reality can become clear; and if my understanding is correct, the functionalism which dictates how world creativity is perceived (from the people—or culture groups themselves) can be looked at as an example of the highest form of creative alignment. For the totalness of a vibrational approach—encompassing the elements used in a particular manifestation—is also the form. Thus, a given creative manifestation in world music is a profound example of a living, breathing culture, rather than a factor that can be separated and studied by itself. The end result of this phenomenon is that world creativity sustains the agreed reality of its cultures' lining in extended spiritual terms.

It is necessary to search even further into the functional reality of world music if we are to understand the vibrational position of each participant in the actual creative process. For the factors that determine the composite reality of a given form in the world group are also manifested in the individual reality of the participating musicians, dancers, etc., in that same form. In other words, while all of the factors which determine a given reality of form are operative throughout the total gamut of creativity in world culture, the nature of what this phenomenon means embraces other factors as well (that being, with regards to the participating individual—while he or she is functioning in the creative act). It would be to our advantage if these factors are examined on as many levels as possible.

The consideration that most interests me is the reality of the creative person with respect to how a given form is executed. In other words, I have already written that any given form dictates the nature of what elements it is to utilize—as well as how that utilization is to take place. But since the functional realness of form in world culture is not constructed on any one-dimensional empirical system, we are forced to examine what this utilization means. This is so because there is another factor that must be looked at—a factor whose importance carried multi-complexual implications with regards to the question of form in world creativity. In other words, to deal with the realness of form in world creativity would also imply some understanding of the consideration we call "improvisation." We are thus forced to examine what this consideration really means, for the actualness of improvisation permeates every level of world creativity and how it is manifested—regardless of form or time period. The realness of improvisation is the single most apparent factor that separates how world creativity is perceived, as compared to western art music (at least in physical universe terms). Thus an examination of improvisation could help establish some criteria for the whole of the book (affecting how creativity is perceived on every level regardless of culture or category). Moreover, an investigation of this subject can also help establish the nature of how functionalism is perceived in world creativity—with regards to either the actualness of a given functional alignment, or the meta-implications underlying what that alignment means—in both actual or conceptual terms (even applying to documentation).

Improvisation—as it is "ised" in the world group aesthetic—has to do with the ability to function in a given context in accordance to each individual's own vibrational flow. In the functional context of African creativity where the form is ritual, each individual, while utilizing the language content of the occasion, is in the position of interpreting the nature of what that given reality means subjectively and objectively (or bi-jectively). The totalness of this relationship can be viewed as individuals creating in "actual time" from a composite essence alignment that also affirms the meta-reality of the culture in the "doing" (creating). The realness of this condition thus affects the individual, communal, and spiritual well-being of the culture. This then is the actual "isness" of improvisation as conceived and offered to us from the progressional continuance of world culture—as opposed to present-day concepts which view this subject as an end in itself (or as a factor that promotes a kind of freedom alien to its base aesthetic). It is important that this factor is understood if we are to view the realness of world creativity as a potential transformational tool. This is so because there are now attempts in this time zone from certain circles in western culture (e.g., the post-Cage school or the emerging improvisational movements) to declare that improvisation is a form that can function only in certain contexts (and any other use of this consideration constitutes another functional approach)—but this is not true. The actualness of improvisation, as it has been defined through the progressional continuance of world culture, transcends any one approach or application. I am writing of a discipline that really shows the proper relationship between given functional approaches and aesthetic agreements, as well as a consideration that reveals the functional dynamics related to its own utilization.

Moreover, I am not focusing on the consideration of improvisation and its relationship to functionalism in world creativity as a means to declare innovation. Rather, the use of improvisation can be traced to culture groups thousands of years before the Christian era. It would be more realistic to view the use of improvisation in world creativity as the culmination of what has been learned/experienced throughout the progressional actualness of life on this planet (and beyond—relating to the realness of the "is"—or original knowledge, etc.) rather than the product of isolated innovation—as the word is now used in this time zone. This information is important to understand, because the realness of improvisation promises to be the next source-transfer factor in the western documentation cycle. It should also be noted that the utilization of improvisation in world creativity was dynamic—extending throughout the total spectrum of creativity. There are as many different forms of improvisations as there are cultures (not to mention that every culture necessarily found many other ways to deal with this consideration in its own way of being creative). Add to this the natural realignment of functional process that takes place in the course of time and one might have some understanding of the dynamic realness of improvisation and how it has been utilized in the composite thrust continuum of world culture. Any attempt to negate this most obvious fact is ridiculous, for the progressional use of improvisation is documented for all to see (yet we will probably have to deal with this very subject in the next time cycle).

I believe the study of world culture is very important especially in this time zone. We, as earth people, are in the position where great tasks await us in practically every area. The importance of the historical progressions leading to this time zone can shed light on how we can develop in the future. This section of my book is primarily concerned with re-establishing the underlying principles which define the personification of the world group aesthetic—nothing more. The real research has yet to be completed, for without doubt, there is much more for us to learn about world creativity.

(Level One) WESTERN ART MUSIC

THE SOLIDIFICATION OF WESTERN ART MUSIC would mark a new cycle for creative music from the trans-European aesthetic. For the next three hundred years this thrust would detail the progressional continuity of western creativity and reshape world music as well. Moreover, the dynamics of this thrust would also provide many new avenues of explorations for the creative musician composer to work in. It is fashionable in this period to simply dismiss western art music as a bourgeois or elitist music, but in fact the solidification of classical music would revolutionize western creativity. Every period of western art music would thus reveal to us the changing meta-reality of western culture and every juncture of this thrust would also shed light on the nature of the next transformation. This can be understood by tracing the spread of art music throughout Europe and the Americas and detailing the many changes which have affected the science of creative music. The solidification of western art music would also comment on the thrust continuum of western civilization and give insight into what this continuum would mean with regards to the changing meta-reality of western culture. In other words, it is possible to investigate the composite progression of western art music as a means to detail what factors contributed to the present juncture we are now living in, because every period of the music is related to some aspect of that change. That is: the thrust continuum of western art music can be viewed with respect to the social-political implications surrounding its progression or the thrust continuum of western art music can be viewed with respect to what it reveals about the vibrational actualness of western culture. This is true because the vibrationaltory lining which dictates how events are perceived and acted upon—regardless of period—is directed related to—and in some cases the direct result of—the meta-reality of its creativity. To understand the nature of this relationship is to gain insight into western art music as a separate creative thrust from that of the world group, but this is only the beginning. The meta-reality of western art music is significant because of how it participated in shaping the present period we are in as well—and this is true on many different levels. Moreover, the seriousness of where we have arrived at present, with respect to both creativity as well as politics, gives us little choice but to attempt an all-out examination of what this relationship means. In other words, an examination of western art music can help us understand what is happening at present in western culture—that is, what is really happening (regardless of level).

To examine the vibrationaltory lining of western art music would only accent the diversity of this thrust as a multi-dynamic continuum quite separate from the reality of world culture. The body of music that has come from this thrust represents what is best about western civilization, and the multitude of forms realized through this continuum can be viewed as a unique testament to western ingenuity and creativity. To experience the spectrum of this thrust is to be confronted with many dynamic forms and styles. From opera to symphonic orchestra pieces, on through to the development of electronic music, what we see are forms corresponding to the vibrationaltory actualness of given periods in western culture, and forms that also correspond to the technical developments related to how that period was affirmed. The diversity of this thrust, as much as the actual number of works, attests to the substantialness of western art music as a form that has expanded, and the nature of this phenomenon also sheds light on what that expansion will mean in future terms (i.e., the nature of source-transfer with regards to transformation). To view the actualness of western art music is to be confronted with the seriousness of what it poses—as a thrust separate from that of the world group—with regards to the concept of thrust affinity alignment. For it is understood that we are not simply discussing an existing thrust (which means nothing in itself) but rather an affinity alignment of profound importance. To deal with the actualness of western art music would imply that some effort is made to understand what that alignment is. For it is clear that the success of the next transformation is directly related to what we are able to understand about this transformation (time zone)—in other words, it is useless to work for change if we are ignorant of what we are changing from. The seriousness of western art music—as a thrust projection manifested from the affinity alignment of western culture—must be dealt with and understood (on some level) if we are serious about transformation.

To view the composite projection of western art music is to have some understanding of the progressional flow of western culture. By this I am saying the path western art music was to take is directly related to the solidification of western culture as a composite affinity alignment after the destruction of the Egyptian Empire on through the forming of Greece and Rome. The solidification of what this alignment was to mean would move to establish western thought, and the fruit of this movement—in projectional terms—would help actualize western art music. The emergence of western art music would thus establish the thrust projection of the western vibrational and affinity alignment—from the previous transformation cycle after the decline of Egypt—as well as what this would mean in functional terms (with regards to both system and methodology). The thrust continuum of this projection would play an important role in shaping the development of western creativity (i.e., progressional continuity or process) and would also detail the nature of the next continuum towards transformation. In other words, the solidification of western art music—as a composite projection of western creativity—commented on a multitude of factors related to western culture, as opposed to only music. It would be to our advantage to examine some of these factors as a means to acquire an overview of this subject and also as a means to establish the broadest possible basis for understanding western art music in its separateness.

When I stated that the solidification of western art music is directly related to the meta-reality of western culture it might be necessary to elaborate on what this means with regards to the progressional development of western creativity. My point is that the establishment of western art music can be viewed as an affirmation of a particular attitude—vibrational attitude—and the reality underlying how this attitude was perceived is not separate from, and indeed directly comments on, the philosophical position of western culture. To understand this relationship is to view the progressional solidification of western culture after Egypt—from the affinity adaptation of new ideas (how a given universal consideration is colored in accordance to the thrust alignment of a given culture group) through the embracing of dialectics onto the many new schools of philosophic thought and what this would mean for the culture. In other words, the thrust continuum of the western affinity alignment (with regards to what this phenomenon means in the establishment of a composite philosophy) is directly related to how the solidification of western art music would be perceived, and moreso, the establishment of western art music can be viewed as a phenomenon affirming the vibrational state and dynamics of the western philosophical position. By this I am saying the solidification of western art music would establish a functional and creative thrust in accordance to the vibrational affinity nature of western culture; and moreover, this establishment would be directly in accordance to how events were defined and "ised" in the western philosophic position.

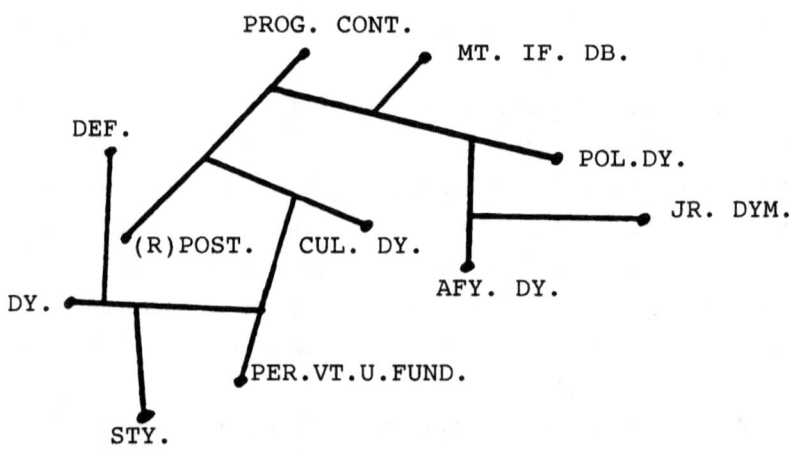

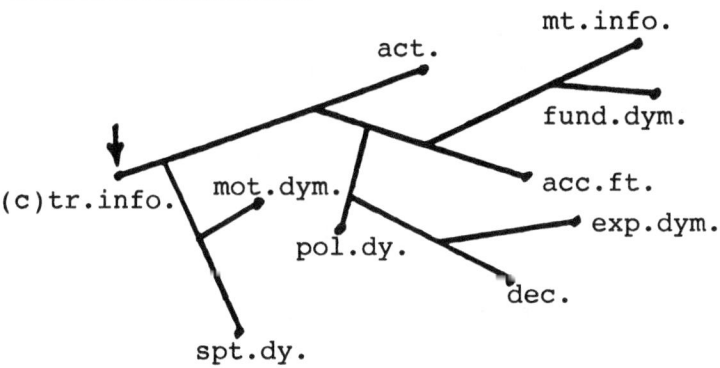

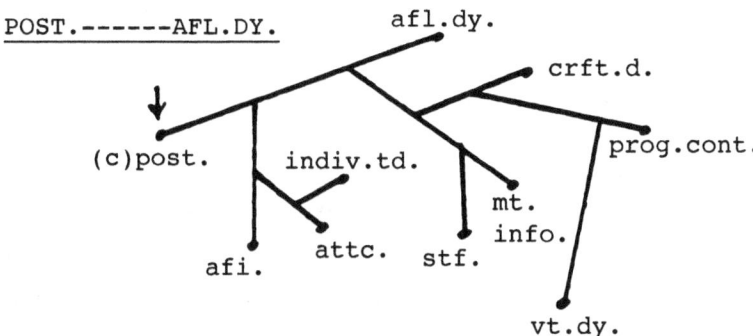

Thus, the creativity would celebrate the philosophic position—which of course is the natural position for creativity—and yet there is more here. For if the relationship between the creativity and composite philosophic attitude does indeed function as a unified thrust then any attempt to examine the essence factor of western art music would shed light on the thrust continuance of western culture—from its early formation until the present. Thus, if the essence factor of western art music can be viewed in a progressional context, it might be possible to examine what has happened in the last three hundred years as a means to understand why this thrust is separate from the world group and also as a means to understand what this difference might mean with regards to transformation. Whatever, it is important to understand that no matter the diversity (i.e., spectrum of styles from the western creative thrust)—we are really dealing with a single projection—or vibrational affinity and/or attitude which directly sheds light on the state of western creativity. The solidification of western art music would substantiate the next cycle of creativity from the western vibrational thrust since the completion of the last transformation in Egypt. The solidification of this thrust must be viewed as an important factor related to the state of the planet during that period: that is, the composite formation of western art music signaled the nature of the next path for the western affinity alignment, and what this path would mean in vibrational and projectional terms.

There are several reasons why I have chosen to separate western art music from that of the world group. One, the nature underlying how the affinity alignment of the aesthetic is perceived and what this viewpoint has necessitated with regards to the composite essence umbrella of western art music; two, the progressive development of the music can be viewed as separate from that of the world group; three, the vibrational and philosophic realities western art music seeks to affirm can be looked at as separate from the world group; four, the understanding of process in western art music can be viewed as separate from that of the world group; and five, the resulting situation western culture finds itself in during this period in time can be looked at as separate from that of the world group. The effectiveness of any examination of western art music would reflect to what degree these five considerations are dealt with, yet it might be necessary to clarify my approach in cosmic terms, for I have not meant to give the wrong impression about the "realness" of any creative thrust. I have instead formulated this approach as a means to clearly write about how I see the many different types of creativity we have on the planet. It would be wrong to assume that my reason for separating western art music—or for that matter creative music from the black aesthetic—implies a lack of respect for these musics, or a lack of belief in whether or not these thrust continuums can be of use in helping to establish transformation, because this is not true. My reason for separating western art music is to help establish a basis to look at the composite identity of world creativity—and in particular creative music—so that we might better understand the present situation of the planet.

In its early period the formation of classical music was very closely tied to the church. Many of the great composers—like Bach, for instance—wrote music for the church, and in fact were employed by the church. To understand the formation of classical music is to become aware of the spiritual base of the aesthetic—which is to say the formation of this thrust was conceived in spiritual and as such cosmic terms. The personification of western art music would establish a new dynamic thrust in creativity, and the progressional continuity of this thrust would bring forth many new forms to celebrate its religious base. Composers like Bach would write new compositions every week for the choir, and on his own, compose larger works. My point however is that all of this activity was related to a composite spiritual base and as such represented the solidification of the next juncture of western culture. Moreover, in its early period, classical music functioned near the same vibrational and aesthetic platform as world creativity—in the sense that the relationship between the creativity and spiritual community was proper (i.e., creativity affirming the spirituality of culture)—and at the same time unique. The establishment of western art music would signify that western culture had reached the next level, and the potential implications of what this level signified could not even be imagined—so new and hopeful was this thrust viewed. Yet there is more to the solidification of classical music, because the thrust projection of western culture is not limited to only this context—there is much more to look at.

Undoubtedly, the factor that most distinguishes western art music as a separate creative thrust from the world group is the affinity alignment particulars of its essence foundation. By this I am referring to how the composite western community has come to view the aesthetic actualness of creativity with regards to the vibrational or functional implications of a given projection. It is my opinion that the nature of this affinity alignment represents the strongest basis for establishing both the separateness of western art music from world culture as well as understanding what has happened in the progressional continuance of the western creative projection. Western civilization has revealed one constant alignment projection since the transformational dissolution of Egypt, and any attempt to examine the underlying principle foundation of its information order would accent the peculiarness of how this "alignment" is manifested. The alignment I am referring to has to do with the nature underlying how western culture has come to deal with "essence"—or "what is" and the realness of what this nature means in actual terms. The affinity alignment I am referring to also has to do with how a given essence is perceived in terms of its conceptual and functional make-up as well as the science constructed to sustain that relationship. The nature of the western philosophical and methodological thrust can be viewed with regards to its unique affinity balance between the consideration of "idea" and the actualness of "spiritual tenets." This alignment also sheds light on the path western culture would take to qualify aesthetic or empirical projections as well as what a given projection would mean (or how it would be perceived). In other words, any attempt to deal with the reality of western art music would imply that the affinity thrust foundation that defines its creativity is examined. For if the significance of a given vibrational continuum (culture) has to do with the nature underlying how its affinity projection flows, then it is necessary to understand how this projection functions—and also what this phenomenon means. Because all of these factors are brought into play when we look at a given "vibrational-identity" or methodological approach. In other words, the most basic factor that differentiates a given group (i.e., race) has to do with the nature of the thrust projection of that group. Yet when I say that the western affinity alignment is separate from the world group it is important that I lay a basis to clarify what this means—with regards both to the affinity projection of western culture as well as to the creativity actualized from this projection.

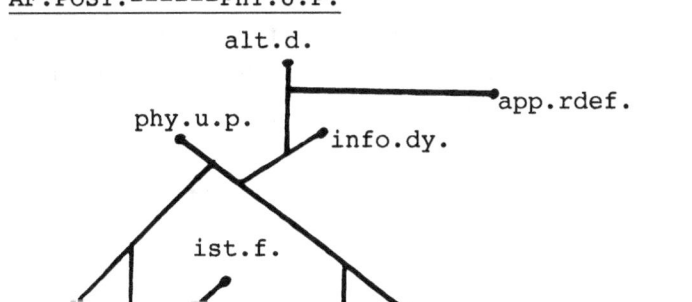

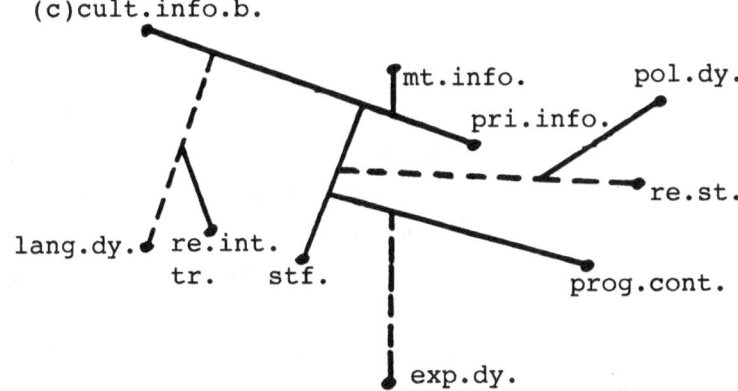

Without doubt, the most basic difference of the affinity alignment from the western principle to that of the world group has to do with what the separation of essence has meant to the western sensibility as opposed to what this concept means universally. For when I state that the understanding of essence in western terms had to do with how separation is utilized with regards to a given set of particulars, I am saying that the vibrational attitude related to this affinity alignment is what has established western culture as a separate thrust from that of the world group. Yet it is necessary to explain this viewpoint more in depth, because I am not simply commenting on an abstraction, but rather an all-encompassing attitude that permeates western culture. To really view the separation of essence into "idea" and "spiritualism" in western terms is to also understand that this phenomenon is only the beginning. For the affinity alignment surrounding this separation also encompasses what a consideration means with regards to its "qualification" or "validation"—or establishing what is to be considered "ised" or not—or "how." In the case of western culture during its early period the affinity alignment I am referring to was directly related to the establishment of the philosophical hierarchy which later would dictate the projectional direction of western culture. The most important factor that would later become apparent about this phenomenon would be the peculiar emphasis on empiricism as a means to validate ideas—in a separate realm from the composite spiritual community. Thus the establishment of the western philosophic and methodological thrust would move to apply this affinity alignment on its total reality spectrum (concerning how western culture would see itself). This trait would move with the understanding that there are certain things in the universe which corresponded to projections that are perfect, and there are other things that are imperfect. "Perfect" in this context would have to do with the alignment of a given particular in a given systematic or logical context, as opposed to how a given particular functions in a total spiritual or cosmic and empirical context. Thus the most basic factor that would distinguish western culture from world culture would be this use of empiricism and the "affinity" result of this application as well. From the early transfer junction concerning the Pythagorean use of number to the gradual forming of the functional science of western music, what we see is the development and expansion of what the affinity thrust of western culture would mean in what I call "actual terms."

The most apparent factor that we can investigate in western civilization—with regards to affinity alignment—would have to do with the nature of systematic alignment in determining how something is to be understood. In other words, we can view the systematic and logical implications concerning how a given essence is perceived as a factor that exemplifies the "stuff" of the western affinity alignment. Without doubt the nature of what this means sheds light on the meta-reality of western art music and permeates how we have come to view phenomenon as well. For the nature of this alignment has not only played a dominant role in shaping how the western vibrational and methodological projection was to move towards knowingness—and establishing culture (and particulars)—but the actualness of this alignment would also dictate the thrust continuum of western creativity. But if the uniqueness of separation and the application of empiricism without spiritual connections would establish the nature of the thrust projection in western culture, then it is important that we understand what this means—with regards to the establishment of the functional arena and projectional thrust actualness of western art music. In short, we are commenting on the factors which helped solidify the "idea alignment" of western culture, and we are also commenting on the affinity implications of this development as well. In actual terms, it is possible to look at what affinity alignment means with regards to the functional arena of western art music. One example of what "alignment" in this context means can be found in the scale formation of western art music. For in the early period of its development western art music functioned from a seven-note scale—later expanded to twelve notes. The understanding of this phenomenon would have to do with the nature of how sound was being experienced (heard) as well as the actualness of the philosophic basis which helped establish it.

    My point however is that in the final analysis the nature of this "affinity" moved to create a situation in western music that was very different from world music; more so, it is only in this time zone that western music has begun to utilize a wider sound spectrum (and to a great extent black music and the development of electronics is responsible for this expansion). To understand this example is to be aware of the significance of affinity alignment—not as a means to proclaim any notion of superiority but only to comment on the nature of how given thrusts "proceed" in accordance to the reality of a given period.

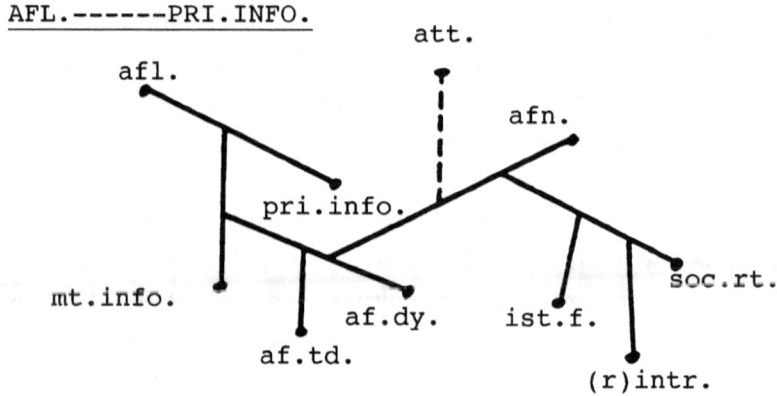

To observe the nature of how separation is utilized in western culture is to view the progressional expansion of this time period. In other words, when I write that the affinity alignment of western culture has a distinctive use of empiricism and separation, I am also commenting on how this alignment has developed in the time continuum of the last three hundred years. My point is this: the most basic factor that has determined the course of western art music can be found in the progressive decline of the church as the vibrational center of culture and the emphasis on intellectualism as a dynamic replacement for center. In other words, as the composite spiritual base of western culture moved towards the decline, the progressive continuance of western art music would move to base its expansion on ideas—as a given notion related to the composite intellectual thrust of each successive period. The implications of this shift would be profound, and the seriousness of this "alignment" would move to separate the western vibrational projection from the world group into a zone of its own. But it is necessary to elaborate on the nature of this separation if I am to be understood. For when I state that the composite spiritual center of western culture moved to the decline, I do not mean this as a negative attack on any given religious community regardless of its sector of the planet. Nor am I attacking any particular religion or group. I am instead referring to the progressive developments surrounding the move away from organized western religion and what this move really means, and I am also commenting on the progressional development of intellectualism as a non-unification factor. Any real investigation of western art music would have to deal with what this "transfer shift" means on a multi-complexual context, because creativity is connected to the base-lining of the culture it takes place in. Thus to gain insight into the essence factor of western art music is to be confronted with the cosmic implications of its expansion—that is, the nature of how this intellectualism was perceived, and what this would mean with regards to establishing the "affinity alignment" of the western vibrational projection. This is what I am concerned with.

When I stated that the most distinguishing factor of the composite affinity alignment of western culture is the nature of how essences are perceived, it is necessary to understand what this means with regards to the solidification of classical music. Moreover, I am not only referring to one aspect of this alignment but rather the total question of what thrust projection means. For if the most basic factor shaping the reality of western culture has to do with the meta-reality alignment of its vibrationaltory arena—that is, the nature of how composite is perceived in projectional terms (i.e., living and doing) and vibrational terms (i.e., thinking and creating)—then we are forced to deal with the effects of this alignment on creativity. In other words, to examine the thrust projection of western art music is to be confronted with the actualness of how "development" came to be perceived—as an intellectual consideration rather than actual consideration (i.e., life—or life of the culture). The nature of the composite western affinity alignment would thus come to view itself in terms of separating its own essence arena: that is, the solidification of western culture would see the development of a clear separation between how intellect and spiritualism would be perceived, and the resulting projection from this development would help establish the nature of the western affinity alignment. On the physical universe level the realness of what this phenomenon means would manifest itself with regards to the forming functional science implications surrounding how process was to be viewed. The emergence of empirical investigation—with this unique thrust alignment—would thus establish how western culture would proceed, and the peculiar nature of western empiricism would assume even more importance after the dissolution of the composite spiritual center of western culture. Intellectual empiricism has played not only the dominant role in establishing the nature of the progressional continuance of western culture, but the vibrational implications of this alignment have shaped the reality thrust for western art music as well.

Empiricism as a means for establishing functional progressions is one thing—certainly when we talk of technology, we are speaking of the inherent functional possibilities of systems—but it is quite another thing to use numbers without spiritual content as a means to establish essence. To understand the development and path of the western vibrational and methodological thrust—after the transformation of the Egyptian Empire—is to begin to see one of the unique traits that would dictate the solidification of western art music. For the affinity alignment of the western vibrational projection would move to reorder how basic aspects of the universe are perceived. From Plato to Aristotle to existentialism, what we see are variations on systems as a means for establishing a composite identity in accordance with the affinity alignment adjustments western culture has had to make because of the unique path it has taken. The realness of this alignment is of extreme importance if one is to truly deal with western art music, because not only has this alignment helped to separate western art music from the world group, but this factor was also directly instrumental in shaping the path western creativity was to take.

```
RT.DYM.-------CULT.INFO.B.
```

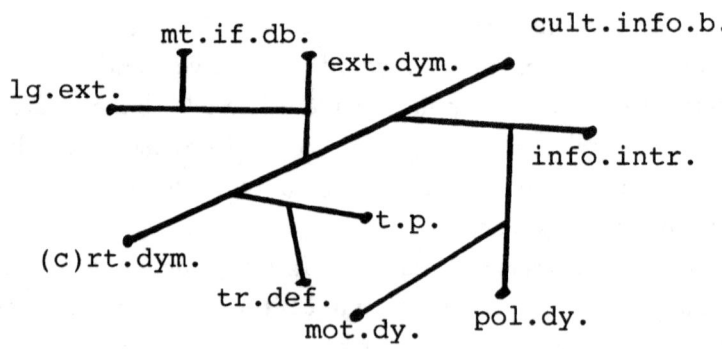

To view the actualness of the western vibrational and affinity alignment is to deal with where this projection has brought us today. Moreso, the end result of this thrust projection can be viewed in both positive and negative terms. For the present reality of western art music can be looked at as directly related to the nature of how it was established: that is, the factors which actualized western art music as a separate projection from the world group are the same factors related to what is happening in the music today. On a physical universe level what this means is that all of the functional developments related to the progressional continuance of western art music can be traced to the "attitude" which defined the aesthetic reality, yet there is more here. For if the affinity alignment of western art music is directly responsible for the dynamics of the functional arenas of classical music, it is also responsible for the spiritual vacuum that the aesthetic finds itself in today, and any attempt to deal with the actualness of western art music would imply that this consideration be examined.

The uniqueness of how separation is utilized in western culture is also directly related to the development of new forms of western art music. To understand this is to see the positive implications of this "alignment." Quite possibly the best example of what this means, with regards to process, would be in the progressional development of notation in western art music. For the expansion of the classical orchestra would open up a new role for notation, and the progressive continuum of the orchestral context would establish a unique and dynamic music quite separate from anything before it. Another feature of this "alignment" would have to do with how it promoted independent development in the arts. In other words, the affinity alignment of the western vibrational projection would create a situation where dance would begin to see itself separately from music, painting, and sculpture, and every area of creativity would function independently. The end result of this alignment would promote the nature underlying how a given thrust would expand (or develop) while at the same time obstruct the possibility of a composite spiritual center forming. Thus on one hand the affinity-alignment implications of the western projection can be viewed as a positive asset with regards to the discovery of new stylistic and dynamic creative routes, and on the other hand the affinity alignment realness of the western projection can be viewed as a negative factor related to the state of "anti-culture" that western culture finds itself in during this period. I do not mean to imply that the overbalance of empirical investigation is the only factor related to the present actualness of western culture in this period, but I do mean to imply that the affinity alignment of the western vibrational projection is directly related to the juncture we find ourselves in—concerning the position of western culture in this time zone, and what this position means with regards to the meta-reality of western civilization and the actualness of western art music. Any attempt to investigate what transformation will mean for the next period would necessitate that some effort is made to gain insight on the aesthetic lining of western creativity: as a means to extract what is most positive from this thrust and as a means to understand the ramifications of the path western creativity took.

It is important that we maintain an "overview" in any investigation on the particular peculiarities of a given thrust projection or we run the risk of obscuring the essence of our inquiry. I state this because while I believe the separateness of western art music from the composite creative projection of the world group does indeed shed light on the special situation of western culture in this period, it is important that we not lose the universality of what any creativity is about. In other words, when I write of the underlying philosophical base determining the course of the western philosophical and vibrational position, in no way does this type of investigation negate the significance and beauty of the actual music. That is, however one chooses to perceive the vibrationaltory lining of western art music, it is important to not confuse the progressional body of the actual music with the nature of how a given projection is presently viewed. Because even the lightest inquiry into the actualness of creativity makes it clear that the progressional body of any creative thrust must be both acknowledged and respected—for any other attitude runs counter to the spiritual realness of what creativity is about. To understand the actualness of what "alignment" really means is to become cognizant of the cosmic implications of creativity—because every projection affirms a spectrum of factors (and all of these factors are related to cosmic forces). To deal with the actualness of western art music is to focus on what this projection has contributed in vibrationaltory terms—and what this contribution means with regards to transformation as well. My point is this: the contribution of the master composers in western art music must be viewed as significant for what they have contributed to both western art music as well as world music. To deal with the significance of a composer like Bach or Beethoven is to become aware of the actualness of these contributions. The point of my inquiry into western art music has to do with establishing the multi-complexual actualness of creativity on this planet—what this means—as well as examining the progressional developments which have shaped the present situation we find ourselves in during this period. The method I have chosen to utilize for this investigation reflects my belief that there is something for us to learn in every projectional thrust of creativity. Moreover, the seriousness of what this means will be accented as we advance into the next time cycle (transformation). For the challenge of the next period makes the necessity of world creativity more critical—that is, our ability to successfully deal with the coming period will be directly related to whether or not we establish both a unified world position—with regards to creativity and politics—and a composite spiritual alignment (on some level). For this reason, it is important to examine the present situation we are now in as a means to establish how to bring about this "coming together" of people. What this means with respect to investigation is that we are forced to examine how creativity has participated in shaping this period, and what this shaping has meant with regards to the course of a given creative projectional thrust. This type of investigation is also necessary as a means to build a composite picture to act from—which is why I have chosen this route. My point is that however an investigation of this type is seen, it is important to keep an overview of what creativity really is, or run the risk of obscuring the very subject we are trying to see.

 The importance of the western affinity alignment can better be understood if the consideration of process is dealt with. To view the progressional continuance of western art music is to be aware of the separateness of its functional arena from that of the world group, and it is from this point that we can begin to investigate. For while the adaptation of notation in western art music would help define the uniqueness of the creativity, this consideration would also establish another thrust precedence for western methodology—that being, the emergence of western art music as a composer's medium. To understand this development is to deal with the break in the composite projection of western culture: that is, the break in the bi-aitional juncture of western culture and the failure of religion to function as a center factor. The thrust progression of the composer is directly related to the affinity alignment development of the meta-reality juncture of western culture, and the subsequent position of present-day western functionalism is directly inspired by how this juncture was perceived. The major difference between a composer like Bach and Beethoven would thus have to do with their position in the progressional continuance of this phenomenon. For the whole of Bach's activity is directly related to the solidification of western culture as a hopeful bi-aitional or "actual" culture, while the activity of a composer like Beethoven signaled the realness that western culture had already come to the next time junction (de-solidification). My point however is that the peculiar nature of the western affinity alignment would dictate what this de-solidification would mean in actual and vibrational terms. Because the transfer shift of western creativity could thus be characterized by what transpired in its meta-structure—having to do with what intellectual and spiritual forces surrounded its separate functionalism, rather than its composite functionalism, and the nature of this phenomenon would commit the western vibrational projection on the path we are presently on. Thus the thrust continuum of western art music would advance from a spiritual to an intellectual force and the actualness of this path would permeate how each subsequent period saw itself. The result of this development would be the expansion of process and the institutionalizing of creativity—as a factor corresponding to the spectacle diversion cycle of western culture. But what does this mean in physical universe terms?

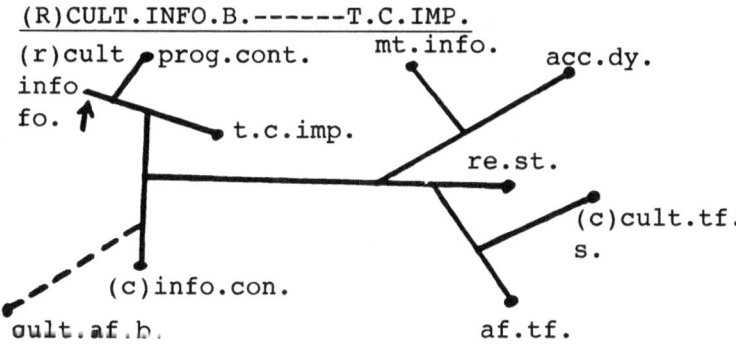

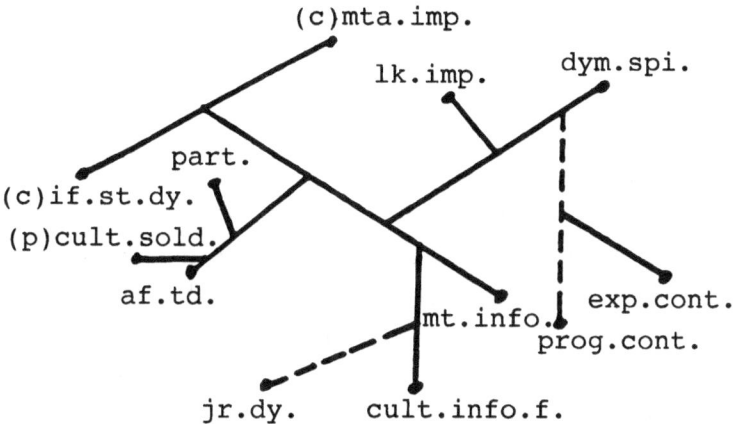

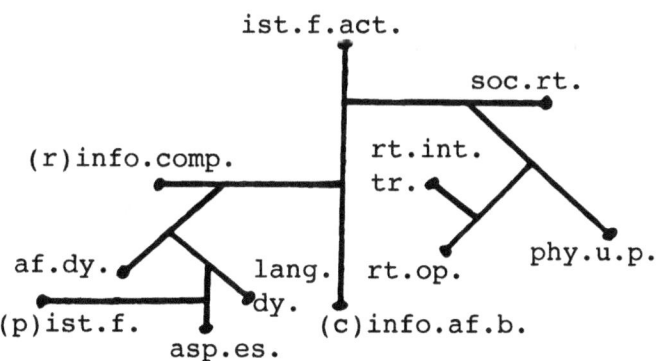

It is generally considered that after Beethoven, the emphasis on process contributed to the general de-solidification of western art music—as a meaning projection affirming western culture—and in many ways this is true. But what this really means is that the western affinity alignment after Bach would establish the nature of the source-transfer continuance of the western vibration in intellectual rather than composite terms. After Beethoven all of the functional particulars of process would move to extension as a means to create in accordance to this unique alignment. Thus the consideration of rhythm would "advance" from Beethoven to Stravinsky, and the consideration of harmony would "advance" from Beethoven to Wagner—or at least this would be the prevailing viewpoint. In other words, after Beethoven the nature of this affinity projection would make itself felt and permeate the "lining" of western art music—in what I call "actual terms." My point is that none of these developments would have been possible had it not been for the uniqueness of the western vibrational and affinity alignment—moreso, my point is that the "actualness" of this development signaled other complications that were happening as well. In other words, if the thrust projection of western art music before Beethoven was related to the solidification (and desire) of the western composite vibrational center, then the reality of classical music after Beethoven would correspond to the source-transfer cycle of western culture. Which is to say, if the composer before Beethoven vibrated to the meta-reality of western culture in its composite state, then after Beethoven the composer would move to "expand" the progressional thrust of western creativity from intellectual considerations—and the tool that accomplished this alignment would be notation.

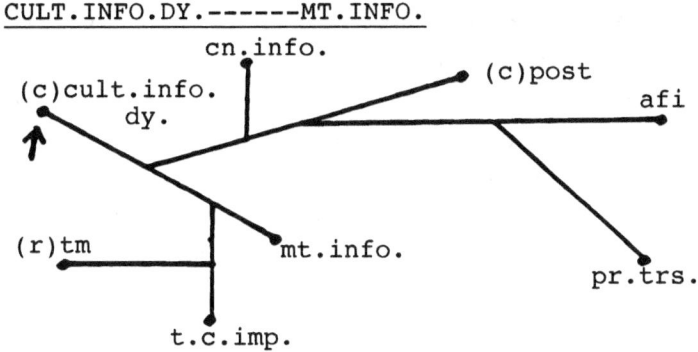

To view the position of notation in western art music is to be aware of the uniqueness of this consideration. For the functional arena of western art music is designed with respect for intellectual scrutiny, rather than composite participation. In actual terms this context has opened up a whole new mode of expression for the individual creative person—or in this context, composer. The dynamics of this medium are limitless and the wealth of music that has come from this projection constitutes another whole approach for creativity. And while it is clear that any attempt to deal with transformation would require that this projection be included as a means to establish a composite alternative creative thrust, there is also another factor related to notation that cannot be avoided. For if notation in western art music is related to the dynamics of classical music, it is also connected to the situation surrounding interpreting musicians in this period. To understand this situation is to view the harmful effects of notation because one of the most basic factors separating western art music from the world group is the nature underlying how a given person is allowed to participate in the creative process. Simply put—western art music has established a projection that corresponds to the dynamics of the composer rather than the total group. The net effect of this application of notation would see the gradual inability of western musicians to function creatively without notation. The realness of what this development has brought cannot be separated from the affinity alignment that produced this situation, because it must be understood that western culture is the only culture group faced with this problem. Yet I do not mean to take away from what has been developed through this methodology because the solidification of western art music must be looked at in positive terms. My reasons for commenting on the negative effect of what has developed from notation is to better understand what this alignment really is—or at least to better view the nature of this consideration—what it means with regards to what role "projection" has in helping to establish "process." The relationship of affinity alignment to the affinity insight (1) principle is extremely important, and the fact that the projectional thrust of western art music has moved to diminish this consideration cannot be taken lightly. The actualness of what this means is directly related to the position of western art music today—as a separate creative thrust from the world group—and the challenge we are faced with in this time zone is directly connected with how this unification is brought about. The negative consequences of western process have to be understood if we are to avoid this problem in the future, yet I do not mean to state that these limitations are natural to a given functional projection. That is, the functional consequences of western process are a reflection of how these considerations were viewed through the western affinity alignment rather than the given projection itself—this distinction is important.

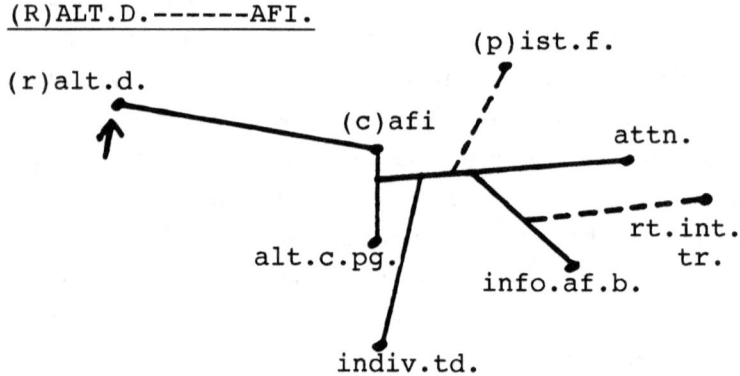

If the emergence of notation in western art music would effect the actualness of the affinity-insight principle—with regards to the reality of the interpreting musician—then the progressional development of each advancing projection thrust (form) can be viewed with respect to how this effect would be manifested. In other words, every progression of western art music, after the dissolution of the composite center of its projection, can be viewed with regards to how a given altered alignment would affect the basic scheme of its thrust. Thus not only would the cycle after Beethoven show the progressional implication of process (i.e., the expansion of aspects—rhythm, harmony) but also, the composite thrust of the western affinity projection would detail the nature of its altered meta-reality. In actual terms this phenomenon could be seen by viewing the vibrational arena of classical composers and understanding the factors related to its solidification. Because under the banner of "positive intention" (or "noble investigation") the composer after Beethoven would move to establish both the intellectual nature of the western affinity alignment in actual terms, as well as the resulting vibrational alignment of classical music, and it must be emphasized that this was a creative position—in fact, this would be the most creative position in western art music. Thus a given composition would be perceived for its intellectual significance as well as its actual sound. The realness of this development has helped to establish another projection for creative music, and the net result of this alignment has helped to establish another type of viewpoint in creative music. The uniqueness of this progression would also establish the nature of the present vibrational arena of western art music, for to understand the present position of the composer in classical music is to view the nature of the resulting science of this thrust as well. In other words, the progressional development of the science of western art music would also be based on intellectual considerations rather than actual considerations (i.e., the science for any given thrust would not develop from the musician's participation in the actual music, but rather by the composer). The realness of this development is related to the separateness of western art music from the world group—yet I am not commenting on this alignment as something inherently negative, because it isn't. The establishment of western art music as a composer's medium has given us the possibility to experience another viewpoint, and this is what is important. Moreover, the most basic factor distinguishing this projection from that of the world group is not the composer but rather the affinity result of basing a thrust development on intellectual premises rather than composite spiritual premises (and the nature of how the west perceives of these considerations).

The progressional continuance of western art music parallels the development and character of the composite thrust of western philosophy—that is, the basic thrust projection of western art music would move to become an existential expansion, rather than an alternative spiritual factor. The resulting development of this attitude would thus manifest how a given idea could be "celebrated," rather than "affirmed," and the spectrum of a given thrust would reveal the dynamics of what this would mean (depending on the time zone a given composition was conceived in). My point is that this continuum can be viewed in a number of contexts (for there is much to learn here)—because the effects of this thrust have been both varied and informative.

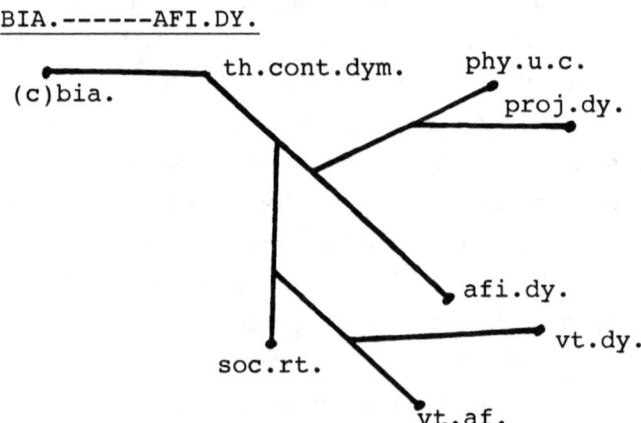

The solidification of western art music as a composer's forum is directly related to the resulting social reality of classical music. For as the progressional thrust of the music moved into expansion, the position of the composer would require less and less dialogue with the musicians. In other words, the alignment projection of classical music—with regards to development—would naturally create a separation between the composer and interpretive musician. The nature of this separation would also be instrumental in establishing the social arena surrounding the music, and the basic thrust of this alignment would promote the emergence of the specialist. After Beethoven the net result of this development would see the utilization of separation as an integral tool in the creative arena of the music, and the seriousness of this development would directly shed light on the nature of the affinity alignment in the western aesthetic. To view the social reality of western art music is to be confronted with the hierarchy of specialization from the composer's reality, through conducting, on to musicians of exceptional interpreting ability—yet in itself this might not necessarily mean anything. But the realness of the social reality in western art music is directly related to the thrust alignment of the creativity—that is, the direction the music was to take, and the resulting position of the composer in western art music. The social implications of western art music are directly related to the thrust political projection of western culture, which is to say the progressional continuance of the social position of classical composers would move to solidify the functional affinity alignment of the western defining community. Thus a given composition could be perceived in terms of its aesthetic and political connotations. To view the actualization of Wagner's creativity and its relationship to the vibrational developments of the post–World War I period (i.e., the relationship of this thrust to the vibrational projection Nietzsche opened up—or the birth of twelve-tone music as a response to existentialism) is to see the intellectual implications of western art music as a factor related to the functional continuance of western culture. The dynamics of specialization that were to change western art music were directly in accordance with the composite projection of western culture—or at least the western defining and controlling wing. By the end of the forties the reality of the composer would mirror that of the scientist in the sense that both junctures represented separate investigation rather than composite insight. Yet I do not mean to simply dismiss the meta-reality of western functionalism, because this would not mean anything. Certainly all of us have benefited from the thrust continuum of western investigation, and creativity as well. My reasons for commenting on the present reality of investigation in western terms is only to understand how this consideration is viewed with regards to the composite thrust of the culture—because if the fruits of what has been established—and understood—through western art music has to do with the nature underlying how a given investigation is perceived—in separate terms—then what does this mean with regards to the western aesthetic—what are we then to understand (when a given composition is labeled successful)? My point is that the concept of separation "ised" through the western thrust alignment is directly related to language, and the net effect of this development has helped shape the present social-political reality we are in during this period.

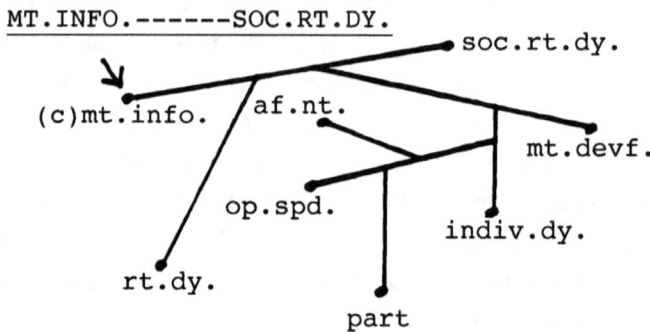

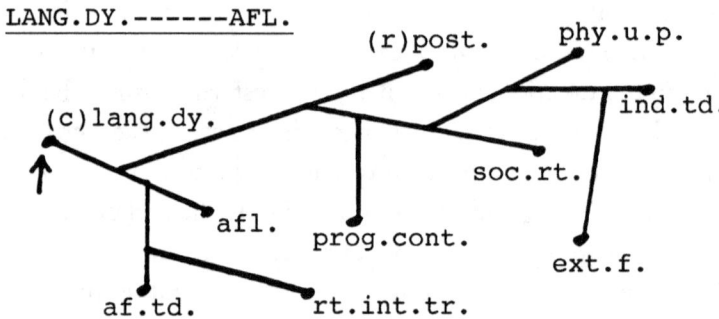

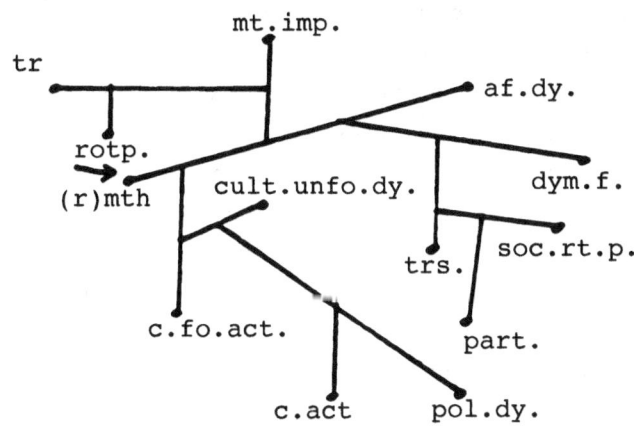

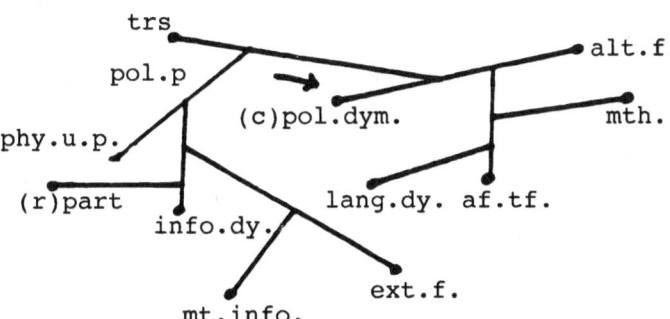

To understand the affinity nature underlying how investigation is utilized by the composite western projection is to understand why the vibrational and philosophic umbrella of western art music is separate from that of the world group. For investigation in the annals of the western position is directly related to the nature of affinity alignment (what this means with regards to projection). The seeds underlying the path of western creativity—and its vibrational and philosophic projection—would have to do with the nature of how curiosity is perceived rather than how the world group perceives of "isness." Thus the consideration of investigation is linked to the vibrational implications underlying how intellectualism is viewed—as a spiritualness functioning factor—in western terms, and the continuance of this development is not designed for unification but rather for "what is interesting." In other words, the most basic difference between the meta-reality of western art music and that of the world group is in the nature of how investigation is perceived. Certainly it is clear that every cultural thrust moves to affirm its projectional reality in its own independent way, and I am not implying that every culture but western culture embraces the same reality, because of course this is not true. I am, however, saying that the thrust projection of the world group can be viewed as moving with the same basic affinity alignment, and I am also saying that this means something.

The most distinguishing feature of the western vibrational projection is the nature of how given particulars are perceived in intellectual terms, rather than spiritual terms. Each progression of western art music can be viewed by its relationship to how a given concept is perceived with regards to systematic logic. While in the world group every vibrational projection is viewed in accordance to what it reveals about the composite spiritual actualness of the culture. The difference between these two thrust alignments does mean something. Because not only does the projectional implication of western culture move towards establishing a vibrational and scientific hierarchy of "separation" in the meta-reality of its aesthetic base, but the end result of this alignment is also actualized on the physical universe level as well. The actualness of the western composite vibrational projection must be looked at as a factor which has designed and promoted the situation the west finds itself in today—and this is both good and bad (depending on what aspect of the planet one wants to look at). Certainly the positive actualness of this phenomenon would focus on the position of western culture in this period—as opposed to that of the world group—with regards to power and technology, and quite possibly the thrust continuum of the western projection was designed to achieve its present political position—or at least this position is the direct result of the alignment of the western affinity projection—as a factor which justified and necessitated the route taken. But the disadvantages of this route would also comment on some aspect of the western projection as well, or at least any attempt to deal with the actualness of western culture—and reality—would necessitate an examination on the nature of the path this projection has pursued, as a means to view the multi-dimensional implications of what has been established through the western vibrational and affinity thrust.

The time-continuum implications of a given projection are another factor related to the path classical music was to take, and the seriousness of this phenomenon is connected to every aspect of the music (and its perceived science). In other words, every juncture of creativity is related to the "time presence" arena (context) that dictated the "real reasons" (or cosmic reasons) for its existence—and inherent in this phenomenon is the "route of its future" (growth or progressional extension).

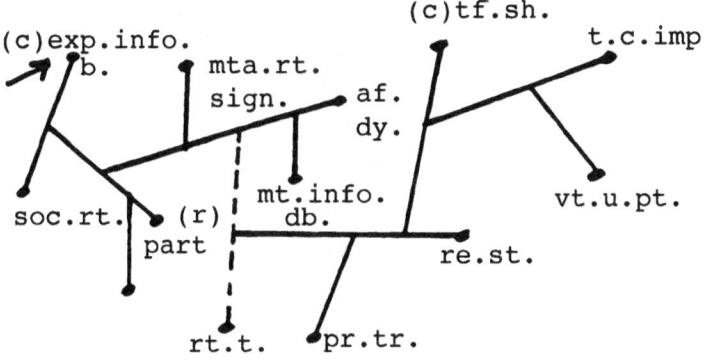

To understand this is to view the actualness of words as a means to disunify the composite potential of a given form   and this is only the beginning. For if the activity of Bach and Beethoven is indicative of the classical solidification of western art music in its early formation, then the post-Schoenbergian juncture of western art music can be viewed as the end of that particular affinity projection. In other words, the aesthetic actualness of western art music is designed to accent the diversionary slant of how a given time juncture sees itself—which is to say, the aesthetic actualness of western art music corresponds to the transient semantical juggling of language. Because of this, many of us have come to view the spectrum of western creativity as a projection of many different thrusts—or a projection that affirms a multitude of realities—but this is not true. The meta-reality of western art music from Bach to the development of the post-Cageian thrust must be viewed as one projection affirming the actualness of western culture—and this is neither negative nor positive. The significance of a given time continuum has to do with how the dynamics of system are perceived, or the significance of a given time continuum would comment on what aspect—of the composite thrust of the activity—is accented (as a means to correspond to the aspect-essence implications of thrust). To understand the realness of this phenomenon is to view the uniqueness of western art music as a separate strain from the world group. For western culture has designed a thrust that can be re-molded according to language—which is to say "never known"—rather than a thrust that is about something (which doesn't change). Yet it would be a distortion to merely say western art music is based on not-knowingness and not clarify what this means, because obviously there must be more to this viewpoint. My point is this: the nature of progressional continuance in western art music can only be perceived in intellectual terms that—while real to the affinity actualness of western culture (certainly the meta-reality of western art music is real to the western affinity-thrust projection it affirms)—do not correspond to the historical and actual reality concerning how the world group perceives creativity. The uniqueness of this position would be that a given projection in western terms can be perceived in any way one chooses to perceive "something"—and thus, this trait would add to the vibrational dynamics supporting how western culture sees creativity—while the weakness of this development would explain the spiritual and vibrational vacuum that western culture has now arrived at—as a factor related to the inability of the western position to establish "center." The net effect of this exclusiveness would establish the realness of western art music as an important and profound creative thrust. Any attempt to deal with the possibility of transformation would imply that the positive implications of this thrust be adopted by the world group—because it is clear that this thrust has much to offer all.

If the thrust projection of western philosophy can be viewed in progressional terms—with regards to the forming of the western affinity alignment on to the actualization of existentialism (as an end juncture commenting on the dissolution of the center factor of western culture)—then the significance of the Schoenbergian juncture of realignment must be viewed with respect to its composite world implications. In other words, the actualness of the dodecaphonic juncture of western art music can be viewed by its relationship to the vibrational and philosophic actualness of western culture in that same period and what this relationship meant with regards to the meta-reality of process. My point is that the thrust continuum of western art music in its "solid" period ended at Schoenberg and, by the same token, the thrust alignment of the western vibrational and philosophic hierarchy ended at existentialism, or at least the establishment of existentialism signaled the most basic shift in how the composite lining of the western projection would be perceived. For any attempt to deal with the significance of progressional alignment would only accent what the "correct" nature of an actual affinity projection is. To understand this is only to view how the thrust-continuum alignment of the western projection moved towards its own dissolution—as a separate affinity projection. For the most basic factor that establishes whether or not a given projection is "about something" would have to do with both the nature of its essence foundation (or center factor) and how this foundation is utilized in extension. The solidification of existentialism, as a word which corresponded to the gradual awareness that the center factor in western culture had advanced into non-beingness, would be the final documented comment on the "isness" of western culture, and this would also be true for its creativity. In vibrational terms, what this means is that the thrust projection we call dodecaphonic or serial music has to be viewed as a western thrust—that is, connected to the source-initiation thrust of western art music—as well as a thrust that is connected to the source-transfer junction of world creativity. In other words, the post-Cageian juncture of western art music has world implications, yet it is important to clarify the nature of what this means (with regard to process as well as the resulting meta-reality of the post-Webern or post-Cage continuum of western art music) because obviously I am not saying that the emergence of serial music represented a gift from Indian culture—just as I have not written that Dixieland music is Oriental. My point is that the actualization of the post-Webern and Cageian juncture of western art music corresponds to the dissolution of the composite vibrational alignment of western culture—as a separate thrust with a substantial meta-physics (having to do with culture)—and that the seriousness of this dissolution is manifested in the lining of how these thrusts were to flow; moreover, because of this relationship, the nature of the western affinity alignment can be viewed with regard to how it promoted a return to basic essences—or to the world group—and the actualness of what was realized through this return can be talked of in terms of its resultant effects on the creativity. That is, the solidification of the post-Webern-Cage projection can be viewed with regards to the implications of source transfer—both in the sense of its reforming meta-reality and in the path this reforming would necessitate (for expansion).

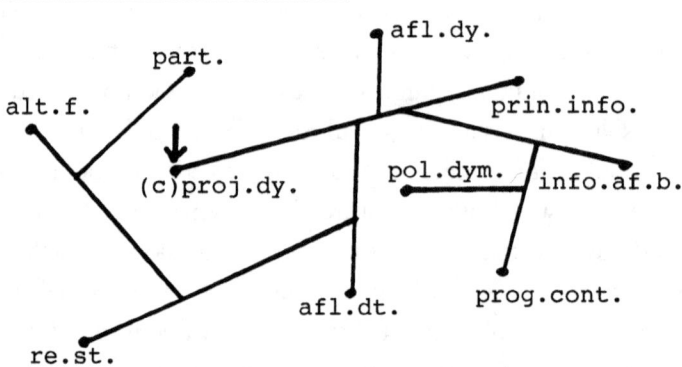

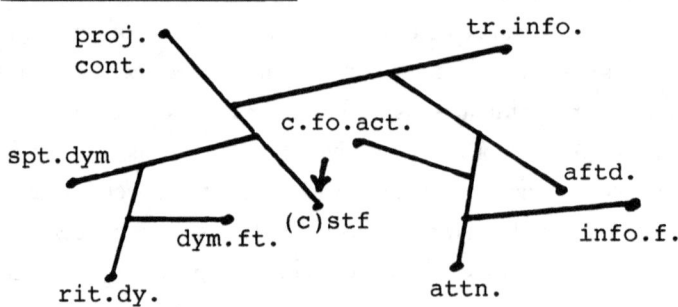

Quite possibly, many people would find the solidification of serial music to be very far away from the creative initiations of the world group, and this is understandable—especially if the surface actualness of the music is experienced. But my reasons for claiming that the post-Webern and Cageian thrusts are connected to the world group would have to do with what the establishment of these thrusts would mean to the existing composite meta-reality and identity of western art music before its arrival. To understand this is to be aware of how the functional arena of western art music was perceived before Webern and what the impact of serialization would mean with regards to the thrust continuum of the western projection. Before Webern, the thrust continuum of western art music—no matter how diverse—could be viewed in what westerners would call a linear progression: that is, the thrust continuum of western art music was constant, and any new variable could be interpreted as an addition to the basic functional thrust of the music—no matter whether that addition was graciously received or not. The activity of Webern would change the basic functional arena projection of western art music—yet there is more here. Any attempt to understand the actualness of serialism would necessitate that some effort is made to deal with the factors which finally persuaded Webern to pursue this route; for it must be understood that not only was Webern a very religious person but the establishment of serialism would be based on the desire to participate in a creative thrust which corresponded to what the actualness of spiritualism demanded. Thus the solidification of serialism can be viewed with this intention in mind, but this is only the beginning. For when I stated that the functional arena of western art music was constant—or a constant projection—it is important to understand what this means. The fact is, the establishment of a constant projection has the benefit of solidifying a particular relationship to process—that being, a familiarity with how process is viewed—and this is both positive and negative (depending on the state of the culture). The solidification of the functional arena of western art music would make it easier for participants like Mozart or Schubert to make a contribution and in doing so propagate the culture. To understand the realness of Webern's activity is to be aware of what the emergence of Beethoven really implied: that being, the significance of Beethoven's activity would have to do with how his activity dictated the establishment of the affinity insight (1) principle—as a factor that signified that the composite continuance of western art music would now reconnect with the world group (and to understand why this development took place, or what it means, is to deal with cosmic matters—my point is that "whatever it meant in cosmic terms," in actual physical universe terms it meant a move towards world unification). Beethoven's activity was the first signal of this shift, and the actualness of his work would power how this phenomenon would materialize (in this time zone it might be difficult for many of us to realize how radical Beethoven was—or was perceived—but in fact his activity would move to reshape western art music). The solidification of serialization would signal that the thrust implications of Beethoven's activity had now moved into the next junction; and once established, the reality-actualness of western art music would never be the same. Because it must be understood that not only would the forming of serial music establish the nature of the path western art music would pursue, but this thrust would also establish what the affinity-insight principle would mean after the dissolution of the composite-center factor of western culture. To understand this phenomenon is to view what the affinity-insight principle really is. For it is clear that not even Webern was able to foresee what the establishment of serialization would mean; for while the functional mechanics of the form would represent no problem, the actual aesthetic implications of its existence did. The solidification of serialism in Webern's understanding would reveal a renewed awareness of universal consciousness, and while this awareness would not necessarily be seen in his perception of its functional science, it would permeate the nature and spirit of its later exploration tendencies.

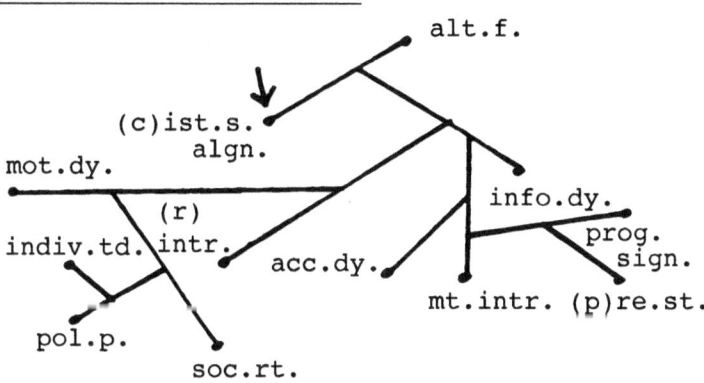

The solidification of serialism as a post–World War II creative thrust would mark a new cycle for western art music. The actualness of this thrust, and the post–John Cage school, would help establish the path of western art music and the basic alignment of this path (i.e., towards world implications). In other words, the time zone of the late forties would be the juncture which dictated how western art music would utilize the source-transfer implications of its position. For if serialism represented the first intellectual manifestation of what existentialism implied, then the affinity projection of this thrust would comment on the nature of what source transfer means in this time zone as well. In other words, it is possible to review this period in western creativity as a basis to understand what is happening now, for the post–World War junction has played an important role in shaping the whole of the period we are now in—or at least the vibrationaltory lining of western culture in this period was established in the late forties/fifties. Yet I do not mean to imply that the thrust continuum of western art music had come to an end because of serialization, for obviously this is not true. The significance of the source-transfer junction in western art music—from the post–World War I and II juncture—would only comment on the nature of cross-sectional influence in this period (i.e., the move to re-investigate world music, or the utilization of world music as an "idea" germ consideration—as a factor to continue the life blood of the western vibrational thrust). Any other interpretation would imply that the consideration of transformation constitutes the juncture where everything stops ("because of unification"?)—and this does not make sense either. My point is that the significance of serialism would have to do with its role in re-adopting the thrust continuum of the western affinity alignment to correspond with the actualness of the post–World War vibrationaltory state of western culture, and also the significance of serialism would have to do with what these changes meant with regards to the world group. The adaptation of serialism is directly related to the changing physical and vibrational universe factors reshaping the planet in both social and political, as well as spiritual and cosmic, terms—during this time zone. And while it is clear that the western vibrational projection still functions as separate from the world group (in terms of thrust alignment), this position is changing—or at least the nature underlying how this difference is perceived is changing.

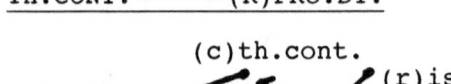

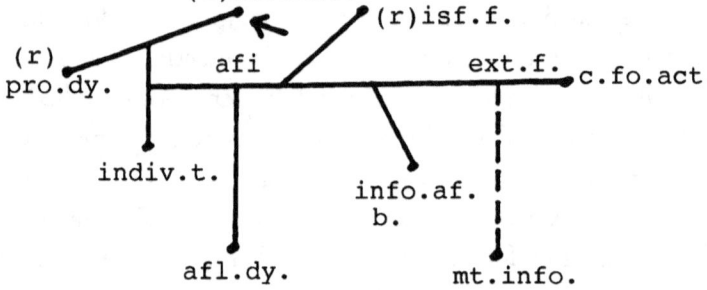

The basic point of this essay is that the thrust projection of western art music constitutes a unique path in creativity. The meta-reality implications of this path also comment on the actualness of the present situation we are now in on the planet. The thrust continuum of this projection is responsible for the dynamic spectrum of classical music, and it would be to everyone's advantage if the fruits of what this means were experienced. My point in this essay has been to accent the meta-reality realness of western art music rather than to comment on the particulars of a given form; this approach is necessary because practically every other forum concerning this thrust over-accents the mechanics of its functional arena.

The realness of western art music is important because of how it will affect transformation as well—that is, it would be to our advantage to examine all of the considerations related to the forming of the next cycle as a means to better assist in shaping what the next period will be. The nature underlying how the functional arena of western art music is perceived might shed light on the dynamic potential of form in helping to secure new paths to establish transformation. In other words, the progressional continuance of western art music has revealed a spectrum of possibilities with regards to both language and dynamics through structure, and it is my belief that some aspect of what this means will be related to transformation. Whatever, the progressional thrust of western art music reveals the spectrum of what the western vibrational thrust means in its separateness—as a factor that could contribute to the world group. I do not mean to imply that this continuum has always functioned without regards for the world group, nor have I meant to give the impression that the source-transfer junction in the late forties constituted western art music's first encounter with the world group, because this is not true either. There have been many transfer junctions in western art music—and for that matter, every creative strain—because no thrust projection can operate in a vacuum. Thus the question has never been whether or not a given thrust can be subjected to cross-sectional influences but rather, what is the significance of this phenomenon—or how has a given transfer junction altered the thrust projection of a given alignment?

This is what I am interested in, and this is also what determines the lining of a given transformation. The progressional continuance of a given creative projection is directly related to how a given period sees itself — moreso, the progressional continuance of a given thrust sheds light on the cosmic factors that really determine how a given period will or can actualize. As such, the cross-sectional implications of earth creativity must be examined with regards to this viewpoint if we are to prepare for the next challenge of transformation. For the thrust continuance of western art music is directly related to the separateness of its position from world culture—as well as the present position of composite western culture in this time zone. Quite possibly, the separateness of western creativity

WAM–38

is related to its linkage implications on the physical universe level—in both political and vibrational terms—and if this is true this must also be examined. But finally, the composite body of western art music must be received as a positive testament of the western vibrational and affinity projection—because, in fact, that is really what it is.

(Level One) TRANS-AFRICAN MUSIC

IF THE STORY OF 20TH-CENTURY MUSIC from the white aesthetic is in great part a story of the progression and annihilation of tonality and the evolution of process to incorporate 20th-century technological gains, then the story of creative black music would be the evolution of process as a means to cast off every remnant of the white aesthetic and re-insert its own definitions. Each progression of creative black music in America must be viewed with regards to its position in the re-formation of a composite African cultural and vibrational thrust and what this means in practical physical universe terms, and each progression of creative black music must also be perceived with regards to its ability to advance the reshaping of the composite world group. In other words, the composite thrust of creative black music must be viewed with regards to the factors that reshaped—and destroyed—black culture (i.e., the raping of Africa and the institutionalization of slavery) as a means to understand the previous transformational cycle that determined the present course of events leading into the present. The realness of what this means sheds light on the essence projection of the black vibration—for the meta-reality of black creativity is connected to many factors. Moreover, the physical universe actualness of black people must also be taken into account if we are to deal with the projectional spread—and spectrum—of black creativity, for I am not writing on one thrust alignment of creativity but rather the composite identity of black culture. We are thus forced to look at the actualness of what slavery really meant in terms of its disruption of the composite black identity, and in terms of the progressional effects of its implementation—that being, the uprooting of a people from their homelands and the gradual implication of having alien forces impose its reality on their given vibrational or racial flow (or way of doing things) and the subsequent sociological and vibrational consequences of that development (i.e., the adaptation of black people to western tools)—and also how this phenomenon was to be understood technically, aesthetically, or vibrationally by western culture. To attempt to understand the meta-reality of black creativity is to deal with all of these considerations and more, for the progressional implications of black creativity have been the single most important re-alignment factor in this time zone.

By black creative music in this section, I am referring to all of the various creative strains that have been produced or defined by black people since their arrival in western culture (yet in its ultimate sense black creative music refers to the composite thrust of black invention—from American or African roots). To deal with what has been developed through black creativity in this time zone is to have some understanding of the profound impact of black people in art dynamics, for the most basic factor that has determined the "isness" of American culture is the nature underlying how black creativity has reshaped the functional and vibrational actuality of composite American creative postulation. Thus my use of the term "black creative music" has to do with all of the various creative projections which have designed the present situation we are now living in—from the early forms of the music until today. I am writing of a thrust projection which encompassed styles as diverse as boogie woogie and what we have come to call "jazz"—a force that has permeated every period in American culture: whether we are talking of the ragtime period, or the use of music in television commercials. In other words, any attempt to gain insight into the actualness of American culture would imply that the realness of black creativity is dealt with on some level. For if there is any single force responsible for how the actualness of American culture has materialized, or if there is any one factor related to the solidification of the vibrational lining of American culture, it would be the realness of black creativity.

To deal with the scope of creative black music is to recognize the dynamic implications of its contribution to American and world culture. For the spectrum of black creativity encompassed a multitude of both vibrational and functional realities. The composite thrust projection of black creativity has provided the alternative route for every sector of western creativity and is also responsible for the total thrust of what we now refer to as popular music. So real is this influence that many of us have come to either take it for granted or—in the case of many white Americans—not be able to deal with it at all. From the very early formation of American culture to the present, it is possible to trace how each period was dependent—and built—upon some aspect of black creativity (and this is still true in this period); however, I do not mean to underrate the many contributions in creativity from other culture groups in America, because it is undeniable that everyone has contributed to the composite solidification of American music, but it is important to put all of these various contributions in the proper context, for the functional and vibrational implications of black creativity have played a role completely out of proportion to the amount of black people in American culture (not to mention the social reality related to the existence of black people in western culture), and my point is that this role does mean something. The progressional continuance of black creativity has supplied the platform for the dynamic development of western art, and this is especially true for music and dance. Nor has this influence been felt on only one stratum, for the composite thrust of black creativity has affected and is affecting the total gamut of world creativity regardless of area—even western art music has been affected by the dynamics of creative black music (much more profoundly than many of us would dare believe). The dynamics of black creativity have completely altered the consideration of vocal music, instrumental music, functional process, the consideration of rhythm and time, the actualness of dance, and the vibrational identity of American creativity, among other things—and this is only the beginning. The realness of what this thrust signified has also reshaped how given creative arenas are perceived—in other words, the progressional expansion of creative black music has redefined the consideration of orchestra, the consideration of small groups—the consideration of harmony as an alternative functioning agent—and the consideration of language. Moreso, the meta-reality of creative music from the black aesthetic serves as the most influential vibrational force in American culture, for at the heart of the composite thrust of black music is the basis underlying both how the next transformational cycle will be arrived at, and what this shift could imply in positive terms. Thus it is both necessary and unavoidable to deal with the special position of creative black music in this time zone. For if the nature of a given transformation can be shaped with regards to what we as a collective people want for the future, then certainly the affinity posture of the present period must be understood on some level as a means to secure some basis for functioning. The fact is, creativity is at the base of what a given culture really is—or could be—and as such the study of black creativity is mandatory as a prerequisite to deal with the present cycle we are in as well as to prepare for cycles we are not in (but would like to be).

The realness of black creativity can better be viewed by dealing with the historical progressions related to the reforming of black culture in America and also by understanding the type of slavery western culture imposed on black people. For all of the factors related to the projectional spectrum of black American music were established in the early phase of America's own transition—from an Indian to western culture—and this is important if we are to really deal with the actualness of black creativity. Any attempt to gain the necessary scope for understanding black creativity would involve examining the state of America in this early period and also how that state affected the composite vibrational arena of American culture. Yet it must be understood I am not claiming America's use of slavery in itself was something innovative—because every cultural and racial group has at some point in time had to deal with this consideration, on some level—but I am claiming that the nature of the bondage black people were put in did not correspond to the accepted definition of slavery that had historically been practiced. The profound implications of America's use of slavery are directly related to the thrust alignment and projection of creative black music and as such cannot simply be ignored. Because the nature of America's utilization of slavery commented on the emerging vibrationaltory lining of American culture—which is to say, the factors that helped solidify the realness of American culture are directly related to the vibrational and physical universe situation in which we now find ourselves. The most basic feature of this slavery has to do with how western culture would choose to justify its treatment of black people and the vibrational consequences of what that treatment would create in the basic life fabric of western culture. The seriousness of this subject is directly related to the meta-reality of creative black music, and the vibrational ramifications of this phenomenon are also related to why this particular section of the book is separate from that of the world group or western art music. Thus before we can arrive at an understanding of creative black music it is necessary to re-examine the factors related to the composite forming of American culture; for the unique dynamics of black creativity correspond to the uniqueness of the physical universe reality of black culture in its transition from world creativity to black creativity (of an exclusive American thrust), yet it would be wrong to interpret my viewpoint as divisive in a "real" sense, because this is not true. The emergence of creative black music in America is significant because of its projectional implications rather than its basic essence factor—for the only factor that really separates this thrust from the composite realness of world creativity is the route black creativity has had to take in American culture (because of the resultant vibrationaltory state of America). To gain insight about the nature of projectional continuity in black creativity is to better understand the position of trans-African composite progressionalism in this time zone. We are now in a period where many of these questions have to be dealt with so that the next cycle can be pursued. The actualness of creative music from the black aesthetic is related to the total realness of this period of time. Any attempt to deal with the potential of creativity—as a positive functional tool for transformation—implies that some effort must be made to deal with the reality of black creative music (as "ised" in the American vibrationaltory theatre).

The reason I have chosen to separate creative black music from the underlying philosophical bases which determine world creativity or western art music has to do with the position black people are in during this cycle—especially with regards to western culture. For it is important to understand that when black people were forcibly brought to America all of their ties to Africa were necessarily realigned. Moreover, the actualness of this realignment would shed light on the meta-reality of creative black music; for the realness of the vibrationaltory lining of western culture is very different (or at least different) from that of Africa—which is to say, this realness would also be reflected in the projectional thrust of black creativity in America (i.e., the route black creativity would have to take for both expansion and transition), and this is important. However, I have not meant to imply that American black creativity is separate from the composite thrust of both black invention and black culture, nor have I meant to separate the essence realness of black creativity into African versus American—or something along these lines—because this is not true either—rather, I have introduced this viewpoint only as a means to focus on the peculiar position black people are in in American culture (as a means to deal with the dynamic implications of black creativity). Certainly it is clear that many aspects of black creativity were transmitted from Africa to the new physical universe space in America, and it is also true that many factors related to the mystical spiritual secrets of black creativity were and are passed through various sectors of the black community, but for the majority of people the separation from Africa would mean a break in the basic spiritual and cosmic hierarchy of what the actual creativity meant in its "pure" state. For if the most basic characteristic of world creativity has to do with the utilization of ritual as a necessary factor related to a given cosmic order—then the emergence of American black creativity (and its various projections) would establish a necessary re-routing of this phenomenon. In other words, the distinguishing factor dictating the thrust projection of American black creativity could be characterized as postulation that seeks to reestablish the composite implications underlying what its thrust projection really meant in its original state—that is, American black creativity flows as a force to re-establish ties with the collective wellspring (thrust) of trans-African continuance (as a means to move towards positive functioning for world transformation).

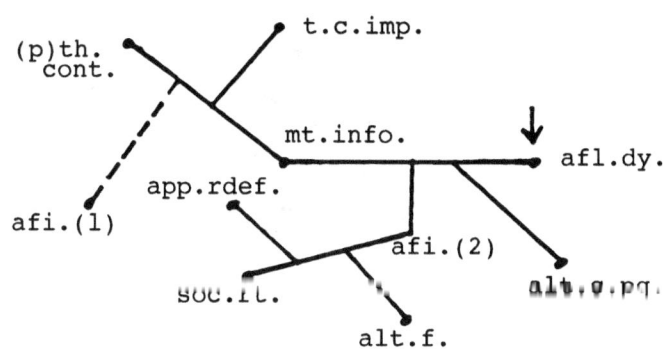

The most basic factor related to how given culture aspects are abandoned is the consideration of time itself. In other words, by the second and third generation of black people it was only normal that many factors pertaining to African ancestral knowledge would be forgotten; because to understand the early period of black people in America would encompass how given families and tribes were separated—which is to say, even communication between black people in the early period (in their original languages) was controlled. With the industrialization of slavery accenting the need for cheap labor, the first, second, and third generations of black people were not in a position to maintain the essence secrets of their given tribal group—or families. Thus for the majority of black people the meta-implications of their creativity were redesigned to deal with the particulars of the new environment, and while some of the traditional cosmic knowledge in the creativity was able to be passed to each generation, much of this knowledge was also lost.

T(AF)M-8

TR.INFO.------T.C.IMP.

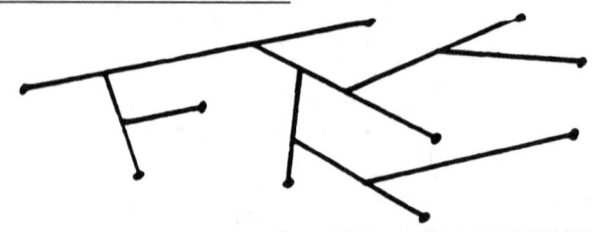

INFO.TRNS.------ALT.C.PROG.

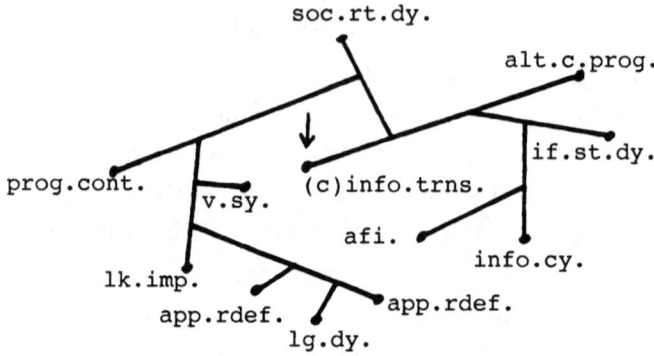

LANG.DY.------PRO.TF.C.

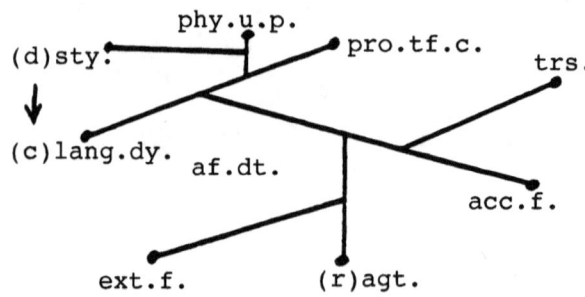

Thus any attempt to deal with the realness of black people after the initiation of slavery would reveal the nature of how systematic oppression was utilized as a means to wipe out any trace of African heritage. Without doubt, one of the most serious crimes committed against black people was the refusal of the controlling forces of western culture to let given families stay together, as well as what resulted from that refusal (e.g., the loss of traditional African language). For with the loss of language the most basic cultural chain was broken and in a period of twenty to thirty years the majority of black people, from the second and third generations, would begin to think of themselves as Americans—rather than Africans. Of course I do not mean to simplify this most complex subject, because obviously there is much more to deal with (understand, I am writing of the slavery of 53 million people to an alien environment)—for the study of slavery would require a twenty-volume set and a lifetime of research, and of course I do not pretend to be qualified to deal with what this period really meant. But if we are to gain any insight into the realness of black creativity, it is important that all relevant considerations be dealt with, for the nature of the slavery imposed on black people is directly related to the progressional continuance of creative black music and culture. Because there has never been a slavery of this magnitude imposed on a people, and this is important to understand. I am writing of a form of slavery that sought to both wipe out any trace of one's base heritage as well as a slavery that justified itself with the notion that black people were not human—and as such, this "special slavery" did not violate any cosmic laws. Moreover, the dynamics of American slavery are also related to the abandonment of African musical instruments—and art; which is to say, the scope of slavery touched on every aspect of life in the emerging black community. The most basic effect of this condition would move to discontinue certain areas of black sculpture and art, instruments and instrument making, ceremonial jewelry, mask making, etc., etc. In short, any attempt to deal with the transition of Africans to the new world would reveal the scope of what was altered in the natural black affinity projection, and also what this loss would necessitate in projectional terms. Yet I do not mean to imply that everything was lost, because this is not true either, for there were many other factors related to slavery which had to do with both cosmic and functional moves to establish this period in time (because it seems that everything makes sense on a cosmic level).

My point is this: the actualization of slavery can be looked at as the juncture which dictated how the dissolution of the composite thrust of black culture would take place, with regard to the basic unification of black people as well as their awareness of the essence foundation of black creativity—what it celebrated in its original state. To this degree many of the factors related to the essence awareness of black creativity were lost, yet I do not mean the vibrational lining of black creativity was lost, but rather changed. In other words, the vibrational realness of black creativity in the time zone of slavery merely underwent surface changes to correspond with the particulars of its immediate context. The utilization of western language as well as western instruments was the only logical move for black people, and it would be this junction that would determine the nature of the post-African vibrational projection: that is, adaptation as a means for survival and adaptation as a necessary factor to rebuild and thus re-create the source-initiation realness of black creativity. It must also be stated that the reality of vibrational transfer through creativity encompasses many factors, which is to say, it would be incorrect to blanketly assume that the meta-reality of black culture (and creativity) was lost in the transfer cycle surrounding slavery (i.e., what a given thrust projection meant in its pure or natural state). For to deal with the dynamics of the slavery period of American history is to also be aware of how certain areas of black creativity survived intact—and even today exist separately from the composite western thrust and observation platform. What we commonly refer to as voodoo is a perfect example of my position concerning the reality of source transfer—that is, much of the original cosmic and functional knowledge related to given African projectional thrusts was able to survive—even if the majority of a given sector of black people were not necessarily aware of its existence. To understand this is to understand that the fragmentation of the composite reality of trans-African creativity is no one-dimensional consideration, for while the solidification of black creativity was dissolved in slavery, the actual seeds underlying African culture were still transferred into the next cycle according to the progressional implications of source transfer. In other words, the vibrationaltory lining of creative black music is the same as the composite thrust of black culture—whether African or so-called American—yet the meta-reality and science of creative black music is separate from Africa or the world group, because of the nature of the path American black people have had to take (on the physical and vibrational universe level). The seriousness of this position sheds light on the real situation of black people in western culture, for the dynamics surrounding how the source transfer shift of black culture would integrate into the composite western culture would determine the thrust projection implications of black creativity, and this is important.

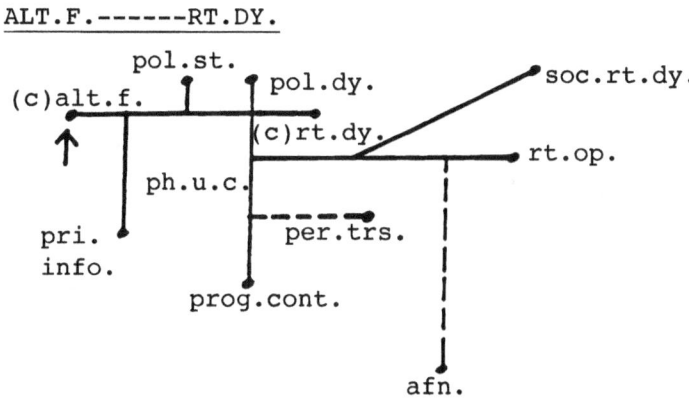

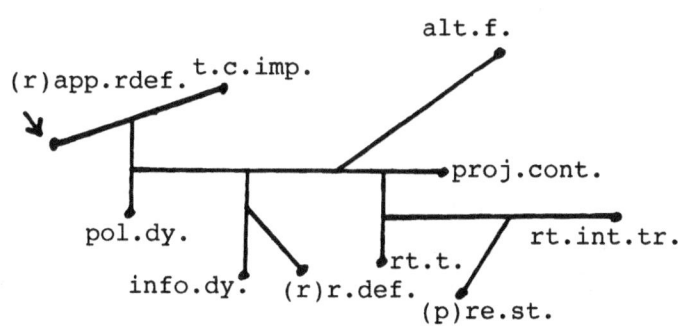

T(AF)M-12

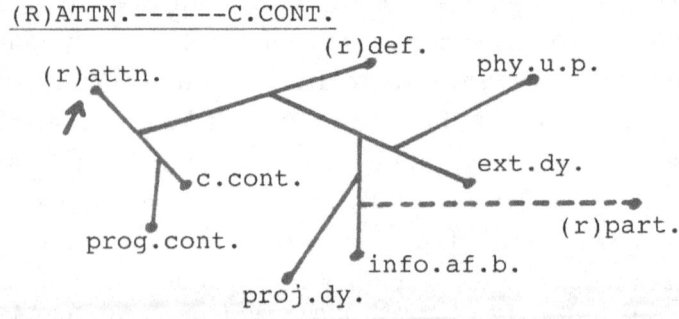

Rather than continue to deal with the implications of slavery and run the risk of obscuring the totalness of this section of the book, it would be better to comment on the relationship of early American culture to the present position black people are in during this cycle. In other words, the dynamics of the slavery black people have undergone must be viewed as a factor related to the establishment of the source-transfer (African to European) junction as well as the junction which provided the source alignment for black vibrational and methodological thrust projection.

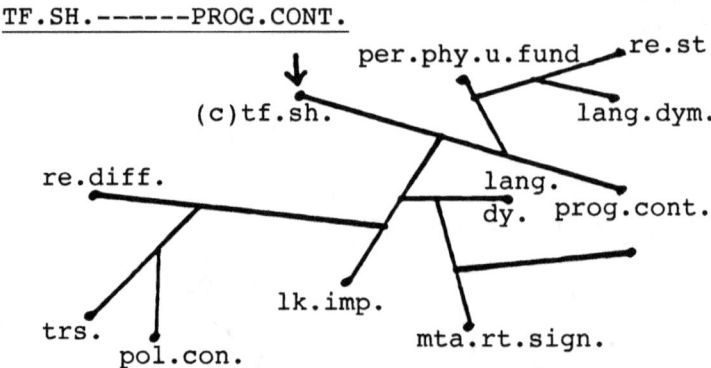

In physical universe terms what this means is that the solidification of black culture in America must be viewed as a separate thrust projection—or new continuum—with its own expanding vibrational hierarchy and with its own dynamic identity. I say new continuum because the scope involving what black people have had to deal with since arrival to these shores involved the complete realignment of their composite vibrationaltory thrust—a complete realignment of language, creativity, and finally culture. The seriousness of the transition black people have had to make since being brought to America is nothing less than a total re-dressing of basic vibrationaltory instincts—whether it concerned the spiritual actualness of that move (i.e., the adaptation of western religion—or at least religions we were told are western, whether true or not) or the functional realness of that move (i.e., the use of western tools as a means to survive). I say new continuum because the situation surrounding how slavery was practiced on black people transcended the limits of what the word is supposed to mean. In other words, the bringing of black people to America, and subsequent destroying of their ties to Africa, created a race of people—whose vibrational make-up had very little to do with western considerations—suddenly having another aesthetic imposed on them to the degree that their most basic vibrationaltory alignment was altered. Which is to say, to understand the position of American black people in western culture is to understand the path black culture had to take for expansion and survival. That path being, the composite projection of the American black sensibility must be perceived as a thrust affirming the restoration of black culture while at the same time adopting western methodological tools to do it—or another way to say it would be: the composite thrust of American black culture can be viewed as a synthesis of the black-essence umbrella with the adaptation of western functionalism as the first junction in establishing transformation (transformation with respect to the situation non-white people are in, and transformation with respect to the situation of the composite world group). Thus it follows that if the physical and vibrational realness of this situation can be called new (and as such black culture in America constitutes a new thrust), then it also follows that the thrust implications of American black creativity can be talked of in terms of it representing a new projection (hence, new music—or new dance—or new art, etc.). For not only did the projectional dynamics of American black creativity develop new languages—in every creative context—but the basics underlying what each projection would mean in its cosmic context were also new, because black people's arrival in the west constituted the

T(AF)M-14

solidification of a vibrational alignment that was not there before. The creativity which has come from black people in America can be discussed in terms of what we refer to as "new aesthetic"—new in the sense that the creativity initiated through the composite thrust of American black culture celebrates a completely new physical and vibrational universe reality (as opposed to the concept of new music derived from intellectual restructuralism). The spectrum of creative forms from trans-African progressionalism has served as the strongest alternative route for western culture because of the vitality of the essence realness of its foundation, for I am not just writing of a new form in the isolated sense that this word is used in the west, but rather the newness of the spirit factor behind the form is responsible for the distinction of American black creativity as a separate thrust with its own meta-reality.

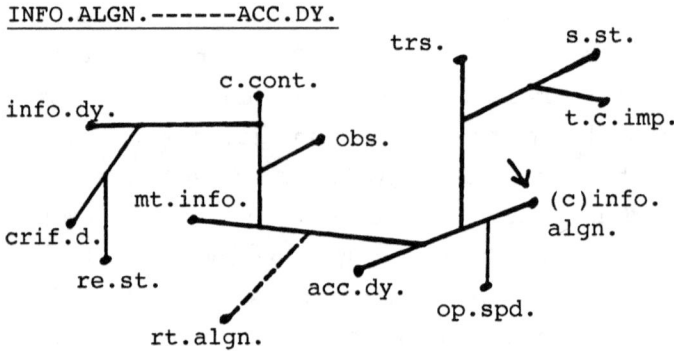

It is not the purpose of this book to investigate the specifics related to every individual creative thrust which emerged through black creativity—from either the early period of black music or the present—because this is a task for musicologists and other specialists. I am looking for something else. One problem that has permeated the study of creative black music is the inability of the controlling forces of western culture to make what I believe are the proper distinctions between the nature of methodological inquiry into western art, and what this means, and the use of this same affinity posture on creative black music. For the end result of much of the research that I have read on black creativity leaves much to be desired—as far as having to do with something really true. The distortions of the defining and controlling wing of western culture have helped to obscure every area of creative black music—either because of a general insensitivity to the actualness of what black creativity really is, or because of deliberate intent (and both of these reasons seem to be true). It is my opinion that while any examination of the composite actualness of a given thrust is useful for what it can reveal to us about the dynamics of particular projections, this kind of examination might not necessarily help us to deal with the composite significance of what that given thrust really is. This is especially true in the case of creative American black music, for the factors underlying the expansion of black creativity are related to the basic vibrational tone lining that black people deal with in American culture, and that lining has not changed since the inception of America. We are usually taught that the work songs which developed in the early period of the music are related to the work black people were doing in the South!!!—which is to say, so what! Because in actuality this tells us nothing. Obviously there is a relationship between a given thrust projection and the particulars of a given physical universe space, but this is only the beginning of any real investigation, and in itself means very little. For if the significance of a given phenomenon derives its real meaning from what aspect of essence it affirms, then to single out the early slaves' relationship and gradual drift towards western technology tells us nothing about the music but only about the sociological context surrounding how given thrusts were actualized—and this is already obvious. With the separation of black people from their mother country it was not only natural that western instruments were adopted to continue creativity, but it was also the only option available (i.e., either adapt to the reality you are in or cease to exist—or at least, adaptation on this level was the only possible route for both survival and moving to reorder). Musicologists have come to view the utilization of western instruments by black people as a means to redocument the significance of black creativity—that is, the fact that black people utilized western instruments is used to over-emphasize the significance of western culture—as a way to apply gradualism (and

T(AF)M-16

thus distort the solidification of creative black music as a form projected through the progressional continuance of black culture). And while I do not intend to dismiss the use of western instruments—and the contribution of any particular group—it is my belief that to overemphasize the sociological context of a given creative thrust is to obscure the essence of the subject.

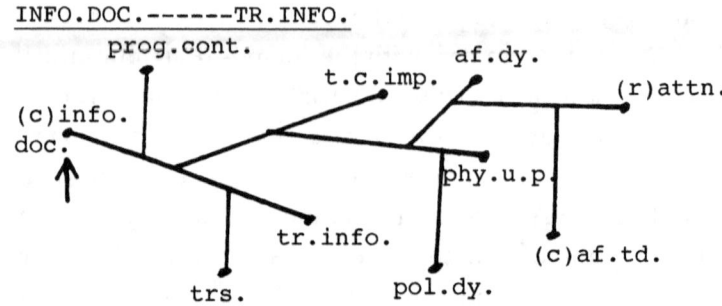

My argument is simply this: however we choose to look at the so-called progressions of creative music from the black aesthetic—in all of its various projectional strains—it is important to understand that the composite thrust of black creativity is one music—or another way of saying this would be: however we choose to perceive the dynamic spectrum of black creativity, it is important to understand that all of the various manifestations of black music represent the same essence factor. In other words, regardless of its various strains, we are basically dealing with the same aesthetic with different permutations reflecting the sociological dynamics of given parts of the planet (or time/space). This is true whether the tools of western or any other cultural strain are adopted. For the most basic factor that connects black creativity is the insight each projectional thrust advances with regards to both the journey black people have taken from Africa through slavery, and what this journey will mean with regards to the nature of the next transformation. The nature of how a given projection materialized is of course important, but the projectional significance of a given creative thrust is not about its materialization but rather its assignment.

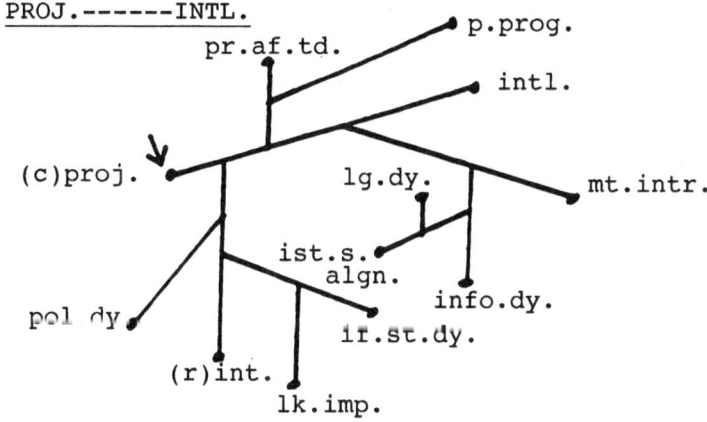

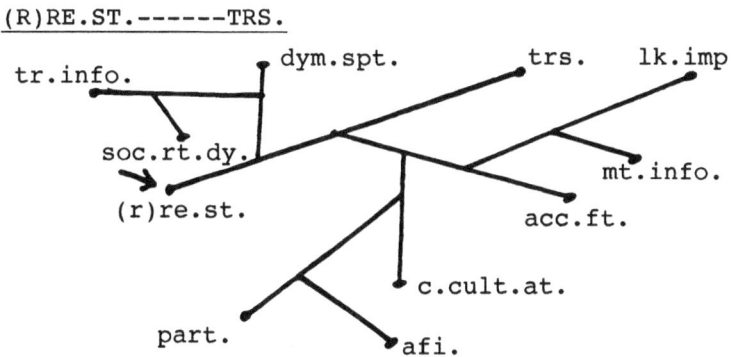

To deal with the realness of black creativity in this cycle is to understand the dynamics of American creativity as well, for the progressional thrust of black creativity has affected the total vibrational arena of American culture on every level. In fact the actualness of black creativity functions as the most efficient generator for American creative culture, supplying either the base dynamics or vibrational identity for practically every American creative thrust involving music or dance. So real is this influence today that many of us have yet to deal with what this phenomenon means for the vibrational lining of American culture, as well as the future solidification of American culture. For the dynamic effects of black creativity are changing every stratum of American culture—affecting all of us (because everyone is subjected to and shaped by the creative thrust of cultural and vibrational dynamics)—and

T(AF)M-18

in doing so this phenomenon is providing clues as to the next transitional progression (to real transformation). Moreover, if the seeds underlying black creativity can be seen as the foundation of composite American creativity in this time cycle, then this viewpoint must also imply that the thrust projection of the European and/or Asian aesthetic can't be isolated from what this influence means as well—or at least the basic divisions we have come to accept concerning what constitutes western or oriental projections do not necessarily correspond to what is really happening on the physical universe planet (which is to say, the dynamic interconnection of humanity is not one-dimensional). Thus any attempt to deal with the realness of black creativity would imply that some effort is made to understand the progressional continuance of black creativity as well as the subsequent effect of its projections—as applied to source projection (i.e., the dynamics and particulars related to how given projectional thrusts were able to expand and what that expansion would mean to black people—whatever period) and also applied to source transfer (as a thrust whose natural projection affected the composite lining of American culture).

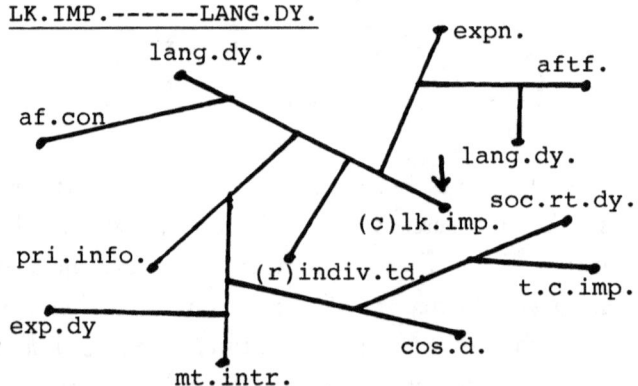

On the physical universe level this attempt to understand would involve viewing the projectional continuance of various projections of black creativity as a means to view both the dynamics of style, as a factor related to functional application (i.e., dance)—what this would mean in the black community in various periods (for example, the migration cycle after Reconstruction to the North and the various changes this spread would necessitate in both music—blues to rhythm and blues—and dance) and also what this phenomenon would mean to the white community (that being black creativity as a primary factor to generate the spectacle-diversion cycle of American culture and as such a force which functioned as an alternative to the basic thrust alignment of western culture). The source-transfer implications of black creativity would also provide the strongest vibrational platform for reshaping American culture. For the natural thrust of black creativity would utilize every sector of western dynamics including the adaptation of western functionalism regardless of level—and while doing so also provide a transfer-junction agent for world participation—and this is important.

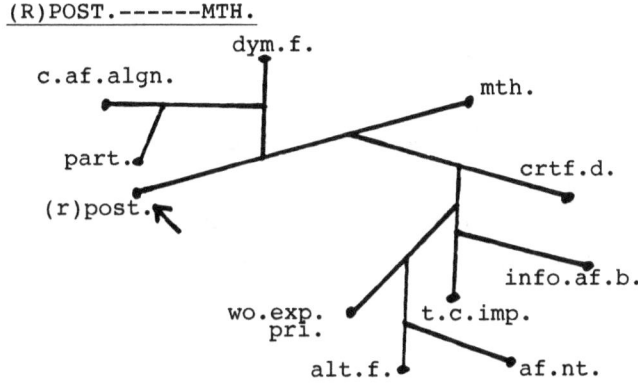

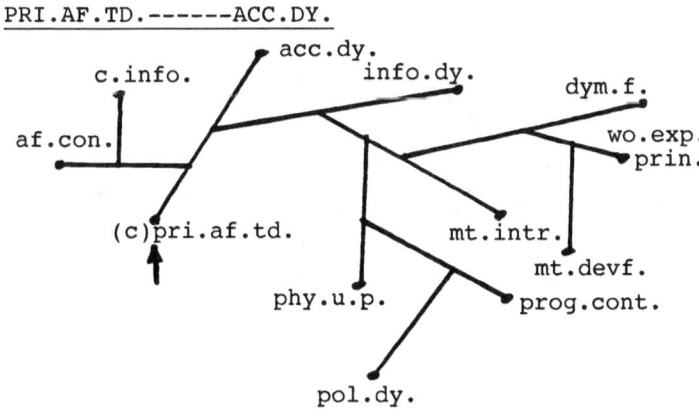

T(AF)M-20

For to deal with the source-transfer implications of black creativity is to understand its attractiveness to the composite realness of American culture, for the meta- and functional reality of creative black music was "ised" with regards to the physical universe arena of composite American culture and history (however one chooses to look at the particulars of that progression). In other words, the realness of black creativity is the most basic generating stimulant for American creativity because it was the only thrust projection that drew its dynamics from the composite American vibrationaltory arena. For this reason, the thrust implications of creative black music were necessary for both black and white Americans—or people—and for this same reason black creativity must also be viewed as a composite transformational factor for America—to western culture continuance. I am talking of a thrust whose vibrational projection absorbed whatever particulars that came in its path (i.e., the western, or so-called western functional arena of classical art music) and maintained its basic essence foundation and alignment while doing so. Thus the basic effect of this projection must be looked at in terms of affinity transfer. In other words, the projectional realness of black creativity, in its natural flow, is related to the nature permeating vibrationaltory transfer for the composite realness of American culture.

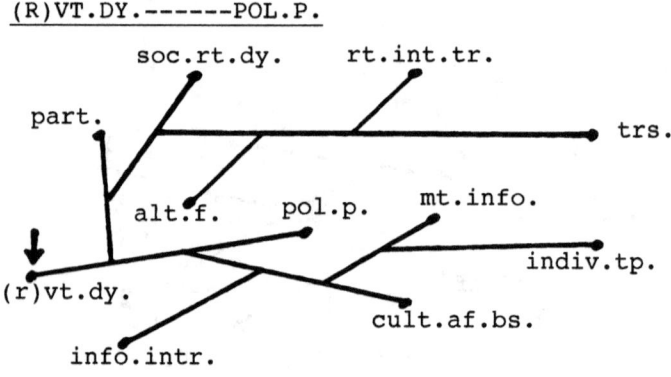

(R)INDIV.TD.------EXT.F.

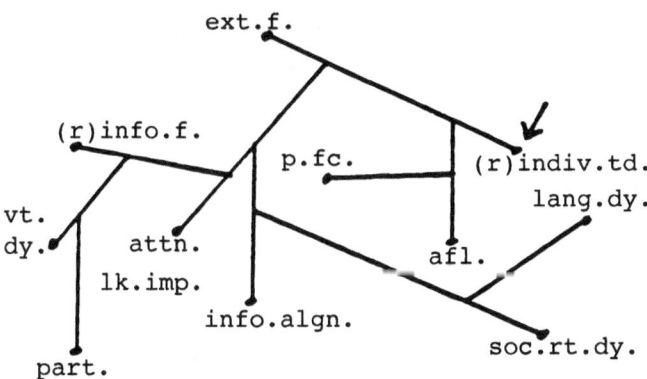

Moreover, the realness of this viewpoint is not one-dimensional, for if every junction of creative black music has seeded physical and vibrational ramifications—with regards to the forces attached to its hierarchy of form—then the ultimate effects of the music are changing everyone—which is to say, the composite thrust implications of black creativity are not limited to its source-transfer implications on western culture (or white people) alone, but rather the actual effects of this phenomenon are reshaping black and white people—or black, white, and Asian people—or simply people. The seriousness of this distinction is important if we are to understand the present realness of western culture, or the inevitable transformational junction we will soon be faced with (if we are here or if we aren't here). Because the seeds underlying the realness of black creativity serve as the strongest single creative factor reshaping the western world in this time period. And as such, our ability to utilize functional creativity for positive growth is directly related to what we are able to understand about this phenomenon. For the potential of black creativity as a healing and positive functional tool has yet to be understood to its fullest extent. If the realness of this subject can be viewed with regards to its composite potential for reshaping earth life, then we might be able to understand the nature of what source transfer really means as a transformational tool. At present, we are forced to deal with the progressional continuance of black creativity as a platform to view the present cycle we are now in (i.e., what is really happening in the source-transfer junction of black creativity), and while this information is important, it is still only the surface of what could be unearthed from the real secrets (and challenges) of the music—from its own terms (source initiation and trans-African mysticism and spiritual dynamics), and what that information could reveal about what we call swing.

The projectional implications of source transfer can be seen by tracing the solidification of creative black music from its early juncture on through to the present cycle we are now in concerning what has come to be called "jazz." It is my opinion that the progressional continuance of this phenomenon details the clearest example of creative black activity and its role in shifting the basic vibrationaltory alignment of American culture—yet I do not mean to imply that this strain (i.e., bebop) is more significant than any other strain of creative black music, but rather, the relationship of this projection to the defining and controlling forces which dictate policy for the composite American information complex has always been very interesting—to say the least. For the meta-reality of this projection (Dixieland to jazz) has long been subjected to extensive interpretations by the collective controlling forces of American culture as a means to better utilize both source-transfer and spectacle-diversion interpretations (for the controlling and philosophical communities' own interest, rather than what is "most true"). For this reason there is more misunderstanding surrounding the composite thrust of creative black music than most of us realize, because the basic interpretations (or reinterpretations) of the western power structure have affected the total reality underlying how black creativity is understood—or not understood. Every period of creative black music has been touched—and as such affected—by the collective defining forces of western culture, and the basis of this phenomenon—regardless of focus—has also affected the progressional development of the music.

The net effect of this phenomenon is related to the emergence of creative music from the white aesthetic, and the net effect of this juncture is also related to the dissolution of the composite-center factor of American black culture. All of these considerations must be looked at if we are to gain the proper perspective for investigating the actualness of creative music from the black aesthetic, for to discuss this subject is to be faced with many considerations from a multitude of standpoints. One fact remains clear: the multi-complexual implications of creative black music cross every cultural and/or ethnic barrier because the projectional implications of its essence spread have revealed the profoundest understanding of cross-sectional participation and/or adaptability; that is, the significance of creative music from the black aesthetic transcends particulars on the physical universe level and is directly related to the vibrationaltory realness of transformation—regardless of section of the planet. As such, the basic interpretations of the western defining and controlling community must be perceived as a factor related to how given aspects of creative music are utilized for source transfer (whether or not those interpretations are correct), and the challenge of this period is directly related to whether or not other efforts are made to balance this phenomenon.

The distortions surrounding the meta-reality of creative black music are related to many factors, and any attempt to deal with the actualness of what American black creativity signifies—as a potential transformation factor—implies that some effort is first made to understand how this present cycle has come to be—which is to say, the present misconceptions surrounding creative black music are not to black people's advantage. For when I wrote that at every juncture western culture has tried to dissect black creativity, it is important to understand what this means. The fact is, the route western culture has taken to examine black creativity runs parallel to the nature of the black aesthetic—which is to say western culture has dissected and analyzed every juncture of black creativity using the same tools used to analyze western art music. Moreover, the basic interpretations handed down from generation to generation concerning the actualness of black creativity—by the collective thrust of the western defining community—have become the tenets underlying how most people now perceive of black creativity, which is interesting because the reality of interpretation surrounding how black creativity is taught (and thought of) by this sector has very little to do with what is really happening in black creativity, because the particulars underlying how given aspects of the music are viewed in western terms have nothing—or very little—to

T(AF)M-24

do with how those same particulars are viewed outside western definitions (or what that same particular means outside of western definitions). The significance of this distinction is profound. For the sophistication of the western defining and controlling community has helped to produce a situation where the transfer-shift implications (interpretations) of black creativity have assumed more importance than the principle thrust projection responsible for the subsequent transfers (the leaf is more important than the tree)—and while every transfer-shift interpretation related to black creativity is important—certainly I have not meant to imply that any focus or reality and/or affinity platform is "less" than another platform—in the final analysis the realness of black creativity is being both distorted and "undermined."

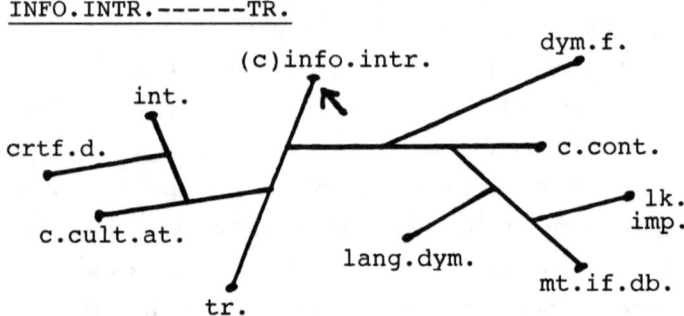

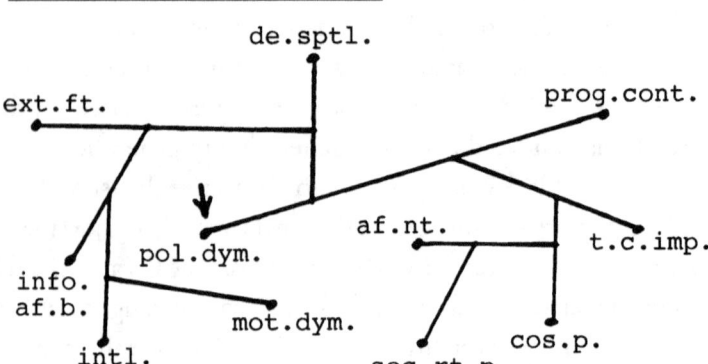

What is black creativity? Which is to say: what is the principal factor—if any—that sustains the actualness of black creativity—what does it mean, and how does it function, and what is its relationship to the composite realness of American culture as well as the composite realness of the world group? These are the questions we are forced to deal with if the challenge of the next cycle is to be met. The seriousness of these questions can also serve as a factor to challenge the composite western controlling forces surrounding the music, for while I do not believe any one creative thrust on its own is more than any other thrust, the position of black creativity in this time zone is too important for the wrong interpretations—and thus usage—to lessen its potential for real transformation. We are forced to deal with these questions.

If what we call black creativity has to do with an essence projection of knowingness (as made real through the historical thrust of black culture in terms of vibrational center) that is transmitted through doing (in terms of both vibrational and methodology alignment)—which also comments and aids the unification of culture (or individuals), concerning the spirit factor of its arena as well as the projectional path related to where that culture (or individual) is going—then the nature of the essence projection affirming creative music from the black aesthetic—as "ised" in the Americas—has to do with the projectional realness of the black aesthetic (source initiation) and its encounter with the composite thrust of western culture (whether concerning "particulars" or given the weight of the vibrational significance of that encounter). Moreover, if my understanding of the black aesthetic is correct—in the sense that however given aspects of its thrust are viewed, in actual fact the composite thrust of black creativity is related to the nature of the composite world group sensibility—then the emergence of creative music from the black aesthetic (as "ised" in the Americas) signals the cyclic realignment of western creativity back into the meta-reality of world culture. (Either this is true or the emergence of creative black music signals some kind of cosmic readjustment having to do with something outside of surface observations.) Whatever, the present situation of creativity in the west can be viewed from this context (whatever its real cosmic purpose—or "not purpose"). But I do not mean to imply that this definition of black creativity satisfies every aspect of what is happening on the planet—because it doesn't. It is possible to use this definition as a means to examine the nature of progressional continuance in creative black music if this viewpoint sheds light on the meta-reality position of black creativity. There is however still the position of black culture in this time zone—that being recessed at the expense of the nature of western expansion—which must also be looked at. My point is this: the essence implications of black creativity must be viewed as in the same position of all black "actualness"—suppressed; and as such the progressional implications of black creativity must be perceived as related to this phenomenon. In other words, the thrust projection of creative black activity moves towards rediscovering the essence foundation of black postulation (i.e., what it was before the decline of black culture—what this means either vibrationally or functionally) as a means to restore order. The basic thrust continuum of black creativity must be viewed from this perspective if black creativity is indeed either a tool for transformation or a positive reconstruction factor. Yet this definition still has to be expanded to include the composite actualness of the world group—including western culture.

In other words, the thrust implications of a given projection cannot be perceived as separate from how that projection is utilized—or from who utilizes it. Thus, while my definition of creative black music can be applied to the essence realness of black creativity in its pure state—and this is necessary—there is also the realness that everyone participates in the fruits of what this thrust has actualized. In other words, the meta-reality of creative music from the black aesthetic must also be viewed with regard to the participation of white musicians as well as its utilization by the world group. This is so because obviously the use of black creative music by white musicians cannot be talked of in terms of its insight into the profoundness of black essence (in its source initiation state). Rather, the utilization of trans-African vibrational dynamics by white musicians has to do with other factors (just as the use of western art music by black composers cannot be viewed in the same reality context as the composite western projectional thrust). The utilization of black creative projections by the creative white musician signals the realness that a given projection's implications—and meta-implications—are not limited to one stratum (even if that stratum is based off the relationship of a particular projection to source initiation) but instead this phenomenon has multi-complexual implications that go outside of so-called racial or cultural (or vibrational and mystical) boundaries.

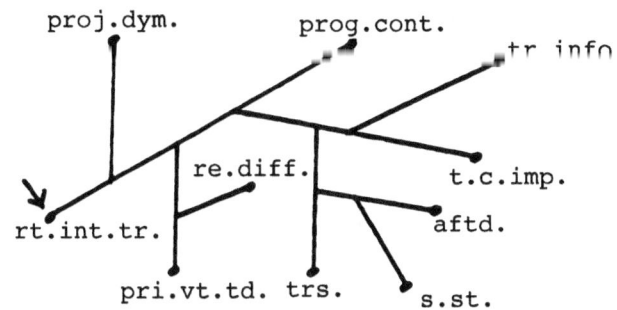

That is, the realness of a given projection must be looked at in accordance with two basic criteria—the actualness of that projection with regards to its basic assignment (i.e., creativity and the culture and vibrational thrust it affirms), and the potential of what that projection really means with regards to the world group (i.e., which comes into play in the transfer-shift realness of given time junctions). Thus the participation of white musicians in creativity "ised" from the black aesthetic can be viewed as a factor related to the dynamic potential of what that form really is (without superficial boundaries and meaningless separation)—which is to say, the participation of the creative white musician must be viewed as a phenomenon that comments on the reality dynamics of black creativity as a composite thrust continuance. Because in the final analysis the reality of a continuum is not limited to only one aspect of "how it seems to be manifested," but instead a given thrust continuance has relevance for the composite planet. The phenomenon of "cross-participation" can also be viewed as a signal about the path nature of a given thrust continuance, for the adaptation of black creativity by the creative white musician also signals that the assignment implications of a given projection have been completed in their own source-initiated sense (that is, the reality of a continuance as it proceeds to secure its cosmic destiny—from its own definitions). For the meta-implications of black creativity's adaptation by the creative white musician must be viewed as the most significant consideration in this time period that has aided the realignment of western culture to the composite affinity-insight dynamics of world culture. The realness of this phenomenon has provided the strongest balance to the vibrational route western culture has taken. To understand this use of black creativity by white musicians is to understand that it is not a question of whether or not anyone has the right to utilize a given creative thrust; rather, the dynamic realness of a given creative thrust is designed for the composite utilization of the world group—and this is important to understand if we are seriously interested in viewing the essence realness of a given projection.

The cross-sectional realness of creative black music also implies that the vibrational and meta-implications of its various projections have double assignments as well. I have already written on the vibrational implications of black creativity in its separate state (applying only to black culture) and what this means with regards to the progressional expansion of American black culture—but it is important to understand that the inclusion of western culture as active participants also changes the vibrational implications of what a given projection means as well. It is important to understand that the utilization of black creativity by western culture really signifies the utilization of black creativity by the world group (for in a given potential state, a creative projection is apt to be utilized by any number of cultures for a variety of reasons—thus, the significance of western culture's use of creative black music has to do with this context— that being, a phenomenon which signals that the use of a given projection does have extended implications). The meta-implications of this expanded participation move towards the solidification of a composite spiritual and vibrational basis as a means to participate in both unification as well as transformation. The cross-sectional implications then of a given transfer-shift junction in creativity in this context can be evaluated by what zone it aims to secure for the world group, as a means to establish the possibility for transformation.

C.CONT.------PHY.U.P.

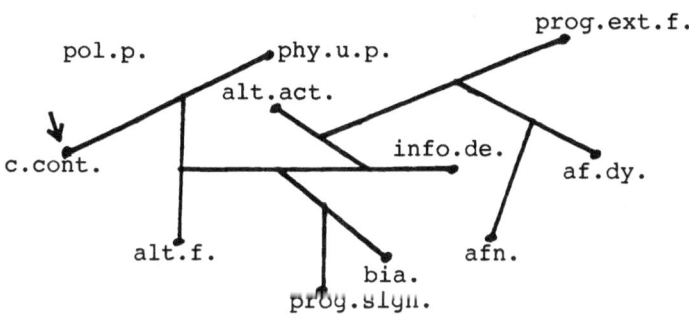

To look at the total progression of creative music from the black aesthetic in America from the early period until the present is to have some idea of the profound effect this thrust has had on western culture. The realness of this effect has moved to reshape the vibrational thrust of western culture—which is to say, the progressional flow of black creativity has affected black and white people alike in American (and western) culture. And while I do not mean western creativity has not also helped to create the present vibrationaltory arena that exists in American culture (certainly there are many factors responsible for the present state of affairs concerning creativity in the west), it is undeniable that the profound implications of black creativity have provided the strongest single alternative foundation for composite change (and dynamics) for American and present-day western culture—and this is true no matter what period in American history we choose to focus on. For whatever the superficial changes that have taken place in black creativity—having to do with the nature of how given functional adjustments have actualized—we can now see the emergence of trans-European creative artists who no longer limit themselves to the reality of interpretation at the expense of total participation, and we can also see the emergence of white artists released from the shackles of the western philosophic and vibrational chains to the degree where their participation in creativity can now have something to do with extended postulation (as perceived by the world group—including western culture—before the solidification of present-day specialization). Trans-African creativity, as a tool for humanizing the western aesthetic, is a real consideration that

T(AF)M-30

must be dealt with if we are to understand the progressional effects of what has happened in American culture during the last two hundred and some years.

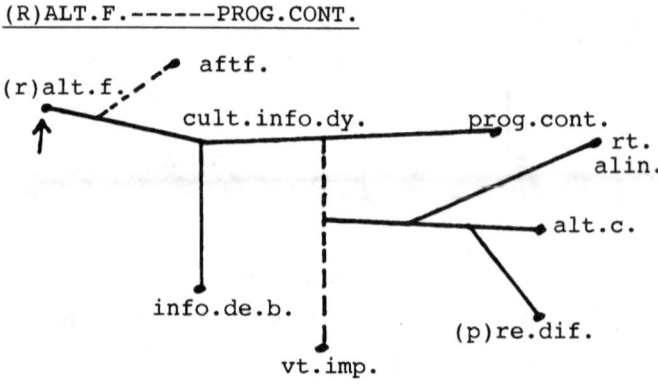

Before an examination of black creativity can take place, it is first necessary to dismiss the present reality of present-day interpretations—that is, it is necessary to separate the realness of this subject from the traditional interpretations of the composite western defining and controlling community. For the reality of black creativity interpretations have long suffered distortions from this sector—and the weight of these distortions involves every area of its involvement or focus, whether we are commenting on the reality of black creativity's methodology or its aesthetic implications; whether we are focusing on the dynamics of a given projectional route or the particulars of its formation—and the extent of misinformation does not even stop on this level; which is to say the dynamics of distortion in black creativity have even touched the reality implications underlying how its projections are viewed in their separate independent realness—and this is true whether we are focusing on the reality of country blues or the significance of stride piano. In actual terms, I regard the activity of a musician like Louis Armstrong to be as "ised" as that of Charlie Parker—which is to say, I do not accept the basic divisions which have been constructed around the total progression of the music. (I have in this series of writings, however, continued to use the established nomenclatures that have been assigned to given projections, but I do not accept the establishment's view concerning what those projections are.) Moreover, I do not accept the argument that it is possible in creative black music to isolate one or two people as a means to claim innovation for the nature of how a given restructured cycle in the music was arrived at. For the thrust continuance of creative black music is directly related to the physical and vibrational universe factors surrounding the position of black culture in western society—that is, the progressional thrust of creative black music has never had the same relationship to essence as defined in western terms. What this means is that no given progression of creative black music can be isolated because of its idea alignment as a means to claim separate innovation because every strain of black creativity possesses the same properties. The real factors which distinguish how given projections are viewed in the progressional continuance of creative black music have to do with the vibrationaltory actualness of cosmic considerations—rather than the genius of one or two people. As such, I am writing of a thrust continuance not seated in the same intellectual arena as western art music—even the consideration of innovation has to be revised if it is to be meaningful. Certainly it is clear that given groups of individuals can be viewed as solidifying certain functional considerations as a means to establish different projectional routes in the music, but my point is that there are many other factors related to how this phenomenon is arrived at (not to mention that history tends to only accent certain individuals at the expense of the whole picture), and the idea of one great master pointing the way for the rest of humanity is misleading.

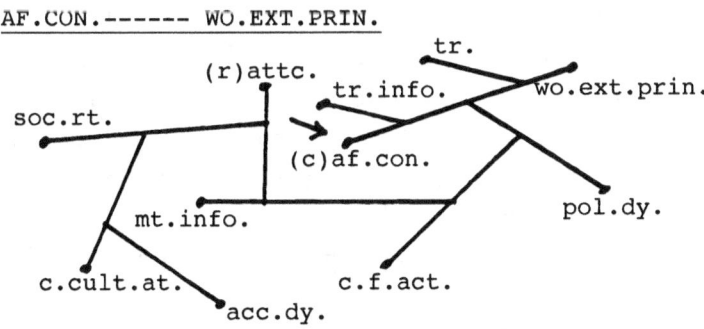

T(AF)M-32

    The progressional thrust of creative music from the black aesthetic can be viewed from many other perspectives—rather than a narrow concept concerning innovation. For the progressional significance of each projectional expansion in black music comments on the physical universe actualness of black people's struggle—with regards to the potential realness of what black culture could be, as well as the progressional shift of the social and political position of black people in American culture. Moreover, the solidification of every projectional expansion sheds light on the nature of what factors from the composite actualness of black culture have been re-secured. To understand this viewpoint is to understand that while a musician like Louis Armstrong is wrongly given credit for the establishment of a complete projection of the music (because in actual fact, many musicians helped to shape each given projection in the music), in fact, the realness of his creativity did comment on the changing position of black culture in that period. That is, Louis Armstrong can be viewed as the personification of the factors that were secured for the creative black musician in his time period. Moreover, the nature of that personification had to do with the progressional exposure of the American black man to western functionalism (in this case, instruments) and what resulted from that encounter. Because in the final analysis, Armstrong's creativity signaled the realness that an American black man had now arrived whose utilization of western instruments transcended the definitions concerning what that instrument meant with regards to its functional and aesthetic realness before his arrival. The dynamics of Armstrong's activity would make this arrival clear, but this should not be confused with innovation because the music is not dependent on any one person—then or now. The solidification of the Armstrong period would clarify the progressional continuance of creative black music in terms of projectional particulars. That being, the utilization of what has wrongly been labeled the western functional aesthetic, as a tool to re-establish the meta-reality science of black music for re-actualizing culture.

    Without doubt the best way to approach dealing with creative music from the trans-African aesthetic is to look at the actual forms "ised" through its projection. It is possible to look at given projections like Dixieland music and clearly see the dynamic realness of composite black music. Rather than focus on the science of this form, the best understanding we can have of Dixieland music concerns the spiritual and vibrational implications this projection opened up. In other words, a real understanding of Dixieland music would involve human beings coming together and celebrating their communication through the music. The functional science related to how that celebration works is at best a secondary consideration, for the social and vibrational realness of Dixieland music would solidify the progressional continuance of creative black music which is to say, regardless of whether or not the functional arena of its form was reshaped. The realness of this "communication" would open up another informational and vibrational spectrum for western culture—but I do not mean to confuse its implications with "it." For the solidification of Dixieland music is an important chain in the progressional thrust of creative black music in more ways than one. The realness of this projection would establish the nature of the source-transfer cycle between the African and western sensibility, and the dynamics of this thrust would clarify the affinity lining of its projectional continuum (Dixieland on through the bop period to the present) with regards to both black and white culture. Moreover, this alignment (and solidification) would be actualized in accordance with black sensibility in the defining position. Any attempt to view the composite realness of creative black music would imply that some effort is put forth to deal with the realness of what we have come to call Dixieland music.

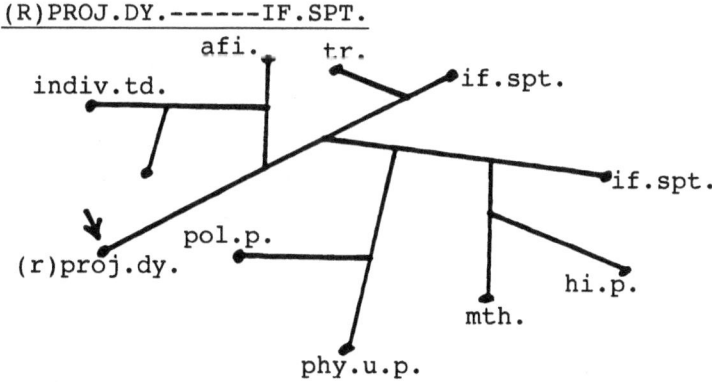

T(AF)M-34

Dixieland music, as a pivotal factor related to the nature of the source-transfer shift of creative black music, supplied one of the most influential projections in the composite thrust of American culture. The solidification of this one projectional thrust would help transform American creativity. Like ragtime music—which is just as significant—this form would establish the nature (and affinity implications) of creative black music, and also manifest the nature of the affinity lining of the black aesthetic—commenting on the changing social, political, and vibrational state of black culture. The dynamic of this thrust (i.e., language) would solidify the projectional realness underlying how improvisation and composition could, in a bi-aitional context, help shape extended functionalism for both form and musical science. I am then referring to a form which, in its natural thrust, comments on the actual physical universe realness of black culture as well as a form that established the meta-reality dynamics of composite black culture (i.e., from a cosmic, spiritual, and dynamic perspective). On the physical universe level, Dixieland music would also function with regards to its social functional responsibility (i.e., dance and creativity as a dynamic or positive social consideration) as well as a vibrational tool for investigation (i.e., improvisation as a tool for probing the reality of source initiation), and while all of this was going on Dixieland music also functioned as a positive ritual factor (i.e., structure as a means to establish the nature of what aspects of what zone—magic—could be utilized). Any attempt then to deal with the realness of Dixieland music would imply that all of these factors are really understood, because I have not mentioned any of these contexts as one-dimensional considerations, but rather, as a point from which to begin research. The solidification of Dixieland music would also shed light on the nature of improvisation in creative black music—or at least the realness of this phenomenon (Dixieland music) would further help us to understand extended functionalism—yet I have not meant to imply that the use of improvisation in creative black music started with Dixieland, because this is not the case either—the utilization of improvisation in black music can be viewed as an integral factor in every period of the music (moreover, this inclusion also corresponds to the underlying philosophical basis of world culture functionalism)—for the dynamic application of improvisation in Dixieland music would accent the social and cosmic realness underlying what alternative functionalism means in the essence lining of black invention. The ritual actualness of Dixieland music would thus reveal a projection that, while allowing for each individual participant to help shape the actualness of the music at any given point (and as such have a role in the total picture of the music), also maintained a basic point of origin or personality (with regards to composition). A given performance of the music would bring forth a dynamic alignment involving the total culture, as well as a signature of the participants in that culture. The composite actualness of black creativity is directly related to what the establishment of this pedagogy means.

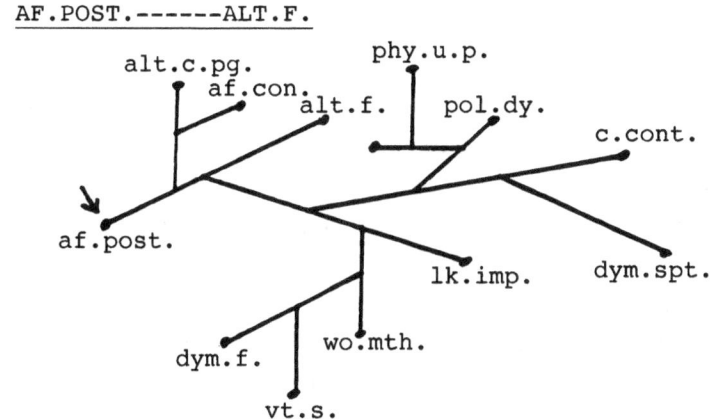

The nature of the thrust continuum of black creativity is related to many factors, for the dynamic implications of a given projection are not limited to one stratum—either with regards to its position in a given thrust alignment or its effect on how that alignment proceeds in its natural state. Thus it would be impossible to view the progressional continuance of black creativity without understanding its effect on the collective defining and controlling forces of American culture. My point is that the realness of black creativity, at every juncture, goes outside of the western affinity and vibrational information reality position. I am not saying that the significance of black creativity is too profound for western culture to understand, nor am I saying that the realness of black creativity is too far from the white sensibility to be received, but rather, the combination of the western affinity alignment (as manifested through its philosophy and methodology) as well as present-day racism serves as a barrier for real perception into the actualness of creative black music. Because of this, the interpretations surrounding the composite thrust of black creativity have tended to diminish the realness of the music with regards to its sophistication as well as its importance. Musicologists have long attempted to break down creative black music using the same systematic tools designed for western art music, with the understanding that through investigation it is possible to comment on whether a given participant in the music is playing correct or not correct—or even worse, "which player is the best." And while I do not mean to give the impression that there are no standards in creative music from the black aesthetic—obviously every form has a functional and vibrational reality (and as such, a science)—in the final analysis, the work of the collective forces of western culture can best be viewed as an outside controlling factor that has very little to do with what is actually happening in the music. Because in the final analysis it is important to understand that any given criticism of a performance (or happening) of creative black music is nothing more than a comment on one's ability to have an affinity with the creativity of another person as it happens or happened in that fleeting moment—nothing more. Dixieland music, and for that matter every projection related to the composite thrust of creative black music (from the zone which involved the synthesis of improvisation and composition in this fashion—i.e., improvised ragtime music, blues, boogie woogie, bebop, etc., etc.), not only didn't have anything to do with the notions of correctness being handed down from western controlling groups—regardless of time period—but the actualness of the aesthetic runs contrary to this type of information platform. For the essence factor of trans-African music is built on the actualness of "individuals being as they are in the music," because this is essential to the projectional continuance of the black aesthetic.

I have not meant to imply that there is no standard of excellence in creative black music, because of course this is not true. Certainly the progressional realness of creative music reveals the highest levels of discipline as well as invention. My objection to present-day information tenets has to do with the nature of how western culture perceives of criticism, rather than what this consideration means for the world group. Because the progressional application of western criticism on trans-African music from its early period until the present clearly shows that criticism as defined in the annals of the western position serves as a life-choking factor rather than merely an observation criterion. In other words, criticism as defined through the western position serves as a choking device on the lifeblood of the music—and its use has been extremely dangerous to creative black music and how it has come to be viewed. My position is that this type of activity has nothing to do with the meta-realness of creative black music. Certainly every thrust projection has a science, and of course part of any learning process involves learning and practicing that science. But the nature of what that science really means—with respect to the aesthetic foundation it seeks to affirm if it is to be in accordance with its aesthetic foundation—is not outside of the actual life realness of where/how its discipline was formulated. In other words, the realness of any given projection would necessarily reveal many different levels of participation, and all of those levels are indicative of some aspect of what its principle foundation really is—which is to say, the fact that some players would interpret a given composition one way, and other players would interpret that same composition in another way, has nothing to do with anyone being better or less than anyone else—not to mention the natural interchange that takes place between musicians (which is also an integral factor related to how given viewpoints—compositions or projectional routes—solidify the reality of black and world creativity). In other words, the actualness of a given projection is a natural factor having nothing to do with the nature of investigation as perceived through western methodological and critical channels. For the most basic attitude underlying how investigation is perceived in western terms involves a kind of separation that is not natural for the realness of black creativity. Because the nature of the western critical alignment is based on isolating a given "idea," rather than experiencing the actualness of the music (which might not have anything to do with the narrowness of what in western terms is called an "idea"—depending on the occasion). Moreover, I do not mean to under-rate the realness of technique in any form. Certainly the projectional continuum of creative black music has seen many excellent technicians come and go, but I believe this consideration must be re-understood. For it is documented very clearly that in every stage of the music the consideration of technique was looked at by black people in a very different way from the forces controlling western culture. Even in New Orleans—when certain projections were solidifying—it was common knowledge that the classically trained Creole musicians who were given the opportunity to study music from white teachers (or institutions) in the final analysis had to come uptown to their more "primitive" brothers to learn how to really play creative music. For the question has never been "how" a given individual played, but rather "what" an individual had to say in his or her activity. It follows then that the sophistication surrounding one's technical mastery of the mechanics of a given thrust (either with regards to instrumental or language ability) was not perceived of in the same stratum as western culture views functionalism. The fact is, the actualness underlying the aesthetic foundation of creative black music is designed for both ensemble and individual dynamics as well as what this means with regards to growth and development (or anti-development)—that is, the aesthetic is designed in accordance and with respect for the life factor of the people participating in the aesthetic. Moreover, the fruits of this alignment are the foundation which really supports creative black music, for the strength of the composite realm of one's participation in creative postulation is both responsible for the dynamics of the aesthetic as well as the realness of the aesthetic—as a positive force having to do with the community. In short, the realness of creative black music has never been separate from the community, nor was it ever intended to be. Even today we are constantly bombarded with the question "is this jazz or not?"—with the understanding being that the dynamic realness of black creativity can only utilize a narrow functional spectrum (and it must be understood that the many definitions surrounding black music from the white establishment are directly related to the defining and controlling forces surrounding the music). In the early period of the music, no one in the black community was asking "is it jazz?" because everyone knew what was happening. The progressional development of western controlling techniques is directly responsible for the many misconceptions surrounding creative black music. However we choose to call the music, in the final analysis, it is really nothing more than human beings affirming who they are through their creativity under a common vibrational reality. That reality encompassed from the very beginning more than just the consideration of what we now talk of as blackness, but was more a reflection of the natural creativity which takes place in a given reality—whatever the physical universe environment. The whole idea of jazz at some point is a grave distortion.

If Louis Armstrong's music can be spoken of as the personification of black people in their first encounter with the white sensibility, Charlie Parker's activity can be talked of as the epitome of the second transformation of black people in America in the sense that his creativity not only completely utilized western techniques with a black aesthetic, but in his activity we can also see a developed reaction and awareness of the whole position of black people—in the physical and vibrational universe context. Charlie Parker's activity can be viewed as the activity which personified the shift (and progression) of the affinity insight dynamic principle in creative black music. I define the affinity insight (1) principle as the vibrational phenomenon which moved towards reaffirming the spiritual-essence factor (or the vibrational lining) of "air" postulation and/or participation. There are two basic principles which creative music functions from (no matter what culture). The first principle would establish creativity as a social factor which moves as an underlining force to establish both functional unification as well as social interchange and harmony. When this first condition is met, it is possible to look at this principle (affinity insight [2]) as the vibrational flow that moves towards "composite knowingness" on the physical plane. The second principle (affinity insight [1]) flows as a vibrational factor which moves to solidify the correct spiritual and vibrational alignment of the culture. This vibrational phenomenon determines how the intellectual and spiritual affinity relationship with the culture is to be "affirmed." It is possible to write of the first principle (affinity insight [2]) as "celebration,"

T(AF)M-40

while the second principle would be "affirmation"—if the first vibration (affinity insight [2]) moves towards stabilization as a factor which allows for the building of culture, the second principle (affinity insight [1]) would be the agent which dictates how transformation is to be arrived at (if a given situation is out of phase with its own "essence factor" in a given phase)—whatever the reason.

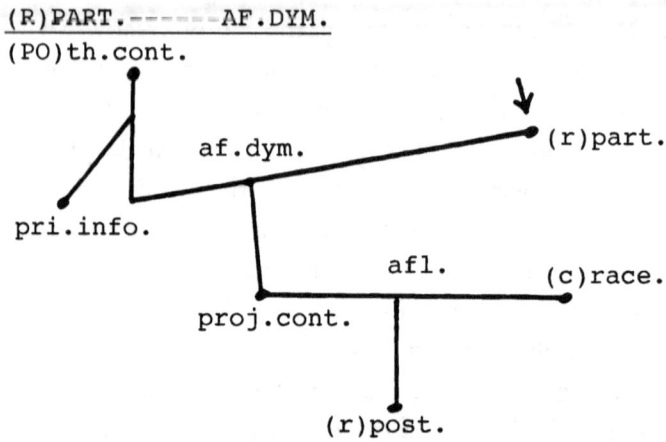

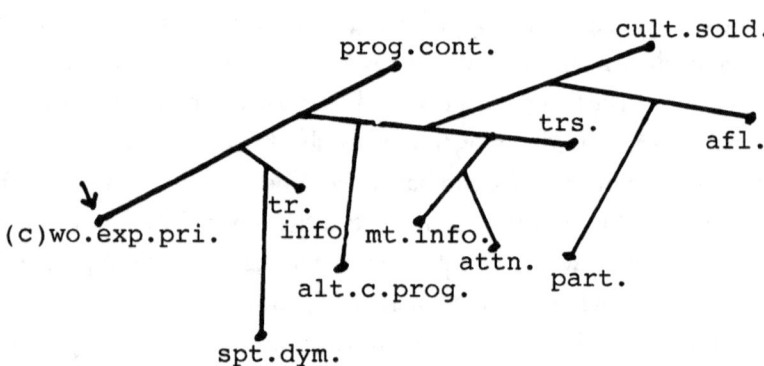

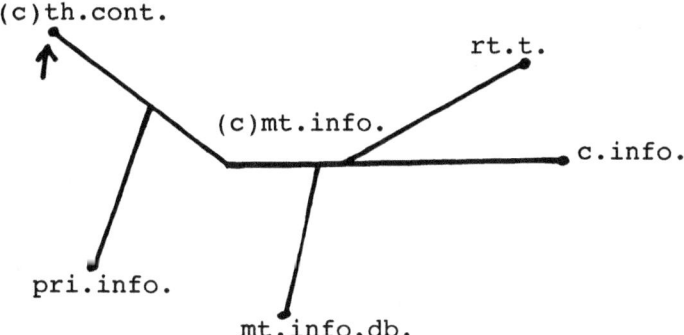

Charlie Parker's activity can be seen as the embodiment of the second transformation of black people in America, because his activity documented the emergence of the affinity insight (1) principle after World War II (which represented a transformation period to black Americans). Parker's activity also represented the junction where white people found the necessary conceptual factors to employ source shift as a means to have creative music from the black aesthetic correspond to the dictates of what is commonly referred to as "art music." In short, the sophistication of western language has long been a tool for realigning alternative factors in accordance with the establishment's reality. It is bebop's relationship to what western culture refers to as an art music which personifies the nature of the transformation which occurred in the forties. The most basic difference between early improvised music and bebop was that while both musics contain the same aesthetic make-up, bebop had to do with understanding the realness of black people's actual position in America and understanding the seriousness of what was being raised in creative music as a separate entity in itself. To understand bebop as the first entry into what America calls "art music" is to understand what in fact was the beginning of a new consciousness on the part of white people. Because in actual fact every projectional continuum from the composite thrust of black creativity functions with regard to what vibrational assignment it corresponds to, concerning the realness of black—and white—culture (and its related information dynamics).

T(AF)M-42

The most obvious understanding of improvised music developed in the forties (bebop) would have to do with the source-transfer implications of both the African and western functional aesthetic filtered through the black sensibility. Moreover, the thrust actualness of bebop could be viewed as a logical functional progression from the period which preceded its development. The solidification of bebop would have to do with its ability to participate in the "particular" lining of that time zone—as well as representing the first actualization of the affinity insight (1) principle (as a composite movement solidification). Any other interpretation of this phenomenon would risk over-accenting the realness of its dynamics. Certainly Parker's use of flatted fifths and extended harmony was not that radical from what was being done in world creativity—for this type of activity can be found in the music of even Bach or Beethoven. Indeed, it is clear that many of these considerations were developed long before black people arrived in America (in fact, the functional arena surrounding western art music did not begin even at that junction, but is also connected to the world group). What is unique about bebop—and for that matter about the composite thrust of creative music from the black aesthetic—are the dynamics surrounding how it utilized the basic functional properties of world creativity. Any attempt to deal with the actualness of creative black music would only accent the contribution this thrust has made with regards to black culture, western culture, and the world group. The effect this thrust has had on creativity in this time zone is so real that any attempt to deal with the actualness of composite creativity—as a factor related to shaping the future or correcting the past—would imply some knowledge of creative music from the black aesthetic.

(Level Two)

IT IS IMPORTANT THAT ATTEMPTS ARE MADE to examine the composite realness of creativity regardless of strain. For the actualness of this subject transcends vibrational and cultural boundaries—which is to say every culture has contributed something of worth for us to experience. Thus in the spectrum of earth creativity is to be humbled by its magnitude—so much has been created for us to experience, it is impossible to not be affected. Because in its own way each culture group has contributed a special viewpoint about what this phenomenon means, and all of these offerings are related to where we, as a collective people, have come from and where we are going. So much has been done that it is impossible to experience it all and go on with the business of living as well. For when I write of the world group I am talking of every cultural and racial strain on this planet as well as the cross-sectional results of this phenomenon. Thus it would be impossible to even speculate on what this subject means in terms of numbers. To write of the world group—and the creative forms that have come from the world's composite culture—is to comment on activity from Alaska to South America, from the Soviet Union to Africa, from Turkey across to Japan. There are so many different kinds of creativity that one could spend his (her) whole life examining this consideration alone. Moreover, it is important to understand that the actualness of given creative strains is not dependent on the size of its country, but rather, what has happened or is happening in the culture. Some of us would be quite surprised to discover that the base projection which established many of the forms we have come to now accept was "ised" in small corners of the planet—"ised" from culture groups we would consider quite small. The realness of what this means can be seen in actual physical universe terms because there is a creative thrust that corresponds to whatever is happening on the physical universe level. Wherever one journeys on the planet this most basic fact can be substantiated—and to recognize this phenomenon is to begin to understand the realness of creativity.

Any attempt to deal with the composite actualness of creativity would shed light on what this consideration means with regards to its cosmic implications. In short, to participate in creativity is to become aware of its universal implications—that is, creativity as a reflection of the spiritual universality of existence—or creativity as activity that "in the doing" celebrates the universality of existence—and this is true regardless of form. Thus the dynamics of a given projection are related to how that celebration is actualized. Our ability to relate to what this means is directly connected to who we are, what we are, where we are (really!—as opposed to only one aspect of "where") and where we would like to be. Yet I have not meant to imply that any particular creative thrust is "more" than any other thrust—because this is not what I believe. My point instead is this: the realness of whether a given projection is "experienced" or not is related to the basic alignment of the person experiencing the activity—that is, the actualness of affinity-alignment has nothing to do with the intrinsic worth of the thrust itself but rather the person experiencing it. In this period of time it might be useful to keep this in mind, for many of us have come to view creativity in quite the opposite manner; and while there are reasons for this, we are still left in a somewhat interesting state. The fact is, in this period many of us have come to evaluate a given creative strain in terms of what that strain does for us rather than the other way around. The end result of this alignment is that if a given projection feels alien to us, we are apt to perceive of it in negative terms—for the nature of how we have come to view phenomena has promoted this type of insensitivity. Thus our "education" in many ways has made it somewhat difficult to experience the composite thrust of world music, and it would be well to understand that this inability is just that—"a barrier" having to do with the inability to risk perceiving and experiencing phenomena in ways unfamiliar with what we think we know. The end result of this condition is that many of us are blocked from experiencing world creativity.

To view the composite thrust of what has been offered through creative music is to have some idea of the multi-complexual significance of world dynamics. For while many of us would like to believe that it is possible to completely separate humankind as a means to either draw comparisons or claim innovation, in actual fact the composite thrust of world creativity is inter-related on a gamut of levels. So profound is this relationship that it is difficult, if not impossible, to separate who initiated what and how—or to tell when a first initiation surfaced in actual terms. The fact is: no creative thrust is really separate from any other, or at least what we call separate is not really separate. Instead this experience (existence) seems to have basic vibrational realignment "tendencies" as a phenomenon to reflect surface particulars (concerning how a given culture group sees itself). The composite quilt of creativity permeates how the nature of a given projection is viewed as well as what that viewpoint necessitates in functional terms. Many musicologists are quite surprised to discover musical instruments from one part of the planet that are directly related to instruments on the opposite side of the planet—but in fact this is what we are dealing with. Not only is the composite spectrum of the music linked together by the functional nature of its utensils, but the vibrational context underlying how these instruments are utilized is also similar—in many cases—as well. My point is that while it is true a given culture thrust can be viewed in its particular state, it would not be to our advantage to perceive of what this means in limited terms. For the basic underlying factors of a given culture can be perceived only in universal-cosmic terms—and this is so because no one group is alone, or no one thrust derives its essence in separation from the composite community of earth. To view the actualness of earth culture is to become aware of what this natural unification means—both with regards to creativity and what that creativity is celebrating (meta-reality implications). Any attempt to deal with the multi-dynamic implications of creativity necessitates that some effort is made to place this consideration (creativity) into its most real context. This is important if we are concerned about the future.

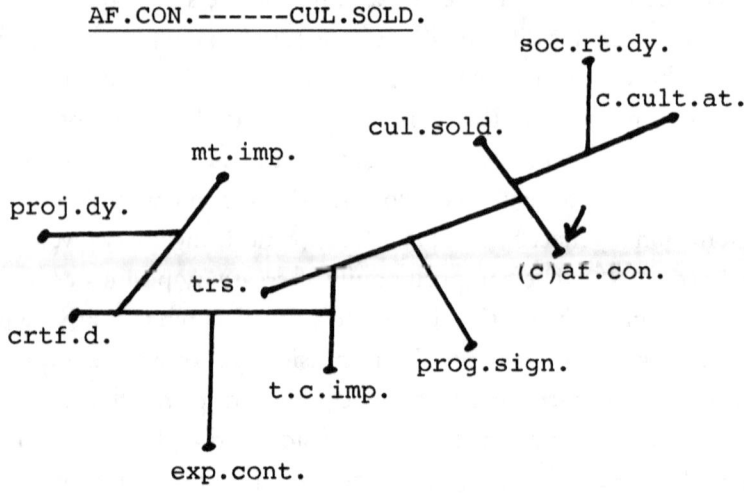

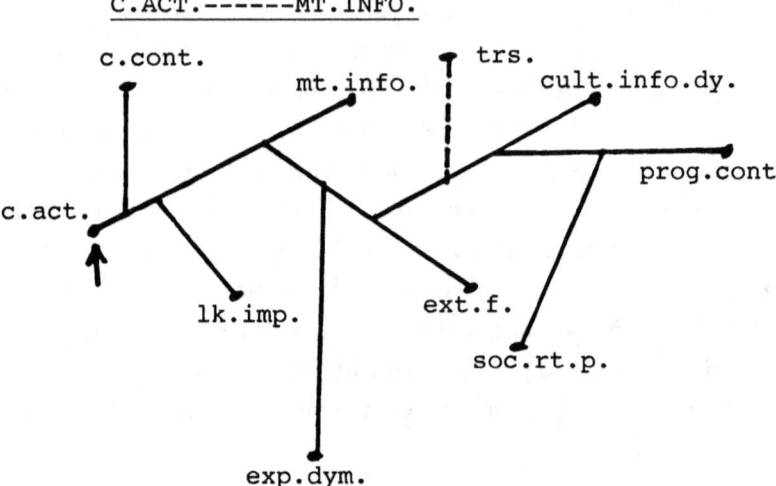

Quite possibly, the best way to approach understanding the composite thrust of creativity on earth is to view the progressional implications of this subject in both vibrational and physical universe terms. For the spread of creativity is related to the spread of humankind, and the aspects of creativity that we perceive as similar are related to how this spread developed. It is also necessary that I state my central position—in terms of what I am basing my assumptions on—or risk the possibility of obscuring this section of the book. All of my attempts to deal with the composite actualness of world creativity are based on my belief in the solidarity of humankind—in other words, I believe that no matter how the surface aspects of human beings (and earth) are perceived, in the final analysis we are not only all one, but we are also from one. Thus any attempt to deal with the composite actualness of creativity would involve dealing with the thrust alignment particulars that have helped to solidify the present physical universe situation we are in—yet I do not mean to imply that this book will attempt to piece together the total universe. My point instead is that to deal with the realness of creativity on earth is to be forced to look at the multi-dynamic diversification which has taken place on this planet, because creativity is not separate from the people who are creating. To understand this is to understand that the spread of creativity is in accordance to what direction a given group took—or what part of the planet a given group settled in. My point is that however we choose to look at a given creative thrust, it is important to recognize that every culture group has basically had to deal with the same universal essence factors as a means to establish culture—or identity. The universality of creativity has to do with what essence factors really are, as much as how it is utilized—which is to say, however the surface difference of a given creative strain is perceived, it is important that we recognize its position with regards to the composite thrust of all creativity. Since I have not yet developed to where I can talk of the universe as a realness, I am only left with speculation as to what a given projection means with regards to its spiritual and vibrational actualness, and because of my ignorance about these matters, it is necessary to not attempt this route of investigation (i.e., claiming that a given projection means this or that)—instead, the thrust of my writings is conceived to lay a basis for real observation. Nevertheless, the spread of humanity is directly related to the nature of how creativity has formed, and any attempt to experience a cross-section of earth creativity would reveal what that spread has meant in vibrationaltory and cosmic terms. This is true because creativity is about something—as opposed to merely being something to do. To experience what this "something" is is to gain insight about the realness of existence on this planet, and the weight of this information can hopefully reshape how one perceives of events on both the vibrational and physical universe levels. From the dynamic sound textures of Tibetan music to the uniqueness of Swiss Alpine music, what we have is the actualness of the collective experience of earth life. Only an idiot would proclaim cultural superiority when confronted with the real facts of world creativity—for the most basic fact that seems to be true about this juncture in space is that no one has a monopoly on creativity, nor is this consideration (creativity) even a consideration.

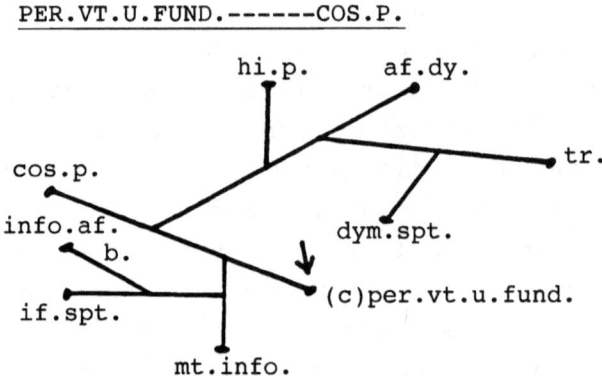

In actual terms, creativity is only one aspect of a much greater consideration—having to do with the actualness of life itself—and any attempt to deal with the multi-dimensional implications of this subject would necessitate that some attempt is made to deal with the essence of what this viewpoint means. This would also apply to the underlying philosophical and vibrational realness of creativity as well—which is to say, to investigate the essence-factor lining of creativity is to be involved with many other related considerations. This is so because creativity is not separate from the underlying factors which dictate how we move in vibrational and cosmic terms in our actual lives. Nor does the reality of creativity to its essence factors depend on how we choose to interpret it. My point is that what we call creativity is actually the thrust phenomenon that has to do with "doing" as a means to celebrate and "affirm" the vibrational forces that dictate "living"—or the "actual" vibrational forces that sustain this experience. When a given person participates in the creative process, what is really happening is "cosmic"—or when a given individual participates in the creative process, the end result of what this participation means has to do with "cosmic matters." The actualness of creativity can be viewed as a vibrational projection which—in its utilization—puts the participant in affinity with particular cosmic realities and cosmic truths—yet I do not mean this in a light way, or as a joke. The fact is, a given participant in creativity does not participate because of "nothing," and the actualness of creativity does not exist as simply a toy—these considerations mean something. Nor am I saying that the surface dimension of a given creative projection in itself is not "enough"—for obviously the person who participates in music does so because he or she has some affinity to music, which is to say "the individual likes music" (I am not disagreeing with that "like"). My point is that the music, in this case, represents, in cosmic terms, the projection or affinity object that that given individual was able to utilize, and what is actually happening in the creative process "is not about music." In other words, music is not about "music," and creativity is not about "being creative" because a given activity in itself is interesting or time-consuming, but rather music, sculpture, dance, painting are connected to "cosmic zones" and have to do with "cosmic matters." To understand this is to deal with the actualness of what creativity is all about—or at least to understand this viewpoint is to understand how I perceive of creativity (and as such to be in a better position to follow this book). It is for this reason that I have formulated this section of the book, because at the heart of my viewpoint is the belief that the reality of creativity is related to the vibrationaltory particulars of a given projection—which is to say, creativity corresponds to the cosmic secrets of what a given projection potentially is about—in its highest state (with regards to both the consideration of culture and the actualness of spiritualism). The seriousness of this belief is related to every observation I have and will make in this book, and the significance of what this relationship really means—with regards to what the aesthetic and cosmic ramifications of this viewpoint hold for creativity and life—can give insight about the composite essence realness of world creativity.

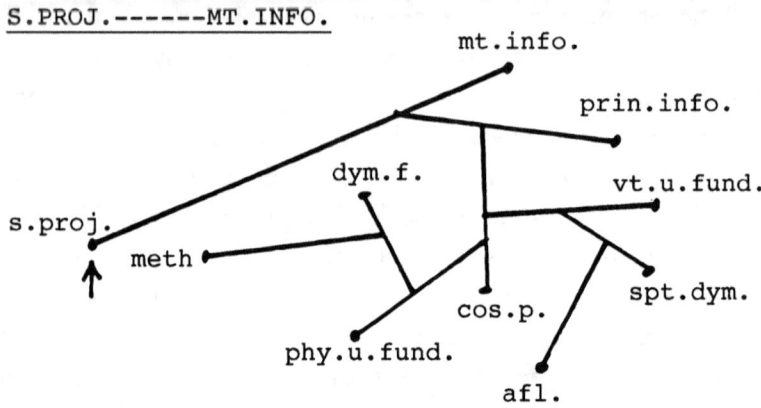

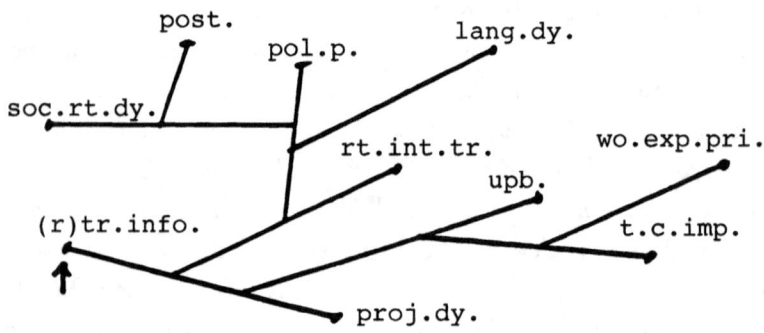

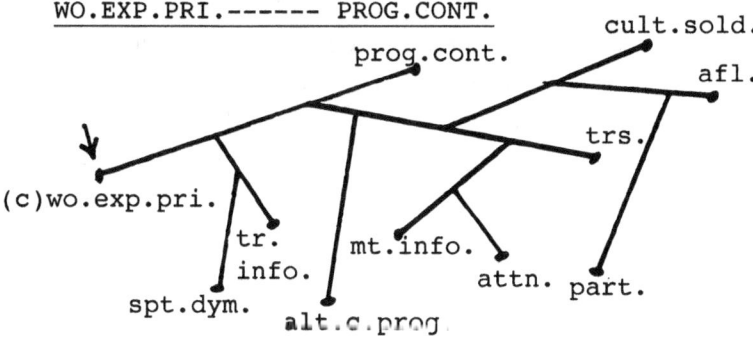

If the basic vibrational breakdown of cosmic forces, as manifested through people, can be viewed in the context of progressional continuity, and if on the most basic level this breakdown has traditionally found itself focusing on the concept of race as a means to establish certain definitions—whether true or not (with regards to what is happening on the physical universe level)—then quite possibly this point of inquiry would also be the most appropriate junction to begin an examination as to the actualness of creativity. For the most apparent factor that distinguishes how we have come to view ourselves has to do with the consideration of race in this time period, and there are many reasons for this. Because the concept of race is directly related to the concept of "vibrational thrust alignment" and also the actualness of "affinity alignment." Moreover, any attempt to deal with the concept of race would also accent what this concept means on a practical and cosmic level. Because to understand the actualness of "race" is to understand that this consideration is directly related to what factors solidified a principle state's meta-reality. It is important that we understand what the uniqueness of a given so-called race's vibrational alignment means with regards to both thrust alignment and world consciousness. This is what concerns us. In other words, what is the significance, if any, of the concept of race to the planet in projectional terms and/or physical universe terms, and also what does this significance mean with regards to the actualness of world creativity? For the concept of race is directly related to the solidification of given thrust projections in accordance to what those projections reveal about their "actual" state (with regards to its position on a given area of the planet). In other words, the actualness of race is directly related to the spread of people on the physical universe level, as well as the addition of given cosmic multi-ingredients (or vibrational alignments), and also this concept has to do with the nature of what spot on the planet a given people inhabited. All of these factors are involved in the establishment of a given thrust projection—or culture—and all of these factors are also involved in the gradual nature of the "particulars" that would affirm what that culture group "is" in postulation terms. Yet it is important to understand that I have not implied that every consideration related to how given cultures solidify must be viewed in its separate state, nor do I mean to limit the concept of "race" to one dimension, because obviously there is much more here. My reason for pursuing this particular course of thought has to do with establishing some basis for inquiry. It is clear that even the forming of a given culture cannot be solely perceived in its separateness, because there are universal considerations that affect every culture group, regardless of strain, and this must be respected and dealt with. To view the actualness of a given culture group is to be confronted with the dynamics related to what the separateness of that group means in cosmic terms, and to view the actualness of a given culture is to also see how the universality of that given group is manifested. But this phenomenon is only one aspect of what "race" is, and a limited aspect of that. For the actualness of this subject really goes much deeper than how the characteristics of a given thrust are manifested. The significance of creativity encompasses this consideration of isolated race and more—but we have only touched the surface of this subject.

I have not reduced the consideration of race to a one-dimensional concept, because this consideration is much too significant to obscure—especially in this time period. Certainly there is much more to be said about this subject on all levels—and it is important to emphasize this point (or risk giving the wrong impression). This is a subject that must be dealt with on some level if we are to establish some basis for perceiving world initiations—on whatever level—and this is a subject that is also directly related to the spread of creativity (involving how certain creative strains have arrived at their present reality juncture). Quite possibly, further definition of the concept of race is necessary if this subject is to be properly established. For it must be understood that I have not introduced the concept of race in this section as a means to establish whether or not a given group is superior or inferior to another—and indeed I haven't done so because I am not interested in this type of investigation. In cosmic terms, the actualness of race has nothing to do with any group being of more importance than any other group, and this is the position I have taken—that being: I have introduced the consideration of race as a factor to establish a basis for perceiving the actualness of affinity and projectional alignments with regards to what these concepts mean for investigation—nothing more. It is my belief that every sector (and hence race) of the planet can help reveal to us what the composite actualness of earth creativity really is—and could be; which is to say all of us are necessary (and important, if we choose to use these words). For it must be understood that the consideration of race is directly related to how the dynamics of earth creativity are manifested—and this is true regardless of region. Every racial group has thus participated in the solidification of the composite identity and alignment of earth creativity—and while this is hardly a profound statement, many of us have come to not see this most basic point.

When I wrote it would be wrong to apply a one-dimensional definition to the consideration of race, it was not because this consideration can't be understood on some level, but rather the actualness of this concept is connected to many other factors of equal importance. For while I have conceded that consideration of race is the most basic factor by which human beings in general have come to view—with regards to separation—themselves, it must be understood that the basis underlying "race" really is cosmic. For the factors which dictate the cross-spectrum of forces related to what race really is permeate the dynamic spectrum of existence on every level of observation (or at least this seems to be so). Because to understand that race is the personification of the solidification of a given vibrational projection is to understand that this consideration is also linked to the actualness underlying how principle cosmic forms are manifested. In other words, the actualness of race can be perceived as one junction which reflects how given forces are manifested with regards to the physical universe particulars of that given reality's particulars—thus the concept of race would also have to do with the dynamics of a particular alignment, and how that alignment flows with regards to its particular physical universe developments (and forces)—and influences. But there is more here. Because even before we deal with the actualness of race as a factor related to how the particulars of a given physical universe space are "ised"—as a vibrational thrust projection—we must also look at what this consideration (race) means before its application (on the physical universe level). My point is this: the actualness of race has to do with the "isness" of particular cosmic forces—which is to say, even before one deals with the influence of particulars on a given racial group it is important to recognize that the concept of race starts before its physical universe application. On the most basic level, I am saying that the actualness of race in itself has to do with how a given force is actualized, and to understand this is to understand why I have had to qualify this consideration on so many different levels. Because I have also stated that there are other factors related to the actualness of this concept which are manifested in other ways—and those factors can also give us some insight into the nature of how the cosmic arena seems to be. The factors I am referring to have to do with how given forces are manifested in zones that do not—on the surface—correspond to how we have come to view primary zones (primary with regard to how we have come to view the concept of separateness in one-dimensional terms). The fact is, a given force is manifested (through people) in a number of ways, and this phenomenon is so complex that it is impossible to put one definition on "what a given group is supposed to be about." For this reason the historical progressions of earth culture are constantly dealing with cross-sectional activity—and while many of us see this phenomenon as something against the natural order of how given culture groups—and projections—are perceived, in fact it is not. The best example of what I mean by this can be found in this period: for example, many of us have come to think of what we call the blues as a projection having to do with the thrust-affinity alignment of black people, and of course this interpretation is true, but only partly true. For the actualization of blues really has to do with the forces the form affirms—thus the entry of a musician like Mose Allison screws everybody up: "is he fake?" (obviously not); "does he have the right to sing the blues?" (does who have the right!)—and it goes on. My point is that the forces which seem to be dealing with this planet cannot be put in a mono-dimensional harness and defined on narrow lines; not only because narrow definitions don't seem to correspond with what is really happening on the planet, but also because this type of bias does not help us deal with real understanding. I have not meant to imply that the vibrational affinity alignment of a given race means nothing (not to mention I have not meant to imply that every racial strain has the same exact vibrational make-up either), but rather, I have meant to imply that none of these considerations can be locked tight and separated from the world group. Principle vibrational alignment would have to do with many other factors as well (and none of these factors are on a level I can deal with) because this subject is related to the actualness of life on this planet. One factor is clear however: the actualness of considerations like cross-sectional flows (transfer shifts) seem to function with regards to both the composite dynamics of essence as well as an agent to reinforce the world implications of given thrust projections. Moreover, the actualization of a given transfer shift comments on the space continuum we are moving through on earth (i.e., how something is actualized and integrated into the composite lining of the planet).

ACT.TR.------COSP.

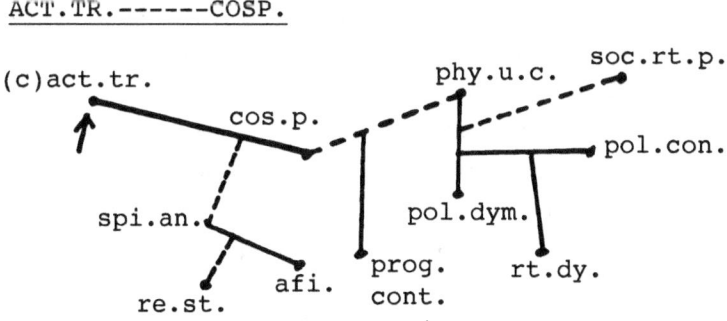

UPB(II)–14

```
RC.------VT.DY.
                             af.dy.      mt.info.
             vt.dy. post.
                                      t.c.imp.
  (c)rc.
    ↑                       phy.u.c.
         pol.
         dy.    mt.dev.f.
```

To understand that given thrust projections are related to higher forces is to begin to deal with the mystical actualness of creativity. For while I do not mean to take away from the notion that creativity is fun or entertaining—which it is or can be—the realness of a given projection sheds light on the actualness of creativity—as serious activity related to cosmic factors. To view the realness of this relationship is to begin to see the position creativity has on the planet—with regards to both the individual as well as society. For in its most functional state, creativity moves to help vibrationally solidify the composite reality concerning how a given culture group sees itself—which is to say, creativity functions as a unification and affinity factor, but there is more here. For to understand the actualness of creativity is to see that this consideration is really a cosmic consideration; that is—all creativity is spiritual on some level. Moreso the dynamic of creativity is not restricted to any one zone but instead permeates the total lining of the culture—which is to say creativity is also related to functionalism (i.e., making things happen on the physical universe level). To understand the practical application of what this means is to begin to view the significance of form—as a factor designed with regard to transmitting certain types of forces. In other words, the most basic factor that has determined how the spectrum of world creativity has progressed has had to do with the dynamic application underlying how form is utilized—and what a given thrust was conceived to mean in its original state. The functional arena of a given thrust must be viewed as related to this consideration as well—and this can become even more complex if the composite spectrum of dynamic functionalism is also included. For rhythm is not just rhythm, nor is harmony only a coloring factor—all of these considerations are connected to factors that are cosmic. Nor am I suggesting that any given culture is better than any other culture (nor does any given group represent something higher than another given group—how many times am I going to keep writing this?). My point is that the actualness of any given thrust is related to how its projections are realized, and the science that determined how the functional arena of that form is to proceed has to do with what forces are controlling that science. In that light, creativity can be viewed as a manifestation of a given cosmic, social, and vibrational (cultural) alignment, and the science which determined how a given form is actualized is related to spiritual, mystical, and functional considerations with regards to what I will call higher forces. Thus the effects of a given form can be viewed through what aspect of the force it affirms—or the actualness of a given form is related to how that form manifests its thrust projection with regards to its essence factor (i.e., primary force), or the realness of a given form is related to how that form utilizes some aspect of its primary force. In other words, the consideration of form means something on a number of levels, and is not merely a vacuum consideration—not having anything to do with anything.

To deal with the actualness of form is to be confronted with the mystical and cosmic implications of creativity. For the significance of a given form (i.e., language, type of structure) derives its meaning from spiritual considerations—even if those considerations are not understood (as in the case of creativity in this period). The nature underlying how a given form is viewed is thus related to the dynamic of each particular culture group—yet I believe every cultural and racial group utilizes the same principle forces, which is to say that basically there is no real difference between people on this planet. I say this because however we choose to perceive the surface dynamics of creativity, in actual fact, every aspect of a given projection can be traced back to its primary language (or form) projection: which is to say, the composite thrust of earth creativity is built from the same basic awareness. To understand this viewpoint is to see the similarities that connect world creativity, and to understand this viewpoint is to also view the similarities related to process as it applies to rhythm, harmony, etc., and I do not mean to imply that all creativity looks and sounds the same, because obviously it doesn't, nor have I meant to imply that the spirit factor of the world group is the same—because this is not true either—but I have meant to imply that there are basic fundamental factors related to the science of all creativity, and I have also meant to imply that while the utilization of a given functional consideration in a given culture group is of course different from that of another group, in actual fact the essence basis of that consideration is universal. In other words, the foundation related to how a given thrust is actualized is universal—and this is important. For any attempt to deal with the seriousness of form would also imply that the consideration of transfer shift is also dealt with. The fact is, the progressional development of the function arena of creativity has not been an isolated development—having only to do with how a given race or culture progressed in its separate state. But rather the historical progressions of creativity are permeated by the occurrence of transfer shifts and cross-sectional activity. Throughout the whole of recorded history it is possible to look at given culture groups being affected by other culture groups—that is, it is possible to see how different aspects of culture are adopted by other cultures. Moreover, the nature underlying how given transfer shifts take place is as varied as anything else on this planet. For the progressional transfer of process has to do with one group being influenced by another group, or one group conquering another group, or one group finding the historical and/or documentation records of another group—intermarriage, changing cultures, etc., etc.—which is to say I am not writing about a narrow consideration but rather a universal feature related to the nature of composite change on the physical universe level. To understand the dynamics of transfer shifts is to see the nature of how given forms are related, and to understand this relationship is to also deal with my original point—that being, the dynamics of a given form are related to the factors which helped solidify the meta-reality of its culture group, but the essence implications of that form derive their ultimate meaning from what that form really is in universal terms. Thus as a dynamic projection, a given form celebrates its natural affinity alignment, and as a cosmic affirmation of universal forces, that same form also gives insight into the actualness of its primary force.

When I stated that the thrust implications of a given form must be viewed with regards to its mystical and vibrational connotations as well as its dynamic consequences, I was referring to the cosmic realness of this phenomenon. For if the actualness of form can be viewed as a projectional vibrational thrust connected with the vibrationaltory lining of a given culture as well as an aspect of some basic cosmic force, then what this means is that the realness of form is related to a primary essence factor with regards to the force it affirms. Which is to say, the significance of what we call form would have to do with what it reveals about the mystical connotations of the force it affirms. Thus, the consideration of form must also be viewed as a spiritual factor—yet I do not mean this in one-dimensional terms. Because if form does have a relationship to the consideration of force, then we must understand that this relationship also implies that form is related to every aspect underlying its force's manifestation on the physical universe level. Which is to say, the actualness of a given force can be viewed in both what we would call positive and negative terms (although in actual fact, positive and negative really have nothing to do with what is really happening on this planet). In other words, a given force might be manifested by its ability to assist in helping life-giving considerations happen, while another aspect of that same force might manifest itself in ways that we would call not life-giving (i.e., tragedy or difficult periods—violence). Thus a given form can be perceived by its ability to assist in some form of functionalism—though the end result of that functionalism might not necessarily benefit humanity if wrongly utilized or misunderstood (yet I do not mean to paint such an intense backdrop on this subject since the consequences of a given form might not always have such a profound impact or a repercussion—moreover, this consideration should not be limited to only one or two types, because there are incredible amounts of forms—and forces as well—or so it seems). Moreover, my point—and reason for bringing this subject up—is to state that creativity is related to functionalism, both with regards to the meta-reality of a given culture group and the actualness of particulars on the physical universe level. It is also my belief that the dynamic consequences of form are not dependent on whether or not the person utilizing that form is necessarily aware of its vibrational implications. For the realness of a given projection is established in its early alignment, as opposed to the notion that each period represents something totally unique in itself. To understand what this means is to deal with the composite thrust of creativity, as well as the vibrational realness underlying what this subject really is. Because if the consideration of dynamic functionalism is established in the actualness of postulation dynamics—in its forming state (or rather with the forming state of "this planet's existence"), and if the actualness of that forming dictated the progressional continuity of particular vibrational tendencies—then what does this mean with regards to the surface changes underlying how particular cultures are "ised"? In other words, if a given thrust projection cannot be viewed as "new," what does this mean with regards to progressional continuity—and what does this mean with regards to the consideration of process in creativity (and is there a distinction between how process should be viewed in creativity and in technological development)?

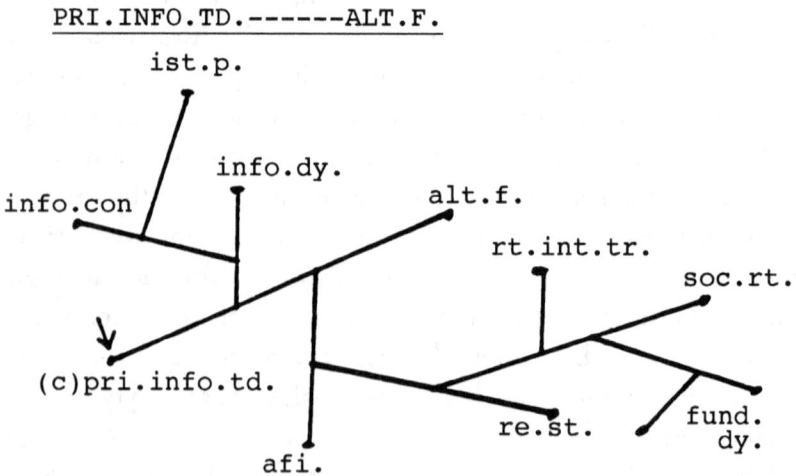

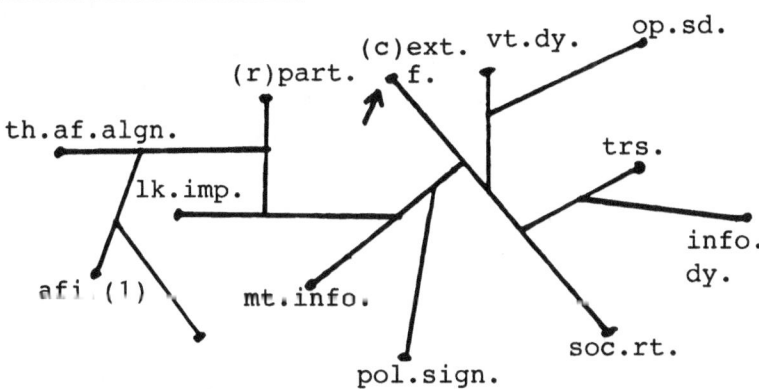

Any attempt to deal with the vibrational actualness of process in creative music would necessitate that some effort is made to deal with the historical progressions surrounding how given aspects (e.g., process) are understood. The seriousness of this consideration can also shed light on the role of process in creativity, for it is fashionable in this period to think of the reality of process in national rather than cosmic terms. Moreover, the historical factors related to how a given form is actualized can also reveal the nature of what its primary force means in its most basic state. My point is this: the political, social, and economic forces which dictate the vibrationaltory lining of western culture in this period would have us believe that the functional arena of western culture—and its subsequent creativity—can be viewed as innovative rather than restructuralist. In other words, the concept of innovation has been embraced by western culture as a means to portray isolated advancement with regards to its progressional continuity as opposed to the collective achievements of world culture. And while the basis of this change is related to the collective controlling and defining forces surrounding western culture—and as such must be dealt with in another section of this book—the essence of what this viewpoint means reflects an attempt to obscure the realness of process as it pertains to the composite solidification of world creativity; this is so because the progressional continuance of creative music has been equally shaped by the world group. It would be impossible to separate every juncture or contribution with regards to process, because all of these considerations were "ised" before our present system of record keeping (or at least before the information and transformation cycle that brought in Egypt as the dominant culture thrust after ... quite possibly Atlantis?) and there is no way to know all of the specifics of a given offering. My reason for stating this viewpoint is only to say that the functional and vibrational actualness of creativity was established much earlier than this particular time cycle—and indeed this phenomenon was not even an intellectual instigation, but rather the result of dealing with "natural" factors—"natural" in the sense of dealing with life and adjusting to what this experience dictates (with regards to functionalism). Thus it is not really a question of who came first as much as viewing how this consideration of process is restructured in accordance to the particulars of a given culture's dynamics. The realness of what this viewpoint means must be taken into account if we are to deal with the present reality of western information dynamics, because many of us have come to believe that the realignment of process alone is sufficient to validate the notion of innovation, and many of us have also come to believe that through the extremities of analysis it is possible to instigate new music. The historical continuum of creativity suggests otherwise.

To view the progressional continuum of world creativity is to be made aware of the spectrum underlying how given creative thrusts are manifested—that is, the composite thrust of world creativity has utilized every conceivable structural arena and premise. Moreover, the composite thrust of world creativity has also—through doing—revealed the thrust implication underlying how given aspects are to be properly utilized (with regards to what a given aspect means to its essence foundation). The consideration of rhythm is only one example of what I am referring to (that being, the dynamic implications underlying how "functional particulars" were and are to be utilized—and for what occasion)—nor is the actualization of ritual music or "storytelling" unique (or music as a healing consideration—which is to say, the science related to what aspect of creative functionalism is activated in this context)—and this is only the beginning. My point is that the meta- and functional reality of creativity—as manifested in music or any of the related continuances—was established and utilized long before what is now generally recognized, and my point is also that the actualness of what this solidification means challenges our present notion of innovation as a phenomenon that did not exist before it was brought into being. Present-day historical documentation seems to reveal that by the time the transformation projection after Egypt solidified, the basic foundations—whether vibrational or functional (in terms of both principle information and its subsequent manifestations)— that were to solidify the present meta-reality of this time continuum were actualized, two thousand, five hundred years before we even arrived at this junction (or time period). Either that is true or it means that even now these factors aren't actualized (or it means that the factors not actualized are not about being actualized)—in other words, the concept of innovation being perpetuated by the west in this time zone is misleading, to say the least. This is so because the consideration that really governs the realignment of process is not about innovation (as this concept is now viewed).

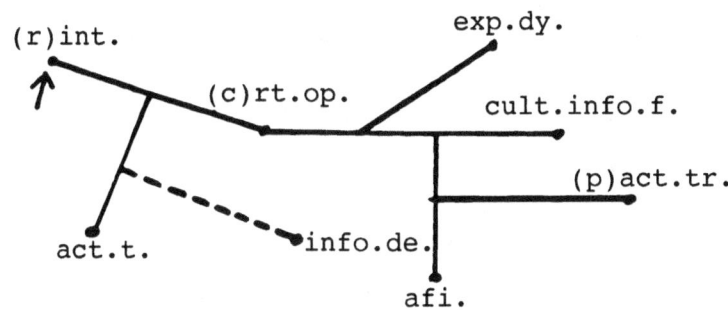

The universal actualness of creativity is a factor that must be dealt with if we are to truly understand this consideration. Any serious student of creativity—no matter what area—would do well to research the composite thrust of this subject as a means to gain real insight about "being"—or life postulation. It is important to not simply become the effects of one viewpoint on this consideration, because at present our educational system is not designed to accurately comment on any other creativity outside of western art music. The basic effect of this situation is that many of us are left with no awareness about the composite thrust of world creativity—and this is unfortunate. We must also avoid the pitfall of present-day interpretation about world creativity and its significance (whatever period) by the established western educational institutions, for many of the accepted interpretations that are taught concerning world creativity have very little to do with what is true about this subject. Yet in the final analysis we have no choice but to utilize whatever resources are available, because if we choose to wait for completely accurate information it might mean waiting forever. Nevertheless, the universality of creativity is a subject that must again be re-established—both for humanity (with regards to life in the present and what can be gained by vibrating to composite creativity from the world group) and also for the establishment of a composite vibrational and spiritual stance to establish transformation. For if our ability to establish positive alternatives (on both a vibrational and physical universe level) is related to what information we have been able to understand about the present as well as the past, then we have no choice but to investigate the seriousness of world creativity. On the first level, this investigation must begin by experiencing the music (if music is one's point of entry). For the realness of a given creative thrust is not about words but rather about the "isness" it conveys when experienced. The profound realness of world creativity must be dealt with sooner or later.

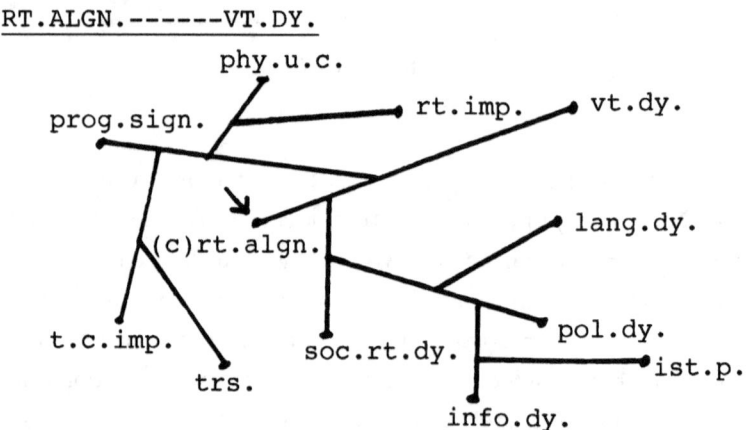

The functional implications of a given creative thrust are also directly related to the meta-reality of creativity. In other words, the science related to what effects a given creative thrust will have—no matter if applied to vibrational or physical universe considerations—is directly related to the essence foundation of its vibrational base. The realness of what this relationship means can be traced to the collective efforts of the world community—that is, the dynamic implications of creativity are related to the composite efforts of world culture investigation—yet I have not meant to give the impression that every culture group has worked on the science of creativity in the same way—or time—because that is not true. My point is that the collective efforts of different culture groups are responsible for establishing the functional science of earth creativity—that is, given groups have contributed different aspects of what this information means, and the composite assimilation of this knowledge is related to the rise and fall of culture groups and also transfer shift progression cycles. In this time period many of us are not aware of the functional implications of creativity, and there are many reasons for this. One—the educational institutions in this time period do not really explore these questions on even a surface level; two—for the most part, western art music has not established its own meta-functional application; three—the separation of western science in this time zone has moved to create a situation where functionalism is perceived in separate terms from creativity (or at least the present vibrationaltory state of western culture has chosen to accent other aspects of its functionalism rather than its relationship to composite information); and four—we are still moving from the viewpoint that creativity is only concerned with "fine arts" (with the most narrow viewpoint of fine art), and as such this subject has only been perceived in aesthetic terms having nothing to do with affecting the physical universe in direct ways. Only in this period are viewpoints being re-examined in the west with regards to these questions, and in the last ten years or so there have been some attempts to deal with creativity as both a functional and dynamic tool. Nevertheless, the seriousness of pedagogical dynamics must be dealt with on some level, for the composite continuum of world creativity leaves no doubt as to the realness of what dynamic functionalism must mean if properly understood.

The thrust-projection dynamics of world creativity seem to indicate that one role of creativity has to do with its ability to function as a vibrational regulator with regards to how a given culture flows (or should, or could flow). In other words, one function of creativity in world culture terms is to help maintain order with regard to the emotional and vibrational state of the people in the culture, and the significance of this use of postulation sheds light on the dynamic role of extended functionalism. For if culture is the solidification of particular vibrational alignments, then quite possibly the realness of a culture group is based on its ability to control alien forces—or to at least utilize those forces in a way that will not threaten what that basic culture's alignment means. To understand this use of functionalism is to deal with the potentiality of sound as a consideration related to many factors—some of which are in accordance to the vibrationaltory lining of a given culture and some of which are not (or at least this is true on the surface, for even the forces not conducive to culture can be realigned and utilized so that some aspect of their projection can be of some positive use)—and to deal with what this viewpoint means is to focus on the seriousness of sound (as an aesthetic vehicle for creativity as well as a functional tool for making things happen on the physical universe level). There are many ways this subject can be dealt with, for the dynamic of creative functionalism is related to the whole of a given culture—applying to more areas than what is generally acknowledged. As we move into the next cycle, the realness of this question will assume even more importance, for the composite thrust of world creativity seems to suggest that the functional implications of creativity are as significant as its aesthetic implications—which is to say, the non-utilization of composite creativity might be directly related to many of the factors that are wrong with western culture in this cycle.

To deal with the functional implications of creativity as "ised" through the progressional continuance of world culture is to focus on the nature of elements a given creative thrust utilizes. In other words, every creative thrust is based on ingredients that serve both aesthetic and functional purposes. In the case of painting we are dealing with color and shape as factors which carry multi-dimensional overtones—that is, the net potential of what these considerations really mean transcends their use in any particular setting—and in the case of music we are dealing with sound and rhythm as factors that carry multi-dimensional overtones. My point is that the net effect of the elements comprising a given creative thrust can be observed by looking at the multi-complexual realness of those elements—with regards to its aesthetic and practical physical universe effect. Thus if we would focus on the actualness of sound—as a major element in creative music, we would have no choice but to deal with what this consideration means in its totalness. For when I say that the consideration of sound has multi-dimensional overtones, I am saying that the effects of that given sound can be viewed with respect to its aesthetic use, as well as its scientific application. For example, the volume of a given sound can be viewed in terms of what effect its dynamic curve would have on the physical universe level. In short, if a given sound is experienced at too high a volume then the person experiencing that sound might also experience physical effects—and the higher the volume, the more acute the physical ramification. Thus the volume of a given sound can be sectioned off with regards for what this effect might mean (for it is understood that when I say the higher the volume, the more acute the effects, I am also implying that the sound can go as high as necessary to get whatever effect is desired). Nor is this most basic example limited to only one context, for the consideration of volume alone, if utilized in a given way, can also be instrumental in affecting the environment of a given space. My point is that the dynamic application of even a consideration like volume extends to its ability to physically affect an individual as well as—in its most increased application—destroy a building (or rupture a given physical universe space)—and this example is only the beginning of my point. For the science that governs what has been established throughout the composite thrust of world creativity has barely been touched upon. When I wrote that the dynamic potential of a given element has multi-dimensional overtones (that is, related to what that given creative strain is about) I was referring to matters much more significant than the science surrounding "volume" (although I do not mean to imply that this one consideration is not important).

UPB(II)–26

To understand the dynamic actualness underlying the properties of a given creative strain is to begin to see the science of that strain. In other words, the science of a given creative thrust corresponds to the aesthetic and functional particulars related to how that thrust is perceived. Thus on a vibrational level, creativity through sound (music) is conceived to be instrumental in establishing the meta-reality dictates underlying what a given culture is vibrationally supposed to be "about," and at the same time the science related to that establishment permeates the functional affinity solidification of its technology. In actual terms, creative music, through its use of sound (and the science related to what this use is to mean), functions as a factor to assist a given culture to vibrate in accordance to what that culture could be in its most advanced (and positive) state. And while the tools of that science can be reduced to the reality dynamics which govern the consideration of sound and rhythm, the actualization of what this understanding means pertains to the meta-reality implications underlying what sound and rhythm really are with regards to its multi-dimensional implications. For the consideration of sound in this context can be viewed as a spiritual consideration that relates to what the affinity thrust of a given cosmic zone implies (or its reason to be)—which is to say, one aspect of sound has to do with its ability to be a functional spiritual factor. Meanwhile all of this activity represents only half of what a given creative thrust really means, for as a given thrust participates in establishing the vibrational and spiritual alignment of its culture group, at the same time the science related to how this alignment was actualized is also related to the basic physical universe scheme of its essence factor. In other words, a given cultural utilization of creativity would reveal (if that culture has functioned from what has been established through the progressional continuance of world creativity—with regards to "gathered" information) the use of sound as a spiritual alignment factor—sound as a spiritual cognizant factor—sound as a ritual cosmic factor—sound as a cultural solidifying factor—and at the same time the actualness of that alignment would also directly relate to sound as a factor to make objects move through space (or at least sound as a factor that challenges basic laws of motion vs. gravity)—and sound as a tool to help sustain mental health—sound as a healing tool—sound as a cutting force—sound as a warning signal—and sound as communication. In other words, the composite actualness of a given creative thrust—as viewed from what has been learned through the collective effort of world creativity—encompasses much more than one aspect of its utilization. All of these factors are the result of the basic affinity platform of a culture—with regards to how given particulars are viewed from its essence foundation—and as such, this understanding of creative functionalism can be viewed as the dynamic inherent implication of form (or the dynamic implication of composite methodology—or, in my terminology, the reality of thrust continuance).

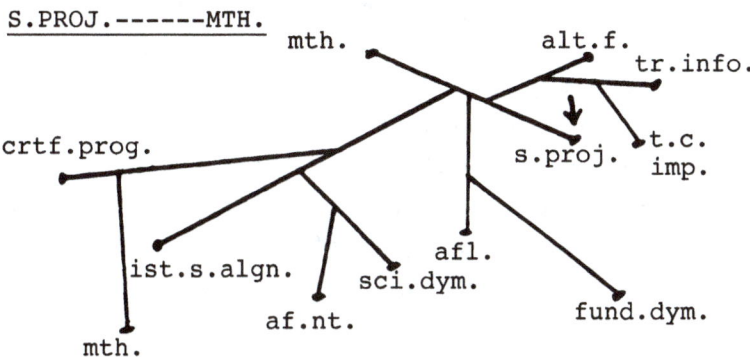

The seriousness of the multi-dynamic realness of creativity cannot be ignored, especially if we desire some real understanding of what this phenomenon (i.e., projectional thrust—music or painting, etc.) really means with regards to transformation. For if the most basic task ahead of us has to do with preparation because of the composite effects of what this period has brought forth, it would be to our advantage if this most basic area of information was again re-examined. For the multi-dynamic realness of creativity is perceived—in world culture terms—as not separate from its aesthetic center, or at least the composite thrust of a given projection, in this context, is not separated from the totality of its essence factor. Moreover, the importance of this viewpoint can be viewed with respect to the present state of creativity in this period (or at least present state of western creativity). For the fact that western culture has lost the insight necessary for dealing with this subject can be seen in the present shape of our culture in this period. In other words, the refusal to deal with composite creativity has helped shape the present reality of western culture in this cycle (or at least, the inability of the collective forces of western culture to establish a dynamic spiritual and/or center factor is directly related to the present route western culture has taken).

Without doubt one of the most important things we can learn from the composite continuum of world creativity is the realness of creativity as a humanistic and unification consideration. For if every aspect of creativity can be viewed with regards to its ability to affect the vibrational lining of a given culture group then it would be to our advantage to view the seriousness of what this ability means in actual terms. Because any attempt to deal with creativity would also accent what a given thrust means with respect to the reality of its responsibility as well—responsibility in the sense that if a given projection does have multi-dimensional implications then it must be utilized correctly (for the wrong usage of a given projectional thrust could have serious consequences for everyone involved). My point is that any attempt to deal with the composite thrust of creativity—as it is "ised" by the world group—would imply understanding the seriousness of what that given projection "is"—which is to say, this awareness must also encompass what that given projection "is not." Thus one of the most basic prerequisites to deal with the meta-reality secrets of a given creative thrust is the awareness of the responsibility underlying how different thrusts are to be utilized. I am not saying that every person who participates in a given creative thrust must first study the science of that thrust in some educational institution, because obviously this is not true—because the creativity of a given culture is "ised" to be utilized by the people in that culture; but I am saying that the people who designed and dictated the solidification of given creative thrusts must be looked at as "masters" in that regard, and I am also saying that the position of the "master musician" carries multi-complexual responsibilities. To understand the reality of a master musician would encompass more factors than I would be able to deal with (for I am only a student of creative music in this period myself), but it is possible to comment on what this position must be about in general terms (and in doing so draw on the comments and writings of different master musicians), for this is a subject that sheds light on the essence lining of world creativity. Yet even in this area I am forced to make important value judgments with regards to how the nature of "responsibility" is to be perceived in creativity (for many master musicians do not necessarily agree with each other either—at least on the surface). Ultimately I have based my judgment on what I believe is the right viewpoint—with respect to what I have been able to understand in this period. In the final analysis the thrust of my examination into world creativity is not so much about declaring any specific areas of information to be cosmically true or false, instead I am interested in establishing alternative basis for re-investigation.

My point is this—the composite thrust of world creativity, regardless of time zone, can be viewed with regards to its ability to function in accordance to the ethical implications of its position—which is to say, any real attempt to understand the essence factor of creativity would also encompass understanding the responsibilities related to what this consideration means—in its most highest state. For when I write that the science that surrounds a given projection has to do with the meta- and vibrational secrets related to its force—or the particulars underlying what a given thrust alignment celebrates—I am also implying that there is more than one aspect of that force which can be utilized—yet it is necessary to elaborate on what I mean by aspects in this context because I have not meant to give the wrong impressions about this subject (and I have not meant to imply that some aspect of a given force is not important or worthy of utilization—this is not my position at all). The fact is, to deal with the spectrum of a given force is to be aware of its dynamic application with regards to both its ultimate effect as well as what this effect means with regards to language. For while in the cosmic sense of the word there is no such thing as positive or negative (at least in the present way we perceive of these words), for our purposes (on the physical universe level) these words do have meaning. Which is to say, any attempt to understand the projectional realness underlying how given forces are actualized on the physical universe level would imply that the whole of that force is taken into consideration. My most basic point is that the totalness of a given force would encompass projections whose ultimate effect on the physical universe level could be talked of in terms of it representing "what is most positive" (as far as our language is concerned) all the way to projections having to do with what is "most negative" (or what in our reality seems to be most negative). Thus the implementation of a given projection can be viewed as an important cosmic responsibility that affects the totalness of its composite culture group. In this context, the spirit factor surrounding how projections are "ised" becomes important—that is, the vibrational and cosmic arena of a given culture group is directly related to what forces that culture group draws from—or has drawn from. Furthermore the actuality of a given culture group can also be viewed with regards for both what that group was able to understand from its utilization of a given projection alignment as well as what that alignment was able to understand about that culture (but possibly this is not the best way to write this). My point is: the utilization of a given thrust alignment can be viewed with regards to what the meta-reality potential of what its alignment could mean if realized, or the actualness of a given alignment can also be viewed with regards to its consequences if not utilized correctly. (Not to mention there are other variables related to this subject which must be dealt with as well, for the utilization of a given force can also be viewed with regards to the realness of cosmic change cycles—that is, the realness that no matter how given forces are perceived and utilized, at some point given cycles come to natural conclusions—or surface conclusions—as opposed to actual conclusions which do not seem to have real meaning.) Thus any attempt to deal with the actualness of creativity as it has been collectively defined through the composite continuance of world culture would imply that these questions be dealt with and understood. Because when I write of the responsibility of creativity—as a factor related to the composite thrust of world creativity—I am not writing about a joke.

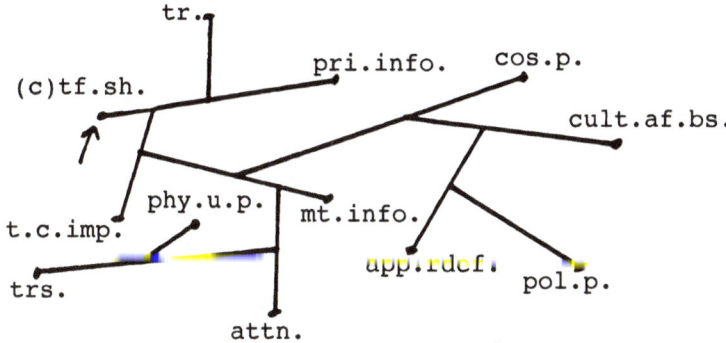

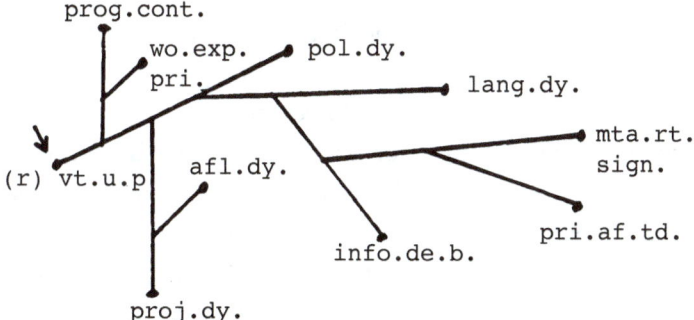

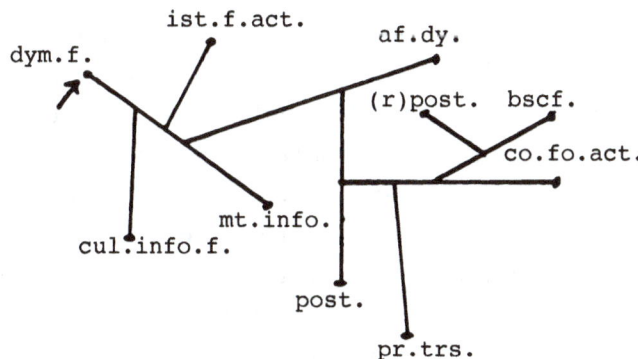

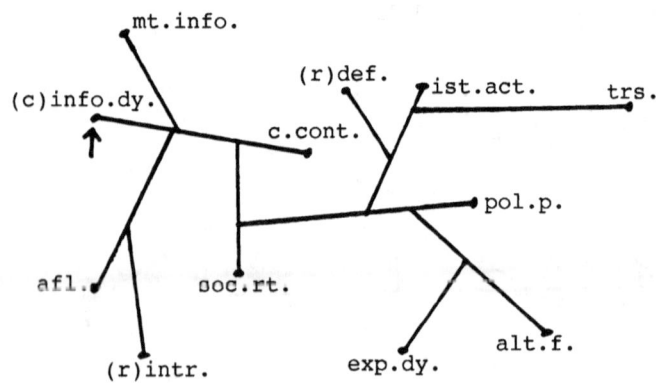

Ultimately a given thrust projection can be viewed with respect to the basic vibrational attitude related to its coming into beingness—which is to say, the actualness of a given projection is directly related to the spirit-factor lining of the culture or person that utilizes it. To understand this is to be aware of the realness that forces simply exist as neither positive nor negative but rather as actual factors, and the realness of what this phenomenon means is directly related to the culture or people in the culture which summons up that given force (or forces). In other words, when I wrote that creativity has to do with the solidification underlying how principle vibrationaltory forces are utilized, I am also saying that this affinity relationship is established by our efforts (or its efforts) and as such constitutes one of the most sacred alliances we can enter into. The seriousness of what this relationship means—with regards to its potential effect on a given culture's direction, or for that matter a given person's direction—implies that some degree of awareness is necessary before entering into given vibrational realities or thrust projections, because if not understood, that culture (and person) could possibly expose themselves to cosmic actualities (and "matters") that could cause serious harm. The realness of this phenomenon implies that some level of awareness must be attained about the use of particular agreements, and also that some level of responsibility must be recognized as well. Yet I have not meant to imply that the actualness of participation in cosmic forces stops at this junction, because it doesn't, nor have I meant to imply that the totalness of a given force projection can be so thoroughly understood before its utilization, that a given culture or person can thus practice its information without any risk whatsoever, because this is not my viewpoint either. Moreover, there is another factor of equal importance related to this subject which must also be dealt with, if this section is to correspond to what I believe is real. That factor is that the realness of cosmic forces—in terms of its actualness and all-knowingness (compared to what we know anyway)—seems to also suggest that however one prepares and researches its meta-implications, that in the final analysis many of these things cannot be known—or at least, known in the way we use this word. Thus in the final analysis our success in dealing with given cosmic forces is directly related to what we have researched about a form as well as the spirit factor related to why we have chosen to deal with that form. In other words, the reality of a given participation with given cosmic forces is related to our primary intentions for pursuing that force—with regards to both our motivation as well as the spirituality related to why we decide to utilize whatever we decide to utilize. In short, the actualness of "intention" is a factor that must be dealt with if we are to deal with the nature of affinity alignment—nor have I introduced this consideration in a one-dimensional context. For the responsibility actualness underlying dealing with cosmic forces can be viewed in a number of different contexts. Certainly one example would be Einstein's discovery of relativity and the progressional effect of what this discovery would mean for western culture. For while many positive things have been made possible from his discovery, the composite thrust of western culture has yet to demonstrate the real responsibility—as manifested in decision-making—that this offering has posed—and thus, if this challenge is not corrected we will have to deal with the effects of what this failure will mean (which is to say we will have to "deal" with the effect of what this failure will mean).

```
(R)SCI.DYM.------SOC.RT.
                soc.rt.
(r)sci.dym
                              c.cont.
        prog.cont.
         trs.                tr.info.

   alt.f.  mt.info.         af.post.
            spt.dym.
```

I have not meant to make light of the necessary research that has taken place with regards to the science surrounding the meta-reality of process in creativity, for obviously this factor must be both respected and utilized if we are to make use of creativity—as a positive vibrational factor. The challenge of creativity in this time zone is directly related to our ability to utilize the science of each given projectional strain as a means to attempt restoring order—and to that objective, the consideration of positive research will be extremely valuable. Yet the multi-complexual actualness of this time period is beyond whether or not it can be understood; for at present so many things are happening on both the vibrational and physical universe levels of this planet that quite possibly present language and concepts are not equipped to deal with (or understand) what this subject really means—which is to say, in the final analysis we still have to deal with "intention"—as a factor that hopefully will affect what we might be able to understand, and also intention as a factor that hopefully will color what we do. For the nature of the transfer shift junction we are now in during this period seems to limit the actualness underlying how investigation (with regards to how concepts and intelligence are perceived in this period) can be utilized. Which is to say, the actualness underlying what is happening in this period is directly related to what I called the multi-complexual responsibilities of the master musician. For when I stated that the vibrational implications of a given progressional thrust transcend one-dimensional concepts and as such must be dealt with in terms of intentions and research, I was attempting to focus on the actuality of the creative process—with regards to its relationship to the consideration of responsibility (what responsibility really means when applied to the actualness of culture and what it really means in itself) and what this consideration also means with regards to why creativity cannot be separated from its humanitarian implications. Thus the reality of responsibility underlying how given thrusts are to be interpreted and utilized must be viewed as a serious subject—which is to say, the sector of the community that participates in shaping cultural direction and decisions has to be viewed as important. For creative music, this area of information involves the master musician for painting, we are speaking of the master painter—science, etc., etc. (and by master I am not commenting on some sacred state that is not attainable by normal people, but rather a state having to do with what a given individual is able to understand about his or her desired area—or zone—after an extended period of research—or at least effort). If we are to understand the realness of creativity, then it is necessary to at least deal with the composite information handed down to us from the progressional continuum of world creativity.

The most basic viewpoint that seems to be constant—with regards to the composite world group—is that the responsibility of creativity seems to necessitate that the creative person pursue his or her activity from a desire to participate in what is most positive for both him- or herself as well as the culture. In other words, the most basic factor that permeates how a given master deals with creativity—especially with regards to establishing different projections related to the dynamics of particular cultural thrusts—has to do with the spirituality underlying how that decision is arrived at. For to deal with the natural limitation of objective and deductive interpretation, and to also deal with the realness of what "intention" really means, is to understand the vibrational need for cosmic assistance to help make the right decision (what to do and how to do it). To understand the spiritual reality of creativity is to be made aware of the difference between intelligence—as a word having to do with the ability to collect information and recall that information when desired—and wisdom—as a word that corresponds to understanding whatever is "actually" being dealt with and thus integrating that knowledge into both its practical and cosmic applications, and thus be able to act on that knowledge and also act on that knowledge in alignment to what is understood to be correct in spiritual terms (for the greatest good). It is for this reason that the composite thrust of creativity is based on its essence alignment with spirituality rather than intellectualism—for the essence implications of spirituality are concerned both with what is true and what is "correct" (as a means to proceed). For the essence lining of creativity must be concerned with what is most positive for culture—and I do not mean intellectual positive but rather cosmic positive—because in actual fact nothing else matters if this criterion is not established—or attempted. Thus the science that determines the solidification of a given thrust projection in world culture terms can be viewed as the resulting methodology related to what has been learned about the essence particulars of that projection's primary force, and also how that force can be utilized for the greatest good—both in vibrational and physical universe terms. The seriousness of what this means can be understood by dealing with the surface negative realness underlying what happens when the wrong force is utilized—for the wrong "actual" situation. The solidification of creativity, as a spiritual tool functioning with regards to culture, also aligns it in the proper context to what religion really is, and as such the meta-reality of creativity is not separate from that of the composite group it affirms. Nevertheless, any real attempt to deal with the nature underlying how creativity is solidified—with regards to the thrust development of world creativity and also with regards to what this question means for viewing the underlying vibrational and philosophical basis concerning how creativity is perceived—would accent the role of spiritualism as an important consideration related to how the establishment of a given creative projection is arrived at. So real is this relationship that one of the main responsibilities of the creative restructuralist (in western culture) is to find and develop new ways for this affinity solidification to occur—as a means to establish a basis for positive transformation. If this challenge is not met then creativity in this time zone will not have met the responsibility of its position.

DYM.SPT.------ AFI.

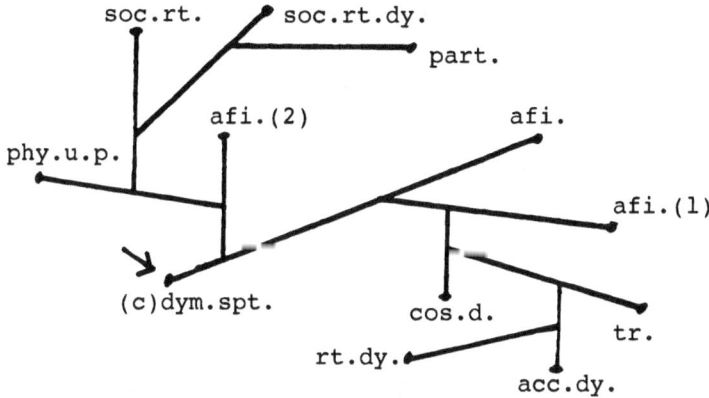

Certainly there are many factors that must be dealt with if we are to understand the actualness of world creativity (this is a subject that would require a separate series of books on its own)—but it is important that we start from somewhere (yet I do not mean to imply that I have started something, because I haven't). The challenge of the next cycle seems to suggest that it would be to our advantage to research the composite progression of world creativity, as a means to prepare for dealing with the coming change cycle. The composite vibrational and philosophic realness of world creativity is directly related to where we have come from and also where we are going. The ability to positively function for transformation is no simple task and I have not tried to put the complexities of present-day culture in one-dimensional terms—because this would help no one. Moreover, I have also tried not to give the impression that my viewpoint is the only correct viewpoint, because obviously there is much more to say about world creativity—what it is and could be. But it is important that we begin to deal with some of these questions if we desire real change. If nothing else, some of these concepts might serve as a springboard for further research, and by doing so also promote the cause for greater understanding. In the final analysis, I believe the inability of the world group to function cohesively for composite transformation has something to do with misunderstanding (at least on some level anyway), and the end result of this state has led to contradiction—with regards to the present state of basic vibrational forces (and also with regards to given countries' ability to deal with other cultures). Any effort to re-establish some level of understanding must be viewed as significant—on some level—because present-day miscommunication is one of the most important problems we are dealing with. Yet I have not meant to sound pessimistic, because I'm not. The realness of the present time we are in seems to suggest that much work will have to be done if we are to correct the many levels of separation that now exist.

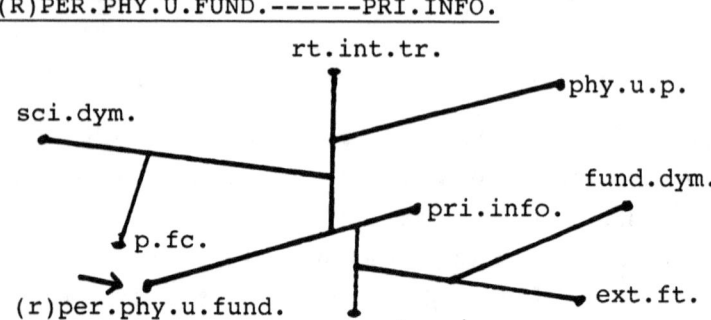

In this period the concept of world unification seems to be far away—certainly not in our lifetime anyway. Yet the cosmic realness of this concept seems to imply its inevitability—that is, at some point people are going to have to see the oneness of what is actually happening in both the physical and vibrational universe and as such come together. Moreover, I do not mean "come together" and all will live happily ever after—or that life stops at this point—but "come together" as a means to finish the cycle we are in now (and thus be in the position to begin new expansions, on hopefully higher levels—if I can use "levels" in this context). To deal with the realness of transformation is to view what the creative process is all about. For the most basic vibration underlying every creative strain (in its ultimate manifestation) has to do with its position in the cosmic hierarchy of "what is"—which is to say, the thrust actualness of a given projection has to do with what that projection really means in its cosmic context (and in all cases that context is positive—or "what is"). In every case, all of these considerations pull towards its world responsibilities—that is, the source actualness of a given projection is manifested in every culture and racial group, and the dynamic implications underlying how that phenomenon is "made real" are related to world creativity. My point is that we are very different from each other but we are not very different from each other—in other words, our surface difference only accents the dynamics of our particular space rather than who we "really" are—and this difference is important. World unification will be achieved when we are able to make that distinction—or at least, world unification will be more possible when we are able to make accurate distinctions. And while it is clear that people have been talking about this subject for thousands of years, in no way does this belatedness obscure the realness of what unification can and will mean. The task for each generation of creative process is to advance how this "coming together" can be achieved—in functional terms, and the realness of what this phenomenon means will also affect the cosmic actualness of our composite situation—on this planet. The underlying vibrational and philosophic realness of world creativity is directly related to how transformation can and will be achieved.

To understand the realness of world creativity is to be confronted with the uniqueness of its position for positive action. Because regardless of culture, everyone participates in creativity—both as creative people and those who are able to experience creativity (and these positions are constantly changing). It does not matter from what part of the planet a given person comes from—everyone can appreciate creativity on some level. Many of us have heard or read the statement that music is an international language, but the actual fact is—it is true (because all creativity is international). The realness of what this means is helping to reshape the planet, and the potential of what this means promises to bring us closer together. For at the heart of every creative thrust is the universality of what that thrust really means. The responsibility of creativity is directly related to its potential for building vibrational bridges across cultural and ethnic groups to establish a unified aesthetic and spiritual base (yet again, I do not mean this as an end junction, but rather as a basis for beginning anew—on a higher level). All of the activity that we have come to label cross-sectional (or fusion) can be looked at as one route leading to transformation—moreover, we must not fool ourselves into believing that cross-sectional activity is manifested only in certain areas (i.e., jazz rock, fusion music, or Indian and jazz fusion), because this is not the case at all. The realness of cross-sectional activity permeates the total spectrum of all earth creativity, involving every kind of music or dance, etc., and the effects of this activity are transforming not just western culture—but rather every culture. In just the time zone of the sixties it is possible to view the transfer shift implications of cross-sectional creativity as the most profound factor reshaping western creativity in that decade. The emergence of groups like the Beatles represented an actualization of cross-transfer activity (from black music to a fusion of black and English music), while on the other end a musician like John Coltrane can be viewed with respect to his utilization of Indian and African forms. The effects of these two examples alone have been enormous, yet only the beginning of what I am trying to communicate about cross-sectional creativity—and its implications. For it must be understood that not only are the surface aspects of these forms affecting the composite lining of earth culture, but also the meta-reality implications of these forms (this has been the basis of what I have been trying to communicate throughout the whole of this section). Thus to experience western art music—to really experience western art music—is to become closer to that reality; and by the same token we would be quite naive to pretend that the spread of black music—and its resultant effects—throughout the composite spectrum of American culture carried no multi-complexual implications as well. For the fact is, creativity does affect us—much more than we generally acknowledge—and this is positive (or not positive). The actualness of cross-sectional creativity must be considered as a major factor related to the spread of world creativity and the strongest signal yet that people will never accept limitations on what is supposedly relevant to their lives—with regards to creativity. Because in actual fact, all creativity is relevant to our lives—on a spectrum of levels—and none of us are isolated from what this relevance means. Moreover, the move towards cross-sectional creativity does not seem to be diminishing, but rather the last twenty years has seen this phenomenon affect more and more avenues of creativity.

It is important to understand that no one factor has dictated the situation of creativity in this time zone, but rather the realness of this subject is the result of many different factors. Without doubt the seriousness of technology has to be considered one of the primary factors related to how the spread of creativity has materialized in this time junction. For when I write that the sophistication of high-speed travel and rapid communication has affected the composite reality of creativity, it is important to understand what this phenomenon means in actual terms. Because if only the consideration of records is dealt with, we can see the dynamic role technology has played in the last thirty years. It is now possible to experience any kind of music in this period, from classical music in the western art music tradition to sacred African music, by simply putting on a record. The realness of this invention alone cannot be measured, for in one scoop the development of the recording industry has totally wiped out the consideration of time and space. It is now possible to experience music that we could never have heard unless we were in that particular country, at that particular time—and while this one invention is now taken for granted (like it was always here), quite possibly its existence might be the most significant development in this time zone. For to deal with the actualness of the recording industry is to be aware that we can now play any kind of music, in any kind of sequence. It is not unusual for people to play rock music and go on to jazz, on to Japanese music, etc., in one given listening setting (and who among us can say that the person experiencing all of this music is not in some way affected by the multi-spectral realness of that experience). Add to that experience the cross-sectional activity of a given so-called fusion music and it might be possible to really understand the position we are now in with regards to creativity. There can be no doubt that among the factors influencing the directions we as a collective people are taking is the composite thrust of world creativity—however manifested.

To view the position of western culture in this period is to also be aware of its potential to elevate the state of human existence (from a positive perspective)—with regard to both its own citizens and the world's community. The present actualness of the planet only accents the position western culture has in this cycle (and this is true both for its economic and functional positions)—and it would be a great tragedy if the vibrational implications of this position were not dealt with. My point is that the underlying vibrational and philosophic actualness of creativity could serve as a factor that helps us see our total relationship to the composite physical universe situation of the planet. For if the progressions of the last cycle have tended to over-emphasize the concept of nationalism—as this concept relates to what is most unique about "who we think we are"—then quite possibly we have come to the next junction of what this phenomenon implies. My point is that the cross-sectional activity happening in this time zone is too substantial to be viewed as only representing the normal amount of activity from this juncture, but rather this phenomenon seems to hint at the nature of the next transformation. My point also is that because of its present social and political position, western culture has been able to benefit and experience the full spectrum of cross-sectional creativity—and this position should not be taken lightly. For if the spread of cross-sectional activity carries vibrational and affinity-alignment implications (transfer shift) then we must understand that this phenomenon is not separate from its dynamic responsibility implications as well.

My point is that technology has helped to create the possibility for inter-vibrational transfer on a global level—and this is the first prerequisite for establishing the realness of world culture. For the major thrust of creativity in this cycle seems to incorporate more and more of world creative initiations (and while this assimilation on the surface has to do with the spectacle-diversion cycle surrounding how western culture works, in the final analysis the basic effect of the music is felt anyway). In other words, even the adaptation of Indian music by the Beatles on their *Sgt. Pepper's* album served to open people to Indian music—and the cross-transfer shift of that projection as well—and this is positive. The realness of technology can be viewed as an agent reshaping our sensitivities on many different levels—which is to say, the significance of western culture in this period is related to what is done with this reshaping: that is, the transfer-shift implications of world creativity can be viewed in two ways: (1) world music as a factor to realign our sensitivity and serve as a force for unification of the world group; or (2) world music as a spectacle-diversion factor related to the progressional continuance of western culture as an exclusive thrust (and/or world music as a factor related to gradualism). Both of these views seem to be true, and the challenge of western culture in this cycle is to resolve this problem positively. For the potential of western culture in this cycle is nothing less than serving as a primary force for establishing the solidification of composite world creativity—and thus the establishment of earth creativity. The realness of whether or not we are able to deal with this challenge is directly related to the nature of the next transformation—which is to say, transformation in this context is not dependent on whether or not we choose to affect its basic shape. Our ability to shape a given cycle must be viewed as optional.

The solidification of world creativity will not only affect the vibrational realness of the present cycle we are in, the realness of this achievement will also affect the composite physical universe level with regards to functionalism. For the composite thrust of world creativity could serve as the most dynamic factor for re-examining the meta-reality of all processes (with regards to its functional application)—and also with regards for its functional implications. To understand what this means on the physical universe level is to see the actualness of process integrated into the composite meta-reality of its culture, and the net result of this realignment would also expand the potential of trans-process. The net effect of the solidification of world creativity in this context would have to do with its ability to reshape and redefine what functionalism really is—moreover, the dynamic implementation underlying what this would mean is not separate from the culture; in other words, if the center-factor implications of composite aesthetic are established, then the actualness of functionalism can be accurately redefined in accordance to what that factor is. The establishment of this condition is directly related to the potential of what western culture could achieve in this period with regards to how dynamic functionalism could, on practical physical universe terms, assist in rebuilding and reshaping the composite world area. Yet I do not mean that the solidification of the composite world group necessitates the destruction of any one projectional thrust—or culture—because this would be "anti-what-is" or "reverse constructivism." To deal with the potential of world creativity is to see the importance of every creative thrust—or culture—and this is important.

In the beginning of this section I wrote of the fundamental relationship between all creative projections from the world group as a means to elaborate on the realness of this subject. To understand the realness of what this means is to view the progression significance underlying how process has come to be viewed: that is, the relationship of a given projection to what it actually means with regards to its essence lining. My point is this: any attempt to deal with the actualness of world creativity—as a necessary juncture to solidify changing life on earth—would reveal that the nature underlying how solidification is to be attained does not imply that any given projection be excluded or lessened, but rather the reverse. The significance of the forming composite world aesthetic has to do with its ability to incorporate the dynamic spectrum of composite vibrational information (as a means to continue expanding). For the basis of cross-sectional activity does not erase any given aspect of its principle ingredients, but rather the significance of any given transfer shift is directly related to how that consideration integrates the affinity nature underlying its given thrust projections (or participants). In short, I am not writing of a consideration involving contraction as a necessary move for survival; I am commenting on a consideration that involves expansion as related to unification (or an expansion so dynamic that it erases cultural and vibrational barriers). For the ultimate success of a given projection is related to that projection's ability to function with regards to actual change—positive change. Yet the dynamic implication of a given thrust projection can only be evaluated in terms of whether or not its continuum is designed with regards to the meta-reality of composite humanity (or another way of stating this is, the realness of a given projection corresponds to how many people are allowed to benefit from its existence). The possibility of a world aesthetic forming should not be taken lightly, for solidification of this phenomenon would affect the progressional continuance of all earth culture—and dictate the nature of the next transformation as well. It is necessary for us to understand that this new forming can and must integrate the essence lining of composite humanity if it is to mean anything (or be successful).

The unification of world creativity must be looked at as only the first junction related to preparation for transformation, and in itself is only one factor related to isolated transition. For the dynamic implications of this subject must also imply that the projectional realness of earth knowledge be shared and unified. In other words, the solidification of world creativity would affect the consideration we call knowledge—as an actualization of a given projectional science—and necessitate a cohesive and composite coming together (and sharing) of all people and things. For not only is this coming together necessary, as a means to share in what has been learned throughout the progressional thrust of given projections, but the composite thrust of world culture could open realities to us never possible before—realities arrived at because the composite realness of earth culture has been understood on some level (not understood empirically—but understood). Which is to say, with unification we could begin to deal with the real problems and real questions relevant to our zone.

(Level Three)

1. *What is your opinion on the significance of black creativity and its encounter with western culture?*

I feel the significance of black creativity has to do with what it has posed to the reality of western affinity dynamics and progressional continuance. For the realness of black creativity has supplied the vibrational realignment implications of western postulation, and this phenomenon has also supplied basis for the composite reality of western continuance. The thrust of black creativity has provided the dominant impetus for helping western culture to regain world culture information and spiritual dictates—and this is true on many different levels. The functional implications of black creativity have helped to accelerate the nature of western alternative continuance—having to do with the rediscovery of individual dynamics and dynamic ensemble participation—and the extended use of improvisation in black creativity has supplied the basis for a new attitude about future continuance and creative multi-dynamics. I believe the solidification of transitional black creativity, since the bringing of black people to America, will one day be viewed as the most dynamic stimulant for composite western creativity in this time cycle. This is true regardless of focus or so-called style, and this is also true regardless of functionalism. Certainly I have not meant to imply that only black creativity is significant, nor by citing its particular dynamics have I meant to either discredit the wealth of contributions offered through world creativity, or undermine the brilliance of any particular projection. To do so would distort the realness of what creativity is. Every projection and thrust alignment has helped bring us—as earth people—to where we are now, and this cannot be over-emphasized. Still—since this question is directed towards black creativity—the realness of what has been offered through this continuum (black creativity) has profoundly changed the nature of composite western creativity—and this is important.

2. Have you somehow implied that western art music is less than black creativity because of its relationship to process?

    In the section on western art music I have most certainly placed emphasis on the particulars of western functionalism—what this consideration means with respect to the path western music has taken, what this consideration means with respect to dynamic functionalism, and what this consideration has posed to the aesthetic lining of western art music. I have attempted to write of these matters as a means to re-establish a broader basis for understanding what creativity really is—as opposed to "is." There is no such thing as a creative form or reality that is "less"—when compared to anything—and nowhere in this book have I tried to foster any kind of supremacy attitude—for any projection. In place of this concept I am saying that every projection has something special, and we should learn to seek out what this means. To somehow believe western art music is less than black creativity and/or world creativity is to really be participating in either a nationalist or racist concept, or to be simply misguided. If we are really concerned for what is true, then we cannot afford to deal in "petty accusations" or narrow bigotry. Creativity is not about the "winner" but rather the "cosmics"—and this is what interests me. I have, in this book, most certainly critically examined the progressional continuance of western art music—with respect to what I feel are its positive and negative implications—and there is reason for this. The thrust of this continuance has long been enshrouded in both misinformation and misdocumentation—the effects of which have profoundly reverberated throughout the composite reality of earth creativity. In this context I have characterized the western philosophic basis as out of phase with the dictates of world culture—and from this viewpoint I have tried to isolate the particulars of its dictates, both with respect to its philosophic particulars and its creativity (which is an affirmation of its philosophic and vibrational position) as a means to better understand what has happened—why, and what this (the reality of western philosophic alignment) could mean for transformation.

3. Historians would have us believe that the solidification of black creativity and its resultant aesthetic was accidental. Do you agree?

Western historians would, if unchallenged, have us believe that black people have never contributed anything to anything—unless a given person's lineage reveals some amount—no matter how small—of white blood. As such, the challenge of the next cycle must involve either challenging this sector of documentation, or creating a new information order of some kind. Whatever, it will not be easy, because the progressional application of misinformation and misdocumentation has been around for quite some time, and all of us have, at some point, seen the effects of what this has brought about. As for the question under consideration, I am not quite sure how to respond—because I do not really understand the question. Certainly the black people who were forcibly brought to America did not think, "at least we"ll invent jazz here!" Which is to say, the dynamic solidification of American black creativity did not actualize from a preposition but was instead the end result of the composite experience black people encountered. But the realness of any phenomenon is not separate from what this relationship means—or there would be no reason to do anything. In other words, if Edison knew how he was going to invent the electric light there would have been no need for doing any experimentation—because experimentation presupposes that, whatever the objective, the route of discovery is taken in the darkness as a means to move towards knowingness. Thus the discovery of a given information line in this context is an affirmation of the nature of one's research as well as one's luck—because if discovery isn't an accident (that being a planned attempt to understand what is not foreseeable), then what is? The solidification of black creativity whether planned or not can be viewed as a consistent phenomenon that—however it happened—is in accordance to the composite affinity dynamics of black invention and affinity dynamics. This is true regardless of the particulars of its given encounters—whether that encounter is western culture, so-called western functionalism, or so-called life particulars in western living. The survival and continuation of the music is not separate from the survival of black people—and no one has yet to imply that black people's survival was accidental.

4. *How do you feel about the word "jazz" to describe the projectional alignment area of black creativity which accents the affinity insight (2) principle for continuance?*

I have generally tried to avoid the word "jazz" whenever possible because, among other things, I have never understood what the word means. I have also neglected this word because somehow the word doesn't properly comment on the dynamic diversity of the reality it seeks to label. In the seventies there were many arguments as to whether or not a given form is jazz—and this is understandable on certain levels. Because it seems to me that everybody has a different definition of the word. I do not rule out the possibility that my disalignment with the word "jazz" is possibly only my problem—and if this is the case, so be it. But somehow I believe a better definition of this music might help vibrationally satisfy its diversity as well as its reality identity. One thing is clear, the word "jazz" does indeed serve as a separate term from any other form of music, and this is true for all of the forms actualized from black creativity in America. Dixieland music, boogie woogie, blues, rock (yes, rock!), rhythm and blues—all of these names are quite dynamic. Quite possibly I am wrong to not vibrate to the word "jazz," maybe my inability to feel good about this word is related to the natural chains of any aesthetic—as well as the racism that has progressionally disrespected the music. I have long preferred the term "creative music from the black aesthetic" or simply "creative music." I prefer these terms because there is more room to breathe, and whenever possible, I plan to broaden these categories even further.

5. *If the source vibrational pull of black creativity is separate from that of western art music, what does this mean with regards to black people in America?*

First of all, the source vibrational pull of black creativity is so diverse that some areas of its projectional spread are received as alien even to particular sectors of black people. Second, the vibrational scan of western art music is just as multi-dynamic as black creativity in its own way—because, contrary to popular belief, all white people do not vibrate to the same information reality either. Finally there are many regions of black creativity that intersect with western art music, and vice versa—which is to say, the present idea we have of separation does not really reflect what seems to actually happen on the physical universe level—either with music or with people in general. Nevertheless, since this period in time is viewed with respect to what is most different about humanity, rather than what is most similar, the dictates of thrust alignment and cultural creative lineage do indeed comment on what a given information transference means with respect to doing. As such, we can say that since the composite informational alignment of black people is outside of the dominant cultural focus that being, the reality affinity position of composite white America—actual living has been made more difficult with respect to both information transference and alternative political activism. Finally, the reality of information and vibrational continuance is also related to what a given cosmic objective poses for participation. In other words, the composite vibrational pull of the black sensibility functions as a force for world transformation and the emergence of new spiritualism, while the composite vibrational continuum underlying western culture expands as a force to sustain its present position on the physical universe level. Both of these dynamic positions are reflected on the vibrational and physical universe level.

6. *What is the progressional reality of source-transfer extensions from black creativity?*

The progressional reality of black creativity has seen a source-transfer extension from every period of its encounter with western culture, and the reality of this phenomenon has always adhered to the same most basic formula. Each source-transfer extension from the white community is viewed with respect to how it has modified some aspect of a given projection, and in every case this modification is viewed as superior to its original model. It does not matter whether we are referring to the Original Dixieland Jazz Band or Elvis Presley—this cycle follows the same pattern. The reality that makes this phenomenon possible most certainly involves racism and social reality, but the dynamics dictating the need for this mentality are economic. The progressional use of this technique usually moves to restructure the composite reality of its transferred projectional continuance, with the eventual understanding being that "this form has had nothing to do with black people and/or black culture." In other words, something has been created from nothing—or the "American dream."

7. Have you implied that white people have no right to utilize and participate in black creativity?

Not only have I not implied that, but this viewpoint is completely beside the point. I have in this series of books tried to comment on creative music—especially creative black music—from as many different levels as possible. By citing the particulars of social reality there is no way to not also comment on the reality of racism and how it works, as well as what it has necessitated. There is no way that the social reality particulars surrounding black people can be discussed without also commenting on the dynamic injustice related to the very fabric of western culture. Nowhere in this series of books, however, have I violated any individual or questioned anyone's right to participate in anything—because not only does this way of thinking mean nothing, but it is also not what I believe. I have commented on what I perceive to be the reality of progressionalism—and the nature underlying information transference—in itself, as well as its relationship to sustaining the unfairness of western culture.

8. Is there a tradition of improvisation in western art music?

Yes—and many people are very surprised to discover this most basic fact. Before the acceleration of extended functionalism in western art music, improvisation was a necessary feature in performance. Composers like Bach and Beethoven were renowned instrumentalists even before the dynamics of their compositions were realized. At present there are many compositions of early western art music which call for some use of improvisation—if it is to be played correctly. To my knowledge, however, western culture had never developed a composite improvisational aesthetic for the dynamic ensemble—or large ensemble. There was no use of collective improvisation in the way we have come to view this concept today. Nevertheless, there was a real awareness of improvisation and this discipline was greatly respected and admired. The history of western art music is full of the success of its brilliant improvisor instrumentalists—having to do with great musicians challenging each other for both invention as well as technique. Bach himself was a great organist who improvised every week in the church and wrote music at the same time for the choir. I doubt very seriously that he would be happy about what has transpired in the functional continuance of western art music—especially involving the decline of improvisation as a meaningful discipline.

9. You have written about the inevitable reaction inherent in the logical progression surrounding western art music. Would you explain what you mean by reaction with regards to that progression?

I have used the word "reaction" in this context as a means to (1) show how each period of western art music has advanced and why; that being, the reality position of form and what effect the extended composer would have on the music, as well as what "reaction" would mean in the isolated focus of functional ingredients (i.e., language and rhythm—and design); and (2) I have also used the word "reaction" as a means to comment on the ultimate implications that each successive cycle of creativity pose to the lining of the western art music aesthetic. Which is to say: the inevitable reality of this phenomenon must also give some insight as to the composite reality position of western information dynamics—which is really what interests me. My point in this context is: the reality continuance that brought us Bach and Beethoven is also responsible for the activity of Cage and Stockhausen—which is to say, contemporary western art music, in its documented conscious reality purpose, is a natural affirmation of the composite lineage and inheritance of western culture. In other words, the philosophical position that dictated the reality of western continuance has remained constant. The present dissolution of western pedagogy—and essence basis—is directly related to the reality of reaction. This is not to say only one criterion can be applied to view western art music, nor have I implied that the whole of this continuum has not also brought forth much of beauty—because of course it has. Rather, the reality of reaction is a concept that does have bearing on western information continuance, and this is my point.

10. Why do you not accept the idea of innovation in creative music?

I reject the idea of innovation because to merely change the surface particulars of a given function in itself means nothing. If that criterion is to be called innovation then every musician who has ever played is an innovator because each individual in the final analysis does something different. I believe the vibrational base of a music determines the real reality function of its coordinates—as well as its dynamics (or potential way of growing). As such, when I commented on the nature underlying how western art music solidified, or creative music from the black aesthetic, I wrote about the solidification of a new way of living, or a different vibrational climate for living—no matter the nature of its particulars. In other words, the establishment of the aesthetic was innovation, or the establishment of the physical universe living space was innovation, and this is what concerns me. Certainly in narrowing the use of this word it might appear that in the final analysis I have no respect for the many individuals whose work has helped to advance the particulars of progressional continuance—but this is not true, because I do. But the concept of innovation has now come to be utilized as only an ego-oriented feature, rather than a dynamic cultural achievement indicator. Because the realness of what this consideration really means transcends any one person—and even culture, for that matter. Because the "reality of functional extension" or "realignment of functional dynamicism" is directly related to the cosmic realness of the greater powers—having to do with what "zone" responds to the will of a given cosmic period—in other words, we are always given what we need (whether or not we know how to use it). It is for this reason that I reject the terms "new music" or "old music" as well as "better or worse"; because in the final analysis we have come to use these terms as weapons, rather than for what the words really mean. The whole of this phenomenon is also related to the misuse of the word "innovation"—that being, innovation as a means to claim the creation of something new. My point is that there is no such thing as new music in a vacuum.

11. Ultimately, does music reflect the social-psychological and spiritual development of humanity and, if so, what significance does creative music today have in relationship to this phenomenon?

Ultimately, music does reflect the social-psychological and spiritual developments of humanity—or at least music (and all creativity for that matter) comments on the social-psychological and spiritual reality position of humanity—since development is open to question. Yet the realness of this relationship is manifested on many different levels—depending on both focus and affinity nature—and should not be viewed as mono-dimensional. For the reality dynamics of each culture group determine the particulars underlying its vibrational and meta-information structure, as well as its spiritual and ritual information (i.e., what significance a given actualization will have in its multi-informational position and in its meta- and infra-information reality). The realness of this phenomenon is very exciting, especially if we are to view the present reality position of earth existence. Because we are slowly moving to the juncture of composite world solidification—which is to say, the reality implications of creativity will also be a factor that will comment on how this solidification takes place, and in what form. The thrust of this phenomenon has defined the nature of what we now call fusion music—which is the dynamics of source-transfer participation. The realness of this phenomenon will also comment on the route re-unification will take. If the reality of creative music in this time period is in any way accented from its normal vibrational position, it is undoubtedly because of the acceleration this phenomenon (source transfer) activated.

12. What problems does the white musician encounter by participating in creative music from the black aesthetic?

This is a difficult question to answer because in the final analysis we are talking about individual people. There are many white musicians who have been able to penetrate into the composite lining and reality of so-called black creativity, and on the other hand there are many musicians who have undoubtedly been denied real opportunities—because of their skin color alone. As such, the dynamics of social reality must be included in any attempt to understand the struggle of the white improvisor. There is also a vibrational struggle that has been created for the white improvisor—involving whether or not one is made to feel that he or she has the right to participate in black creativity, because of the nature of western racism and imperialism—and this argument is serious in that many potentially dynamic musicians have made the decision to not participate in the music because of the misconception that possibly "he or she might not have the right." Add to this the natural struggle that anyone has in approaching anything, as well as the reverse racism that does exist, and one can begin to have some understanding of the situation of the white improvisor. Hopefully the next cycle will see less concern about a person's skin color and more concern about the person. However, in reviewing the particulars of the white improvisor's struggle it is important that the tenor of my response not give the wrong impression about social reality and social advancement. Because however one chooses to view the particulars surrounding the white improvisor's struggle, it should not be confused with the real reality tone of this time period. In other words, I do not believe that the particulars of the white improvisor's struggles are accented to the degree that he or she has any less chance to be successful than the black musician. In actual fact, I see the reverse as true—which to me makes sense—because when we comment on western culture, we are in fact commenting on white people and their culture. The reality of decisions and decision-making in western culture is about "white people" and for "white culture"—this is not to say given individuals, whatever their so-called race, will necessarily not experience any cycle of struggle in their lives, because most people do encounter many levels of struggle—including the white improvisor. Even the concept of transformation does not rule out the dynamics of struggle on some level. As for the question concerning whether or not the white improvisor has the right to participate in the music, it seems to me that if a person sincerely has a need to participate in a given area of creativity, he or she also has the natural right as well.

13. What influence has traditional European art music had on creative music from the black aesthetic?

It is impossible to separate the contribution of European art music from the composite continuum of creative music from the black aesthetic because the relationship is both great and complex. The thrust of European functionalism has affected every projectional strain of black creativity, since the beginning of slavery—from the dynamics of western harmony to the instruments (however, the real reality of this transference is even more complex since nine-tenths of the instruments which came to solidify European art music can be traced to Africa). The dynamic interaction between European art music and its effect on black creativity must also be viewed with respect to the reality implication of source-transfer information continuance. For even musicians like Charlie Parker utilized material from composers like Cole Porter, who utilized the fundamentals of composers like—whoever (I imagine there must be someone—what about ?)—my point is that Porter's music was a logical affirmation of western art music fundamentals. Nevertheless, the dynamic synthesis between black creativity and European art music is much too interrelated to separate—regardless of time period or focus.

14. Creative music from the black aesthetic has drawn from many different cultures—with regards to both style and form. How has this affected the aesthetic?

All of the various creative musics which have interconnected to black creativity have helped to advance the forming of a world creativity. For the thrust of a given source-transfer phenomenon does not only affect one aspect of its encounter—which is to say when you are really touched by someone, that person becomes part of you and you of him or her. It is also important to understand the dynamic acceleration of multi-information and fusion information convergence. Because the realness of this phenomenon is profoundly altering not only so-called black creativity but composite earth creativity as well. I believe the accented position of black creativity is related to what its solidification in the west implies (with respect to the implications of the affinity insight principle). The next twenty years promise to see even greater occurrences of source transfer information conversion—and this will also profoundly affect the essence balance of earth principle information lines. If this is true, there will be no such thing as black, white, or Asian creativity (just as now, only we don't seem to know it).

15. Does innovation by definition imply a separation between the actual activity and the physical universe environment it was created in?

    Well . . . yes and no. Innovation, as this concept is understood in this time zone, implies that something new or different has been created as an entity rather than something which has emerged as a natural result of a greater context—or greater reality context. So the answer to this question is yes if we choose to accept these terms—which I do not. I have long rejected this reality position because I do not believe that the concept of "new" corresponds to what is really happening in life. The western culture concept of innovation doesn't take into account both the composite nature and multi-dynamics of cultural postulation (and people's lives) as well as the multi-complexual significance of vibrational realignment (or cosmic resolidification of information dynamics and cultural direction). Instead western culture defines innovation from the one-dimensional standpoint of the phenomenon itself, or the individual who is supposed to be responsible for this innovation. To make matters worse, usually only one individual is given credit for a postulation that has involved many different areas and/or people—because the cosmic state of information dynamics and vibrational change is always compositely manifested throughout the environment or planet space—touching those of "like sympathy" (or those who are "in tune" with this aspect of "what is"). In short, the music is in the air and no one person has his or her receivers on at any given time. Moreover, no one person has any monopoly on or special insight into the challenge of accurately interpreting what a given informational or vibrational line poses for world change—because in the final analysis these matters are cosmic. And finally, the vibrational arena and imprint of cosmic information is reflected on so many different levels, both within and without the meta- and physical universe plane, that any one-dimensional interpretation of innovation can be very misleading.

16. What factors have most stimulated the progressional continuum of western art music?

I would say the most basic motivation factor that has helped to propel the thrust continuum of western art music is the nature of its philosophical base—especially the consideration of "interesting." The move towards "interesting" has provided the impetus for investigating the dynamics of rhythm and harmony, as well as technical modifications and extensions. In other words, the concept of "interesting" I speak of represents a primary factor in the composite quilt of western intellectualism. I have also chosen the word "interesting" because of its semantic position as well. For the vibrational dictates of the word "interesting" serve to address it more to the intellectual needs of western investigation—as opposed to its emotional needs. This is not to say the thrust continuance of western culture has flowed without emotional needs—or emotion—because obviously it has. Rather, it is my viewpoint that the reality of the western vibrational sensibility, when viewed in the context of world culture, does manifest an overbalanced shift towards isolated intellectualism—at the expense of emotion and spirituality. And I view this phenomenon as a problem, not a virtue.

17. You have stated in this book that western culture inherently moves towards separation—which you view as negative. Do you also see any positive attributes from this phenomenon as well?

Yes and no. Certainly I believe there are many positive aspects of western culture and its affinity alignment, and I have not consciously tried to negate the realness of what has been offered through this continuum. To do so would be not in accordance to what is really true—or proper, for that matter. The nature of western continuance has made the dynamics of living in this period very . . . interesting. In every area we are able to experience dynamic functionalism, and this is positive to some degree. My problem with this phenomenon has more to do with what separation has posed to the actualness of our humanity. Because, even though many isolated advances have been made in western culture, it has not really helped its people to deal with real living. Nor have these gains been necessarily achieved for the whole of humanity—or distributed for the betterment of humanity. Yet it would still be wrong to simply dismiss the dynamic gains that have come from the western information continuum. I believe the dynamic of separation cannot only be viewed for how it has promoted and advanced the nature of its special functionalism, but must instead be viewed in its composite context—and if this is true, then the nature of dynamic separation lies at the heart of what is most wrong in western information dynamics. I write this because my viewpoint is this: if a given phenomenon has the potential to bring about dynamic functionalism while, in the process, making us—as a collective people—less human (or affecting us in ways that promote less concern about humanity), or if a given phenomenon, to be achieved, necessitates the conscious use of injustice to any area of humanity as a means to bring about so-called technological advances or comfort to only one sector of humanity, then I view that phenomenon as inherently negative.

18. Can musical sensitivity be taught, or is it an inborn characteristic of the individual?

I believe every person is born with a relationship to information and information dynamics, and when tapped that person can achieve whatever goal or objective is desired. I believe this is true for creativity, science, history, etc. We are usually taught in this period that "either you have it or you don't," but I cannot agree with this idea. I believe all of us possess many different talents, and that the challenge and beauty of life is to somehow realize as much of that talent as possible. I believe any person can achieve whatever goal he or she desires. This is not to say that at eighty-five years old one can decide to be a brain surgeon—there are of course limits, but not as many as we have been taught. There is no such thing as musical sensitivity; or another way of saying this is, there is no such thing as non-musical sensitivity. All of us are possessed with some aspect which can be musical—which is musical—it is really a question of understanding what one wants to do in life and moving towards that. I completely disagree with any viewpoint that tells someone they cannot do what they want to do because somehow they were not born gifted in that way. What we need are teachers who care, friends who care, and families that care.

19. *To what extent does the musical experience have the power to change the perspective of the listener to other aspects of his or her life?*
I believe the power of creativity is much greater than what we are aware of. Music has the power to transform a person's life, music has the power to heal and uplift the spirit. The power of music can also connect people to particular zones. Contemporary western science is slowly becoming aware of the dynamics of music and I see this awareness increasing in the coming years. Every culture has always placed much emphasis on its creativity, because creativity is about "something else." It is because of this power that we must re-examine our relationship to creativity—with respect to what this consideration means aesthetically as well as its dynamic functionalism. Because music—and all creativity—is dynamically interconnected to the composite laws of this sector in space. Which is to say, to really move into the reality of creativity is to become more and more aware of areas of beingness that have nothing per se to do with music—as we use this term now. Music has to do with spirituality and "life realness"—and has the power to change everyone—to every extent.

20. *Does creativity manifest what the future vibrational arena will be—with respect to culture vibrational cycle or individual living?*
Yes, but I do not mean this in one-dimensional terms. There have been many examples of this phenomenon in the last fifty years even. For the composite thrust of dynamic restructuralism from the post-Webern period, John Cage period, and Charlie Parker period all preceded what the composite vibrational context would be for their respective reality positions. It was possible to see the intensity that would characterize the sixties by viewing the thrust of John Coltrane's music—because it was all there, in his music. The work of La Monte Young would precede the move towards world culture and the interest in Indian music, and the AACM would forecast the move towards re-examining the composite tradition of, first, black creativity, then world creativity. There is, however, another viewpoint

equally real, but the reverse of what I have already stated—one that also seems to be true. That being, creativity is a reflection and affirmation of "now"—but most people have been taught to not be in "now," and so they are surprised. This viewpoint goes on to say contemporary music is viewed as the future by the greater public because of the state of the planet in this period—not the music itself. The thrust of this viewpoint has taken the position that life in western culture is somewhat akin to being in a time warp complex. As such "present time" creativity is perceived as being the future. I believe both of these positions.

TRANSITION

(Level One) WESTERN ART CONTINUANCE

TO REALLY VIEW THE TRANSFORMATIONAL POTENTIAL of a given creative thrust is to first have some understanding about the reality nature of its vibrational center. For the composite expansion of a given projectional continuum reflects both the dynamic implications of its reality base as well as the greater vibrational dynamics of world culture. As such, the particular information route of a given projection cannot be separated from the reality position of composite earth information—because, finally, everything has affected everything, and no one projection has solidified in isolation from the world community. Moreover, the particulars of a given continuum can also help us to understand the nature of the next change cycle. For the dynamic position of earth in this period transcends any one factor: that is, the nature of the next change cycle will involve many different factors from every sector of the planet. As such, it is important to understand the role of creativity in transition, because the composite implication of this subject is not separate from the dynamic nature which dictates how information and affinity alignments are actualized. Which is to say, the nature of any transition and/or transformation involves many different factors—this is true whether we are focusing on the reality of transition as it involves economics, politics, social reality, and/or information exchange. The progressional continuance of earth creativity is directly related to transition and/or transformation. For, like the spread of humanity itself, the meta-reality of earth creativity can be reduced to the utilization of principle information dynamics, from the collective wellspring of universal knowledge. As such, the progressive developments which have brought us to this time juncture have also moved to establish the nature underlying how given information routes reveal particular interpretations (of "necessary" earth knowledge). The fact is, the concept of transition is directly related to the nature of how progressional continuance is sustained. For unlike real transformation—that being, the total resolidification of the composite vibrational reality of a given time—progressional transition can be viewed as the most basic planet change factor involving the particulars of natural expansion. It is through this concept where we can move to understand how given isolated changes have moved to eventually reshape the composite nature of particular time cycles—and more important, it is through the concept of transition where we can better understand the dynamic implications which dictate the ultimate significance of a given creative projection—as it moves through its natural route. For the transition of physical universe information is directly related to how the spread of creativity has come about. This is true for western art music and this is also true for black creativity—Indian creativity—and world creativity (regardless of sector). Thus if we are to really understand the reality position of creativity in this time zone (the late seventies and eighties) then it is important that some attempt is made to view both the cosmic factors which determine a given projection, and the physical universe implications of its particular route.

There are two most basic contexts from which the progressional continuance of a projection can be viewed—(1) the reality of expansion as it relates to the continuum lining of source initiation, and (2) the reality of expansion as it relates to the composite world platform. If we are to understand the dynamics of western art music then it is necessary to view its progression in each of these contexts. For the solidification of western art music—and its accelerated dynamics—would move to greatly affect the reality of earth creativity in many ways. By "reality of individual expansion" I am commenting on the nature of how a given expansion principle is practiced in its given culture group. For in western art music the "reality of individual expansion" would have to do with the relationship between a given projection and the changing dynamics of its vibrational (and philosophical) pedagogy, as well as the nature underlying how empirical and scientific investigation would come to be viewed in transformational terms. As such, the reality of western art music expansion can be viewed with respect to how given developments would accelerate the composite nature of these factors. But the composite significance of western continuance would involve many other factors as well, because as

I have stated—the dynamics of a given initiation have multi-dimensional consequences when viewed in a composite context. Thus to view the continuum of western creativity within the "reality of composite world expansion" is to attempt understanding what effect a given development in western art music posed for the greater world community—and vice versa.

The "individual dynamic reality" of western art music can be understood by examining the dynamics of functional realignment in the early 1900s. This would be the time cycle where the basic continuum of western methodology would exhaust its established methodological application. The two paths that would emerge in this period would solidify the dynamics of post-Schoenbergian activity. Those routes being: the work of Anton Webern and the move towards serialism, and the creative route of Stravinsky and the neo-classicists. Yet I do not mean to oversimplify. For the Schoenberg-Webern expansion was very separate from the work of composers like Olivier Messiaen. Messiaen would move to establish a music that would clarify the source-transfer dynamics of progressionalism—that being, his activity would demonstrate a dynamic extension of western methodology in its use of "world music" material. In doing so, Messiaen's activity would also establish another affinity attitude for western art music with respect to the question of methodological dynamics. For it must be understood that the progressional continuum of the Schoenberg-Webern creative route would accelerate the existential nature of western affinity dynamics—in the sense that the solidification of serialism can be viewed as a logical extension of the same attitude (and information affinity position) that preceded it. Yet I do not write this as something inherently negative—because it isn't. My point is that the reality of transition involves the nature underlying how various zones of information are brought from period to period, as well as how those zones are perceived, practiced, and reinterpreted in their natural spread throughout the world community. This is true for every information line—whether we are referring to science or music.

WAC-4

AF.DY.------C.INFO.

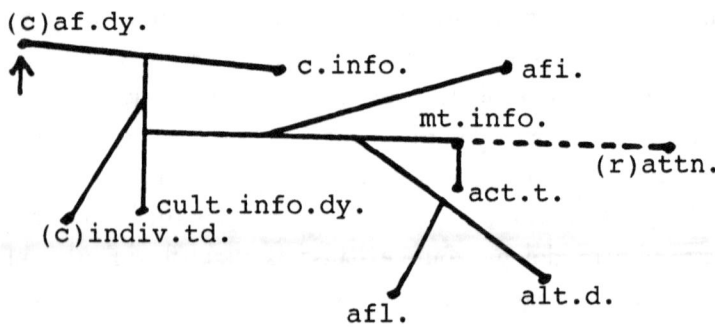

The solidification of serial music would establish the realness that western art music had moved into transition. The dynamics of this technique would dictate the nature underlying how expansion could be brought about in actual terms. As such, the progressional application of this approach would see the post-Webern movement solidify the reality implications of transitional functionalism. For the nature dictating how serial music would expand is not separate from the composite developments reshaping western functionalism. The dynamic implication of post-Webern activity must be viewed for what this relationship implied, because the resolidification of extended functionalism—as practiced in this technique—was perceived in accordance to the composite factors related to western expansionalism. Contemporary western creativity in this context would move to affirm the reality of composite western dynamic investigation—and in doing so also move to change the reality position of its methodological dynamics (i.e., the interrelationship between creativity and science). The nature of how this expansion would be brought about gave insight into the reality position of western art music.

The transfer shift implications of western art music must also be viewed with respect to its social reality position as well as what it implies about progressional continuance. For the dissolution of the composite reality of western art music coincides with the composite factors reshaping the total planet situation—in terms of world information and political expansion. It is clear that one of the considerations behind the solidification of serialism was Webern's desire to find an independent strain of creativity that was uniquely western—as a means to expand in accordance to source initiation. The solidification of pointillism as a concept would thus establish a particular route of both investigation and expansion for western art music. The progressional continuum of the creativity actualized from this viewpoint would utilize the extremities of the western affinity dynamic information position—that being, investigation and participation with respect to the reality of information dynamics as made real through the nature of western methodology. As such, the reality of post-Webern activity could be viewed as an affirmation of the western information continuum—the idea being that there is a creative route related to the particulars of any investigative route (which in itself is a world culture viewpoint, and does describe an actual criterion). To view the reality position of contemporary western art music is to understand the particulars underlying how these factors would move to solidify the next cycle of extended western art music—and this should not be over-simplified. For the progressional continuum of western art music, as it progressed through the post-Webern continuum of its development, has been affected by many different factors. The last thirty years alone can be viewed as extremely dynamic for the nature of how extension in this continuum has been brought about. The force continuum of this thrust (western art music) has profoundly contributed to the total reality of earth creativity and as such, it is important that attempts are made to understand the reality of contemporary western art music—as well as its progressional expansion.

There are four basic information focuses which must be examined if we are to understand the reality of western creative extension in the early 1900s. Those focuses are: the reality particulars of the second Viennese school; the reality particulars of the neo-classicists; the source transfer implications reshaping American creativity; and the dynamic changes reshaping western composite functionalism. All of these factors would move to transform the vibrational reality of western creativity and its role in world culture. Moreover, the reality implications of these four factors would also establish a basis from which the dynamics of progressional extension could be viewed (with respect to world information dynamics). As such it is important that some effort is made to clarify the dynamics of these basic divisions.

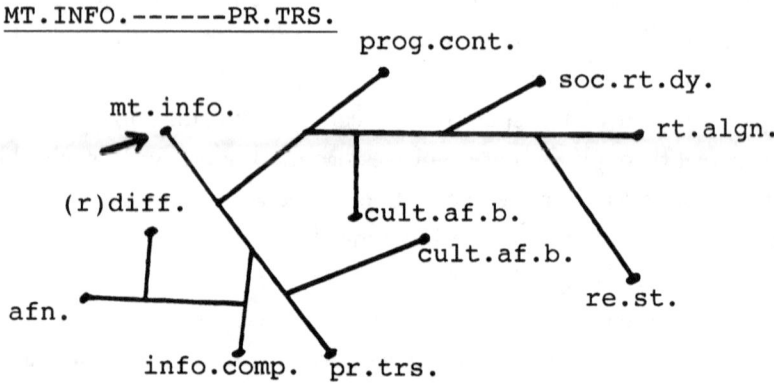

The reality of the second Viennese school can be viewed with respect to the dynamics of "principle information tendencies"—that being, the underlying factors which determine what aspect of a given information line is to be utilized for expansion—and also the concept of affinity dynamics. For the collective music that would emerge from the activity of Arnold Schoenberg, Anton Webern, and Alban Berg would move to solidify the nature of progressional extension with respect to "restructuralism" (which is the word I use instead of innovation since innovation does not semantically give enough emphasis on the progressive route of a given information readaptation). This is not to say that Schoenberg, Webern, and Berg functioned from only one context, nor have I meant to imply that their collective activity shows only one application of extension—because this is not true; rather, the collective participation of their activity would move to solidify the nature of extended functionalism—with respect to the separate reality dynamics of western culture (as made real through its unique affinity dynamics). Yet in actual terms, each of these composers had a very different relationship to principle information and information dynamics. Which is to say, each composer would perceive of

WAC-7

restructuralism in very different ways even though all embraced the same basic techniques—which in this case was the expansion of creativity with respect to the realignment of process as developed in what came to be called twelve-tone technique (and later serialism). Schoenberg's activity could be viewed with respect to the stylist reality of creative western art music, in the sense that his application of twelve-tone music would reveal the dynamics of restructuralism with respect to the basic reality lining of western art music—in that time period (i.e., the use of thematic material in accordance to the dynamics of extended functionalism in that period), and in doing so, his work showed the progressional possibilities of the technique. This approach would be very important for how it would naturally reveal the extension possibilities of restructuralism, while not threatening the basic reality of the music.

The dynamics of Berg's relationship with extension could be viewed as very different from Schoenberg's in that the thrust continuum of his adaptation of twelve-tone (and later serial) technique would show another affinity perspective of applied functionalism. The basic thrust of Berg's activity would move to incorporate the expanded reality of western methodology with the composite continuum of western tradition. Berg's activity would thus reveal the dynamics of integration as a factor to sustain source initiation. For by solidifying the traditional continuum of western art music with the dynamics of expanded functionalism, Berg's application of methodology moved to affirm the isolated reality position of the composite continuum of western art music. Source initiation in this context can be viewed as understanding the nature of applied functionalism. For the reality of methodology after the dissolution of the meta-reality of western continuance had to do with the dynamics concerning what factor (or factors) could be utilized as a means for establishing center. The breakdown of the spiritual basis of western culture would move to establish the nature of transitional affinity dynamics—which is to say, "the reality" concerning how given areas of information would be interpreted is the direct result of the nature of the crisis western culture underwent. This "reality of interpretation" would have to do with how information dynamics—as separate from their meta-implications (regarding both the vibrational and spiritual implication of principle information lines)—would come to be viewed as a basis for expansion in its isolated state. As such, the reality position (of information dynamics) which solidified the particulars of western art music, in its traditional context—as made real through the practice of its great master composers—actualized a particular vibrational relationship with "principle information" (which is to say the actual functional specifics of western art music are not the "reality position" of the aesthetic, but instead the "functional operatives" related to how methodology would be perceived and applied in the music's science). The meta-implications of Berg's activity would reveal how the real "reality position" of western information dynamics could be expanded without disturbing its dynamic position.

EXT.F.------PROG.SIGN.

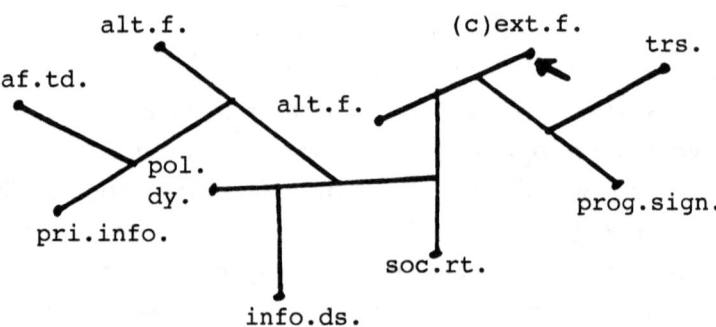

SG.------ FUND.DYM.

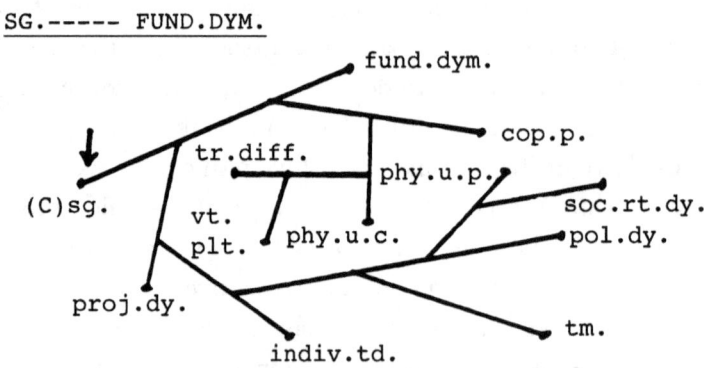

Berg's activity would thus move to solidify the composite continuity of western art music—and this solidification was brought about by his utilization of the transfer specifics of traditional functionalism. To become acquainted with his activity is to experience a dynamic continuum which in its natural expansion was able to incorporate many of the factors associated with tradition. As such, his music would utilize thematic development as it was practiced in the traditional continuum of the aesthetic, and while doing so also maintained a particular sensitive vibrational reality. In fact, in many ways Berg's music could be viewed as an equally romantic and visionary music—which is to say, the dynamic realness of his activity would reveal a profound understanding of transitional methodology and vibrational dynamics. Berg would move to apply his use of expanded functionalism on the total reality of western art music—from the early string quartets to the completion of two operas (or near completion since "Lulu" was not completed—by Berg anyway). The reality of his activity would establish an important contribution to transitional western art music, for this music would profoundly show the projectional and progressional continuum of western art music in all of its various states, and while doing so also give insight as to the future continuum as well.

Anton Webern's activity would move to establish the dynamics of extension with respect to what this consideration poses for restructuralism. The thrust of his activity would solidify the realness of both alternative functionalism and extended methodology—which is to say, the expansion implications of Webern's activity would forecast the nature of the next reality cycle of western creative music and western applied functionalism. This is so because Webern's use of serialism would establish the solidification of an extended language and conceptual context for western investigation. The dynamics of this development would alter the composite reality of creative music, and while doing so, also establish a diversity of routes for world investigation. Moreover, the solidification of both serialism (the process) and pointillism (the concept) would fulfill the progressional implications of traditional western expansion—as initiated by Beethoven—which is to say, the solidification of serialism would clarify the reality position of western continuance. For the development of Webern's activity would finalize the progressional reality of western art music (that being, the solidification of serial music made clear that the era of traditional methodology, as practiced by the master, was over—as an exclusive pedagogy)—and also its meta-functional and reality basis as well. In other words, the work of Anton Webern would have a profound effect on the reality of western creative expansion, and it is important to understand what this means.

It is important that the reality of Webern's activity is viewed with respect to his position in the collective offspring of both Berg and Schoenberg. For if the reality of Berg's activity could be characterized as an attempt to function for extension with respect to the traditional continuum of source initiation and its related definitions (involving western art music and/or culture), and if Schoenberg's activity constituted the nature of extension with respect to the position western art music found itself in (in the early 1900s), then Webern's activity must be viewed for what it posed for the dynamics of alternative functionalism—as this concept is made real through applied transitional methodology. As such, Berg's activity was to the past as Webern's activity would be to the future. This is not to say that the reality of Webern's isolated application of functionalism would dictate the composite reality of contemporary music—either from the western art music continuum or world continuum—because this is not true. Rather, the dynamic implications of Webern's activity would clarify the vibrational reality of western culture continuity. The progressional practice of serialism and/or pointillism would establish a definite thrust in western creativity, and the nature of its expansion would profoundly alter the vibrational implications of the composite planet's relationship with creativity. For the solidification of the post-Webern continuity is not only about the particulars of a selected group of isolated theorists; rather, the expansion of post-Webern creativity would move to dictate the nature of the next source-transfer world integration. Yet it is important that this point is clarified: for in itself the dynamics of serialism would only establish a particular continuity, and the dynamics of extended functionalism (as a concept) would establish only another continuity. But the solidification of serialism would profoundly affect the vibrational continuum of western art music and applied definitions—and this is what ultimately must be understood.

The work of the so-called second Viennese school must be viewed as necessarily significant for the dynamic continuum of western art music. This is not to say that every projectional route of future activity would emanate from post-Webern activity—because there were other movements gathering in that same period that would be just as important—but the dynamic implications of the second Viennese school did significantly comment on the composite reality underlying where western creativity had positioned itself. Moreover, the solidification of Berg's, Schoenberg's, and Webern's activity would establish the progressional dynamics of "source continuance." For the emergence of serialism would be revealed in a multi-context rather than only with regard for one sector (or vibrational sector) of the community. In other words, the initiation of serialism would not be perceived as the only process relevant for the restructuralist and/or restructuralism. The composite application of serialism by Berg, Schoenberg, and Webern would show the realness (or importance) of "composite transition" (or compositely realigning the established continuum) without destroying the dynamic nature of "principle-affinity tendencies" of the creative community. The importance of this mass application of "source continuance" would move to clarify the reality position of western art music and western creative methodology. As such, even the artists who did not move to utilize serialism would come to recognize the dynamics of the crisis in western culture (and creativity)—and this acknowledgement is not separate from what the collected impact of the second Viennese school would make. For the solidification of serialism—when viewed with respect to its mass application (as applied to the tradition—or present dynamics—onto the future)—would establish an alternative methodology that would serve to affect the composite reality of western continuance—which is to say, the realness of this development would directly affect the composite nature of western extension.

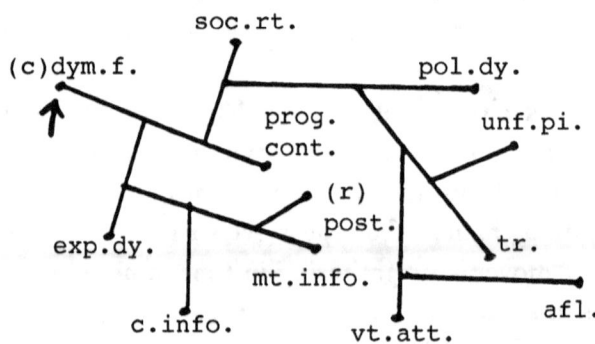

Thus the emergence of serialism would move to accelerate the nature underlying how extension would be dealt with in western culture. But it is important to understand that this movement (serialism) was not the only movement involved in progressionalism—with respect to source initiation. For the dynamic reality of Wagner's activity had moved to exhaust the possibilities of "applied extension"—that being, the application of traditional methodology in its most extreme use. As such, the composite community of creative composers in western art music had long recognized the need for other bases from which to utilize the methodological brilliance (particulars) of western creative functionalism. All of these factors would move to affect the composite lining of western art music as the thrust continuum of the aesthetic moved into the "composite transition cycle" involving the whole of that time period (for the transition western art music was feeling was related to the total changes that the whole culture was undergoing).

The progressional continuity of contemporary music after Schoenberg would move to align itself with the dynamics of composite western investigation—and this is especially true of the relationship that would develop between its creativity and functionalism. For after the dissolution of the composite meta-basis of the culture (i.e., spiritualism) there was really no other choice. This would then be the junction that would see the adaptation of new western technology for creative postulation, and the dynamics of this relationship would see the emergence of many new areas for creativity. Certainly the advent of electronic music can be viewed in this regard, and all of us have greatly benefited from the dynamic possibilities surrounding what this change has meant, but the reality implications of western art music are much more profound than its use of dynamic functionalism.

To understand the reality of extension in creative functionalism is to focus on the particulars of its principal figures. For the change implications of expansion could be viewed by examining the work of composers like Edgard Varèse in the early twenties. Varèse was one of the most dynamic individuals in his time period, and the music he actualized would give insight into the progressional implications of composite western expansion. His activity would move to stimulate the dynamics of alternative functionalism, and in its natural extension also transcend isolated methodological boundaries as well. The basic thrust of his vision would move to clarify the extension reality of western art music, and in doing so profoundly affect the "particulars" surrounding the dynamics of alternative functionalism. Varèse would be the first documented musician to call for the construction of electronic instruments—which is to say he would be the first composer to recognize the next utilization of transitional western functionalism. The basic thrust of his activity would greatly affect the composite reality of western art music.

The nature of how a given extension is actualized also gives insight as to the dynamic implications of the affinity insight principle—as it is manifested in given groups and individuals. For it is important to understand that the reality of any extension is not outside of the dynamic vision and practice of those individuals who are functioning. As such, to view the thrust continuum of a given extension is to examine the reality particulars determining both the vibrational state of the composite reality specifics, as well as the vibrational and reality state of the actual individuals whose work "materialized" that change. Both of these perspectives can help us to understand the reality of a given extension—because no one factor in itself has determined the present state of western art music, or for that matter, any given principle state; rather, the solidification of a given continuum is the composite result of a multitude of considerations. Moreover, the nature of the transition which occurred in western art music transcended even any one region of the planet. For this reason it is important that the dynamics of given specifics be presented from as many contexts as possible—because the underlying factors which solidified the realness of extension in western creativity were not separate from the reality of composite extension that the culture itself was experiencing.

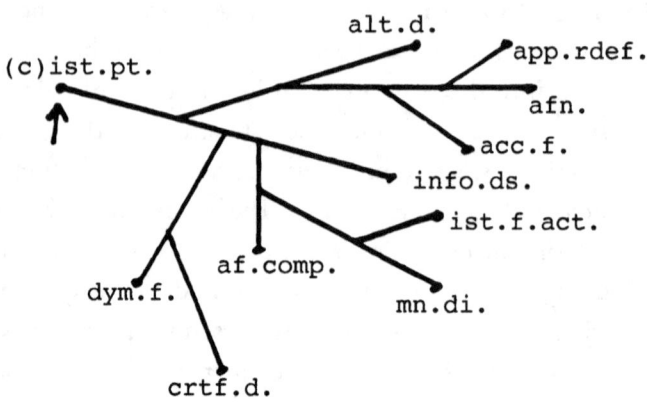

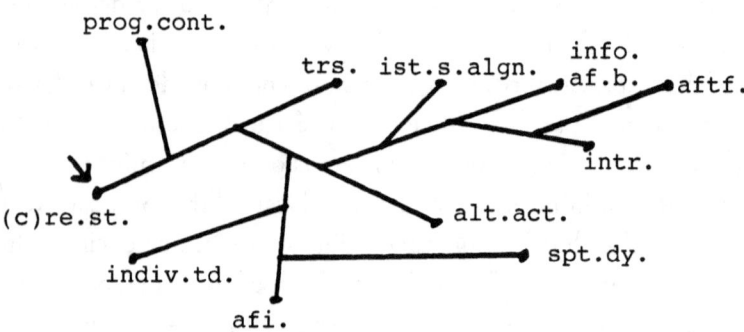

The progressional application of serialism must only be viewed as one approach to extension with respect to source initiation. The basic continuum of this movement would attempt to preserve the exclusive information reality of western culture—as a separate alignment phenomenon from world culture—and to an extent these intentions were successful. But there was also another movement whose activity must be viewed as equally relevant to the specifics of this time period, and any attempt to really understand what took place in the post-Wagner period of western art music transition would necessitate that some effort is made to compositely view all of its particulars. For the reality of serialism was not universally embraced either in its solidification in the early 1900s—or today. Thus the second movement that functioned for source-initiation extension—with respect to the object and/or motivation for restructuralism—is the movement we now refer to as the neo-classical movement. The most basic factor that separated this movement from that of the serial movement would lie in the nature underlying how each movement perceived of procedure—rather than intention. Both of these movements would determine the option dynamics of source-initiation extension—and as such it is important to focus on the reality of this phenomenon in the same context as previously attempted in serialism.

Igor Stravinsky is generally credited as the composer whose activity would solidify the reality of neo-classicism, and the thrust of his activity would generate the same type of enthusiasm that Arnold Schoenberg (and later Webern) generated in composite western alternative functionalism. The most basic concept that would establish neo-classicism was the idea that the natural extension reality of western art music methodology and/or language was not exhausted by any means and that natural extension should instead be directed toward other focuses (rather than changing methodologies). Moreover, the emergence of neo-classicism would pose another challenge for western expansion, for the reality of this movement would also dictate that any change of its principal functionalism could not be viewed as within the correct alignment for western high culture—or high art. For many of the people who practiced neo-classicism would view the nature of serial expansion as signaling the downfall of western culture, and an end to western art creativity as we understand this phenomenon in its separate state (and many of these people still feel this way today). Thus the natural continuance of neo-classicism would move to create a division in the established community of western information control—and a given composer would find him or herself reduced to what "school" their work was so-called related to.

The thrust continuum of Stravinsky's activity would move to create a dynamic music quite unlike that of the serialists. This was a rhythmic music which in its natural flow transformed the dynamics of its period. This music in many ways would be an exciting music and of course an emotional music—as opposed to the concept of serial music as a cold and dry extension. The information focus of neo-classicism would move to explore the natural folk musics of western Europe as an extension tool, and as the momentum of this thrust accelerated, a dynamic body of music would accent the validity of this approach as a meaningful route for western art music to take. Moreover, the use of a neo-classical extension had been prepared through the natural continuance of western creative extension. Composers like Béla Bartók had begun creating works of this type long before the concept of neo-classical solidified as an alternative movement. The reality of neo-classicism can thus be viewed as an extension within the methodological parameters of prescribed functionalism—having to do with postulation which didn't threaten the composite meta-reality position of western creativity, and also having to do with not violating—or leaving—the dynamic continuum of western art music's traditional functionalism.

The significance of applied neo-classicism can be understood by examining the composite reality of western information dynamics. For the thrust continuum of neo-classicism as practiced in the early 1900s, would move to fulfill the information dynamics of the western information focus (of that same time period)—and in doing so, this phenomenon clarified the reality position of western continuance. The reality of this creative continuum would move to clarify the nature of extension for transitional western art creativity as well, for the dynamic continuum of neo-classicism did not pose a new music, or alternative functionalism—rather a return to the fundamentals of classical methodology. The idea being that the nature of extension as practiced through serialism would move to destroy the reality of western art creativity, but a return to the basis could instead result in a new incentive for transitional western culture resolidification. This movement would later fold as a composite continuum by the middle fifties, and even Stravinsky himself would come to terms with twelve-tone technique. For the dissolution of the reality of neo-classicism was inevitable if one would consider the actual planet reality which solidified by the middle forties: that reality being—the emergence of transitional technology and the momentum of existentialism (as a philosophy which signaled that no longer could the progressive wing of the culture pretend religion as a basis for "meaning" and/or justification). In other words, the reality of neo-classicism as it was practiced and understood by the late forties was not conducive for the "real" reality of western continuance. The fact is, the reality of the thirties and forties all pointed to the realness of transition—with respect to technology, with respect to world politics, and with respect to alternative information. The work that Stravinsky completed, as well as the momentum secured by the progressional continuum of his movement—whether we are referring to events in America or Europe (including the Nadia Boulanger school that included such composers as Aaron Copland)—would instead occupy a niche on the composite path of western extension (at least up until the eighties).

Thus the solidification of serialism and neo-classicism would come to actualize the reality dynamics of source initiation extension in western art music. This is not to say that only two schools of extension developed, because many other movements were also functioning for change. But the realness of serialism and neo-classicism would establish the strongest principal source-initiation movements. To understand the other factors which promoted extension is to deal with the multi-dynamics of progressional continuance—which transcend the reality position of source initiation (and this is discussed later). But the significance of serialism and neo-classicism would involve how each of those movements moved to advance the reality dynamics of source initiation—which is to say, how each of those movements advanced the nature of its primary information lines, and its related affinity dynamics.

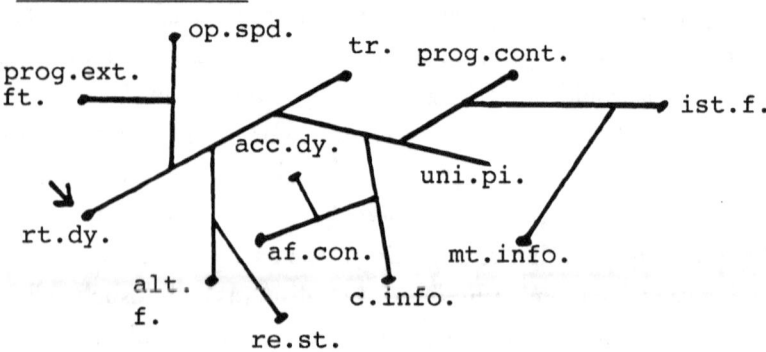

The dynamics of transition in creative music must be viewed in as broad a context as possible if we are to really understand what has happened to establish this cycle (i.e., the late seventies). As such the expansion of western art music after Schoenberg must be viewed with respect to the nature of its information lines: that being (1) the progressional continuum of contemporary music as a factor in accordance to the exclusive nature of its affinity dynamics (having to do with the isolated reality expansion of western art music as a separate creative thrust from world culture that draws on its own information continuum as a source for development), or (2) the progressional continuance of contemporary music as a factor in accordance to the reality implications of source transfer (having to do with the collective inter-relationship of world information lines as a factor relevant for dynamic extension). Both of these routes are important for what they imply about the dynamics of contemporary multi-information, because the reality of information extension transcends particular regions of the planet. The nature underlying how a given extension is solidified gives insight as to the composite reality of its given period—and as such this phenomenon is related to cosmic matters. For this reason it is important to examine the progressional route of a given solidification, because the "reality nature" of a given transition also moves to establish the fundamentals that will underline the vibrational and actual arena dictating what participation will mean in an expanded sense. In other words, the consideration of transition can be viewed as one of the factors which helps signal the "vibrational tone" and "functional identity" of a given time period (having to do with establishing insight as to the "nature" of what a given time period seems to imply as regards to "what vibrations are in the air"—or what forces are determining the dynamics of participation). This is so because the reality of transition has to do with the cosmic design of a given time period. Transition in this context then is related to how a given "zone formation" solidified as a composite reality lining factor. Every time period can be viewed in these terms, for the vibrational lining that permeates given cycles of earth existence also permeates the total reality lining of that same period. In actual terms, a given transition will move to establish the basic informational and vibrational continuum that "actual participation" will function from, as well as the spiritual ingredients that will color the affinity adaptation and dynamics of that information focus. As such, the reality of transition is not a mono-dimensional consideration but instead is related to the total reality of progression cycles. For the nature of a given transition will tell about the ingredients of a given "solidification" (or state of being) and also about what factors will have to be dealt with if that given participation is to fulfill its natural continuance. By attempting to view the reality implications of western art music as it moved into transition, we can better understand the composite world vibrational state—because all of these various considerations are interrelated on a number of levels. In the final analysis, to focus on a given transition is to begin examining the basic cosmic elements at work in the composite world community.

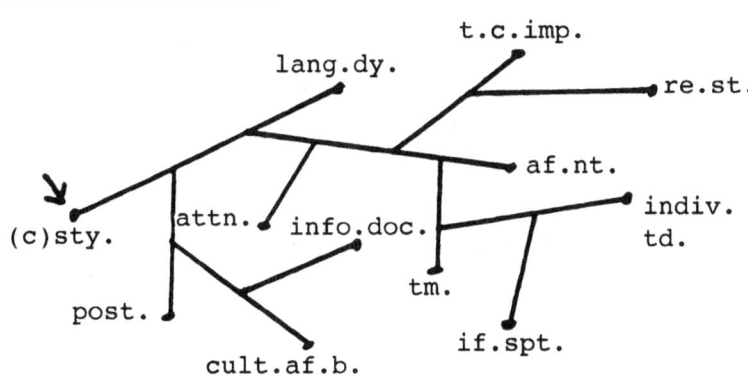

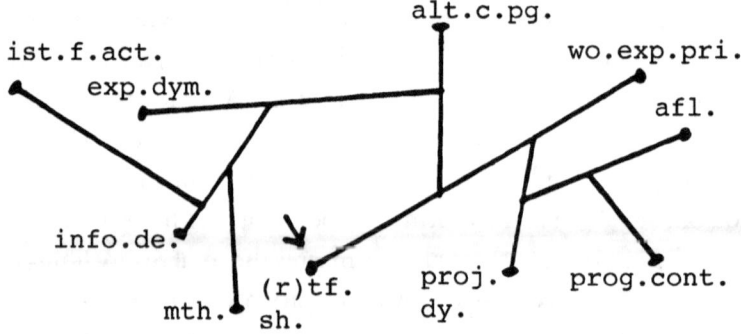

The cross-transfer dynamics of western extension in the early 1900s could be seen forming at about the same period which brought forth twelve-tone music—and its related continuum. By cross-transfer in this context, I am commenting on the reality progression of given information lines—which in this case is western—and how in their natural state these lines move to interact, and draw from, the affinity dynamics of world information as a means to continue (or expand). The reality of cross-transfer initiations would prove to be a valuable route for western expansion, and moreover, the dynamics of this route would also comment on the composite dynamics of all earth transfer cycles. In other words, the nature underlying how given thrusts of information move to expand is not outside of the cosmic factors which determine what "anything is to be"—and "how." As such, the "truth" of a given period is cosmic (or the reality of a given period is "about the cosmics"—or "with respect to what God wants"). Thus, the reality dynamics of a given time period comment on what factors are in the air—and in doing so, those factors also give us some indication of the "nature" of that same cycle. **In actual terms, the route western expansionalism took in the early 1900s would give insight into the "reforming vibrational reality" of world culture.**

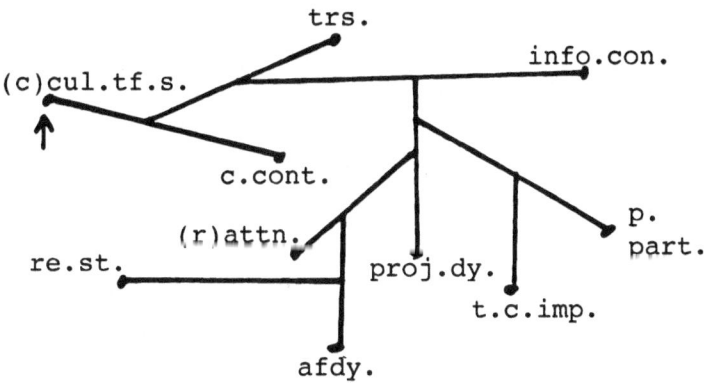

The historical particulars related to how actual cross-sectional extension would actualize could best be understood by examining the effects of composers like Debussy in Europe or Harrison in America. This continuum would function as a dynamic extension of western creativity, and while doing so also move to reshape the vibrational reality of the music. For the cross-transfer implications of extension would involve the nature of change as applied to the reality of form, the dynamics of timbre, the use of rhythm, and the concept of material development. The dynamics of source-transfer extension would also eventually move to become as important a movement as source-initiation extension (although the applied use of this concept would not meet with universal adaptation until the late fifties)—and no doubt the reason would have to do with what source transfer implies as a composite extension factor. The truth is, the future of a given extension is directly related to whether or not that extension can absorb the multi-informational and vibrational demands that relate to composite continuance. This is not to say that a given source-initiation particular cannot in its natural route sustain relevancy—because obviously this is not the case—rather the nature of a given informational continuity must respect the reality dynamic of "natural" (or what I will call natural) change cycles. In other words, if the nature of progressionalism has to do with how information is brought forth, and if—in its natural state—that same information must undergo source transfer—as a means to reflect the social reality peculiarities (the way information is perceived and utilized in different parts of the planet) of progressionalism, then the nature of dynamic extension must on some level function with respect to what this diversification means. It is because of this diversification that the reality of source transfer is perceived as dynamically expansive.

From a vantage point of thirty years we can now begin to understand the implications of source-transfer extension. The work of composers like Harry Partch would have a minute effect on the reality of extension in the thirties, but instead became very significant in the seventies. This is also true for the work of Olivier Messiaen, for as the reality continuum of his work becomes clearer, it is now possible to understand his real position in transitional extension—and it is more significant than is generally assumed. The thrust of Messiaen's activity would move to give a dynamic universal context for western art music extension—and in doing so the thrust of his work would eventually move to affect the source-initiation particulars of the post-Webern continuum. Moreover the reality of source-transfer extension for western art music cannot be limited to any one context. For the reality continuum of western art music, as it moved towards transition, would see the emergence of important developments in social reality. As such, no real understanding of transitional western art music can take place unless the composite reality of its extension is taken into account—this is so because the adaptation of western art music in America would move to become another reality factor in its extension, and also because the dynamics of its progressional spread would move to affect the composite lining of world culture. As such, the nature of source-transfer extension must be viewed with respect to what it has posed to the transitional nature of earth creativity—as applied to social reality in such countries as America, Japan, India, and China. The source-transfer brilliance of western art music and its related extension has played an integral role in establishing the nature of the transition we are dealing with today. It is important that some attempt is made to look at this expansion in particular terms.

Euro-American Tradition

However one chooses to understand the progressions which took place in western art music after Schoenberg and Webern, we should understand that in America quite another situation was happening. I do not mean to imply that American classical music functioned as a completely separate entity from European art music, for that is not true, but the emergence of the American composers' tradition does have a distinct historical progression, and this movement does give some insight into the nature underlying how the next transformation of western art music was to be defined. From a historical basis there has always been a renegade group of creative composers in America whose activity attempted to utilize source material from their own environment. Composers like Charles Ives in the early 1900s were experimenting with advanced concepts which accented the realness of his work as a separate factor from the European mainstream. Yet I do not mean to imply that the majority of composers in America were functioning on the level of Charles Ives either; for it is clear that when we talk of the American art music thrust, we are talking of a movement which, for the most part, flowed directly in accordance to the dictates of the European defining community, and there were reasons for this. But it is possible to trace a clear progressional movement from the time zone of Charles Ives until the present; and while the amount of composers who have sought to move towards an independent creative route are minimal compared to the mainstream of American composers, there can be no doubt that this alternative creative thrust did, at some point, affect the general reality of the Euro-American art music tradition. The alternative activity undertaken by the radical American stylists is an important factor that has dictated the entry of western art music as a factor in the present forming world music. In short, the Euro-American tradition has moved western art music towards the "source-transfer" shift in the forming composite aesthetic.

WAC-24

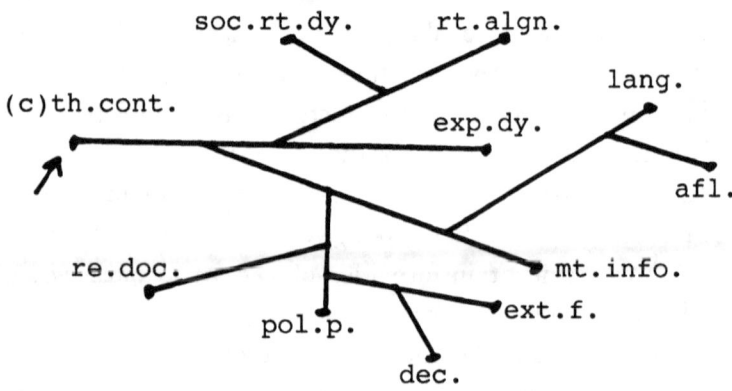

By the late thirties an independent creative continuum could be seen gathering momentum in America, and this continuum would move to later affect the composite reality of western art music. The forward momentum of this continuum must be viewed with respect to the unique developments which were reshaping American culture. For the Euro-American creative community can be viewed as the direct recipients of the legacy of western art music as dictated through the European continuum as well as the dynamics of transitional American society. Moreover, the Euro-American continuance would also be affected by the thrust continuum and accelerated dynamics of Charles Ives' activity. As such, the composite reality of Euro-American art creativity would move to establish a particular vibrational identity—and particular stylistic approach. The reality progression of Euro-American western art music then can be viewed with respect to the dynamic emergence of Ives' activity on through the establishment of the "League of Composers"—on through to the expanded developments of the fifties. Moreover, the reality continuum of Euro-American western art music would also greatly benefit from the many instrumentalists and composers from Europe who would make the decision to move to America. It would be impossible to measure the effect many of these people had on the accelerated momentum of Euro-American creativity. To list the important composers and teachers alone would be staggering, for among the people who would eventually end up in America would be—Varèse, Bartók,

Schoenberg—famous conductors; Toscanini, etc., etc. (even Stravinsky). The importance of this development cannot be underestimated. By the time zone of the late forties America could be viewed as a source-transfer continuum of western art music—as dynamic as Europe in many ways— and this has been the situation ever since.

The dynamic solidification of Euro-American western art music must be viewed with respect to what it posed for the western affinity insight principle. This is so because the reality alignment of American creativity did not have a traditional basis from which to practice extension—that it could call its own anyway. As such, the progressional continuum of extension participation in Euro-American classical music would move to function from the particulars of its own reality dynamics—and in doing so, this difference helped to establish its own isolated information focus. The nature of that information focus would have to do with understanding the reality of transfer extension activity in actual terms—that being, the dynamics of American culture (or anti-culture—as separate from Europe) could provide more than enough material for unique extension—which is to say, the reality of Euro-American western art music would have to do with the source-transfer utilization of indigenous American creativity with the reality continuum of the European information alignment. The realness of this position would greatly affect both the option possibilities of neo-classicism, as well as source-transfer extension possibilities. For the emergence of American participation in western art music would have a profound effect on the reality of composite European art music—yet I have not meant to over-estimate the achievements of any one group or nation (let alone the contributions surrounding how given source-transfer routes of creativity actualized). Because the underlying factor which determines the reality of a given extension has nothing to do with "who is best," or "what is best."

In America, the transition cycle of western art music must be viewed with respect to the reality implications of source-transfer extension. For the progressional continuance of creative extension in this context would focus on the dynamics of its regional members as a means to solidify a composite viewpoint and identity—and of course in many ways this was understandable, because a given creative extension must take into account the reality of its own "particulars." Without doubt the work of Charles Ives would come to be viewed as an important extensional platform for American creative progressionalism, and by the late thirties one could view a significant movement of composers whose work attempted to advance the reality position of Ives' activity. Any study of Euro-American western art music would only accent the contributions of these composers, for the achievements solidified in the late thirties and forties would establish the reality base of America's relationship to European culture (or at least America's relationship with the information continuum of composite western culture)—and this should not be taken lightly. The fact is, the dynamic contribution of composers like Henry Cowell, Lou Harrison, and Charlie Ruggles can be viewed in the same context that one views any source-transfer "real" initiation. For the solidification of their activity in the final analysis profoundly commented on the vibrational reality of American continuance. The activity of this group of composers could best be understood as the solidification of an extensional creativity that functioned with respect to the reality continuum of European culture, as a means to expand the information continuum and reality position of composite western art music—and also as a factor that would dictate the integration principle between American and European culture. Moreover, the nature of this same integration would allow for the development of an informational contingency that would be uniquely American in spirit, and one that would also expand the option spread possibilities of all "source transfer" activity.

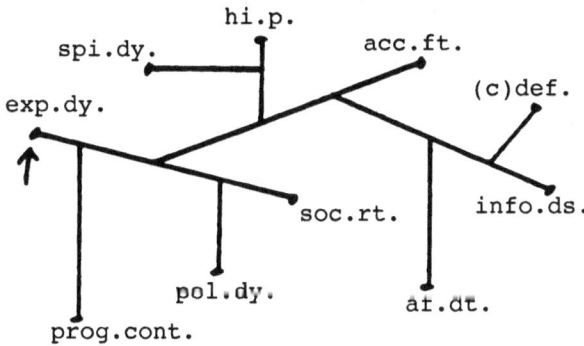
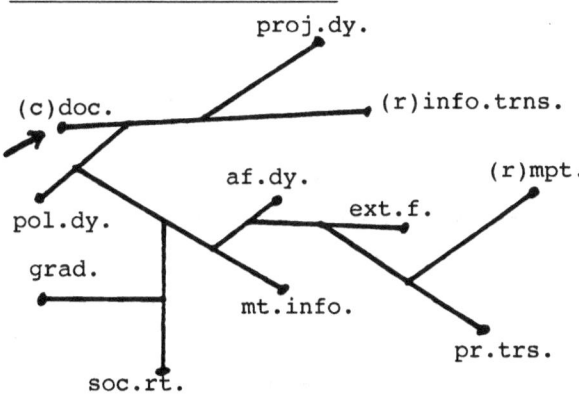
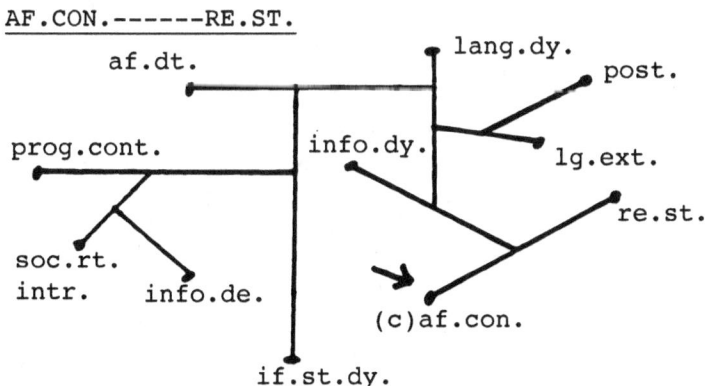

Quite possibly the significance of the American adaptation of western art music would have to do with what that adaptation posed with respect to source transfer. For the solidification of source-transfer extension in America would move to give life blood to the reality of neo-classicism by drawing on the dynamics of its own diversified culture. Moreover, the reality of source-transfer participation in this context—as opposed to serial participation—would move to give strength to the basic lining of composite western art music (giving the impression that "all is well with the aesthetic"—even though everyone knew that the traditional basis of the music would never be the same). Thus the diversification of America's utilization of "source-transfer-related extension" would move to affect the composite reality of the western aesthetic—while at the same time not threaten the vibrational basis of western extension. In other words, whatever processes the post-Ives continuum utilized, there was no attempt to separate the actual vibrational affinity reality of their work from the western art music composite aesthetical lining. The Euro-American movement can instead best be understood as a thrust that found original variations in its approach—rather than a school that was distinct in itself. At the same time, it would not be necessarily correct to state that this movement (Euro-American art music) hasn't affected the total reality of composite western art music in this time zone, for to view the particulars of progressional continuance would seem to suggest differently. In other words, even though the reality position of Euro-American creativity derives its meaning from its relationship to the composite scheme of western reality—and its related information continuum—it would be wrong to assume that the nature of that relationship implies no dynamics. For while the dynamic implications of Euro-American creativity in the thirties and forties affirmed the composite reality of European and western culture—the actual developments taking place on the physical universe level in this same period were changing more than what many people would like to admit. In other words, an American extensional thrust of western art music did gain momentum in the thirty year cycle from 1920 to 1950—and this thrust would not simply echo the reality position of European western art creativity.

If there is one composer whose work must be outlined and singled out—as representing what is best about the Euro-American projectional thrust—that composer would undoubtedly be Harry Partch. In fact, in many ways, the realness of this composer's contributions exceeds the parameter of any one context—or section of this book. Because the solidification of Partch's activity comments on more than just a style (or projection)—but rather on another reality context for creativity. Partch created his own instruments, his own notation—designed a ritual music, and also outlined his own aesthetic. This dynamic individual functioned completely separately from the American mainstream (or European mainstream for that matter) and in doing so allowed new insight into transformation participation. The thrust of his activity moved to reconnect composite functionalism (in western art music) with world music (i.e., Greek, African, and Asian). In my opinion, Partch's activity should be viewed as a cornerstone of transformational pedagogy—and should be required study in any university dealing with creativity.

It is important that some effort is made to understand the source-transfer implications of Euro-American art music. For the dynamic continuum of extension is not an isolated consideration but instead gives insight as to the composite factors forming the next cycle. The fact is, the source-transfer participation of European art music by America has moved to accelerate the composite nature of western continuance. Moreover, the reality implications of source-transfer extension must be viewed in the same context, for in the final analysis I am commenting on how given information lines are adopted for the composite dynamics of world information. The source-transfer extension of American creativity, as well as the work practiced by composers like Messiaen, would move to dictate the nature of the next vibrational extension of western art music—that being: extension with respect to the composite planet. The route then of a given source transfer must be viewed as the route transition and eventually transformation will take—yet I do not mean to over-generalize this important subject. The fact is, the dynamics of earth seem to be held together by the nature underlying how its information expansion is practiced. The spread of a given information line is directly related to how given "reality positions" solidified on the physical universe level—and "vibrational universe" as well. The collective adaptation of western art music by America and also Japan must be viewed in this same context—that being, the route of a given information line, and the nature underlying how dynamic extension is made compositely relevant with respect to its information focus. My point is that the significance of this phenomenon is not separate from the reality of dynamic transition—as regards the world community towards the resolidified world community (yet I do not mean to violate the context of this section)—and as regards the particulars surrounding the nature of a given expansion. As such, the Euro-American tradition must be viewed as a dynamic agent whose ultimate significance comments on the nature of its use of source-transfer extension—as a factor to make its primary information continuum relevant.

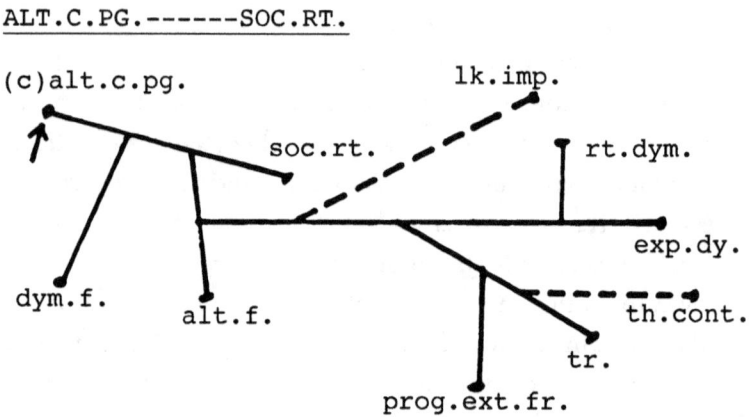

Post-Webern School

The solidification of dynamic post-Webern extension would move to reshape the continuum of western art music, and could be seen gaining momentum in the late forties. This would also be the time zone where many of the most dynamic students of serialism would begin to establish their own activity. As such, the end of the forties would see an important move to extend serialism as the next progressional functionalism for transitional western art music. To view the works which have been completed from the late forties until the middle sixties is to see the dynamic implications of serialism as an important extensional methodology. For the nature dictating how serialism has been utilized was not limited to one application but instead has underlined many different approaches. As such, if we are to understand the reality dynamics of the late seventies, it is important to have some awareness of serialism and the post-Webern continuum, because this movement would be directly related to the composite vibrational factors which helped to solidify the nature of what we are now dealing with in this cycle.

The reality dynamics of serial extension can be better understood if viewed with respect to the activity which took place in France, Germany, Italy, and the United States. This is not to say that only four countries have contributed to the extension of serialism—for many individuals from many different countries have greatly contributed to the thrust development of this phenomenon—rather, these four countries can be viewed as principal centers that moved to establish both unified research and dynamic composite extension lines vital to the continuance of the music. Moreover, many of the composers we have now come to view as representing what is "most dynamic" about serialism have come from one of these countries. Thus, the reality particulars surrounding serial extension can best be understood if some aspect of the various countries mentioned are viewed in their separate context.

There can be no doubt that the activity which took place in France must be considered important. For France has long functioned as one of the most progressive countries in western culture (with respect to how it traditionally has dealt with creativity, and also with respect to the vibrational nature of its environmental supporting dynamics). This is not to say that every sector in France immediately embraced serialism, because obviously this was not the case. The fact is, the progressional continuance of serial functionalism would be a difficult struggle—with half of the critical community against the music and the other half undecided—even worse, very few people really supported this music in its early period, and nothing has changed today. Nevertheless, much activity would take place in France, and the dynamics of this activity would move to affect the composite reality of serial extension. France would eventually move to become one of the best outlets for this music, and by the end of the sixties many of the most successful works of serial music would be premiered in Paris. Moreover, in the course of a given time period the creative continuum of Paris would greatly affect the information continuum of the music—which is to say, the information continuum that would clarify the reality dynamics of the music could be seen forming in centers like Paris.

The educational centers in France would also play an important role for advancing serial extension. A composer like Olivier Messiaen would affect three-fourths of all of the composers we have come to view as representing the first new wave group of serial composers. Messiaen's students would include: Boulez, Stockhausen, Xenakis, Berio, Ferrari—among others. Many of the institutions of France would also advance the reality position of serialism—both with respect to teaching its students about the existence of the music, as well as turning out future interpreters with an understanding of how to play it. The role of educational institutions in this context should not be lightly viewed because the sophistication of total culture support in France would establish a high level of interest in the music and also attract its most prized students. Even more important, given concerts of creative serial music would be performed throughout practically all of the educational creative institutions in France.

The French government itself would also provide many different kinds of assistance to help the music. In the fifties, the government, through its subsidy of the radio, would contribute to many of the collective and individual projects which were undertaken as a means to further the nature of creative serial extension. Some of these projects would involve the development of new instruments for creativity, and some would involve the funding of different compositions and/or performance possibilities. This assistance would greatly benefit the composite reality of the music, and also add to its continuance. By the late sixties, the reality effect of this support could be viewed for how it had assisted the music. For the basic continuum of post-Webern activity has dynamically extended, and in doing so has greatly contributed to the thrust continuum of earth creativity. Yet it would not be correct to only focus on the role of the government in advancing serial music without also commenting on the dynamic participation of given individuals, for the extension of a given projection is not about the assistance given that projection in economic terms, but instead is about the people or persons whose vision and participation are realized.

Certainly if I can cite the work of Olivier Messiaen as important for how it effected the thrust continuum of serial music (i.e., his actual music as well as the instruction he gave to the first generation of post-Webern composers), then I must also mention the important role Pierre Boulez played as well. Boulez's activity would be an important factor for establishing the "nature" of dynamic functionalism in French culture. The implications of his work would affect every area of the culture, for the reality implications of Boulez's activity would transcend mere composition. Instead Boulez would move to reshape the educational reality of creative music in France, and also help establish alternative performing outlets. As such, if any one figure is to be viewed as necessarily responsible for the reality of post-Webern extension in France, that person would be Pierre Boulez.

To view the reality of post-Webern activity in France is to view a dynamic continuum that has contributed to the composite reality of western art continuance. This contribution has been realized throughout the dynamics which surround France's total information focus—that being, the work which took place in the educational communities throughout France, and the move to establish performing outlets for the music.

Germany must also be viewed for its contribution to post-Webern progressionalism. By the end of the forties this country would play an important role in defining the nature of serialism as well as the resulting directions that continuum would pursue. The dynamics of extended electronic technology would begin to form during this cycle, and by the middle of the fifties Germany would have a major center for electronic music study in Cologne (Köln). It would be practically impossible to separate the achievements in serial music and extended functionalism from the particulars that underlined German functionalism during the forties and fifties. Germany must be viewed as important as France—and later

Italy—for its ability to shape the direction and reality of post-serialism. Many composers would come to live and work in Europe during this cycle, and the German government would play an important role by providing assistance for the music. This was one of the first countries to help accelerate the dynamics of the post-Webern continuum by providing performance possibilities and/or financial backing, as well as media exposure. The time period of the fifties and sixties would also see the forming of many new festivals for contemporary music—like the one in Donaueschingen, as well as new courses taught in music schools throughout Germany. One cannot underestimate the importance of this assistance.

The thrust of the fifties would see several basic creative movements in Germany, and the realness of this phenomenon would help to expand the spectrum of contemporary creative music to even greater heights. Composers like Mauricio Kagel would come to live and pursue the activity in Germany, and practically every established figure in post-Webern creativity would have some involvement with the scene in Germany during this period. American composers like John Cage would regularly travel and perform throughout both Germany and France, and this is also true for individual musicians and/or interpreters (e.g., David Tudor). It is unfortunate that so little has been documented about this time period because there were many different movements happening throughout the whole of Europe. For all practical purposes most of this activity has been lost for posterity—and that is unfortunate to say the least. The last decade and some has begun to see some recordings of new composers and hopefully some of this music will be distributed internationally for the greater public. Certainly the works of a composer like Hans Werner Henze must be considered important for the composite musicians and listeners' community, for the thrust of his creativity has opened many new areas for creative investigation.

If there is one composer from Germany whose activity has dictated the reality of post-Webern progressionalism, that composer would undoubtedly be Karlheinz Stockhausen. Stockhausen's activity has clearly demonstrated one of the most dynamic utilizations of post-Webern techniques and extended functionalism in this period. The thrust of his work has moved to re-dictate the reality spectrum of serialism and while doing so has also pointed the way towards future directions. Unlike many of the structuralists in the early fifties who composed serial compositions in either the post-Webern style or the Boulez extension of that route, Stockhausen has continued to develop his own separate viewpoint and information focus. The spectrum of his work clearly has shown the realness of independent creative insight as well as extended functionalism—regardless of context. I believe his activity to be mandatory for any person seeking to understand or experience the particulars of post Webern progressionalism. For the significance of his work transcends one dimension—or style, and instead moves to give insight as to the whole of composite functionalism and creative dynamics.

The reality of serial extension has greatly benefited from the various levels of participation that can be found in Germany and France, and yet I have not meant to give the impression that any one area's involvement with serialism is totally different from the rest of the planet—for the reality continuum of serialism can be viewed as dynamic in all of the countries I previously mentioned.

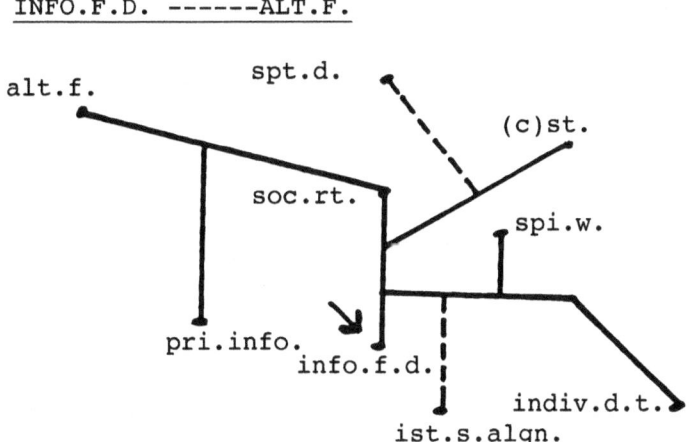

The dynamic acceleration of post-Webern creativity in Europe would see the emergence of many new and exciting compositions. From the middle of the forties to the middle of the sixties, it is now possible to view a spectrum of new works that clearly shows the beauty of this thrust progression. All of these works could be viewed for how they developed the basic idea scheme of Webern's early establishment of a "point"—music—but to new heights. It is unfortunate that this thrust projection was interpreted only in intellectual and/or negative terms to the general public, for many would be quite surprised to discover that serialism and post-Webern creativity is not outside of something that could be positively experienced. Nevertheless, the collective participation of European applied serialism would move to advance the reality of post-Webern activity to the next junction—both with respect to its vibrational dynamics as well as its transfer expansion implications. **In other words, the post-Webern movement which solidified in the late forties would be the group that would vibrationally and functionally move to determine the "reality position" of composite western extension up until the end of the fifties.**

There has also been a post-Webern continuity in America which elaborated on the dynamics of serialism—and it would not necessarily be correct to assume their activity had no effect on the composite reality of post-Webern extension. For the American post-Webern movement would involve many creative composers—from Elliott Carter to Milton Babbitt—and the dynamics of composite post-Webern extension has most certainly benefited from their participation. The focus of this American movement would emanate from various universities throughout the country—in particular, Columbia University in New York City would come to be identified as a platform for post-Webern extension. The work of Charles Wuorinen and Harvey Sollberger would be associated with this movement, and by the end of the sixties the composite reality of transitional serialism would see many dynamic new works brought forth from this juncture.

The dynamics of Euro-American post-Webern extension are not limited to only one section of America, but instead could be experienced throughout the country. Probably the most basic factor that has suppressed

WAC-37

the reality dynamics of midwest or west coast creative post-Webern involvement would be the information focus of American culture. For the collected forces of American society have been designed to effectively comment on the reality particulars of only New York City—and its so-called art community—at the expense of the rest of the country. As such, the work of composers like Ralph Shapey in Chicago has largely been ignored—and this is true for the greater reality of the country as well. But active post-Webern extension—and participation—can be experienced throughout the whole of America from the east to the west coast. Hopefully one day we will have more possibilities to experience this music, for at present the composite reality of American post-Webern activity is distorted and suppressed. There has been only a handful of recordings of this music, and of these records maybe thirty percent have ever really had any distribution. Whenever the reality of this music is finally unveiled many people will be surprised at the volume of works which have been produced. For it is important to understand that the creative continuum of American post-Webern activity has its own reality dynamics—which is to say, this music has not simply echoed the activity taking place in Europe. As such, the realness of Euro-American extended serialism must be viewed with respect to the dynamics of alternative functionalism—having to do with the emergence of alternative technology developments (as a factor directly related to the continuum of extended methodology) and also having to do with alternative moves to expand the structural dynamics of its basic operational arena (i.e., form). One thing is clear: there has been no move towards restructuralism—either in terms of functionalism or philosophy—or expansion (with respect to information focus) that the Euro-American continuum has not been as equally involved in as its European counterpart—moreover, there has been no alternative creative direction embraced by the composite European creative community that has not been greatly affected by the Euro-American school. In short, the significance of the Euro-American schools' emergence in western art music is much greater than is generally recognized.

Thus to view the reality brilliance of post-Webern extensions is to have some understanding of the diversity of activity in all of the countries

I have mentioned previously (i.e., France, Germany, Italy, and the USA). Certainly there is much more to write about this movement, and I cannot pretend that my general outline of this continuum is complete on any level. Hopefully this information can give a more balanced viewpoint about this subject—especially when integrated into the whole of this book—and this series of books. For the realness of post-Webern extension must become better understood because this creative continuum has had an important effect on the reality of composite western creativity (and world creativity) as it advanced to the fifties and sixties. Yet I have not meant to imply that only one projection has determined the reality of any period—for certainly this is not the case. Instead, the reality of a given period has to do with the dynamics underlying what spectrum of vibrations is engaged—and this is true whether we are focusing on the reality of a composite period (i.e., having to do with the spectrum of events that "naturally" take place in a given phenomenon) or having to do with the natural diversity that is inherent in a given thrust continuum (that being, the dynamics of both information focus and affinity dynamics as made real from a principle-thrust reality). As such, **the thrust extension of post-Webern activity can be viewed with respect to the importance of its position in the continuum of transitional western art music—with the understanding being that the phenomenon of serialism was one important additive (or contribution) among many.** For just as neo-classicism can be viewed as one development that determined the reality of western creative continuance— as it was made real in the thirties and forties (on through to the middle fifties)—it is important to not over-elevate any technique as the only factor that determined the composite reality position of western art music (or any continuum for that matter). All of these considerations are only isolated factors that must be compositely integrated into the total multi-context. Because while both of these developments would shape the reality of western art music in its early transition period, the fact is, no one consideration would dictate the later reality of western extension. Even more surprising is the realness that the second extension continuum after serial extension did not actualize in Europe, but instead in America. Thus, to view the reality extension of western art music is to deal with the dynamics of post-Webern continuance as well as that other continuum—which in this case is the movement we now have come to call the John Cage School.

The dynamic emergence of the Cage movement would challenge the reality of western creativity in that its natural dynamics would pose a threat to the composite lining of western pedagogy. This is not to say that Cage's activity was outside of the composite reality of western affinity dynamics—because it wasn't; rather, the significance of his activity would have to do with the implications which surrounded his information reality. For in many ways Cage's activity could be viewed in the same context as the neo-classicists—that being, extension with respect to source transfer. The reality thrust of Cage's activity would move to link the vibrational continuum of western functionalism to that of the world group (or more particularly Indian culture) as a means for continuance. Yet the nature underlying how Cage's activity actualized would create another crisis in the composite arena of western art circles. For the musicians of this continuum (e.g., Earle Brown, Feldman, Wolff) would move to challenge the composite reality of alternative functionalism in every context imaginable. To deal with the composite reality of transitional western art music is to have some understanding of this continuum—and what it posed, because the vibration created by this movement has yet to be properly dealt with.

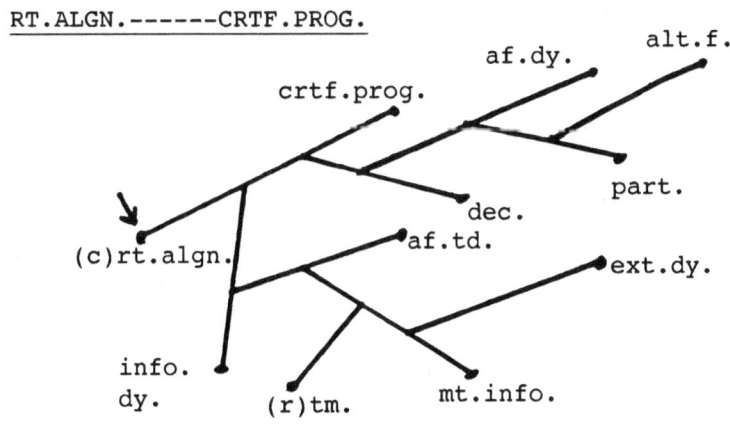

WAC-40

The basic continuum of the Cage movement would move to clarify the reality position of the western aesthetic. For this movement would all but ignore the reality of traditional western empirical methodology and instead move to expand the composite dynamics of western affinity dynamics. The continuum of this group would shed insight into the real reality position of western creativity, for the accelerated continuum of contemporary music since World War I had never really come to terms with the implications of its philosophical basis (that being, the realness that spiritualism for all practical purposes had been destroyed as an actual factor in the vibrational and functional reality of western pedagogy—and "information degrees"). As such, the Cage movement would in its natural continuance challenge the reality of contemporary western methodology. This would be a movement that utilized any- and everything as a means to function. In fact, the reality extension of the Cage continuum would move to re-establish "creativity" rather than real transitional methodology—although Cage's use of the *I Ching* must be viewed as an attempt to establish a spiritual overview with respect to the notion of "doing." But the dynamic momentum of this movement would eventually come to solidify the lunatic fringe wing of western information dynamics. Their activity—and especially Cage's himself—would greatly affect the reality options of transitional creativity, and in doing so, his isolated activity must be viewed as possibly more significant than both serialism and neo-classicism combined (at least for how it would affect the composite implications of extension in the fifties).

To understand the significance of the Cage movement is to also understand the reality situation of western art music as it entered into the time zone of the fifties. For the solidification of serial music would see the acceleration of complexity as the natural extension possibility for procedure. Many of the serial composers would become so involved in the techniques of their work that their actual music would move to become an affirmation of a given system rather than actual creativity. The Cage movement would bring all of this into focus—and in doing so would also clarify the dynamics of methodology (i.e., the dynamics of pointillism as separate from serial techniques—the extension possibilities of electronic music and musique concrète as separate from a formulaic approach). Moreover, the extension dynamics of the Cage movement would move with respect to the western affinity insight principle—as far as how it utilized the inherent creative possibilities of 20th-century earth. Cage has written compositions utilizing the most dynamic spectrum of creative approaches, and he has pioneered the emergence of extended composition. All of these advances have been incorporated into the general mainstream of creative music—and this is true even though Cage's actual activity has never really been accepted.

It is important to acknowledge that all of the individuals who functioned with Cage were instrumental in reshaping the particulars of this movement as well—because Cage did not solidify the reality of alternative extension by himself. Certainly the work of Earle Brown has greatly contributed to the reality of extended creativity. It was Brown who really initiated the concept of extended composition, and it is unfortunate that his activity has been given so little credit and exposure with respect to what he has actually contributed. The dynamics of Morton Feldman's activity must also be mentioned, because he was also involved in many of the changes that reshaped alternative creativity during the fifties. I have referred to this movement as the Cage movement because this term has been the most convenient (and also because this is usually how this movement is referred to), but in fact the dynamics of this movement were not about any single person. All of the composers I have mentioned (and many others I have not mentioned) were equally important for what they contributed. The dynamics of the Cage movement would be the generating factor for creative music extension in the fifties, and the diversity of this movement would greatly add to the vibrational nature of alternative creativity (in terms of perception and practice).

The reality of methodology in transitional western art music would move to embrace several processes—there would be the dynamic continuance of serialism as defined through the traditional solidification of western application—the emergence of indeterminacy, as a concept which utilized extended composition and "actual" (or what is now referred to as "real") time—and the continuing practice of neo-classicism as a source-initiation extension. All of these considerations would establish the reality of transition for creative music from the western art music continuum. Any attempt to really understand the "reality of progressionalism" would imply that the nature of this period of creativity is understood—on some level. Certainly there is more to this subject than what is included in this book—for the reality implications of extended functionalism (as a subject that reshaped western creativity in the fifties and sixties) has only been lightly touched. But the progressional expansion of western art music, as commented on in this section—with respect to what has been dealt with, as far as given movements and their reality particulars—does give some insight as to what has happened, and this information should be of positive use to the reader.

(Level One)
CREATIVE MUSIC FROM THE BLACK AESTHETIC

THE TRANSITION OF CREATIVE MUSIC from the black aesthetic in the 1960s must be looked at from several necessary perspectives: (1) the incredible absorption of the western harmonic and functional arena in a time period of fifty to sixty years and thus the need to go beyond western functionalism and definitions; (2) the gradual acknowledgement among creative restructuralists that the functional arena of creative music did not necessarily meet their vibrational and conceptual needs; and (3) the physical universe particulars that would dictate the composite climate for social reality in the sixties. To really understand the reality expansion of creative music is to have some awareness of each of these perspectives, for the progressional implications of black creativity are not one-dimensional. It is also important that one has some idea as to the relatively brief existence of transitional black creativity—for many of us have come to view the music with the mistaken belief that American black creativity is as old as European art music or world creativity. The fact is, the solidification of transitional black creativity—as actualized in America—is a recent event as far as creativity is concerned, and this should be kept in mind. Moreover, the projectional extension of creative black music has seen one of the most rapid expansions in this cycle—for the emergence of the post-Parker continuum, and the resulting vibrational implications of that thrust, actually only lasted from 1940 to 1960—a span of only twenty years—before the projectional reality of the music would move to its next transition cycle. Thus if we are to understand the transitional reality of creative music from the black aesthetic, then we must attempt to view the reality and vibrational implications of accelerated expansion. Each progression of black creativity in this context must be viewed with respect to what it reveals about the "path nature" of alternative activity—having to do with the nature of what its extension implies about source initiation and source-transfer progressionalism.

CMBA-2

The composite continuance of black creativity in the Americas has been so dynamic that very few people have been able to accurately comment on the music—and there are many reasons for this. Certainly the mis-definitions of the western defining and controlling community have moved to undermine the progressional significance of the music— and this is true whether we are focusing on the reality of creative music in its early period or the present. One of the most basic distortions that have come to permeate creative black music is the notion that every given thrust extension must necessarily represent a breakage in the composite identity of the music. In other words, no thrust extension of creative black music is perceived with respect to what its emergence signifies about the composite continuance of black creativity, but instead extension is used as a vehicle to challenge the reality position of black culture. As such, misinterpretations which have accompanied every extension of black creativity must be viewed with respect to what the white establishment has presumed is the "essence" of black creativity—as opposed to how this "essence" is perceived by black people themselves. The end result of this phenomenon is directly related to the progressional "jazz is dead" death wish that has regularly been a feature in the information dynamics surrounding the music. Every extension of black creativity has been isolated as a means to not deal with the composite transitional implications of alternative functionalism.

To really view the reality continuum of black creativity is to have some awareness of its vibrational and actual spread. For the absorption of western functionalism would not exclusively dictate the reality options of any particular projectional path; rather, the total dynamics of source initiation and/or source transfer would serve to actualize another creative continuum. To really understand the transitional nature of black creativity is to have insight as to how a given principle affected the natural dynamics of a given projectional expansion. This is not to underrate the nature underlying how western functionalism was absorbed into the progressive continuum of black creativity, but only to clarify what this absorption means. Certainly it is clear that the solidification of American black creativity would naturally move to incorporate various elements of western functionalism—for in reality, there was no other option (with the physical universe position of black people being as it was, no other possibility existed)—but the dynamics of this absorption would dictate another vibrational position for alternative functionalism. Thus to view the dynamic reality of black creativity from its early period until today is to see an alternative continuum very separate from the composite reality of western art music—or American music, for that matter. Every thrust development of creative black music would reveal both the expanded dynamics of its principal methodology as well as an expanded affinity alignment with respect to the particulars of its physical universe path. Even more important, it is now possible to view the composite progressional continuance of the music with respect to what this increased methodological acceleration implies about alternative transition. For the progressional spread of black creativity comments on both the linear expansion of the actual music as well as the route that alternative world transition has taken as a means to be "effective" and as a means to be in accordance to the "greater" forces which dictate "real change."

The source-initiation implications of creative black music can better be understood by viewing the dynamic continuum of particular creative routes. For to experience the progressional activity that has solidified black folk music on through to what is now called contemporary extended creativity is to see a clear projectional continuance which has defined its own reality. In other words, the dynamic continuance of source-initiation creativity in black music would move to completely solidify its own methodology—which had little to do with a synthesis between western and African methodology in any applied sense, but instead had more to do with the natural continuance of affinity dynamics (which in this case involved the vibrational continuance of African creativity to Afro-American creativity). Even the so-called use of western functionalism must be seen in the right context, for the harmonies and instruments that would come to make up the reality of black folk music and blues really can be traced back to Africa as well. The fundamentals that would move to solidify American black creativity would be chosen because they either approximated or vibrationally signified some aspect of source-initiated related activity—from the African experience. **There are several creative** routes that we can view as a means to understand the progressional realness of source-initiated black creativity in the sixties: (1) the continuum which established alternative functionalism, (2) the dynamic use of improvisation as a necessary discipline for creative investigation (with respect to the affinity insight principle as it concerns both the individual and the culture), and (3) the transitional implications of alternative dynamics as a necessary factor for composite continuance. Thus to understand the reality position of black creativity—and its relationship to source initiation—it is important that these contexts are understood on some level. For the reality of transition transcends any one principle—or creative projection. Instead, we are commenting on the composite dynamics of a total reality continuum.

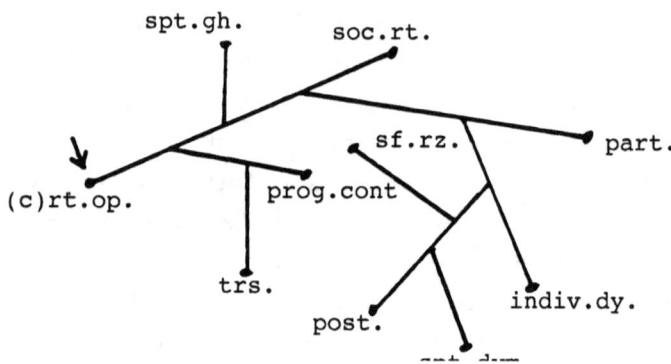

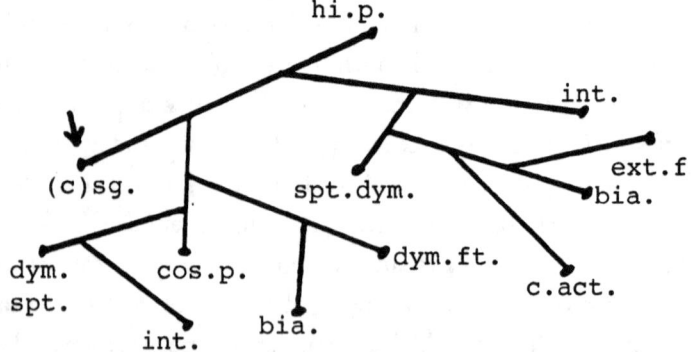

The dynamics of transition can better be understood if social reality particulars are taken into account—and this is especially true if we are to understand the progressional implications of black creativity. For unlike western art music, which provides fuel for the philosophic and defining community that interprets information dynamics for the exclusiveness of western culture, the reality of black creativity is directly related to the factors which are shaping the composite society. This is not to say that western art music has no relationship to the people, nor have I meant to imply that black creativity has no expanded implications—with respect to its pedagogy—rather, the net position of a given creative thrust is directly affected by whether or not that thrust is viewed as representing the reality tone of its cultural group (and clearly western culture does not view black creativity as representing what is most real about western culture). The fact is, the dynamic implications of black creativity are being felt, rather than understood, for no efforts have been put forth to deal with the progressional implications of alternative creativity—and this is true whether we are focusing on the information scan of western education and/or western media interpretation. Thus if one is to view the reality effects of black music, it is important that the social context of these effects is taken into account, because the source-initiation implications of transition in black creativity cannot simply be separated from the dynamics of its total position. In other words, source-initiation progressionalism in black creativity is not so much about a particular form as much as about a vibrational alignment that permeates a given methodology. This is not to say that no given projections of black creativity have emerged to affect the greater reality of western culture in a source-initiation context—because obviously this is not the case—rather, if we are to really understand black creativity then it is important that the "nature" of a given methodology is understood. For the reality of source initiation in black creativity must be viewed with respect to whether or not a given form allows for a particular vibrational nature (and that vibrational nature has to do with the primary information and vibrational continuum which solidifies black culture in its essence state—or most basic state). Thus if we are to view the reality affect of black creativity in transition then it is important that the physical universe response to that change is commented on—on some level.

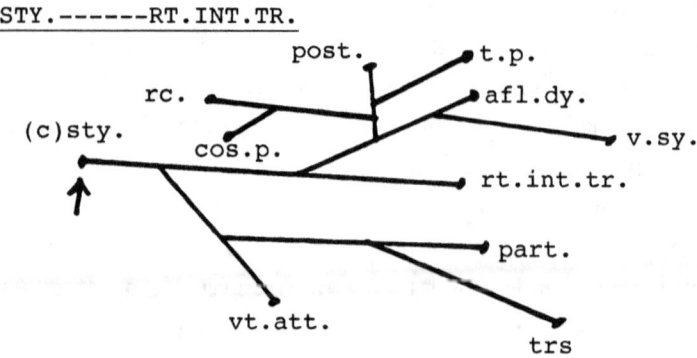

Without doubt the composite continuum of black creativity can be viewed as a profound stimulant for the reality of progressional dynamics in western culture—and this is true on many different levels. Not only has the consideration of language in black creativity been totally adopted by the composite society (regardless of sector) but this is true on several different levels. For the dynamic implications of language in black creativity (i.e., music, dance, and speaking language) has moved to profoundly alter the composite landscape of western culture. Moreover, in every case, the progressional continuance of black language has functioned as alternative functionalism—with the significance of that functioning having to do with establishing transitional applications of the affinity-insight principle either as a means to "is" given periods or as a means to postulate a desired period. Thus it is possible to view the progressional reality of black creativity with respect to the actual music as well as the implications related to what that music signified in alternative terms.

If we are to really understand the reality of transition in the sixties—as this question involves the progressional implications of black creativity—then it is important that some attempt is made to clarify the nature of what extended functionalism posed in this context. For the meta and functional arena of black creativity, in its inception, solidified a dynamic functionalism that was quite different from western art music. The dynamics of this functionalism would involve another level of both organization as well as creativity responsibility (the use of improvisation, as practiced to affirm the dynamics of the individual to the greater reality of the total culture), and this information is essential to the dictates of black culture transition. By extended functionalism in this context, I am commenting on the dynamic meta and functional reality consequences of the new forms that would solidify in the sixties—in terms of what new responsibilities these developments would establish for the transitional musician. Extended functionalism in this context then would have to do with the emergence of these forms to accelerate the affinity insight principle as well as the dynamics that these extensions carried for progressional continuance. **There are several degrees of extended functionalism and accelerated dynamics: (1) for the individual, (2) for the collective, (3) for the society, (4) for transformation, and (5) as a necessary route for world culture to take for resolidification.** All of these contexts can shed light on the reality of transition as it concerns creative black music. In other words, to deal with the transitional consequences of progression, we cannot only look at the actualization of the music—or of a given music—but instead, we must include the reality factors which help define the music as well.

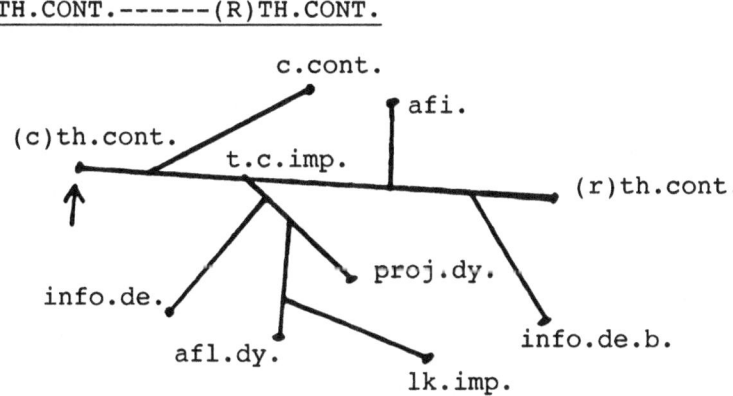

The concept of extended functionalism for the individual involves understanding what the vibrational and physical universe factors in the sixties dictated in terms of "character" or "identity." This time cycle would be significant for how it would establish the reality continuance of composite American culture—and as such, must be viewed as a pivotal juncture in determining the vibrationaltory nature of composite western information dynamics. The intensity of this period can also be viewed as directly related to the emergence of extended functionalism, for the progressional development of the sixties would move to transform the vibrational arena of alternative (as well as commercial) creativity on several levels. Extended functionalism for black creativity in this context can be viewed with respect to the nature underlying how investigation would be pursued—in actual terms. For the emergence of artists like Ornette Coleman and Cecil Taylor would clarify the methodological position of creativity from the black experience—that being, the thrust of their investigation would no longer adhere to any one methodologically imposed criterion (even if that criterion had only to do with source-transfer observations as opposed to real insight); instead, their activity would expand in accordance to the dynamic principles of alternative affinity dynamics (from the meta-reality of black culture). The realness of this new position would have a profound impact on the composite reality of the music, for the dynamic acceleration of extended functionalism—after the initiation of Coleman and Taylor—would forecast the composite reality of earth creativity and life (that is, the solidification of expanded functionalism would not only comment on the music but also on the progressional reality of earth creativity in the sense that western art music and western culture had now come to a decline in terms of their (or its) ability to assert source-transfer definitions on composite earth creativity as a means to make outside initiations conform with its (western culture's) reality position).

CMBA-9

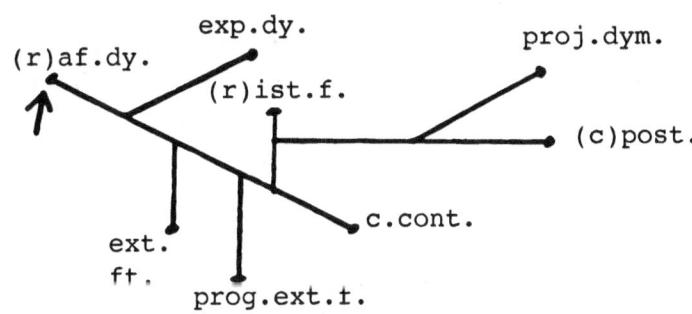

The first degree of awareness in extended functionalism is creativity and creativity methodology as a factor to actualize "self realization" on the part of the person practicing the discipline. Which is to say, the first degree of extended functionalism would see given individuals moving to define their own solutions to progressional continuance in creativity. The reality of this participation would see the development of alternative functionalism with respect to how a given postulation is "made real" through the affinity dynamic principle implications of functionalism. As such, the reality of post-Coleman/Taylor creativity can be viewed as a dynamic move to re-investigate both information dynamics and refunctionalism—as vibrationally motivated through given individual life experiences and feelings. The western press would move to view this movement as a movement with no sophistication, rather than a dynamic movement that established new information lines (and there are many reasons for this—for the collective forces of western culture by their very nature could not be prepared for affinity dynamic re-interpretation from the black community).

The second degree of extended functionalism has to do with the vibrational implications of collected participation in alternative creativity. For the dynamic implications of creative postulation in this context have to do with the nature underlying how given information and vibrational zones are experienced "as a real consideration" by two or more participants. The difference between this degree and "self-realization" is that the reality of collected participation moves towards establishing a greater effect on the composite nature of "functioning." As such, the completion of this degree would establish the thrust realness of the music's existence (as concerns the musicians' community) and the actuality of this juncture would also serve as a momentum factor for all of the future extensions that would follow. Thus the progressional spread of extended functionalism from this context would move to transform the composite reality of creative music in the sixties—affecting both individuals and later the lining of the composite culture itself. It is important that the reality of extended functionalism is viewed as the platform which allowed for transitional creativity to develop. This is true for the post-Coleman/Taylor continuum, and this is also true for every subsequent projection which has followed. In other words, the dynamics of extended functionalism have dictated the composite reality of transitional black creativity—and this is true on every level (whether we are referring to rock music and/or television commercials). As such, it is important that this phenomenon is viewed in every possible context, so that we can better understand the dynamics of progressional continuance.

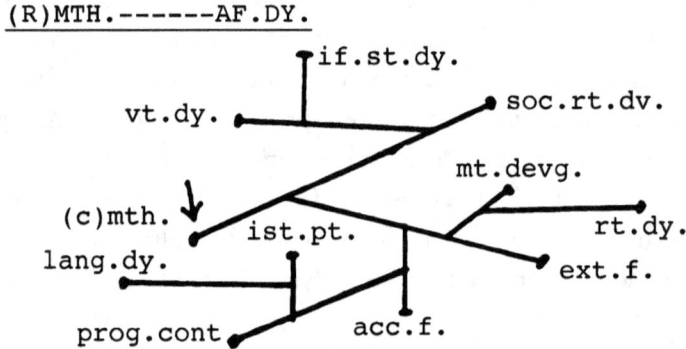

CMBA-11

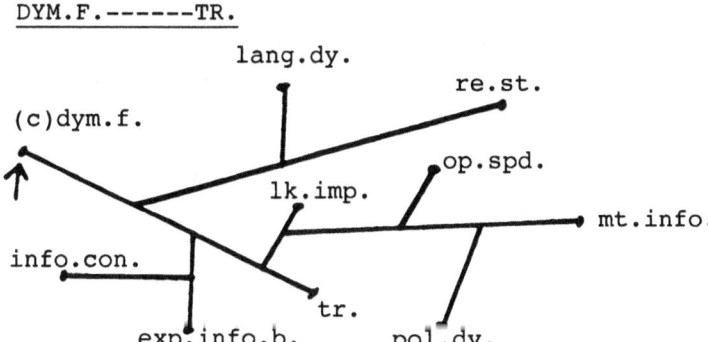

In 1960 several functional and vibrational routes solidified in transitional black creativity, and each of those routes would dictate a particular reality progression as well as a composite dynamic cultural position. All of these particular routes would come to establish the option spread position of transitional black creativity—and in doing so, these routes also established the alternative functional paths that would determine the activity of the sixties on through to the seventies. The projections actualized in this cycle could be separated into several categories: (1) there was the movement which moved towards modal concepts as a means to open up the harmonic complications which had developed by the end of the fifties; (2) there was the movement which moved to completely abandon the conventional harmonic reality of western functionalism as a means to explore the natural or vibrational implications of open harmony; (3) there was the movement which sought to participate exclusively in given reality projections of creative music (and in doing so, establish affinity lines to the composite continuum of the music); (4) there was the movement that abandoned periodicity as an underlying functional tool for transitional methodology; and finally (5) there was the movement which established the nature of contemporary source-transfer extension (that being, the dynamics of available creative routes and what this would imply for the progressional realness of fusion towards world culture solidification). Yet it would be wrong to necessarily perceive of any of these movements as completely separated from each other—because in several instances a given movement would function in accordance to several of these creative route possibilities. This is so because few musicians restricted their development to only one path of creative growth. Instead, the dynamics of the sixties' transition would stimulate the reality of alternative investigation—regardless of area. Thus a musician like Freddie Hubbard could be put in several different categories; for by the middle sixties this one musician had participated in practically every movement in the music before deciding on the path that best fit his needs. The sixties were characterized by the diversity of alternative possibilities that would mark an important cycle in American progressionalism. All of the activity that would emerge in this period would establish the projectional spread of alternative functionalism for the coming decades. By the end of this cycle the only other alternative consideration that would emerge as a dynamic thrust continuum would be the acceleration of "jazz rock" as a source-transfer tool for commercial manipulation. The time zone of the sixties would prove invaluable for solidifying the dynamics of alternative investigation. This period both provided an arena for the emergence of new forms as well as the necessary intensity needed to actualize results. As such, the reality of the sixties' transition must be properly documented—on as many levels as possible.

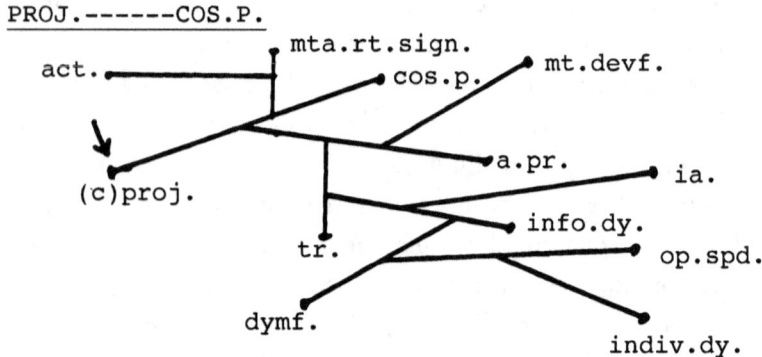

The transitional implications of alternative functionalism in creative black music—as it applied to the consideration of harmony—could be seen forming in the middle fifties. From this transition, two functional routes would emerge, and both of these routes would establish the "particulars" of progressional dynamics in alternative extended methodology—at least up until the sixties. The first route would be the expansion principle related to the natural acceleration of principle information lines. In this context, the activity of a musician like Thelonious Monk would dictate a projectional path for harmonic extension. Monk's music would play a pivotal role in establishing the second degree of information extension (from reality solidification to extended application—and as such shaping the nature underlying how complexity could successfully be utilized). The thrust of his activity would extend the reality of harmonic functionalism as it related to the dynamics of post-Parker re-established functionalism. Moreover, his activity would establish the later reality position of the extended so-called bop school that moved into the sixties and seventies. For the most basic factor that would underline extension bebop would be the use of traditional bebop functionalism with an expanded harmonic and rhythmic application. The dynamics of Monk's music would greatly clarify the solidification of extension bebop, and lay a basis for the next continuum of pianists as well. Thus to view the reality of Monk's music is to see a principle factor whose particulars established the progressional position for such diverse musicians as Paul Bley, Bill Evans, Herbie Hancock, and Chick Corea. This is not to say that any of these pianists play like Thelonious Monk—because they don't; rather, my point is that the reality of Monk's activity has underlined the progressional functional path that all of these musicians have taken (yet there are other factors related to this viewpoint which also must be stated, for the dynamic expansion of applied functionalism—which in this case is harmony—does not necessarily help us understand the diversity of creative applications that have also influenced the composite music—for instance, the work of a musician like Bill Evans can also be viewed with respect to his position in the composite progressional lining of this phenomenon—as regards to his position in the chain of events with respect to Monk—as well as for the influence that his own activity would generate—that being, the reality dynamics of his use of extended functionalism).

But the notion of alternative harmonic extension in creative black music cannot be viewed in narrow terms, for the progressional documentation that surrounds the music does not lend itself to blanket generalizations. The fact is, it is possible to view the dynamic functionalism of a pianist like Art Tatum as the most basic generating source of his period—the effects of which have carried over to even the middle fifties and sixties. Yet to understand what this means is to see the dilemma in attempting to separate the composite reality of black creativity; for Tatum's activity is supposed to be outside of the bebop reality—that is, his work is documented as preceding the alternative Parker continuum. Nevertheless, one can view a clear lineage from the solidification of Tatum's functionalism on through Oscar Peterson (whose activity is labeled bebop) that finally encompassed every pianist from Herbie Nichols to Cecil Taylor. The reality of this lineage can be viewed with respect to the dynamics of transitional harmonic functionalism—that being, the progressional move to explore the dynamic implications of harmony while respecting the basic fundamentals of "the focused" traditional methodology. To view the reality of black creativity in transition is to have some awareness of what this creative route has meant to the music. For the composite spread, and application, of extended harmony from this juncture would help dictate the reality of composite transitional creativity—both in the sixties as well as the seventies.

The reality of progressional extended functionalism can be viewed as a major factor that determines the vibrational position of source-initiated methodology—as practiced in the sixties. Musicians like Andrew Hill would contribute a special viewpoint in this regards, and the dynamics of his music would exist as a separate alignment from the post-Coleman/Taylor continuum of what I will call "atonality" (even though in actuality none of these routes had anything to do with atonality or tonality as defined by western definitions). The basic spread of this projectional route would clarify the reality position of source-initiated extension with respect to alternative functionalism—that being, extended functionalism as a consideration that is conducive for gaining insight into the composite reality position of black culture—and its related forces. Hopefully we will soon enter a period where the functional dynamics and individual contributions raised in source-initiation extension can become better known to the greater public. For the intensity of the sixties was not necessarily conducive to viewing the realness of extended methodology—because this period was more aligned toward restructuralism as a transformation possibility. As such, many of the gains that were realized through "actual participation" were either neglected or distorted. A renewed attempt to investigate this area of musical achievement could be greatly beneficial for understanding the achievements of such musicians as Herbie Hancock or Wes Montgomery—and/or again Bill Evans. For the dynamics of a given composite transition is not about only one sector of its variables, but instead concerns the total information particulars of its zone.

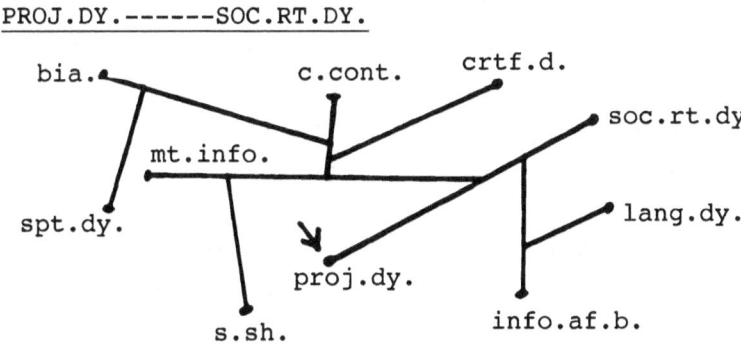

If we are to have a real understanding of harmonic extension then it is important to not limit the nature of what this concept poses for both source initiation as well as source transfer. This is so because no systematic function is indicative of only one aspect of principle information, but instead every given functionalism equally affirms the composite implications of thrust dynamics. Certainly the progressional continuum of methodology from black creativity can be viewed with respect to how its vibrational particulars have been advanced from cycle to cycle, but the dynamic implications of this extension have not occurred at the expense of its cosmic reality. In other words, the natural momentum of the alternative methodological post-Parker continuum would affect the greater spectrum of its affinity alignments—and this phenomenon can be viewed with respect to both its positive and negative aspects. To really understand the transitional expansion of source-initiated methodology—which in this case is the reality expansion of harmony—is to be aware of the natural cycle of applied redefinitions with respect to source-transfer interpretations. To view the acceleration of harmonic extension in the fifties is to see the emergence of transfer definitions as a basis to align alternative methodology with the central composite culture.

As such, **to understand the reality of harmonic transition in creative music from the black aesthetic is to look at its multi-complexual implications—as concerns its own source-initiation and source-transfer extension (from its own terms—as opposed to applied definitions).**

The dynamics of transitional harmonic expansion in the sixties would see the emergence of several other investigation routes, and these areas would also dictate the reality position of extended functionalism in creative music. The first extension route which can be commented on is the source-initiated activity that was characterized by the work of composer-instrumentalists like Charles Mingus and John Coltrane—having to do with the move to establish an extended functionalism that would be all-encompassing in its exploration of methodological extension (and in being so, would move to naturally exhaust the extension possibilities of its own functional arena)—and the second area of transitional extension would be the source-transfer implications that were to be explored by musicians like Miles Davis and, again, John Coltrane—having to do with the move to modal functionalism as a means to establish alternative transitional functionalism. Both of these movements are important.

The dynamic activity of Charles Mingus must be viewed as one of the most essential bodies of work to characterize the transitional route of creative music in the fifties and sixties. For Mingus, along with composers like George Russell, would move to create a dynamic spectrum of approaches. His activity would reveal many possibilities for future expansion, while at the same time retain a clear linkage with the composite continuum of the music. The scope of Mingus' activity would affect every sector of the music—from composition, to solo and/or orchestra music. The reality of his work would also be an important factor to clarify the dynamics of transitional black creativity—for the implications of Mingus' activity transcends any one context. It is possible to view Mingus' activity as a major linkage factor to all of the events that would solidify in the music in the sixties and seventies—this would include his use of open-ended improvisation, extended composition, and world music dynamics. The heart of Mingus' activity revealed the very essence of world creativity, and the thrust of his work would capture the spirit of positive transformation. As such, Mingus' activity can be viewed with respect to the reality of both source-initiation and source-transfer extension. For the thrust of his work would encompass the dynamic implications of transitional expansion—as it relates to the whole of creativity.

If the progressional weight of Charles Mingus's activity can be viewed as a pivotal factor in the restructural dynamics of the music—as a spiritual and emotional offering—then the work of George Russell can be viewed in like terms—with the thrust of his effort encompassing spiritual and intellectual dynamics. Russell, in fact, can be viewed as the first real theorist from the post-Parker continuum of the music. In this musician it is possible to clearly view the nature of what tendencies would dictate trans-African functional dynamics (from the bebop period—including its extensions) and the direction these tendencies would dictate. This is so because every aspect of Russell's music details the route of post-bebop invention dynamics—from the early period of his music to the present. And when in the fifties he solidified a concept of harmony (the "Lydian Chromatic Concept of Tonal Organization") it cleared the way for what was to come—that being: the move to totally re-evaluate both trans-African pedagogy and western information dynamics. Hopefully, the next cycle will see more research on George Russell—and his pedagogy. There can be no real understanding of fifties and sixties (and seventies/eighties) progressionalism unless his efforts are considered and included.

The work of John Coltrane in the middle and late fifties must also be viewed as significant for what it posed to transition. In this period, Coltrane's activity would have a direct bearing on the acceleration of source-initiation functionalism—with respect to both the dynamics of rhythm as well as harmony. Moreover, the implications of his work can be viewed from several contexts, for the dynamics of his work as an instrumentalist can be viewed as related to particular areas, and the dynamics of his compositions can be viewed as affecting still other areas. Certainly the instrumental and harmonic concepts of Coltrane would play an important role in transitional black creativity of the fifties. For the use of what is now called "sheets of sound" would greatly affect the vocabulary of transitional functionalism, and this is also true for his expanded rhythmic concept. Moreover, as an instrumentalist, Coltrane would move to extend the dynamic possibilities of saxophone pedagogy—involving both the diatonic range of the instrument as well as the multiphonic implications of extension. His work in the fifties would move to exhaust the reality of vertical harmonic functionalism, and his compositions in this cycle would also contribute another understanding of harmonic extension—with respect to source initiation. Compositions like "Giant Steps" or "Countdown" would become valuable additions to every improvisor's repertoire, for the thrust of these works would greatly contribute to the reality application of vertical harmony. I believe the reality and functional implications of these compositions have yet to be really commented on and documented. For the solidification of "accelerated changes" represents another application of extended functionalism. There had never been a music quite like this, before or after. Without doubt, one of the major reasons this area of Coltrane's work has not been properly researched (in its most real context) is that the multi-complexual dynamics of his total composite activity simply require more time. Which is to say, Coltrane's activity contributed so much to the reality of creative music that it will be some time before the various stages of his activity can be dealt with. Nevertheless, if we are to understand the reality of transition in creative music, it is important that some of these considerations are examined.

The reality of source-transfer extension in the late fifties is both diverse and complex. So many factors were taking place in so short a period that it is somewhat difficult to accurately comment on the continuum of this period. But it is important that some attempt is made to see the real position of the fifties and its role in establishing alternative functionalism. As such, the progressional route of extended functionalism in the fifties must be viewed on several levels because there are numerous considerations which must be looked at—having to do with the dynamics of source-transfer extension as it relates to alternative functionalism and world dynamics. Because by the end of the fifties another movement would emerge to give real insight on the developing forces which solidified the vibrationaltory arena of the sixties. The realness of this movement would signal the end of the post-Parker continuum as the only extended continuum of transformational value in creative music (at least of the vibrational continuum it is related to)—and in doing so, also establish another option route for creative investigation. This movement would be the source-transfer extension into modal forms and also the solidification of the Coleman/Taylor juncture of extended functionalism. The reality of creative music transition is directly related to what these forms posed.

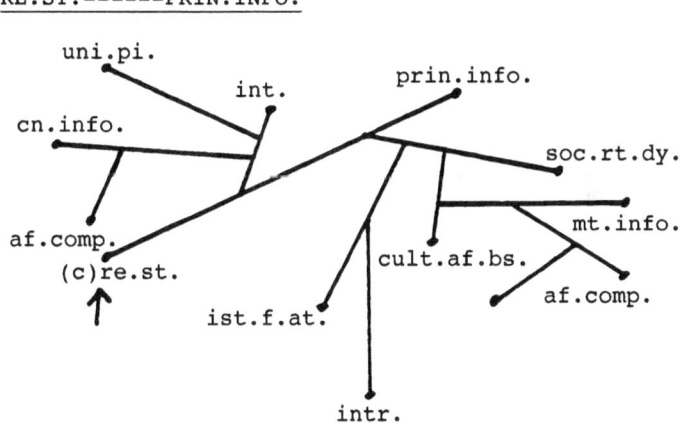

CMBA-20

EXT.F.------TH.CONT.

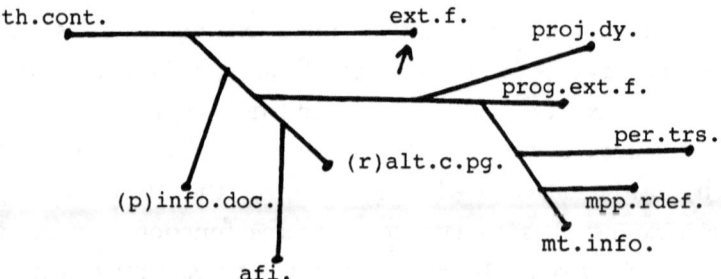

AFI.TF.------STF.

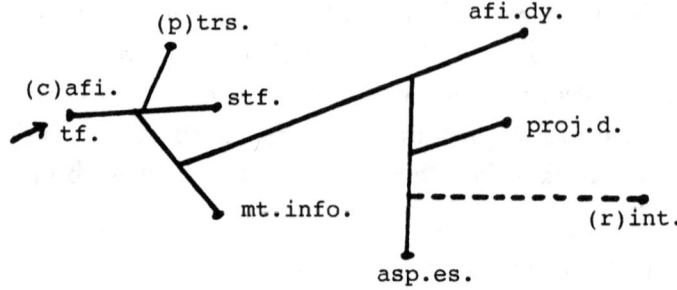

ALT.F.------DEC.

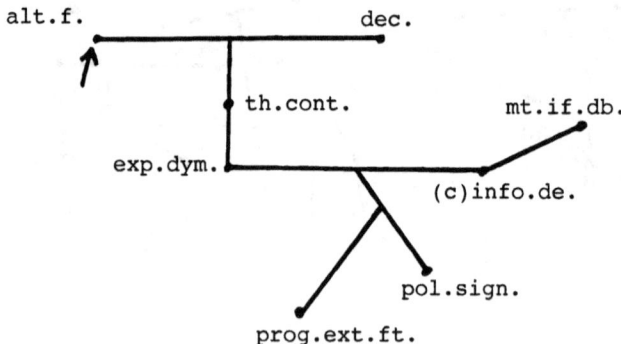

CMBA-21

The dynamics of modal functionalism must be viewed with respect to what this discipline has come to solidify in world culture terms. For the functionalism that we refer to as modalism is manifested in many forms throughout earth culture—from Africa to India. The reality of this discipline would give insight as to the meta-reality implications of transformational methodology, and this is true on many levels. For the essence of modal systems brings the multi-implications of methodology into real focus—with respect to what a given function means in both its cosmic and systematic sense. Thus if we are to understand the nature of the expansion that occurred in the sixties, then it is important that the source-transfer implications of its spread be commented on. The emergence of modality in black creative music would signify that another dynamic extension had solidified in alternative functionalism—and the realness of this development commented on what source-transfer extension poses as a natural progressional factor. Nor have I meant that modality would only be manifested through one given thrust alignment, because this phenomenon would permeate western creativity in several contexts and continuums. There would be three basic thrust continuums which utilized modal functionalism in the sixties and all of these alignments would affect the composite tone level of the culture. The first continuum would be the arrival of modal creativity from India, the second continuum is the source-transfer continuum of black creativity, and the third is the dynamic continuum of popular music. All three of these considerations are important if we are to understand the source-transfer dynamics of extension.

By the middle sixties one could begin to see what amounted to an exodus of great musicians from India to several western countries. This period would represent one of the first cycles in American history where Indian creativity could be experienced—both in live performances and on record. Musicians like Ravi Shankar thus moved to establish the dynamics of Indian music as something "real" in America, and by appearing in many different performance settings (as well as some of the important rock festivals) his activity eventually spearheaded a profound change in western "information dynamics." The vibrational arena of the sixties later moved to be conducive for experiencing world creativity as well—which is to say, not only would western culture focus on Indian creativity, but also Japanese and Tibetan culture. But the continued exodus of master musicians from India would greatly accelerate an accented awareness of Indian creativity in western culture, and in doing so this phenomenon played an important part in the overall vibrational fabric of the sixties. For not only would the dynamics of the music play an important part in reshaping the basic vibrational arena of American culture, but the composite realness of Indian culture (i.e., philosophy, dress, spiritualism) moved to also create a definite vibrational position. The thrust alignment of these considerations was to be important for the transitions occurring in the sixties.

Miles Davis's use of modal functionalism in the late fifties would move to stimulate a whole new awareness of expanded functionalism in the black music community—and there were many reasons for this. For the adaptation of modality by Davis had come to a crucial stage in the extension reality of black music (the other being the complicated functionalism that led to "Giant Steps"). The path of modality would also represent an attractive investigation route for musicians who were deeply schooled in tonal organization but still felt the need to develop into other forms. For the reality procedure of modal functionalism provided an arena that gave each individual musician more room for establishing a particular vibrational thrust statement, while at the same time, fewer restrictions with respect to the demands of the methodology. The particulars of modal functionalism would offer all of these possibilities while also providing the tonal consideration that had become a primary tool of the post-bebop continuum. The work of Davis in this period thus detailed the dynamic implications of alternative functionalism, and compositions like "So What" would become some of the most-performed works of the late fifties and sixties. Nor was Davis's utilization of modal music an isolated adaptation, for the dynamic continuance of his work directly affected the composite reality of black creativity. By the beginning of the sixties practically every group would have one or two modal compositions in their book. A musician like Jackie McLean would later adopt this area of functionalism to create another chapter in his own output of creativity, and this adaptation was not unusual.

Modal functionalism could be viewed in the commercial creativity of the sixties. This continuum basically functioned as a color consideration with respect to a given group's repertoire—yet this usage should not be taken lightly. For modal music in this period solidified as one of the factors that generated the acceleration of what came to be called fusion music. Even a group like the Beatles had one or two compositions that were modal (and one of these pieces was included in their highly influential *Sgt. Pepper's* record—complete with Indian tabla and sitar). Many other groups would later follow this same path—which is to say, by the end of the sixties there would be no denying the impact that Indian creativity had made in western culture. The thrust assimilation of the music could be experienced on radio and television (and television commercials) as well as in the composite fabric of western creative music. The music as well as the culture group it came from must be viewed as directly related to the vibrational implications and dynamics of the sixties. Yet the reality implications of modality did not stop at any one juncture. For the methodological implications of its functionalism would underlie one of the most significant creative inquiries of this time cycle. I am referring to the activity of John Coltrane.

If Miles Davis's adaptation of modality was the major factor that attracted musicians to this area in the late fifties, the work of John Coltrane would move to solidify modal functionalism to an even greater height. For modality in Coltrane's music was not simply a color consideration to be added for a given performance, but instead a methodological platform that lent itself towards a particular type of alternative extension. From modal functionalism, Coltrane would move to create one of the most dynamic musics of this time period—and in doing so establish the third juncture of what had already been an exciting and innovative career. It is important that some attempt is made to deal with the multi-complexual implications of Coltrane's activity in this cycle, for the dynamics of his work profoundly altered creative postulation in the fifties and sixties (nor has his influence diminished as we approach the eighties). Moreover, to view the dynamic application of modal functionalism in Coltrane's activity is to receive direct insight as to the composite factors which vibrationally made up the transition in the sixties. There are several factors about Coltrane's dynamic utilization of alternative functionalism which must be understood: (1) his use of modality detailed the route of source-transfer methodology as a dynamic tool for composite world resolidification, and (2) the progressional continuum of his work would clarify the affinity insight principle implications of transitional creativity, with respect to both the consideration of "purpose" as well as "spiritualism." Thus, by the end of the fifties it was clear that the third cycle of Coltrane's creativity would be just as significant as his previous work—and every extension additive would pose even greater implications for the reality of creative music continuance. Coltrane's use of modality as an alternative transitional methodology would last for over five years.

The physical universe reality position of source-transfer extension can better clarify the nature of progressional continuance—and this is particularly true when applied to projectional changes in given thrust foundations. For the reality of a given extension transcends any one boundary. Coltrane particularly understood this, and he has long been documented as concerned about universal matters, with respect to both his own life as well as the broader implications of creative extension. Moreover, the dynamic nature of his activity would not distort his concern for the cross-sectional brilliance of world creativity—for many times Coltrane expressed the desire to play with a wider spectrum of world musicians. Had he lived longer this might have become possible, for Coltrane was profoundly interested in African music and culture (he also expressed the desire to play with African drummers and on one occasion sought out the possibility to play with Ravi Shankar). As such, if we are to understand the dynamics implications of Coltrane's activity then it is important to view his progressional output with respect to the composite factors shaping the sixties. The utilization of modal functionalism in Coltrane's activity was a conscious adaptation to extend creative music—and its methodological dynamics—and while doing so to also function with respect to world resolidification. In other words, Coltrane wanted to have his activity connected to the greater movement of world consciousness and world universality. To understand the reality of transitional functionalism in the sixties one must deal with the inherent world implications of its dynamics. That is, this phenomenon cannot be separated from the natural reality position of source-transfer progressionalism—even applying to the particular implications of modality. Yet I have not meant to isolate the nature of a given affinity alignment. For Coltrane's use of modal functionalism did not simply imply that he only wanted to connect with Indian culture—this was only one step in what would later be a universal position. **Every period of Coltrane's activity advanced the nature of an expanded source-transfer extension which is to say it is now possible to view the particulars of his expansion with respect to several junctures: involving African music, Mexican music, and Oriental music.** Nor was Coltrane's interest in universalism restricted to one context, because he was also very much aware of and concerned about the physical universe particulars of planet earth (in short, by discussing Coltrane, we are not discussing a limited subject focus).

The vibrational reality surrounding Coltrane's use of modal forms also dictated the nature of transitional spirituality and its relationship with creative music. Coltrane's activity, even more than Sun Ra's, came to actualize and represent accented spiritualism—and this is true in every stage of his music (the progression being spirituality to "applied spirituality"). As such, Coltrane's use of alternative functionalism can be viewed as one of the most vital creative utilizations in the sixties for both establishing expanded functionalism and spiritual awareness—this is true for his actual creativity, and this is also true for the effect his activity would have on the composite culture. So great was Coltrane's contribution in establishing spiritual consciousness that we are still dealing with the effect of what this contribution means today. For in actuality, Coltrane's spirituality must be viewed with respect to what his activity poses for transitional and/or transformational perception (and I am not referring to only one aspect of spirituality or spiritual manifestation—because the real effect of Coltrane's activity is much more dynamic than any one particular application). I am commenting on a music which directly affected and tapped the vibrational factors of its time period, and of its "not" time period.

The work of John Coltrane also gave insight into the spiritual and vibrational situation of black people in the sixties, and while doing so also provided possible directions for functional transformation. The importance of Coltrane's activity in this context cannot be overemphasized, for the reality continuum of his activity served as a beacon in one of the most difficult cycles in America's social reality. To understand the significance of his work is to deal with the dynamic particulars of the sixties, for the thrust continuum of that time cycle would move to disturb the composite lining of world culture. The first most basic effect of the sixties would be the confusion that naturally results when the essence of a given culture's moral and ethical position is exposed as either not relevant or in decay—add to this phenomenon the realness of vibrational transition (and the realness of assassination and war) and one can have some idea as to the "reality basis" of the sixties. Coltrane's activity in this cycle could be viewed as a dynamic alternative continuum which, in its natural spread, gave insight about the vibrational dynamics of progressionalism—and in doing so, served as a positive factor in the total community. The dynamic spectrum of his work cannot be isolated into any one area or context, for the nature of its spread was all-encompassing. If we can say that the reality of what came to be called third stream music has to do with the natural extension of creativity involving the projectional path of black creative music and western art music, then we can view the dynamic implications of Coltrane's activity with respect to the route of source transfer as it involves the integration (or re-integration) of black creativity with what is now called the third world countries—as well as all non-western countries. The solidification and practice of modal functionalism, then, can be viewed as the methodology that would establish the nature of how these changes (and expansions) were brought about.

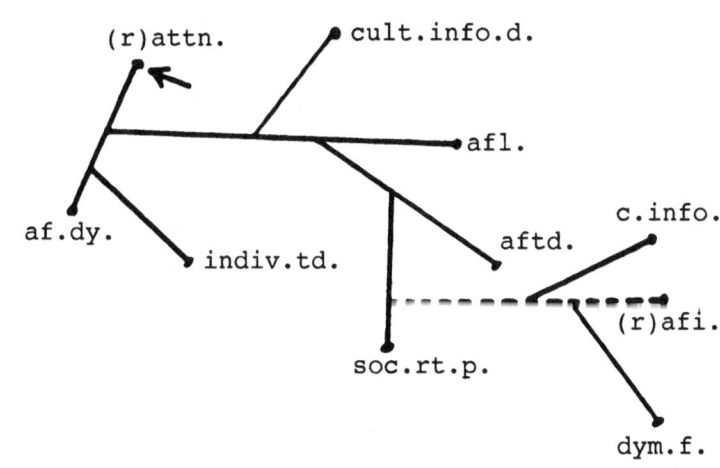

The emergence of alternative functionalism and the dynamics of alternative spiritualism must be viewed on several levels. For the reality tone of events in the sixties was both varied and complex. In actual fact, the solidification of alternative spiritualism (and spiritual consciousness, period) must be understood with respect to what its emergence signified about the reality position of western culture. For the emergence of spiritual awareness is not separate from the factors which solidified the reality position of western continuance. As such, spiritualism could be viewed as a direct response to the nature of intellectualism in the fifties—that being, the over-emphasis on empiricism, and the distortion of essence and what this phenomenon posed to the particular "reality-state" of western culture. Thus the move to embrace spiritualism must be viewed in its composite context—and this is also true for the creativity that would solidify that move. In other words, the emergence of modal functionalism can be viewed with respect to the greater reality of cosmic transition. Moreover, alternative functionalism in this context can also be viewed as the consideration related to how given vibrational terminations—in a given time cycle, as "ised" through its cosmic purpose—are brought about: which is to say, the reality implication of modal functionalism in the sixties would move to be the most conducive factor for tapping the cosmic-related forces that generate change (real change as opposed to surface realignment). The reality dynamics of Coltrane's activity not only determined the particulars of source-transfer methodology, but the progressional significance of this route is still effective—that is, the "reality" of alternative activity has not changed as we move into the eighties. The work of musicians like McCoy Tyner in the sixties and seventies can be viewed as directly extending the path Coltrane solidified—nor is Tyner unique in this sense either, for by the end of the seventies it was extremely difficult to find any younger musician whose activity had not been influenced by Coltrane's work. **The extension route dynamics of Coltrane's activity would establish a particular kind of "world music"—or "world methodology"—that was perceived as directly relevant for transition and/or transformation.** Obviously this was the case, for the dynamic spread of Coltrane's activity has affected every sector exposed to its "reality." The seeds underlying Coltrane's activity could be experienced in Indian to Japanese creativity—and as such, the dynamic move to imitate his music could also be experienced in those same countries—and many others as well. The thrust continuum of Coltrane's activity can be viewed with the same intensity that characterized the Parker continuum of the music—for the actualness of Coltrane's music would bring both a wealth of followers as well as enemies. To understand the vibrational implications of Coltrane's activity, it is important that one views the reality of Coltrane's methodology—with respect to what it posed for the affinity insight principle, as well as for what it posed for progressional expansion. This is so because the reality of Coltrane's activity commented on the factors which were developing on the physical universe plane—involving composite social reality. The thrust of Coltrane's music came to forecast the reality and vibrational position of black people in America, and in Africa. Which is to say, his activity provided great insight into the dynamic particulars of this time period—so sweeping was its scope. Coltrane's music solidified the transitional (to transformational) potential of projectional continuance—both with respect to expansion as dictated through source initiation, as well as expansion with respect to source transfer—and finally as expansion with respect to source initiation.

CMBA–29

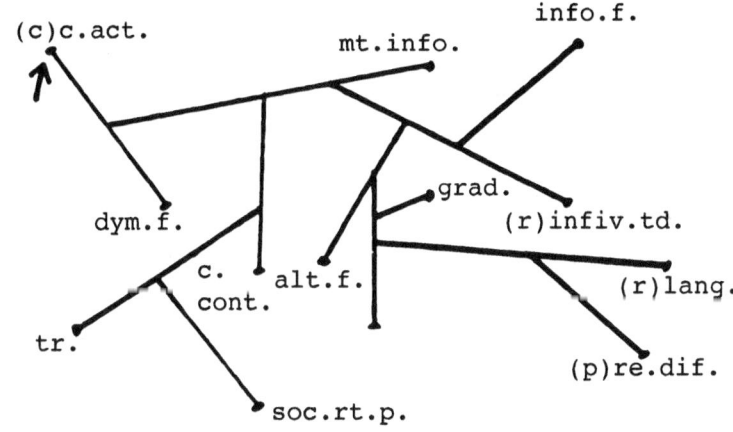

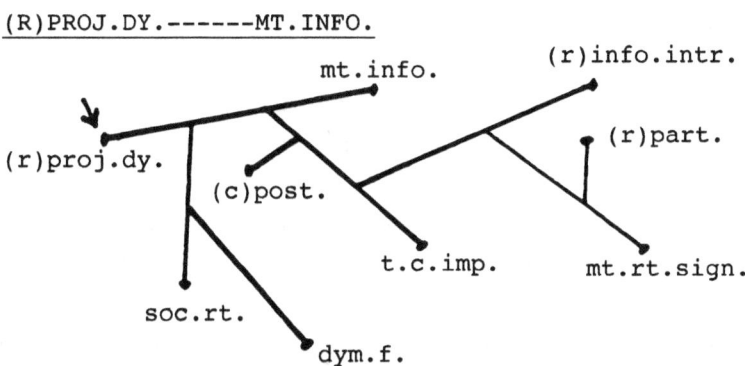

The transitional dynamics of creative music in the fifties and sixties must also be viewed in expanded terms. For the dynamic emergence of alternative functionalism was not actualized through either one person or one segment of the greater culture. Instead, by the end of the fifties several creative routes could be seen forming, and each of these routes would give insight into the nature of alternative participation. As such, the nature of transition in this context should be viewed with respect to the concept of principle information tendencies, as well as what this concept poses for actual extension. The fact is, it is important for the reader to understand the composite reality of transitional black creativity in this period (i.e., the fifties and sixties)—because the dynamics underlying how change was actualized transcend any one viewpoint or approach. Moreover, the thrust implications of change in this cycle would comment on the composite reality position of black people at the beginning of the sixties. Thus to understand the reality of creative transition in this cycle is to deal with all of these considerations and more. It is not simply a question of singling out given individuals or given areas of research; rather, the alternative functionalism that solidified by the end of the fifties can be clearly viewed for how it has profoundly affected the reality dynamics of alternative options. The natural thrust of this activity would vibrationally play an important role for how it affected composite earth information dynamics as well as particular information routes. In other words, to view the dynamics of alternative creative functionalism—as actualized in the transition of the late fifties—is to view activity that played an important role throughout the composite strata of the culture affecting the reality dynamics of progressional continuance as well as information focus—and this should not be taken lightly (especially if the fifties/sixties juncture is considered with respect to what its particulars have meant to present events).

The dynamic implications of transitional functionalism and progressional continuance can be understood by dealing with the restructuralists whose activity solidified—as a real reality position—in the middle fifties, and who emerged as basic forces by the end of the fifties. Those individuals are Ornette Coleman, Cecil Taylor, Sun Ra, and John Coltrane (in his third and fourth cycle). The composite work of these musicians would establish the first movement of transitional functionalism in the late fifties, and in doing so their activity also dictated the reality continuum of "new" trans-African music. All of the music that later emerged on the scene can be viewed with respect to the activity of these four musicians—so overwhelming has been their offering. In a time period from five to six years, the realness of their activity would move to totally transform the dynamic tone-level of black creativity as well as the black community. The thrust momentum of their work forecasted both the social-reality implications of the sixties and seventies, as well as what these implications meant in actual terms—with respect to both information focus and constructive alternative functionalism. Thus it is important that some attempt is made to deal with this movement.

In many ways, the activity of Ornette Coleman and Cecil Taylor solidified the extension implications of transitional black creativity in the late fifties. Their activity would have a profound impact on the progressional continuum of creative music on every level, and their impact must be viewed as equally significant as that of John Coltrane. For the realness of their activity commented on the philosophic and vibrational implications of progressionalism—and in doing so, their activity also dictated the vibrational nature of extension as well as its functional particulars. Coleman and Taylor can be viewed as two of the most daring restructuralists in the sixties. The whole of their activity constituted a complete breakthrough in the progressional expansion of alternative functionalism—and in the progression continuance of black culture. The impact of their activity would transcend transitional creativity—or particular functionalism and/or individual dynamics—and instead give profound insight into the reality and information dynamics of black people—(and/or source initiation in its essence sense). In other words, **the realness of Coleman's and Taylor's activity must be viewed with respect to what it signifies about the composite meta-reality implications of alternative functionalism**. Both of these musicians—through their activity—were able to grasp essential information about the essence reality that underlines world culture—and this is only the beginning.

If we can say that the activity of John Coltrane is directly related to the emotional and spiritual changes that transformed the sixties—regardless of focus—then we can view the activity of Coleman and Taylor with respect to what it signaled about composite and alternative information dynamics. This is so because the dynamic implications of Coleman's and Taylor's activity directly gave insight into the nature of composite information. To understand this viewpoint is to deal with the particulars of the beginning sixties. For the emergence of transitional restructuralism would move to clarify the information continuum that dictated terms for American culture—as well as black culture. The gradual momentum of alternative investigation (and not only in the creativity) would move to expose the flaws of the misinformation that sustains America's social reality. The activity of Coleman and Taylor must be viewed in the same context as that of the black scholars whose activity would begin to challenge the nature of what information was being disseminated throughout the composite culture. For the collected weight of composite investigation is directly related to the events that transpired in the sixties—involving the contribution of scholars, activists, lawyers, doctors, and artists. The work of Coleman, Taylor, and Sun Ra must be viewed in this context as well, for the composite offering of their activity would have a devastating effect on the culture. Their activity gave a dynamic meaning to alternative functionalism, and the thrust of their work would move to uncover new projectional routes for both informational and vibrational investigation and also the forces related to those routes. It is important that these contributions are understood—and not on one level.

The work of Coleman, Taylor, and Sun Ra would give new insight into the expanded dynamics of transitional black creativity in every context. All of these musicians functioned on several levels in the music—from composer-instrumentalists and (just as important) as definers, or redefiners of their work. The thrust of Coleman's and Taylor's activity would also move to function towards an all-encompassing investigational viewpoint—involving one of the most intensive re-examinations of information in this cycle. Their activity is directly responsible for the expansion of the affinity insight principle with respect to its wider investigatory possibilities. In other words, the thrust of their activity gave profound insight into the "nature" of alternative functionalism as well as "source initiation." This can be understood by examining the composite dynamics of their activity, for each of these musicians developed insight into the realness of restructuralism as it involves their separate creative directions. Coleman's activity can be viewed with respect to his use of the affinity insight principle as made real in his own life and also applied to the traditional continuum of composite black creativity (from what is now called blues, on through to notated forms and extended improvisation). Taylor's activity can be viewed with respect to what it implied to the meta-reality of extended methodology—that being source-transfer extension (the move to become involved in world creativity regardless of thrust) as a tool to gain both insight about black creativity (what this consideration really means) as well as resource initiation (that being, after learning about composite invention, applying that information to a transformational viewpoint for black functionalism). Sun Ra's activity can be viewed as a dynamic composite move for investigating black music—with an information scan that focused on both the ancient and future dynamics of given methodologies, as well as a music of ritual vision. To deal with the reality of transition in creative music is to have some understanding of the work of each of these musicians. For the composite thrust of their activity has established the option spread foundation of alternative functionalism in this cycle (in the late seventies).

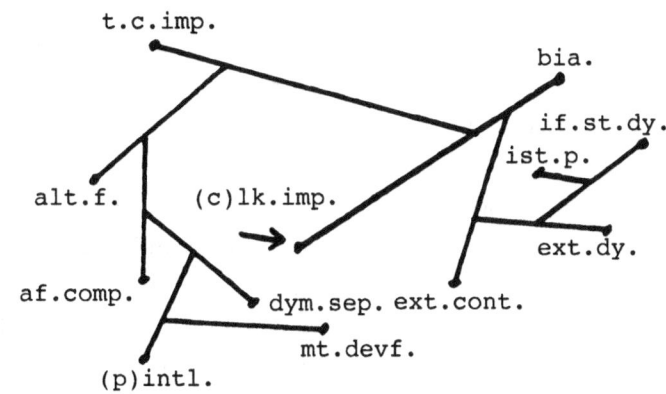

To really understand the dynamic implications of transitional black creativity, it is important that no one context is over-accented. For the realness of this subject has deeply affected the composite reality of black culture on every level. The fact is, the progressional continuance of Coleman's, Taylor's, and Sun Ra's activity forecasted a total re-evaluation of both black ideology as well as alternative functionalism (in creativity as well as politics). The realness of this movement affected changes in the philosophic and intellectual reality of black culture and also served as a vibrational stimulant for new ideas. In doing so, the composite offerings of their creativity clarified the next reality platform for black creativity.

Coleman, Taylor, and Sun Ra must be viewed in the total context of what their activity signified for both the particulars of their approach as well as the progressional implications related to what their work activated. It is important to remember that their activity came into solidification during the time cycle that western interpretations were unchallenged. Which is to say, during the time zone of the middle to late fifties the defining forces of western culture were still able to perpetrate the notion (1) that the functional and theoretical reality of western art music was more advanced than any other culture group that ever existed, and (2) that its methodology—and criteria—was necessarily relevant to every culture group, regardless of whether that group agreed with its interpretations or with western culture's right to impose its definitions on non-western focuses. In other words, because of the vibrational and political reality of American and western culture—from its inception on up to the late fifties—the collected forces of western culture did not have to take into consideration whether or not its definitions (and interpretations) were valid when applied to other cultural groups. Instead, the realness of this sector would function as a suppressive tool for sustaining the present political position western culture now enjoys over the rest of the world culture. As such, the creative solutions of Coleman, Taylor, and Sun Ra would come to shock the total reality of this phenomenon—affecting both the composite community of western information control, as well as the musicians' community. To really understand the whole of what extended investigation really means is to have some awareness of the monumental dynamics that these three individuals activated by simply having the courage and integrity to advance their work.

The work of Coleman and Taylor can be looked at as the terminal point of a vibrational and actual phenomenon which started when black slaves were brought to America's shores hundreds of years before. In other words, the realness of their activity must be viewed as a reconnection to source initiation as the most important factor for re-establishing procedure and culture (unification), and also their work clarified source initiation as a platform for re-establishing an alternative spiritualism. Of course I have not meant to imply that these aims have been secured—for this struggle is still taking place—but the activity of Coleman and Taylor (among others) can best be understood by both their position in this particular progressional objective and also for how their activity has advanced its own dynamic axioms. The time zone of the late fifties in many ways represented the most significant period for the breakthroughs shaping this period (late seventies), and the significance of Coleman's and Taylor's activity is directly connected to what these breakthroughs mean. The transition of creative music in the late fifties could best be understood as the final juncture of the western defining community's ability to stifle the significance of "actual" creative music and have their definitions accepted by the musicians' community—and greater public. This is not to say that the western power establishment has now decided to embrace creative music because nothing could be further from the truth—instead, the time zone of the early sixties was the period which saw the momentum of creative music accelerate, and the time zone of the sixties was also the period that would see a response from the musicians which could not be simply put down and contained. All of the later developments in creative music are tied to this phenomenon—which is to say, the work of Ornette Coleman and Cecil Taylor was instrumental in establishing the composite transition which took place in the sixties and seventies.

I do not mean to imply that either Coleman's and/or Taylor's activity can be evaluated as out-extending or out-intellectualizing the established defining community of western culture, for this is really besides the point. The real significance of their work would lie in their ability to accurately tap the realness of who they "really are" as understood in the separate information reality of black methodology and what this understanding really means in regard to "black essence." In other words, the determining agent that moved these musicians to create the music they made could best be understood as "an honest attempt" to participate in creativity that was, and is, directly in accordance to what they were/are as human beings. **The dynamics of the music that these musicians created in the late fifties was no more than a profound—and independent, as it were—understanding of "source initiation." The significance of** their activity would not only lie in the originality of their actual music but also in the insight that their work transmitted with regards to the implications of "source initiation." The reaction and subsequent developments that materialized in the sixties and seventies were directly in accordance with the implications of this phenomenon and this is why I have isolated this movement from, say, the factors which surrounded modal music, for instance.

The work, then, of Coleman and Taylor directly forecast the emergence of the transition schools that gained momentum in the sixties. The development of what came to be called the "free" schools can be looked at as a direct extension of the work which was done by these individuals, although there were other factors happening as well. Certainly the most distinguishing feature of the forming schools in the early sixties was the functional realignment particulars of their creativity. For instance, musicians like Albert Ayler created a music that further solidified the implications underlying what Coleman and Taylor had activated. This period of creative music from the black aesthetic must surely be viewed as one of the most distorted and misunderstood cycles in creative music. But the solutions arrived at by this continuum greatly affected the course of composite creative music. It was the so-called avant-garde movement in the sixties which extended both the language aspect of creative music and the dynamic principles (and implications) underlying how extended improvisation was to be viewed (and henceforth practiced). **It was the avant-garde movement of the sixties that also solidified all of the later emerging creative developments—in a time zone of about ten years—to a composite collective creative force; and finally, it was the avant-garde movement of the sixties that dealt with functionalism (on the physical universe level) as a means to correct the "actual" situation that separated and "thwarted" the public's inability to experience live creative music.** By the time we entered the time zone of the seventies, creative music from the black aesthetic had experienced many levels of radical change—from the functional dictates of its particulars, to the implication of its aesthetic positions—and all of these changes were related to the actualness of this movement.

The activity of the post-Ayler movement could best be understood by looking at the prominent factors which characterized the time zone of the sixties. Those factors would be the social situation in American society, as well as the intensity that this situation produced. The unsophisticated attempts at revolution in America in the sixties did reflect the isolation and rage that characterized much of that period, and this factor was also present in much of the creativity in that period as well. But the underlying factors that really determined the creativity in this time zone could best be understood as attempts to completely discard western functionalism as a means to instead rediscover the essence factor of creative music. If John Coltrane's activity represented source transfer in this context, as a means to build a unified alternative affinity to spiritualism, then we can look at much of the post-Ayler music as the movement which—because of the physical universe factors in American life—sought to separate from the mainstream what this unification would mean in actual terms.

This was then the group that challenged the total reality concerning how creative music had come to be perceived in western culture. For if Coltrane's, Coleman's, and Taylor's activity outlined the distortions that surrounded black creativity and served as a force for the effectiveness of the affinity insight principle, then the post-Ayler movement fulfilled the task of what that challenge implied on both the aesthetic and physical universe levels. The work that was offered in this period—from both the east coast, and later the movements which emerged in the midwest—will undoubtedly influence the course of creativity on many levels as we move into the eighties and nineties.

C.CONT.------SOC.RT.P.

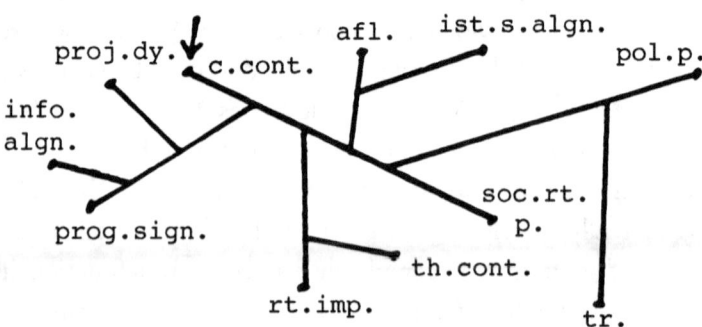

There was also another movement that emerged near the end of the fifties which signaled the forming of yet another creative thrust. That movement has now come to be known as the "third stream school"—that is: the movement which sought to move towards a composite aesthetic utilizing both creative music from the black aesthetic and notated music from the western aesthetic. Among the musicians who have worked in this movement are John Lewis, Gunther Schuller, and Eric Dolphy (although I do not mean to imply that any of these musicians functioned in the same context to this movement). For some reason this movement has had more than its share of criticism—the very idea of a synthesis of western art music and black music seems repugnant to many people—yet many beautiful works of music have emerged from this juncture. The move towards a composite aesthetic in this context can also be seen in Ornette Coleman's activity with notated compositions as well (for the spectrum of Ornette Coleman's activity touches practically every related focus—vibrational and functional—of creative music).

The work of John Lewis with the Modern Jazz Quartet is also an example of what can happen in a composite aesthetic. In the early sixties Lewis began to utilize chamber orchestras with his quartet—and on some occasions also worked with string quartets. The music he produced in this context was both fresh and daring in its design and broad in its utilization of both idioms. The move towards "third stream music" was much more profound than is generally recognized by composite western journalism—nor does that move only pertain to composers. Musicians like Eric Dolphy were very much involved in a "composite" music (which is to say his activity touched on more than one reality of the music—he was involved in Indian and African forms as well). There were even many occasions where Dolphy functioned solely as an interpreter of western art music. The book on Eric Dolphy by Barry Tepperman and Vladimir Simosko mentions the concert where Eric—working with a contemporary classical ensemble—performed Edgard Varèse's flute piece "Density 21.5." On many occasions Dolphy expressed his admiration of Gazzelloni's work in classical music, and there has long been respect between musicians whose creative vision superseded the manipulated boundaries underlying how their craft is politicized.

Nor was the creative thrust towards a world music restricted to individuals as opposed to groups. For in the early sixties, ensembles like "Orchestra USA" functioned as a platform where the spectrum of composite activity could be concentrated on. This was a group that functioned as both an interpreting and creative orchestra—providing outlets for composers like John Lewis and Gunther Schuller, among others. I have no doubt that this period of creative music—and in particular, this area of creative music—will be re-evaluated and received for what it was (and is), for there has been much beautiful and important creativity produced from this arena. The work of Orchestra USA and John Lewis in particular superseded the later developments that were to take place in creative music—those developments being: the integration of the functional arena of contemporary western art music with the creative aesthetic of black music in the move towards the forming world music. The "realness" of what this movement implies can better be understood by hearing the actual music—or by experiencing a musician like Eric Dolphy with Orchestra USA, for example. Yet by the end of the sixties, Orchestra USA—along with many other "composite" groups—was forced to break up. Undoubtedly the social and intellectual climate of the sixties was a factor in the abandonment of this approach, for the music community had broken into many fragmented groups by this period. But I have no doubts that there is much more for all of us to learn from the work that has been done in this sector of creative music.

(Level One) THE WHITE IMPROVISOR

TO VIEW THE MULTI-IMPLICATIONS OF EARTH CREATIVITY is to deal with many different factors—regardless of form. For the study of world creativity transcends any one context. To really gain insight about the reality dynamics of this subject is to examine the composite implications of life itself, because creativity is not separate from who is being creative (or who has experienced a given creative phenomenon). As such, I have tried in this book to separate various information regions as a means to better focus on the isolated reality of its "particulars" with the hope that an approach of this nature could lead to a more composite understanding of creativity. It is important that a world context is established in the near future about this subject, because many of the concepts surrounding earth creativity in this cycle are not necessarily conceived with respect for what is "the most true"—as opposed to simply what is true (about a given level or focus). If we are to ever gain insight about creativity as a positive transformation tool, then we must come to view this subject with respect to what it means on a composite level. I have tried in this book to state my belief that creativity is not about only the focus (or doing) of a given activity, but rather, the reality dynamics of this subject move towards dealing with the all-cosmic realness of existence. If this is true, then it is important that some attempt is made to examine the nature of the information we are dealing with in this cycle. For the nature of a given information line can dictate the reality platform of a total time period—which is to say, the dynamic implications of this subject are much too significant to ignore. This is true for both this time zone as well as the future. If the realness of creativity is to serve as a positive transformation tool in the coming cycles, then some attempt must be made to examine the information underlying our perception of "particulars"—this is important for the music and the cosmic implications which dictate what music is (in vibrational terms).

WI-2

To really attempt to understand the composite realness of earth creativity (let alone "all creativity" as separate from isolation), it is important that the nature of a given inquiry is not over-simplified. For to view the realness of information dynamics is to move outside of the established parameters dictating our traditional relationship to principle information. In other words, the realness of transformational interpretation cannot be either tied to the specifics of a given information focus or seated in the comfort of two million information continuums, because the truth of a given phenomenon cannot be contained by only one interpretation criterion, and no one is qualified to accurately comment on "everything." Furthermore, I recognize only too clearly that there are no real qualifications to write with authority about the meta-reality realness of earth creativity and/or progressional continuance, because this subject really requires two lifetimes of necessary research and spiritual guidance. I have instead moved to solidify a viewpoint that agrees with both my feelings as well as my own affinity nature (or vibrational nature)—which is to say, I have had to rely more than once on what I perceive to be the "cosmic truth" of a given phenomenon—as opposed to what that same phenomenon might mean in its most separate state—since there are no credentials to speak of that validate any viewpoint in either academic or intellectual terms that really mean anything when certain focuses are being observed. But I have not let this awareness of multi-criteria deter my actions, because in the final analysis there is a need for musicians, and other members of society who normally are at the mercy of the professionals, to speak out and act—or in my case, to solidify in writing a composite viewpoint about creativity—even at the risk of not having my viewpoint affect the greater culture. I am restating my understanding of intention in this section of *Writings* as a means to vibrationally establish this section of the book, because at first glance one might wonder why is there the need to isolate and focus on the reality of the white improvisor (especially since I have already stated my objections to the very concept of "race" as it is understood in this period), and what does this section have to do with the music—and this question is valid. I can only answer that no viewpoint would be complete that chose to ignore the social reality dynamics of "participation"—and as such, it is important that the particular reality of the white improvisor is commented on. **Moreover, to view the special situation of the white improvisor is consistent with my attempts to isolate and recombine the composite aspects of world creativity**—this is what I have done in the section **on the black improvisor, and this is what I have done in** *Writings* **2 and 3 on the special situation of non-American creative music, or the situation of the black composer and creative women.** My point is that all of these so-called categories must be dealt with on some level if we are truly interested in viewing the realness of earth creativity—and especially if we are interested in changing the reality of earth life. As such, to view the special reality position of the white improvisor is to have an increased information focus—and in this period we need as wide an information scan as possible.

What of the white improvisor, and why is it even necessary to comment on this subject in a separate section?

The reality of the white improvisor must be discussed in its separate state because it is a separate state—that is, the underlying reality dynamics which solidify the information particulars of the white improvisor are distinct enough from those of the black and Asian improvisors that they should be commented on. This is not to say that the music of the white improvisor is "less" than that of the black or Asian improvisor, because this is not true—nor does this have anything to do with what I am looking for. Rather the separate reality of the white improvisor is important for what it signifies about its "path" nature—that being, the particulars of its route. Throughout the whole of this book I have tried to take the position that if we are to ever really view the realness of creativity then we must first move to open ourselves as to both the dynamics of composite earth creativity and also the realness of transformational spiritualism. To view the reality particulars of the white improvisor is to be in a better position to understand the meta-implications which surround his or her work. In other words, I do not believe in the concept of a given sector's creativity having anything to do with being better than any other sector's creativity—this kind of thinking is usually either racist or nationalist. Yet it is true that we can learn particular information by examining particular focuses—or in this case, particular routes of creativity. The dynamic implications of the activity of the white improvisor are important for what they can tell us about the nature of its path, as well as what that path poses for the concept of affinity dynamics (that being, the vibrational implications surrounding principal areas of information).

Quite possibly by providing an overview, the significance of particular routes of creativity can become clearer. In other words, if humanity is not about the diversity of human beings but instead simply about human beings, then the particulars outlining how a given area of information expands should be of concern to all humanity—because that "particular" is part of "us." Thus to view the specifics of a given information line is to deal with what that focus contributes to a composite viewpoint—or "state of things." By attempting to view the separateness of the white improvisor we can focus on the nature of what has been offered to the world community from this route (understanding, too, that every route is both important and necessary). It is for this reason that we have no choice but to examine every aspect and context of creative music—that is, if we are looking for what is true "about things."

It would be easy to ignore the dynamics underlying what this subject really poses—for surely the reality implications of the white improvisor can be a sensitive subject, and touches on many different factors. And it would also be easy to ignore the realness of this subject with respect to what it poses about social reality—this is true even though everyone has discussed this subject on some level. **The fact is, many white improvisors feel rightly or wrongly that their activity has not been dealt with on the level it deserves, and on the other hand many black musicians feel that the work of white musicians has received more credit than what it merits with respect to the composite reality of the music.** Without doubt, both of these views are indicative of the present reality dynamics of this cycle, yet there is still the realness of what these sentiments provoke. For how can we ever postulate world consciousness and unification if even the creative community can't come to terms with what this consideration means? In other words, if the challenge of real change is to be made, then surely this change will call for another level of responsibility—and this is especially true for the creative community. There is now a need for these questions to be dealt with once and for all—that is: there is now a need for dynamic attempts to solidify a universal platform for alternative functionalism—and we must do it in this time cycle if possible.

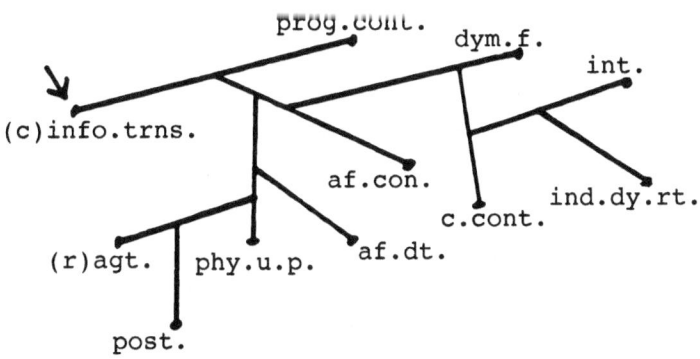

At present, to speak of so-called jazz is to comment on two distinctly different realities: that being, the reality continuum of the black musician and the reality continuum of the white musician—that is true even though the composite basis for so-called jazz has been designed by black people. For the most part, if questioned as to their influences, the majority of black musicians would speak of musicians like John Coltrane, Sonny Rollins, Miles Davis, Max Roach, Bud Powell, Paul Chambers, etc., but there is a reality group of white musicians who, if asked the same question, would reply Sal Nistico, Stan Kenton, Buddy Rich, or Chuck Mangione. Furthermore, in many instances neither group knows about the musicians of the other group—but this is only the beginning. In actual fact, many white musicians have come to view their activity as completely separate from the reality of black music and/or black culture—yet this cannot be stated as an absolute rule because it isn't (there have always been musicians, both black and white, whose activity and participation transcends any one definition or criterion).

WI-6

Nevertheless, if we are to understand the reality of the white improvisor, then it is important that the dynamics of this subject are not avoided.

The reality division between black and white musicians reflects the physical universe landscape situation that permeates present-day social reality. For the reality continuum of the last two to three generations of black musicians reflects a very different pedagogical alignment to both learning and participation from that of the white musician. In other words, the dynamics of social reality in this period have solidified two very different life experiences for white and non-white people, and this difference is essential to understand if we are to properly view the reality of creative music as we enter the eighties. For the black musician, learning and functioning in creative music had to do with growing up "and listening" to the composite spectrum of black creativity—from what we call blues on through to church music, popular music to so-called jazz. This experience was and is directly related to the affinity dynamics of expanded functionalism, and more important, this experience also lends itself towards the possibility of gaining profound insight as to the vibrational and dynamic implications of creative music (from the black projection, that is) with respect to its essence, and expansion possibilities. By the same token, the white improvisor attracted to the same activity in many cases had to function from a source transfer learning position—in that, the reality position of the white community did not lend itself to experience (to any real degree) the dynamics of composite black creativity. As such, the social reality implications of separation have seen the last two and three generations of white musicians come to rely more and more on educational institutions as a means to gain relevant information about improvisation—and in particular improvisation as practiced in black creativity. The difference between these two paths of learning should not be lightly viewed, because the meta-implications of this phenomenon lie at the heart of the reality position of the white improvisor. If we are to understand the reality of the white improvisor, then it is important that his or her activity is viewed from a relevant context. Because not only has the white improvisor had to establish alternative routes to study the mechanics of creative music and/or improvisation, but the reality dynamics of this phenomenon did not necessarily mean the same thing to the white musician as they did to the non-white musician anyway. In other words, the reality position of expanded functionalism does not imply only one application or participation. This is true not only for the black or white improvisor but also extends to the nature of affinity dynamics—regardless of group (pertaining instead to the zones that people are born into). If we are to understand the dynamic position and contribution of the black, white, or Asian improvisor, then it is important that all of these considerations are dealt with, because in the final analysis we are commenting on people (which is to say, "people" are much too complex to generalize about). Whatever, the role of education and the significance of affinity dynamics should not be overlooked, because both of these considerations are directly related to the present factors that are reshaping the cosmic dynamics of world "creative participation" and/or source transfer extension.

C.INFO.------PROJ.DY.

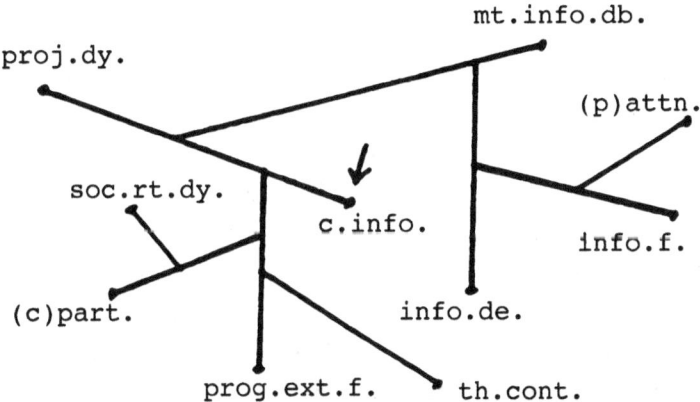

WI–8

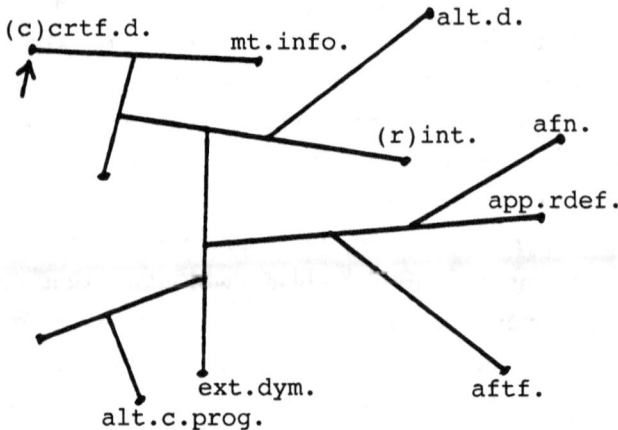

The educational route of the white improvisor must be viewed on several different levels. For the nature underlying how information is viewed and interpreted in the established institution is very interesting—to say the least. In short, the information-affinity interpretation taught in the university mirrors the information position of western culture—which is to say, this position (or affinity alignment) moves to affirm a particular relationship with information that in many cases is very separate from the vibrational alignment of world culture information dynamics and/or black culture information dynamics. The fact is, the "normal" focus of information transfer in nine-tenths of the educational institutions in the west promotes a distorted view of black creativity at best—which is to say, for the white musician who has just become aware of black creativity (who had no real understanding or exposure to the music in his or her early upbringing), the college experience does not provide any insight about the "real" significance of past or present "masters" of the music (black masters, that is). In its place, the university has moved to instill a concept of "correct" that in many cases is only consistent with the affinity-dynamic-information position of western information dynamics exclusively—having nothing to do with the essence umbrella of black creativity. As such, this juncture (the university) has not been a completely positive tool for composite information transference—and the importance of this "unsuccess" cannot be lightly dismissed. Yet I have not meant to imply that the present divisions existing in social reality between black and white people are the sole result of the university—because to imply such would be one-dimensional indeed. Rather, the reality implication of western education is only one factor among many.

Without doubt, the disease of racism must also be viewed as an important factor that has helped to shape the present reality of "creative participation"—and this is true on several million levels. The nature of the various divisions between white and non-white people can be directly traced to the expanded implications of what this phenomenon really is. **In actual terms, the resultant social reality position of the white improvisor cannot be separated from the composite position of all white people in general—which is to say, to view the reality of the white improvisor sheds light on the composite reality position of all white people—regardless of sector—during this time cycle.** As such, the social political position of white people in this time cycle has given the creative person an "option spread" that is on another level from that of the non-white creative person. Nor does this advantage limit itself to any particular sector of the community, for the advantages (or option range) of the white improvisor, as compared to those of the non-white improvisor, are no different than those of the white school teacher compared to the black school teacher—or those of the white businessman, politician, or factory worker as compared to their black counterpart. This is not to say that a given white creative person cannot produce necessarily relevant creativity, nor have I meant to imply that the creativity from any sector of the white community is necessarily inferior to that of any other community—because to believe either of these charges would be to engage in both prejudice and stupidity. But to simply pretend that these advantages don't exist would also be to ignore reality. The fact is, the white improvisor must be viewed with respect to all of these considerations—and others as well. It is not simply a question of attempting to over-apply social theories in a vacuum; rather, the actual reality position of the white improvisor must be seen with respect to the composite factors of which his and her work are part. This is true for the white improvisor and this is true for any other improvisor.

WI–10

Gradualism

In 1975 I recall watching a program on television with one of the more celebrated white jazz musicians on a talk-show variety program format. The thrust of the discussion that took place on this program would clarify my understanding of information documentation or redocumentation—having to do with how the present "state of things" has come about in western culture; and the realness of this experience helped to solidify my concept of gradualism. Basically the particulars of the program involved discussions about the reality of jazz music, and since the musician being interviewed had performed with practically every important musician in the music, the talk-show interviewer spent the thrust of his program asking questions about the whole of jazz music. What interested me, however, was the nature of the famous musician's answers—both for what it implied about his viewpoint of black creativity, and also for what it implied about composite information continuance. I can still recall the interviewer saying, "Since you have played with all of the big bands, Ellington, Basie, etc., what can you tell us about this wonderful experience?—and what band or bands did you feel to be the best overall band?" And the musician answered something like "Well, that's a difficult question, but of all the bands I have worked with, I would say Woody Herman's Big Band was undoubtedly the best." To the question of jazz vocalists, the musician replied, "Well, I've worked with them all, Eckstine, Williams, Rushing, etc., etc., and without doubt Tony Bennett is the best jazz singer in history." And throughout the whole of the program the standard of every area of excellence, in this musician's opinion, was the offering of the white musician. I recall feeling that opinions of this nature are the only opinions transmitted to the greater society, and even more amazing is that after a given time period, people come to accept these interpretations as true. **In other words, the perpetuation of a given viewpoint, in a given time parameter, can be solidified as true, if not successfully challenged—and this phenomenon can have very ominous implications for black people (and all non-white people), because ideas do not simply become implanted and accepted as true; instead, the propagation of a given interpretation involves the "gradual" transfer of documentation and affinity transfer.** This is what has happened to the information that was transferred from Egypt to Greece, and this is what will happen to present-day achievements as well, unless something is done. For instance, slowly but surely ragtime music has been redocumented, Paul Whiteman has been installed as King of Jazz, Goodman—King of Swing, Beatles—King of Rock and Roll, Joplin—Queen of the Blues (in *Time* magazine), Springsteen—Savior of Rock and Roll—and while one might view these examples as not necessarily indicative of anything, at the same time the success of a given cycle of gradualism is directly dependent on this very phenomenon, as it involves hundreds of years of unchallenged documentation. As the present stands, in a thousand years when someone goes to study or teach rock and roll, will that person teach about the dynamics of Martha and the Vandellas, or the Beatles and Rolling Stones? The realness of gradualism is no more complex than this—that being, the point of an interpretation shift.

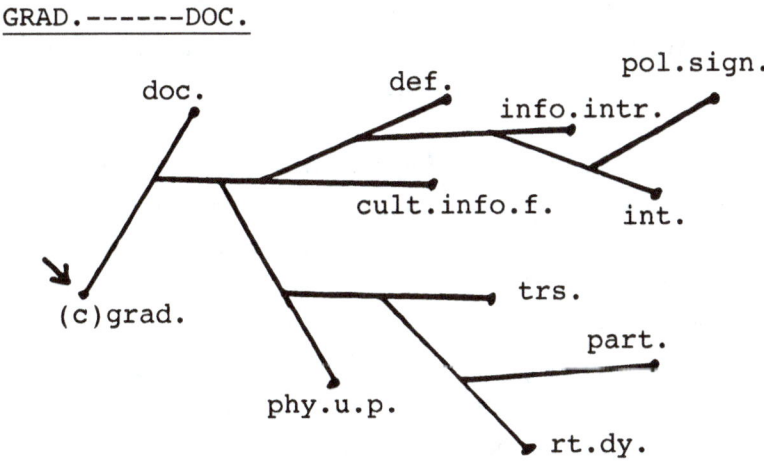

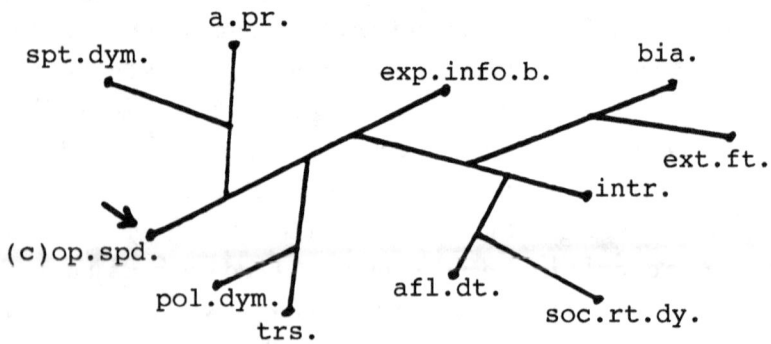

The present social political order of this time period has moved to solidify an extremely complex situation for creative music—and this is especially true if one attempts to deal with the dynamic implications of racism. For the nature of this time zone has progressively seen the white improvisor become the commercial recipient of public focus on one hand, while viewed as an undeserved beneficiary—who has not really contributed anything to the music—on the other hand. Both of these positions are serious and must be examined.

To write that the white improvisor is the commercial recipient of public focus is only to comment on the natural advantage one has in his or her own country. This is the natural advantage that the white improvisor has enjoyed in the west—nor am I commenting on any recent phenomenon. The fact is, every projectional thrust of black creativity, from the early forms to the present, have experienced a cross-transfer response (that being an offshoot continuum practiced by white musicians—sometimes exclusively). It is for this reason that the Original Dixieland Jazz Band was to become as successful as it was in the twenties, and it is also because of this reason that the progressional continuance of the music has cyclically experienced the practice of redocumentation. Yet I do not mean to imply that any of these groups were in themselves not creative—and deserving of support from the greater public—because they were. My point is that the history of so-called jazz must be viewed as extremely

WI-13

complex in that the progressional documentation surrounding each area of its expansion has always seen more focus on white musicians—in what has been essentially a black music. The misdocumentation I refer to is clear: Paul Whiteman, King of Jazz, Benny Goodman, King of Swing, etc., etc.,—nor am I only referring to the past, because nothing has changed as I write this book. One has only to read any of the so-called jazz poll results in the last thirty years to understand my point. To even lightly view western historical documentation is to begin to understand the advantages the white improvisor enjoys by simply being in his or her own country. In other words, in many instances black people, and especially musicians, are mistakenly guilty of viewing the option spread implication of the white improvisor as something outside what is normal in western culture—when in fact the white improvisor is only enjoying what all white people in the west enjoy: that being, affinity focus and support. The fact is, black people have yet to understand that western culture is not "about" black people and, in its natural state, will never be. In other words, one cannot make the mistake of viewing the reality dynamics of the white improvisor as something foreign or unfair (even though, in objective terms, the present reality of western culture is ridiculous) because the white improvisor only enjoys that which was created for him or her. To say that the white improvisor has unfairly gained more commercial acceptance and/or economic leverage from his or her activity is to only comment on the design of the normal physical universe situation as it is in the west. The white improvisor's situation in this regard will not change until the composite reality of the culture is changed—on every level.

But to simply believe, because of the social inequalities permeating western culture (and as such the whole of this planet), that the white improvisor has not contributed to the composite body of creative music (jazz, or whatever else the music is now called) is to take a somewhat... interesting position—that is outside of what seems to be true. To really take that position is to put oneself in a somewhat difficult position, both actually and cosmically, for to comment on the white improvisor is to be commenting on a whole group of people. The fact is, many musicians have contributed to the wellspring of creative music—regardless of projection, and regardless of focus. Moreover, the nature of a given contribution transcends the concept of race, sex, or origin. **To simply not acknowledge the dynamics of world contribution is to isolate a given phenomenon past the point of what is real. It is not a question of whether or not the white improvisor has contributed to the music; rather, it is a question of whether or not one's contribution is to be received with respect to what it is.** In this period of social and political unrest it is important to not lose our sense of what is both cosmically and vibrationally real. I write this not for the white improvisor, nor have I meant to over-focus on the spiritual implications of this question; rather, because of the actual music. **To simply state that the white improvisor has not contributed to the music is in fact a lie—and it is important that it is understood as such.** The realness of these questions, however, is much more profound than "how one's participation is to be viewed." Because the social reality and creative implications of the white improvisor involve many more considerations— considerations that touch on the very nature of the times we are living in—and if we are serious in our concern for creativity then we cannot afford to let blind prejudice and ignorance block our ability to learn what really is.

The reality of the white improvisor defies any one focus and is instead connected to a multitude of factors—and this should be remembered. For the dynamic implications of this subject are not separate from the composite implications of present-day earth. To accurately comment on this subject is to necessarily view it with respect to the nature of present-day earth life and participation—because there are several important assertions related to this subject that must be dealt with and understood. This is so because it is impossible to really view the reality of trans-European dynamics in creativity without also viewing the reality of the white improvisor in composite physical universe terms. Yet I have not meant to imply that there is nothing of substance to comment on by viewing a particular focus or area of the white improvisor's work, because there is much to discuss in this area as well (to really understand the seriousness of this subject is to approach every aspect of its dynamics). But the reality implications of the white improvisor are not separate from what has transpired on the physical universe level in the last two and three thousand years—and as such, cannot be ignored. There are several basic questions related to progressional continuance that must be dealt with, for the vibrational nature of this time period has solidified several "interesting" vibrational positions related to the subject of the white improvisor. These positions translated into questions are: **(1) somehow there is the understanding that the consideration of improvisation is totally alien to white people, and as such whenever utilized signals that some aspect of black creativity is about to be stolen;** (2) the idea that white people have not really contributed to creative music (or so-called jazz) and that if their offerings were separate from the thrust continuum of the music, nothing would be lost; (3) that for a white person to be attracted toward black music is somehow out of the natural order for positive expansion, and instead only signals either a deceptive means to "get over" or source transfer redocumentation. All of these considerations have come to color how the reality of the white improvisor is viewed (and of course there are other questions as well). To examine the reality position of creative music in this time cycle is to deal with what these questions mean—with respect to both the dynamics of alternative functionalism, as well as transformation. Yet I have not meant to imply that the option-spread particulars of the white improvisor can be viewed in one-dimensional terms, because the reality position of the white improvisor is much more profound than any one series of questions; we are forced to examine this subject on several different levels.

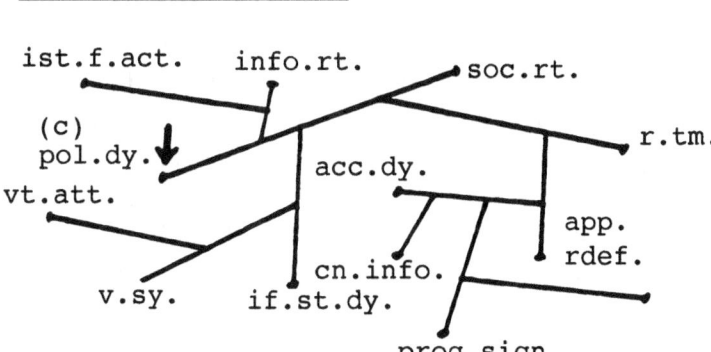

The question of whether or not the white improvisor has a right to participate in improvisation is really related to the concept of "which came first, the chicken or the egg." In other words, the validity of a given creative participation in this argument is related to whether or not that participation has historical relevance, either as a means to proclaim the false notion of superiority or as leverage to deny the "actualness" of a given offering. In other words, the participation of the white improvisor in improvisation is viewed to be alien because improvisation is not documented throughout the composite progressional continuance of western creativity—and this is only the beginning. The expanded use of this argument moves to create profound vibrational divisions concerning what vibrational areas are to be perceived as legitimate for given sectors of humanity. The question of who practiced improvisation first or last is also really only the beginning of a much more profound attitude that has crept into the mainstream of composite American information documentation, and if unchecked this phenomenon threatens to become a major social reality barometer for both social and vibrational obstruction. What of the chicken-and-egg analogy? History does seem to document that the solidification of dynamic improvisation (as a discipline) developed in the high-culture cycle of Egypt—which in that period was a black nation. If this is so (and there is no reason not to believe this information if we choose to believe anything about the past—SINCE WE WEREN'T THERE TO SEE FOR OURSELVES) then all of us can be thankful that the progressional dynamics of this consideration (improvisation) has been handed down for humanity to utilize. Obviously this is so, just as we can all be thankful for the positive dynamic changes which have expanded information in this period—in every area of technology. But if the white improvisor's activity cannot be received as real, on the basis that western culture did not solidify improvisation as an expanded functional methodology, then everyone is in serious trouble. Because this same logic must also hold that black people today have no right to study and hopefully advance contemporary science, medicine, computer technology, and any of the other unique information routes advanced in this time cycle by the people we now call white people—and there is still more to this argument. Because to really study the dynamics of a given information line is to see both its historical and contemporary interdependence—which is to say, the basis which supports any contemporary information line has to do with the meta- and progressional reality underlying that line—in other words, without the past there is no present and without the present there is no past—not to mention what happened before Egypt anyway, and what happened before that—who was really first (not to mention, does first have anything to do necessarily with earth anyway)—in other words, which came first, "the chicken or the egg" or the "or"?

If we are to ever move towards a more just planet, then three-fourths of present-day information lines must be re-examined. It is also important that our traditional documented definitions—vibrational and actual—are understood with respect to what they pose about social reality (for it is clear in the final analysis that many of these considerations really have nothing to do with positively forwarding either the planet or the music). The vibrational and actual position of the white improvisor is directly related to what has transpired through the progressional continuum of western culture. Which is to say, by citing the vibrational innuendos surrounding the scene in this time period, I am only commenting on the natural result of a much deeper campaign that has helped shape present-day sensibilities. For obviously there is much deception between normal people in any culture—which is to say, there are both good and bad feelings between all kinds of people, regardless of focus and/or so-called classification. My point is that the composite reality of present-day information manipulation is not controlled by "the normal people," but instead information dissemination is directly connected to the powers which really regulate events in the west. In other words, **the peculiar position of the white improvisor in this cycle is not the result of black people who are angry over the composite scene, nor is it the work of what in this period is called "reverse racism."** Rather, the reality position of the white improvisor is directly related to western expansionalism over the last five hundred and some years. To view this phenomenon is to focus on one of the most important developments responsible for solidifying this cycle. My point is this: **the reality of the white improvisor is related to** the "grand trade-off" that was solidified with the forming of America and the institutionalizing of slavery.

The concept of the "grand trade-off" concerns the nature underlying how various vibrational and cosmic maneuvers were justified—involving both particular physical and social universe reality events—as a means to solidify a composite culture vibrational position. To really understand this concept is to re-examine what has taken place in the last two to three hundred years. The fact is, it is important for the reader to understand that the present reality particulars of planet earth have not come about as the result of a particular move to establish (or re-establish) "intention." It is important that this viewpoint is understood, for to view present-day earth is to see white people in a particular position (with respect to the power this one group wields over the entire planet) and non-white (and in particular, black) people occupying another position. The solidification of the "grand trade-off" is directly related to the events that helped to establish these positions, yet I have not meant to over-generalize this most important subject. Certainly the favorable social reality position that white people now enjoy in this time period must be viewed as a testament to their ingenuity and cultural achievements as well—and this position must also be viewed as in accordance to the greater design of the all-cosmic pattern to—"things" (which is to say: nothing can happen unless it expresses some aspect of the greater realness of cosmic purpose and unfolding truth). But at the same time, the social political domination related to how this phenomenon is maintained has also dictated the reality position for all of those people (or individuals) who are not of its perceived contingency—or at least, the dynamic solidification of present-day social reality has produced necessary consequences for "all of those outside of its benefits." This is not only true for black people in America, but this is also true for all non-white people all over the planet (I write this generally, understanding that there are several sections of the planet that are outside of western reality and/or vibrational domination—like China, North Korea, etc., etc.). In other words, the realness of present-day western expansionism and continuance has necessarily produced particular consequences for all non-white people of the world group—and this is only the beginning. The solidification of

WI-19

the "grand trade-off" can be understood by examining the nature underlying how western expansion was brought about—especially the events that characterized the dissolution of composite Africa. For the essence intention that necessitated the vibrational need to establish the "grand trade-off" had to do with political expediency—as opposed to labels related to the "spectacle-diversion cycle." To understand the progressional solidification of the "grand trade-off" is to understand what has happened to all non-white people in this time cycle (and I do not write this as something that will last forever because it, like everything, will change)

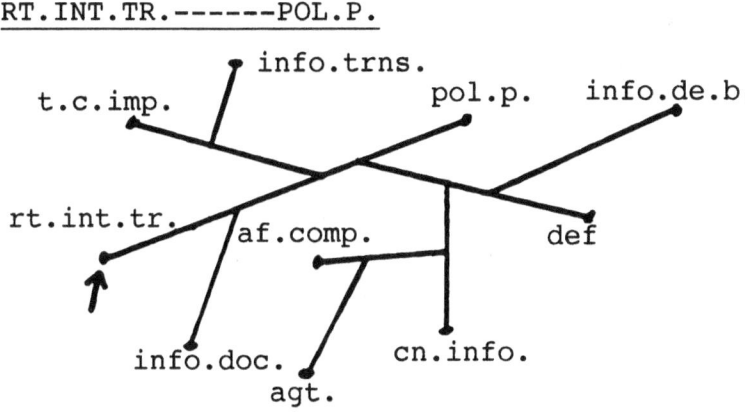

I have not mentioned the historical dynamics of early Africa as a means to simply rant and rave about this sector of the planet; rather, the historical position of this continent is directly related to the nature underlying how this time zone solidified. The fact is, Africa is documented in every information continuum as having played an important role in human evolution (and not only in one context, rather having to do with the development of the arts, sciences, the concept of law, and the awareness of dynamic spiritualism, etc.)—and any attempt to understand the progressional implications of this time period would imply that some attention is given to what transpired in this region—and why. Since this is not a historical essay, there is no reason to investigate every aspect of this most important subject, but the dissolution of the composite African-affinity cultural and political position has been the most significant factor to determine the course of composite events in this time cycle—and this phenomenon is also related to the vibrational solidification of the "grand trade-off." **My point is this: the nature underlying how Africa was dissected is directly responsible for the present reality position of non-white—and especially black—people. This is true with respect to the reality dynamics of politics and this is also true with respect to the overall vibrational position that black people are now dealing with today (1979).** Yet I have only begun to deal with this most important subject, for the seriousness of composite African progressionalism is much more than any one aspect. It is important that this subject is not overly generalized because I have not meant to conjure up the image of the "nice guy" who was done in by the "bad guy." History has recorded very clearly that transitions and/or transformations are in themselves nothing new. Which is to say, the particulars surrounding how given "changes of order" are brought about have been constant for the whole of humanity (those instruments being war, and the enslavement and brutality of human beings). As such, it is important to understand that by citing the dissolution of black Africa, we are not focusing on something that is unique in the annals of human behavior—which is to say, the success of "those we now call white people" cannot be viewed as out of context with "what this planet has experienced before." But it is also possible to view the "particulars" of Africa's destruction with respect to several contexts that have not been "in keeping with the historical dynamics of transition," and this is what concerns—or should concern—us.

The fact is, the nature underlying how Africa was plundered has established a unique vibrationaltory stance quite separate from world history. For the progressional and vibrational solidification of so-called black inferiority has expanded to proportions that cannot simply be ignored. My point is that the destruction of Africa and the later institutionalizing of slavery has necessitated that some greater viewpoint be utilized as a means to validate "present-day contemporary life," and this is where the "grand trade-off" comes in. In other words, many of the ideas we have now come to accept—even vibrationally—concerning both the reality of humanity as well as "the nature underlying given segments of humanity," are nothing more than collected responses that have been vibrationally planted as a means to serve as a basis for either rationalizing or justifying the "present state of things"—and this is true on many levels. The seriousness of these vibrational and actual concepts have come to color our understanding of practically everything, including the reality dynamics and dynamic implications of both the black and white improvisor. To investigate the nature of this phenomenon is to gain insight as to what factors have contributed to our present viewpoint of the white improvisor, yet to really investigate this phenomenon is to move towards viewing the composite nature regarding what has transpired in the last thousand and some years.

The "grand trade-off" is this: slowly but surely the collected forces of western culture have moved to solidify a viewpoint concerning humanity that has nothing to do with anything but maintaining the present social and political "state of things." In this concept, black people are vibrationally viewed as being great tap dancers—natural improvisors, great rhythm, etc., etc., etc.—but not great thinkers, or not capable of contributing to the dynamic wellspring of world information. White people under this viewpoint have come to be viewed as great thinkers, responsible for all of the profound philosophic and technological achievements that humanity has benefited from—but somehow not as "natural" as those naturally talented black folks. The dynamic implications of the white improvisor have never really been dealt with because this juncture was "one of the sacrificed categories"—but I have not meant to over-generalize. Surely, say, western art music is perceived as a great contribution to humanity, and of course this thrust is also viewed as an exclusive offering from white people (with respect to the greatness of western culture)—which is to say, I have not meant to imply that white people cannot respect the creativity of white people. And it is also true that even in improvised music, the white improvisor has long enjoyed greater acceptance and respect (for reasons I have already mentioned, as well as others I have not). But the concept of the "grand trade-off" pertains to the essence lining that determines the vibrational nature of events in this cycle. For western art music is not viewed as a so-called natural thrust, but instead the solidification of a "high culture" thrust (what we now call art music)—which is to say, western art music is perceived as "more" than the "merely natural." This is also true of the white improvisor's work—for every progressional period of music from the white improvisor has always been viewed as a more "sophisticated offering" from that of their black counterparts. This is true from every period of creative improvised music, from Dixieland to the present (witness any of the books written on the music before the fifties). In other words, the concept of the "grand trade-off" is not merely a hip phrase to comment on the nature of progressional continuance in the past one thousand years; I am instead referring to an all-encompassing vibrational and actual attitude that permeates the composite lining of this time period.

The vibrational particular implications of the "grand trade-off" have produced a very interesting situation in this time period, and the reality position of the white improvisor is directly related to what this concept has posed. For at present, the particulars of the trade-off are that "no white people have ever contributed to so-called jazz"—which to me sounds somewhat strange. I mean out of all the white improvisors who have functioned in the music, no one is credited with any real degree of restructuralism? To really investigate this position is to move towards viewing the real "under vibrational structure" of western culture.

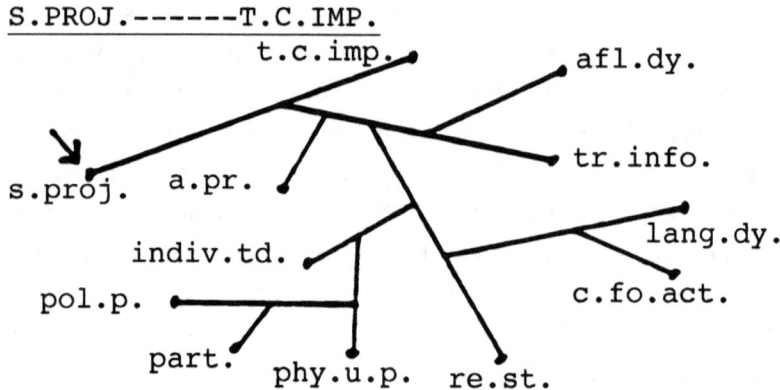

WI-23

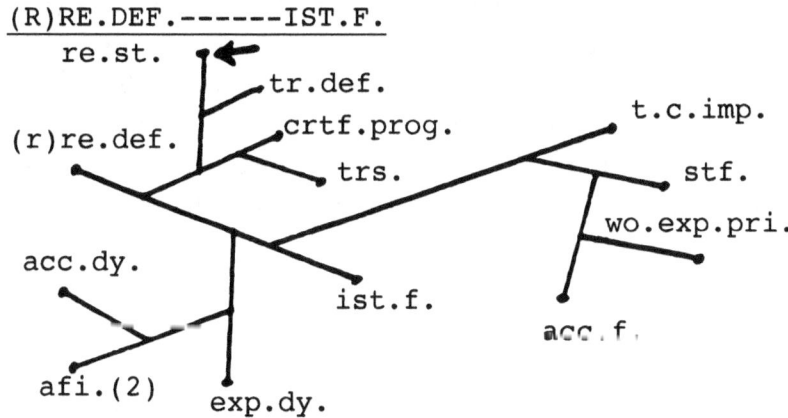

The achievements of black creative people in so-called jazz are now acknowledged because the western power structure doesn't regard the music as significant. These achievements are now recognized (and remember, even twenty years ago all of the books, and jazz polls, were focused—even in that period—on the white improvisor exclusively... which is to say, the acknowledgement of the black improvisor in this period is even a recent development) as a means to not focus on the many other areas of achievement that have been solidified through the black community. **The fact is, black people have contributed—like everyone—to the composite solidification of this time period and culture, but this is not now, nor has it ever been, recognized.** Instead we are dealing with an attitude that has progressively been reinforced—and shaped—that moves to vibrationally and actually solidify how the affinity dynamics of black and white people are to be viewed (which is to say, this attitude is subject to change depending on the focus, and in every case the beneficiary of positive interpretation in the long run will be western culture)—this must be understood.

The concept of the "grand trade-off" is also related to the concept of "elastic definitions." For the progressional utilization of a given participation is only valued for as long as that participation satisfied some aspect of the "greater information manipulation" of western culture. In other words, the present reality position of the black improvisor should not be viewed as unchangeable on any level. Because as long as western culture has the power to define the reality of black culture, then they also have the power to change a definition—and this is exactly what is happening. My point is this: **the achievements of black people, even with respect to black creativity, are being documented in the wrong way—with emphasis on the wrong focuses, having very little to do with what is actually happening.** Unless this is changed, the solidification of the next cycle promises to be extremely interesting—concerning black, white, and Asian creative people. In actual terms, it is possible to focus on the particulars substantiating the nature of these definitions as a means to better understand what has happened to the white improvisor. For instance, practically every so-called writer that commented on black creativity in the last fifty years (and more) has helped to distort the nature of the music's functionalism. In particular, the concept of rhythm in black creativity is taken all out of proportion to what is really happening in life. As a result, many of the current vibrational notions that surround contemporary creativity have nothing to do with what is really happening in the music, because in actual fact, the concept of rhythm is manifested on so many different levels in creative music that no one function can accurately house it. The realness of this example can be better understood when the dynamic offerings of the white improvisor are taken into account, because how often has one read about the inability of a given white musician to swing, or a given white movement of style to swing. This is ridiculous. There is no such thing as swinging in the way that this consideration is now used. But the reality implications of the white improvisor are much deeper than any one example. It is important that this subject is expanded as a means to view its composite dynamics.

If we are to understand the meta-reality implications of alternative functionalism (which is what black creativity really is), then we cannot make the mistake of ignoring what this question poses when viewed with respect to its greater focus—that being, what this consideration means for composite earth. In other words, I have already written about the significance of black creativity in this time zone, and I have already commented on the role black creativity has played in accelerating the affinity-insight-principle dynamics of western culture. To reject the initiations of the white improvisor is to in fact really be rejecting the meta-implications of the music. For the essence of black creativity and alternative functionalism—in the creative process—has always been "activity" that in the doing moves to vibrationally and dynamically give one insight about both him or herself, as well as the greater culture. In other words, the essence of the music has always been "to be as you are" or "to be as you are becoming." As such, to neglect the activity of the white improvisor is to run against one of the most basic tenets of the world music aesthetic—and this is important to understand. To simply claim that the vibrational particulars of alternative creativity have to assume a particular affinity posture is outside of what world creativity has long postulated in its essence-aesthetic foundation. This is so because the meta-reality of world creativity has always insisted that a given phenomenon, above all, "be true" as a vibrational actualization of doing. It is important that this is understood because many of us have come to view the meta-reality of black creativity in the wrong light. The greater vibrational reality of black creativity has never had anything to do with western words as an essential focus; rather, music (and all creativity for that matter) was viewed as one part of the collective life experience. For this reason, Africa at every juncture has always attempted to share her creativity—and information—with every visiting group (whether from Europe or the Orient). This is documented in every period of her history. My point is only this: **the spread of black creativity has been brought about because of "real attraction" to the music, as well as political manipulation—but the meta-reality implications of the music have always been receptive to the greater world group.** This is true on every level (yet I have not meant to imply that Africa [and Africans] view their creativity as "supreme" or more advanced than any other group—because the consideration of creativity is not viewed in that manner in Africa). One is only asked to enjoy and/or participate "if you should so desire." The music, in other words, is "given," and has been "given to the world" (without any false qualifications, as to whether or not a given person or group has the "right to participate"). But this has somehow been forgotten in this cycle.

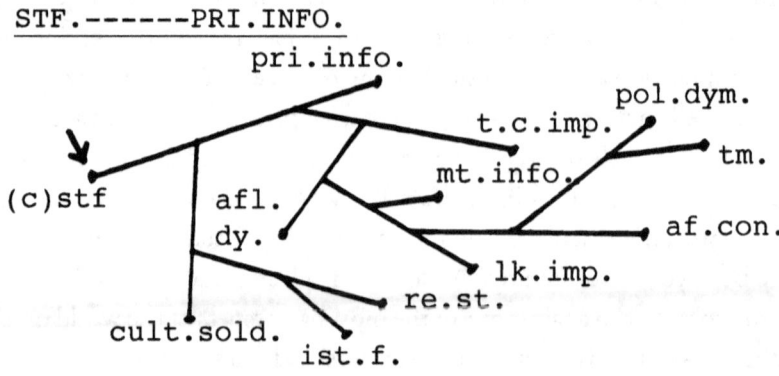

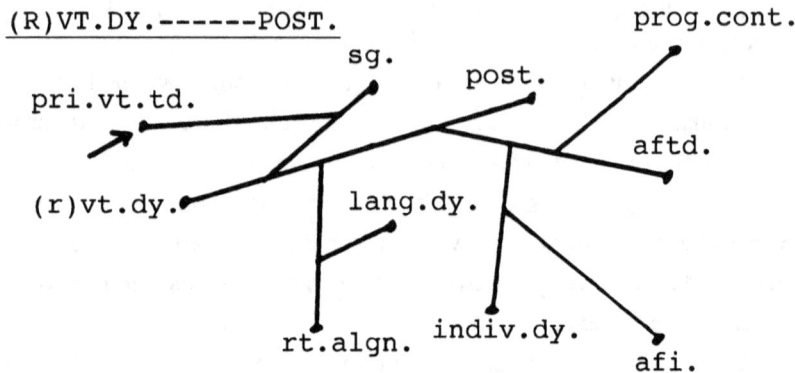

The affinity-dynamic implications of the white improvisor must be viewed in his or her own terms, without respect for preconceived notions as to vibrational properties. At present there are two vibrational perspectives related to expanded functionalism that directly relate to this consideration. In this context the white improvisor is viewed by how closely their activity approximates that of black music (with the added feature being, if a given musician utilizes a vocabulary learned from a given black master musician, then he or she is accused of "stealing the music" or "trying to be something they are not"). On the other hand, if a given white musician chooses to function from the affinity dynamics that we associate with western creativity then that same musician's work is viewed as "not really playing the music." Moreover, practically nine-tenths of the white improvisors, whose activity has become commercially acceptable, have functioned from a source transfer creative position (which in itself is fine and good—I am not knocking any affinity position, because every position manifests some aspect of "what is") rather than a source initiation position. This is not to say that no original white improvisors have become acceptable, but very few white musicians have been able to accept or acknowledge their European roots without being labeled as "not jazz"—"not good" (or "not really playing the music").

The implications of expanded functionalism in creative music must also be re-evaluated if we are to understand the spectrum possibilities for alternative investigation. For the dynamics of world creativity have long showed that there is no one form of "correct participation"—which is to say, to exclude the activity of the white improvisor on the basis that a given sector's use of improvisation (and/or functionalism) is not consistent with a given time focus is to defeat the composite position of the music. In other words, the reality of the white improvisor (like everyone else) cannot be viewed only in the context of his or her relationship to so-called jazz, but extends back into early western art music. The dynamic implications then of a given participation must be perceived with respect to the route its participants are traveling—this is true for the Asian, black, and white improvisor.

```
WO.EXP.PRI.------MT.INFO.
```

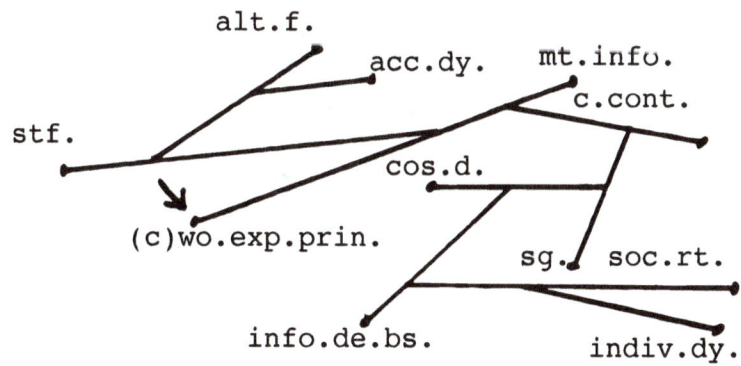

It has been generally accepted that there have been no white restructuralists in creative music from the black aesthetic, and to a great extent this is actually true. But what must be remembered is that there have only been a few innovators in any form—regardless of race. If the realignment of form—restructuralism—is the sole criterion to judge whether or not a given person's creativity is valid, then nine-tenths of all of the people participating in the music could be dismissed—for this measurement would have to be applied universally. On the other hand, if the essence factor of creative music has to do with a person developing his craft to the point where his (or her) activity can honestly express where that person is coming from, then any person who reaches that point has to be respected—and "ised." There is of course more here, and we could expand this way of looking at the music; but I have only written this section to state that it would be a gross error to simply exclude the initiations of the white creative person on the basis of race. Not only would this be unfair but this action is not very different from the current situation happening in western art music (which is to say, very few people would choose to be viewed in that light). In my opinion it is a testament to the music that it has attracted and dictated the attention of all people on the planet. It would be a great disservice to the aesthetic if the initiations from that attraction were simply discarded on the basis of race.

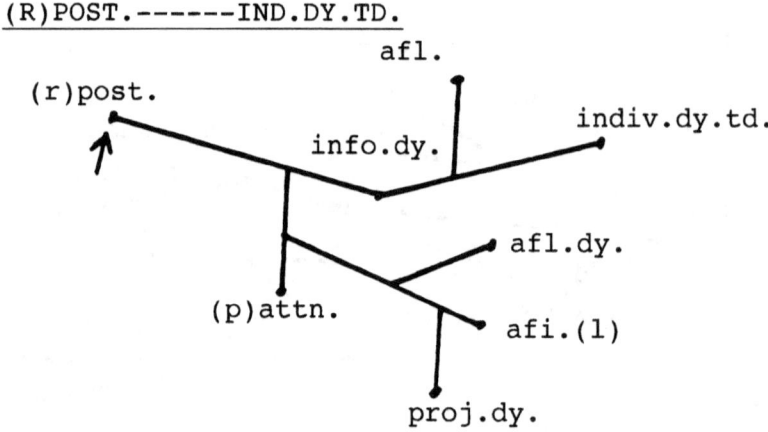

For, it must be remembered, I have previously stated that creative music from the black aesthetic is the strongest factor that has helped to solidify transformation in the west during this time cycle. In this light, creative improvised music represents the strongest aesthetic for the formation of a possible world aesthetic. Yet if this is true, then how can we simply not accept the progressional implications underlying what this statement obviously signifies? There are very clear reasons why black musicians have dominated the meta- and functional reality of the music (having to do with the affinity particulars of the creativity—as well as the historical factors related to how black people arrived in America). But—because the planet is as it is—there has always been a group of white musicians who have felt an honest love for the music, and have because of that love contributed. The fact that we are talking about actual people—and lives—makes it all the more important that we understand the cosmic implications of creativity—as it applies to each and every person who participates. It is not a question of whether any person has the right to participate in a given form—nor is it a question of the worth of a given individual's activity—it is more a question of understanding the multi-dimensional dynamics of existence on the physical universe level.

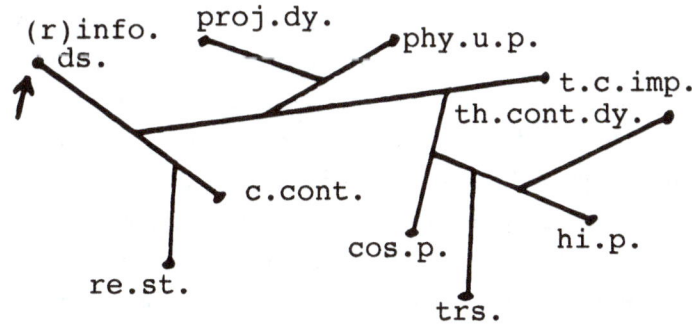

When I stated that there is a body of music coming from the creative white musician that is essential to the entire body of the music, I was not being condescending nor am I trying to be liberal—I am stating a fact. It is not a question of whether or not any individual's creative approach is totally innovative, because if we choose to erect too many barriers we might not ever hear the music. There are simply too many creative musicians who happen to also be white for the standard argument of that individual being a "credit to his race" to apply. For if innovation is as rare as I think it is, then the next level for examination would surely pertain to the originality of the stylist, and if this is true, there can be no doubt that there are many creative white musicians participating in the music. I am not implying that the majority of white musicians participating in creative music from the black aesthetic are original—for that matter, can we say the majority of any race participating in anything is original?—but I am saying that there has been a body of music offered by the creative white musician which is real—whatever the context—and important to the total body of the music. In today's climate this all-too-obvious fact is sometimes forgotten, and it would benefit the aesthetic of the music if—however one chooses to deal with the present physical universe situation—we kept the cosmic perspective of the music intact. Without doubt the universal realness of the music is put off balance by the physical universe particulars surrounding actual living, because I am sure the question of whether or not the white improvisor is creative is not the real factor which has determined the reality focus underlying how his or her activity has come to be viewed (in the black community anyway). The "realness" of the white improvisor's activity is always connected to the social-political physical universe context—and this connection is both valid and not valid—depending on which zone one represents.

If the activity of the white improvisor is looked at in relationship to the forming world group, it is possible to see the implication of alternative process (improvisation) on a global level. In other words, the "realness" of creative music from the black aesthetic can be viewed in terms of its effectiveness for altering aesthetic and vibrational concepts—and what this effectiveness implies for world culture. In short, creative music is the stimulus for a new attitude concerning composite music—which is to say, in this position creative music provides a stabilizing basis for the realignment functionalism towards world consciousness. The actual progression towards this new consciousness can best be experienced by understanding what alternative functionalism means for the black, Asian, and white creative person. In this context the progressional reality of the white improvisor shows only the path towards this inevitable unification— or how it is to be attained. It is not a question of any "thrust" being less creative than any other "thrust," but rather understanding what factors each thrust has to deal with on the road towards unification. One thing remains clear—the emergence of creative music has transformed the total arena of western music and this "transformation" does mean something. But it is also important to understand that the resultant sensibility thrust of this phenomenon will not—and should not—necessarily reflect only one racial group, but instead take on the vibrational properties of all the world's communities and truly be a world music. The work of the white American and European improvisor (as well as the Asian-African and Hispanic improvisor) must be viewed in this context.

The emergence of the white improvisor can also be understood by dealing with the aesthetic predicament of western creativity. For it is important to understand that however sophisticated western functionalism became with the development of notation and its subsequent harmony theories, the actual vibrational reality of European functionalism had a stifling effect on the individual person. To understand that this music came to actualize the "western creative thrust" is to have some idea of the real position of the western creative individual. For it must be clear that the use of improvisation in creative music today is not merely a new use of process but instead the personification of a different vibrational sensibility. In other words, the white improvisor today can be viewed in relationship to European art music and what this continuum posed on the vibrational-thrust arena of western culture with regards to a person's ability to function individually and collectively in a creative non-notated context. The "realness" of the activity of creative white musicians has nothing to do with any notions of racial group superiority or inferiority, but instead only the context from which each group developed. By the same token, it would not necessarily be correct to say that the activity of the white improvisor is "less" because of the route white improvisors have had to take on the way to learning the music. It is really just a question of understanding what factors are at work and what these factors actually mean. It would also be misleading to state that there have never been any western schools of thought in creative improvised music—no matter the connections (if any) to the black aesthetic—because this assertion is not true either.

On the actual physical universe level (playing music and living from day to day), there has always been a great separation between the majority of black and white musicians—and this separation is to be expected. For the vibrational arena of creativity cannot be separated from the total physical universe reality of its real-life particulars. Historically, this type of separation can be viewed as greatly beneficial to the white improvisor, since in a racist society white people would be expected to support only white groups (e.g., record companies and higher fees for performance). And of course this factor alone has promoted much bad feeling between musicians. The actual position of the white creative musician—as this subject pertains to the spectrum of opportunities in western civilization—breeds separateness between the races, for the present-day structure of western culture is designed to basically exploit non-white people—on any level. Yet by the same token, the white improvisor cannot be held accountable—on a one-to-one relationship—for the gross distortions which have been designed by western culture since its inception. For however much the creative white musician has benefited from this situation, there are simply too many factors involved in present-day living to hold any particular person accountable for western culture social reality. As the present-day situation continues, very few black musicians make any distinction between creative white musicians who are attempting to be honestly creative and those individuals who are simply trying to get over—and when generalizations like these occur, we all lose.

(Level One) THE POST-CAGE CONTINUUM

THE DYNAMIC REALITY OF TRANSITIONAL CREATIVITY in the last twenty-five years cannot be viewed in narrow terms if we are to understand the nature of the present cycle. For the progressional factors which have solidified this period of creative postulation have come from many different sectors of world creativity, and there are several reasons for this. The fact is, the accelerated dynamic expansion of contemporary creativity is not separate from the social reality and technological changes reshaping composite physical universe life. In actual terms, the dynamics of creativity in this time zone are directly related to the increased information position of earth culture—and this is true on many levels. To view the composite factors shaping transitional world creativity is to deal with the progressional route of several necessary projectional strains—and this must be understood on at least three different levels, those being: (1) the reality of a given projectional expansion with respect to what it poses for its separate individual expansion reality; (2) the reality of a given projectional expansion with respect to what it implies for source transfer; and (3) the reality of a given projection with respect for what it signals about the composite reality platform of its time cycle. All of these factors must be understood on some level if we are to understand the nature of the transition that has taken place in the last cycle. The present actualness of creativity is too important to view in isolated terms—for the realness of this subject affects everyone on many different levels. To view the reality position of creativity in transition is to move towards hopefully coming to terms with those vibrational dictates which underlie what a given creative reality is—which is to say, the expanded reality position of creativity is not limited to only the actualness of a given sound or style, but instead this subject comments on the meta-reality implications of composite information and vibrational dynamics. In other words, to view the ingredients of a given creative mixture is to view what factors have determined the composite vibrational stance of its given culture. And this stance involves both the reality position of creativity as well as the reality position of the vibrational factors which underlie what that creativity "really is."

The significance of expansion with respect to social reality should not be taken lightly, because this consideration is directly related to how we have come to view "choices." In other words, the factors related to one's discovery of a given creative projection are not separate from the dictates of social reality. In actual terms, this phenomenon is directly related to how a given culture utilizes its information focus—either with respect to general education and/or extending into its information dissemination. Thus whether or not the average person even hears of a given projection is related to the decisions which occur in social reality and social reality politics. This is not to say that a given social reality situation must necessarily be negative, nor have I meant to imply that any particular region must necessarily be better or less than another; rather, my point is that the reality of a given creative expansion is not separate from what projections are allowed to affect and penetrate into its actual culture. Because in the final analysis it is not possible to transform or extend a given consideration if that consideration is not permitted to become known to a person's information reality. In other words, the particular dynamics of a given social-reality position determine what variables will be dealt with for composite culture expansion. This is true for both creativity as well as composite information dynamics. Thus to understand the nature of creativity in transitio, attempt must first be made to deal with the physical universe particulars which help dictate the vibrational dynamics of a given expansion—because creativity is not isolated from the general life and reality principle.

PCC-3

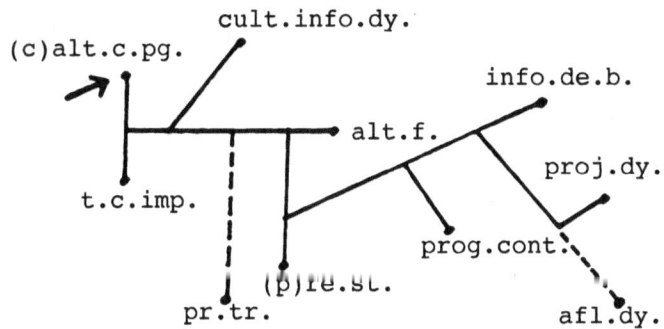

The nature of creative expansionism in the middle fifties to late seventies gave insight about many different factors—concerning both social reality and vibrational integration—and it is important that some attempt is made to really examine this period. This is especially true if we are to deal with the spectacle-diversion reality position of American culture. For the nature of western culture in this cycle has produced a reality position for information continuance—and life continuance for that matter—that is very separate from world culture. The concept of spectacle diversion is only one example of how given events are programmed for the general public in western culture (that being, as a means to produce controlled information and affinity responses). The dynamics of present-day western information manipulation involve everything from the use of television to the rotation of fashion—for what we wear, and for what we vibrate to in creativity. As such, the reality of a given information focus is not separate from how the people in its culture group perceive of particular information lines—or in this case, creativity. Yet by stating this most basic fact I have not meant to over-generalize the reality position of this subject. For all of us have been shaped at some point by the progressional manipulation of given idea focuses. My point is only that this manipulation is an important factor that cannot be overlooked if we are to really understand the nature of creative transition in this time period.

The social reality solidification of events in the late sixties would clarify the creative "ingredients" underlying both commercial creative postulation as well as alternative creative postulation. Both of these variables would determine the composite position of creative functionalism in the seventies and, while doing so, also dictate the projectional dynamics of the eighties. There are several basic divisions which all of these projections can be viewed from—and this viewpoint can also simplify the specifics of this section. The divisions are: (1) the reality of restructuralism and what this consideration posed to creative transition, (2) the reality of stylism, and (3) the extended application of traditional creative functionalism. Each of these divisions is directly related to the composite reality of creative transition in the sixties and seventies. If we are to really view the dynamic implications of extended functionalism and transition, then it is important that some attempt is made to clarify the vibrational context underlying our progressionalism from the past to the present (the late seventies). This is so because the reality solidification of transition is not dependent on any one projectional extension in an exclusive sense—which is to say, the composite realness of transition is not about the reality of only one aspect of its dynamics. Instead, this concept moves to comment on the nature of many factors—some of which have very little to do with creativity in the sense of how the word is generally used.

The first category of extension—that being, extension with respect to the dictates of dynamic restructuralism—can be viewed by examining the dynamics of the post-Cage movement, and the expanded significance of modern technology (the reality expansion of the post-Ayler continuum is explored in the next chapter), and there are many reasons for this. The fact is, however one chooses to deal with the actual specifics of Cage's activity, it is clear that the conceptual implications of his work have functioned as one of the strongest factors to affect alternative methodological expansion in western art music. Certainly I do not mean to imply that only concepts from one area have solidified this period in time—because they haven't. For the reality implication of black creativity has most certainly played a profound role in this context, and the progressional realness of world creativity has also served as a dynamic tool for creative expansion—but this has never really been dealt with—which is to say, the effects of Cage's activity are not separate from the social reality factors which validate what areas can be appreciated and for what reasons. Thus if we are to understand the reality of expansion for restructuralism with respect to what this consideration posed for western art music expansion exclusively, then it is important that some attempt is made to deal with the dynamic implication of Cage's activity.

The reality position of post-Cageian activity in western art music must be viewed from several necessary perspectives, for the dynamic implication of his activity has transcended any one context. In other words, the reality position of Cage's activity must be viewed with respect to many factors that have nothing to do with the exclusive reality of western art music—and there are many reasons for this. For the solidification of this thrust would give insight as to the expanded vibrational position of western creativity with respect to both the affinity-insight principle, as well as the nature of alternative functionalism. To really understand the significance of this thrust continuum is to deal with the multi-implications surrounding what it meant as an extended continuum in social and actual terms. We are forced to view this continuum in several necessary contexts; for example: (1) the realness that "the defining forces which validate what musical areas are to be viewed as worthy of serious consideration" have never been able to deal with any initiation that, in its pure state, was not perceived as being a caucasian source initiated projection (and as such, these forces have never really dealt with the reality implication of either black creativity or world culture), (2) the seriousness of racism as a factor which discouraged any attempt to deal with the expanded meta-reality of world culture, and (3) the fact that the progressional continuance of post-Cageian activity would, in its natural spread, move to utilize source-transfer dynamics from the greater world platform, and as such functioned as a natural tool for "gradualism." All of these considerations are related to the reality position of post-Cageian continuance, and yet I have not meant to imply any disrespect to the actual activity itself—for certainly the work which substantiated this continuum must also be viewed for what it posed to the actual "stuff" which determines what a given continuum really is—that being in this case, its creativity and creative dynamics. But it is important to view the composite implications of the post-Cageian movement, especially if the reality position of the sixties is made clear. Because the reality continuance of the post-Cageian movement would move to clarify alternative functionalism, and while doing so, also give insight as to the vibrational and philosophic position of western culture. The thrust of this continuum has served as the strongest alternative factor after the post-Webern period. Moreover, its natural dynamics provided a unique continuum that paralleled the dynamics of European art music. To view the transition of creative music in the fifties, sixties, and seventies is to have some understanding of the post-Cage continuum.

When I wrote that the dynamic implications of Cage's activity superseded any one application, I did not mean this as a generalization, but rather a fact. The thrust of Cage's activity would clarify the reality dynamics of contemporary western art music on several levels. For the methodological brilliance of his work did not promote a limited viewpoint with respect to either procedures or idea focus; rather, the composite realness of his activity expanded the option range of individual participation. Cage solidified both a reality functional principle for alternative procedure in western art music and a vibrational and philosophic basis to justify future creative postulation—and this should not be viewed lightly. The nature of his activity supplied a dynamic foundation for the route western creativity would have to take from classical to existentialism to transformation. This is not to say that only Cage's activity has established the possibility of future continuance, but there can be no denying the contributions he has made towards solidifying alternative functionalism for either transition and/or transformation. All of the later extensions that occurred in the late fifties, sixties, and seventies could be viewed with respect to what aspect of Cage's activity was isolated—and extended. To view the dynamic continuum of this application is to see an important movement that has yet to be dealt with—in any real sense; hopefully the eighties will be the time cycle that will properly document this subject.

The reality position of the Cage movement would solidify in the middle fifties, and this would be one of the strongest cycles of its documented existence (as opposed to its real existence). The thrust of this movement affected the composite reality of western art music—and this is true for both

American and European activity. This is not to say that Cage's actual music was imitated in all of its various aspects; rather, the dynamic implications of his concepts have long been viewed as equally significant as his actual music (and some would say even more important). Whatever—the end of the fifties saw many of the cornerstone concepts of Cage's activity adopted by the composite contemporary western art community—among those cornerstones being: the use of extended composition techniques, the use of indeterminism (or the use of given aspects of improvisation), and the vibrational establishment of an alternative attitude that would characterize the tone of western art music investigation until the present (that being up until the eighties). The work and reality of the Cage movement must be viewed for what it has posed to the composite reality of western creative postulation. Because the essence of Cage's activity solidified another understanding of "participation" for western functionalism.

The fact that Cage, and the subsequent movement that resulted from his work, was not European cannot be overly emphasized. For the solidification of this movement had a dynamic effect on the composite reality of western art society. The Cage movement would move to create a totally different vibrational stance for alternative investigation in European art music, and while doing so, also move to widen the nature of what credentials were to be observed as relevant. This is not to say that the Cage movement was necessarily separate from European culture—because it wasn't—rather the solidification of this movement commented on the reality expansion position of western art culture: that being, the fact that Europe in the fifties could no longer be viewed as the sole bastion of western creative postulation. But the nature of this relationship cannot be over-generalized, for while the solidification of the Cage movement was perceived as threatening to the reality base of European cultural dominance by Europeans, in fact in America the post-Cageian movement had done everything it could do to be viewed as European—or "of Europe"—or "of white people and Europe exclusively." Which is to say, there was no need for Europe to view the Cage movement as a threat, but rather an expanded arm of western continuance. Nevertheless the progressional continuum of the post-Cage movement established an extended reality position for alternative creative investigation, and this establishment must be viewed as necessarily significant to the composite expansion of western creativity. To view the position of this continuum is to view how the particulars surrounding its expansion were brought about. One thing is clear: the reality solidification of the post-Cage movement established the dynamics of an alternative viewpoint in theoretical and practical terms, and the second expansion of this movement (so to speak) would advance these principles in fundamental and dynamic terms. In other words, the practical application of post-Cageian concepts established a dynamic spectrum for alternative investigation—and the second generation of its composers advanced what this spectrum would mean in actual terms from the time period of the late fifties until the present. Any attempt to deal with the dynamics of transition in the fifties, sixties, and seventies, implies that some effort is made to understand the post-Cage movement.

In many ways the transitional extension of post-Cage functionalism could be viewed with respect to the historical movements that solidified in the twenties and thirties in Europe. For the nature underlying how functionalism was applied in post-Cage functionalism was not separate from the early Bauhaus and Dada movements. All of these movements would move to produce a deliberate reactionary kind of music that in many ways accented the problems of the composite philosophic position of transitional western culture. The most basic thrust of these alternative movements accented the existential dynamics of "participation" with respect to the surface particulars of culture continuance—that being, in this case, the emergence of industrialization and the new awareness of technology, as well as the resulting dilemma of attempting to adapt to the changing vibrational reality of western culture. If seen in this light, the solidification of the post-Cage movement does have precedence, yet I have not meant to imply that this context is all there is. Because while the reality—and idea focus—of the post-Cage movement can be seen with respect to its position in alternative western existential reformation developments, the actual significance of the movement really transcends any one interpretation—or qualification. The fact is, the progressional continuum of the post-Cageian

PCC–9

movement commented on the nature of the affinity insight principle with respect to the expanded position of the western or white improvisor, and also on what that position meant to the possibility of world transformation. This is not to say that Cage or the Cageian movement was necessarily in itself concerned with world solidification (there is much evidence to argue on both sides of this question)—rather, the solidification of the post-Cage movement was not separate from the composite arena which dictated actual and vibrational events in the late fifties—sixties—on up to the seventies. The nature of this post-Cageian movement cannot be separated from the composite reality of its related particulars.

To say that the post-Cage movement cannot solely be reduced to its position in the spectacle-diversion continuum of western culture is to deal with what its solidification posed to the greater reality of planet developments in its respective time period. To understand this viewpoint is to understand the complex reformation which would characterize the vibrational and actual reality of the late fifties and sixties—and seventies. The realness of the last twenty-five years must be viewed as profoundly relevant for the establishing transition. For the dynamics of this time cycle would move to accelerate the nature of information extension and transfer on several different levels. The thrust of this period would see the forming of many different areas of source-transfer extension—and this is true for both creativity and information dynamics. As such, the reality of post-Cage functionalism is not separate from what those areas posed as a transitional consideration—that is, to really view the dynamic realness of the post-Cage movement, it must be viewed with respect to the composite backdrop of its time period, because the solidification of the post-Cage movement posed particular implications that were directly related to the composite reality of events in its time zone. In other words, the Cage movement would establish a dynamic pedagogy that functioned with respect to the composite information transfer that characterized the last time cycle—that information transfer being: (1) the progressional move to examine world culture, and in particular the spiritual particulars of world culture; (2) the move away from traditional empiricism as a means to either re-establish contact with feelings or the "awe" of things;

325

and (3) the expanded functionalism of the individual, that being the use of improvisation or simply "doing." The solidification of John Cage's work, as well as that of his colleagues, would move to touch on all of these considerations, and the realness of the second generation of post-Cageian composers must be viewed for how these considerations were "made real" in actual terms.

The dynamic implications of Cage's activity in the sixties and seventies can be viewed in two most basic categories, and each of those categories gives insight about the reality effect of alternative functionalism. The two categories are: the movement which proceeded to practice Cage's concepts in its defined position (and in doing so, moved to redefine the application or focus of the aesthetic), and the other movement which consisted of those who functioned in Cage's concepts for a limited period of time but later abandoned them (which is to say, the movement that used Cage's concept as a means to find other possibilities for alternative functionalism). In both cases, however, Cage's activity served as a liberating factor from the suppression of established western pedagogy. In doing so, his activity must be viewed as an important alternative factor not separate from the implications of affinity-insight dynamics. To really view the route of transition in the sixties and seventies is to deal with the expanded dynamic implications of the post-Cage continuum, and the dynamic implications of alternative functionalism. Moreover, many of the people who functioned in the second continuum of post-Cage functionalism have now come into their own as creative people (with their own achievements and focus). To write on the reality position of transitional alternative creativity necessitates that some effort is made to comment on their work, as well as the movements generated because of their work. By commenting on the post-Cage continuum it is important for the reader to understand that this is no fly-by-night solidification of events. Rather, the post-Cage continuum is moving into its thirtieth year (depending on how one counts it), and as such has been around long enough so that certain factors can now be discussed. The composite offering of this continuum is important for what it signifies about the present meta-reality position of western culture, and western continuance.

The dynamics of post-Cageian activity can better be understood by viewing particular aspects of its extension—and this is especially true if we are to understand how given information and conceptual schools developed. Certainly a group like the Sonic Arts Group can be viewed as an example of the new developments posed by Cage-like concepts (although I have not meant to imply that no separate individual gains were made from the members of this group, because many were). The Sonic Arts Group (later Sonic Arts Union) represented one of the first of the post-Cageian alternative creative groups to function as a unit. For a time span of twenty years, this collective has functioned in a variety of contexts and has helped to reshape the total arena of alternative creative music. The Sonic Arts Union consists of four extremely creative individuals—Gordon Mumma, David Behrman, Alvin Lucier, and Robert Ashley—and any attempt to really understand the post-Cage continuum of creative music would necessitate that some effort is put forth to examine the work of these individuals—with respect to both the collective and individual work they have contributed. For the most part, the Sonic Arts Union can be viewed as one of the first ensembles that utilized live electronic music spontaneously. In the beginning one could view the creativity of this ensemble as a direct outgrowth of post-Cageian concepts, but by the end of the sixties it was also clear that the group had become a force in its own right—this is true for both the ensemble as well as its individual members. For while the group had been conceived as a composite effort to perform live electronic music, at the same time the ensemble was a vehicle for each composer's separate interests—which is to say, the growth of the ensemble was in fact the growth of its individual members (this was not a group in the sense that all of its members functioned from the same desired objectives or for the same desired objectives). The reality implications of the Sonic Arts Union can be viewed as a significant factor for its role in advancing the dynamics of alternative creative music. This ensemble has performed all over the planet and has been a source of positive influence throughout all of its twenty and some years. The actual activity of the group can be understood by examining what it has posed to source-transfer progressional expansion—because the thrust of its activity produced a positive body of work towards composite reformation, and this is important. The Sonic Arts Union adopted many of the conceptual implications of Cage's activity without also adopting the philosophical and methodological particulars underlying Cage's reality base. Thus a given performance of their work would utilize the dynamics of open compositional techniques for live electronic music—as well as theatre—in a post-Cageian fashion, without utilizing the *I Ching* or time-measuring devices as a means to validate a given work. Hopefully the creativity of this ensemble will one day be documented correctly—because few people are aware of the dynamic gains which have solidified from their efforts. The Sonic Arts Union has been at the forefront of alternative creative music since the sixties (and possibly earlier).

It would be impossible to comment on all of the composers whose activity was inspired from the initiations of John Cage—not to mention, there are many whose work I have never experienced myself. Certainly a composer like Max Neuhaus must be mentioned for the dynamic work he has contributed in the last decade and some (more like twenty years). In his early period as a percussionist, he performed practically all of the percussion literature in his day, traveling all over America and Europe. Later, as a composer, Neuhaus displayed a profound understanding of both extended functionalism and alternative investigation. In the past five years, he has been involved in the concept of "installations"—involving the installation of sound-generating sources in various regions of the community. The work of Neuhaus can be viewed as directly related to the information-affinity continuum of affinity extension—that being, his activity has moved to clarify the transitional nature of alternative functionalism for western art music as well as transformation participation. As such, Neuhaus can be viewed as one of the composers whose activity helped to both extend and clarify the reality position of post-Cageian activity (and what this aesthetic implies for information focus). The activity of Christian Wolff (who was one of the original members of the first wave of composers who functioned from a post-Cage perspective) can also be viewed for its role in helping to extend alternative creative music. Wolff's activity has helped to clarify Cage's reality position—that being, the progressional thrust of

PCC–13

post-Cageian activity is not so much a given approach to methodology but rather the emergence of a transitional and/or transformation attitude—and this difference is important. No one creative route has emerged from the post-Cage continuum—instead what we see are attempts to clarify and gain insight into the affinity-insight-principle implications of alternative functionalism and alternative participation. In actual terms, we can now easily view the difference between the work of a performer like Charlotte Moorman and the dynamics of an instrumentalist like Stuart Dempster, and this is also true of the diversified range of approaches from the post-Cage continuum. The solidification of the post-Cage movement must be viewed for what it posed as a separate thrust continuum from the developments reshaping post-Webern extension (which is to say, as a separate factor from European art music)—and as such, this movement signifies a new development for both western art music extension and definition.

It is somewhat difficult to properly trace the dynamic impact of post-Cageian activity in all of its various contexts, for the reality spectrum of this continuum is both complex and divided. One thing is clear: the reality progression of post-Cage activity has continued to flourish, even though this continuance is both "in" and "outside" what is perceived to be the "acceptable reality position" for western art dynamics. For the most part, this movement is practically all caucasian, and functions with respect to its own separate "social reality" alignment. The thrust of this movement was brought about through the active performing of both Cage and his cohorts in the fifties, and also through the social reality changes which occurred in the late fifties and early sixties that saw many of the first-generation composers attach themselves to universities of some kind. Whatever, many of the participants of the second and third generation of post-Cageian composers have developed their viewpoint from alternative spaces and university-type situations. Because of the nature of this diversification, it is impossible to write of the ultimate effect of the post-Cageian movement (although it is now clear that many younger composers are currently coming forth—which is to say, it is clear that the work of the first generation of post-Cageian composers has indeed affected the next level of composite investigation for the next generation of musicians and composers—as we move into the eighties). It is also clear that the activity of the post-Cage continuum has profoundly altered the composite reality of western art music—affecting the general affinity tone alignment dictating how "things" are perceived—and practiced. This is true for both American creative music as well as European creative music—and postulation.

Musica Elettronica Viva is another ensemble that sprang from the post-Cageian continuum that must be dealt with on some level. Unlike the Sonic Arts Union, which functioned as a vehicle for each individual composer's compositional approach, Musica Elettronica Viva moved to explore the dynamic possibilities of composite music participation. This direction would reveal another projectional extension of post-Cageian activity—even though the basic tenet of its aesthetic was, on the surface, in opposition to Cage's aesthetic (Cage has never been interested in improvisation without controls). Musica Elettronica Viva was one of the first ensembles from the post-Cageian continuum to utilize a more open approach to making music. The dynamics of this group would involve expanding alternative electronic music and also the use of what came to be called "the sound pool" (having to do with the move to create a communal-like music that involved audience participation in the actual performance—the ensemble in this context even provided instruments and encouraged total participation). In its various periods, Musica Elettronica Viva functioned from one of the most expanded operating contexts of all post-Cage projections. This ensemble openly sought to build alliances with the composite world community and encouraged a wider spectrum of dynamic participation. Musica Elettronica Viva has worked with classical musicians from western art music, Indian musicians from Indian classical music, Japanese musicians, and creative musicians from the black aesthetic. This ensemble was one of the first of the post-Cage projections to embrace the realness of improvisation, and also improvisation as a form in itself. The work of this ensemble solidified the realness that alternative functionalism was more than a one-dimensional consideration but extended to dynamic proportions. As such, the dynamic work of Musica Elettronica Viva has played an important role in clarifying the direction of post-Cageian concepts—and dynamics. The end result of this ensemble's activity must be viewed for its role in helping to solidify the realness of expanded functionalism and composite resolidification. In other words, the work of this ensemble signaled the route of post-Cageian expansion and integration—towards a composite aesthetic.

To really view the realness of this ensemble, it is necessary to focus on the individuals who make up its nucleus. For the thrust of its members has never been limited to only their work with this ensemble but instead extends into every area of creative music. The musicians of Musica Elettronica Viva are:

Frederic Rzewski—whose contribution to creative music is documented in every context and medium since the late fifties. As a virtuoso pianist, he has worked with and premiered the works of every important composer from the post-Webern creative continuum. Rzewski's contribution to contemporary piano technical extension is second only to David Tudor, and the dynamics of his music is second to no one in its sheer breadth and beauty. As a composer, Rzewski has also contributed many important works, and his composite offering to world creativity will undoubtedly be viewed as beneficial to anyone seriously concerned about creativity.

Richard Teitelbaum—is one of the first practitioners of live electronic music and also one of the most creative. As a synthesizer instrumentalist, Teitelbaum has brought another level to creative music—regardless of context. Teitelbaum has also been very much involved in advancing world music projects, and the thrust of his work has involved every focus—from Japanese music to projects that utilized the music of the American Indian. He has also been one of the early pioneers in Brain Wave music. The scope of Teitelbaum's work has definitely helped to extend the parameters of alternative creativity.

Alvin Curran—has been a major contributor to creative music for over twenty years—regardless of focus. Curran was one of the first musicians from the western art music sector to begin utilizing improvisation, and the vision and sensitivity he has brought to his work has helped to solidify another reality continuum of creativity. Hopefully the thrust of the eighties will see more attention on this most special composer-instrumentalist.

The reality implications of Musica Elettronica Viva and Sonic Arts Union were significant on many different levels, for the progressional continuance of their activity helped to dictate another vibrational position for post-Cageian activity (and extended functionalism). The dynamics of these ensembles would establish a wider operational and functional methodological basis for transitional western art music, and this should not be overlooked. The thrust of their activity utilized both "open-ended" structural settings as well as improvisation. Thus, while Cage himself never really embraced improvisation as a "real" consideration, his theories provided the vibrational arena that made further investigation of this type possible (for the western art music community). Nor can the implications of Cage's activity be viewed on one level. For the dynamic implications of his work have prepared the present reality position of restructuralism—as this consideration applies to western art music. Yet, at the same time, the work of groups like Musica Elettronica Viva and Sonic Arts Union must be viewed for how they were able to clarify the reality of applied functionalism and expanded functionalism, even though those extensions were practiced from the vibrational basis of Cage's reality platform. The thrust of these ensembles, as well as others who functioned from the same affinity position, helped to establish the vibrational position of contemporary western art creativity with respect to its (1) reality base (the actual situation that western artists were dealing with in particular and vibrational terms), (2) expansion dynamics (with respect to its own individual route of expansion and also its world culture position), and (3) methodological dynamics (the progressional resurgence of new approaches and "focuses"). As such, the reality position of the post-Cageian movement must be viewed with these considerations in mind—that being, the dynamic implications of Cage's own activity (and what it posed for extension) as well as the actual particulars it activated. There are no creative ensembles in western art music which have not been affected in some way—or on some level—by Cage's activity (or by the post-Cageian movement). Many of the avant-garde classical ensembles that now utilize improvisation and extended forms can be viewed as direct descendants of the post-Cage continuum. Even in Europe, it would have been inconceivable to experience a group like New Phonic Art—even twenty years ago—without the work done by the Cage continuum. The effects of this thrust have moved to create a dynamic new creative position for western art music and expansion. Moreover, the realness of this movement promises to permanently alter the course of western art music, and while doing so also serve as a positive integration factor to world creativity. In short, the activity of the post-Cage movement has created a situation that has the potential of rejoining western art music with composite earth music—and this is important.

C.INFO.------TR.

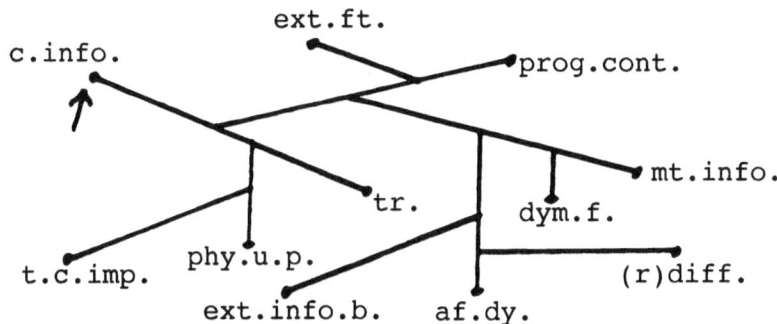

(R)PART.------POL.DY.

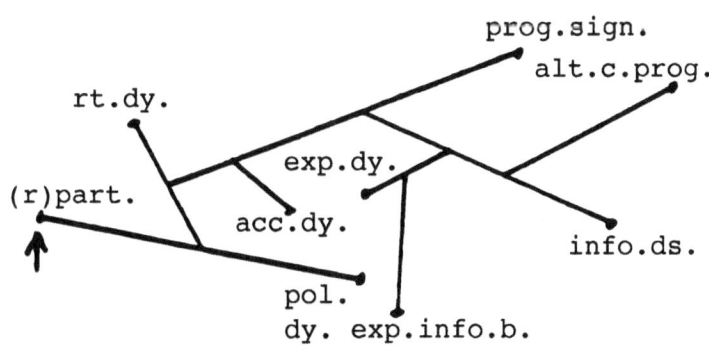

The most significant transition in western art music after John Cage also materialized in the late fifties. The restructuralist whose activity laid the foundation for this transition was a young composer named La Monte Young. It is possible that if Cage supplied the strongest functional aesthetic for the extension of the post-Webern vibrational thrust, the activity of La Monte Young could best be understood as the first aesthetic, after the destruction of the classical vibrational hierarchy, to utilize and reintegrate spiritualism as a real part of the meta-reality of its process. If the works of John Cage—no matter that it served as a liberating factor from the established tradition—served as only an existential exercise rather than a fulfilling creative outlet—then the activity of La Monte Young served as the first creative platform for the post-Webern movement to practice in a substantial (potentially spiritual) creative arena. In short, the spiritual implications of the creative thrust founded by La Monte Young were as important as the functional implications of his work. By the middle sixties, the situation in western art music had begun to see many new creative approaches; for both John Cage and La Monte Young supplied an extension platform that could dictate events in creative music for the next creative cycle.

The movement which emerged from the activity of La Monte Young began to solidify around the middle sixties—although the actual activity which led to this movement was done in the late fifties and early sixties. Young, in his formative period, had been a student of Stockhausen, and like many of the composers in that period, went to Germany to study the post-Webern serial advances practiced during that period—in its high cycle. Nevertheless, the music Young began to create in that period was very different from what Stockhausen had taught him. This was a music which, in its later period anyway, began to draw on non-western influences. By the time Young's activity began to get noticed (in the New York hip press), the distinguishing functional characteristics of his activity had already clearly solidified. For the activity of La Monte Young represented the first post-Webern thrust for source transfer with eastern creative forms—especially Indian music. This was a music which in some cases utilized only one sound (as a drone structure) with the added use of open

PCC–19

singing within given tonal structures. In many ways the work of La Monte Young represented a move towards simplicity and a return to basic values (basic creative and spiritual values), as opposed to the complications which solidified in the functional arena of the post-Webern school. The dynamics of La Monte Young's creative thrust in the early sixties would play an important part in shaping both conceptual and musical attitudes in the next cycle of western art music.

In many ways, the activity of La Monte Young occupies the same position as the work of Sun Ra and John Coltrane. All three men seemed to understand—on some level—the seriousness of the spiritual gap that plagued both western creativity and culture. The progressional particulars of La Monte Young's activity forecasted what factors were to be embraced by the majority of young people in the greater culture—in the move to uncover alternative realities. The embracing of eastern culture, the need to study under Indian masters (as a means to spiritually uncover alternative lifestyles), and the move towards a composite aesthetic were only some of the routes that many of these people took; and Young was among the first of the new generation of composers whose vision would encompass those sentiments.

The realness of this creative route as an alternative functional arena can become apparent when Terry Riley's activity is taken into account as well. For if we can say that the activity of La Monte Young served as a rallying basis for the potential establishment of an alternative creative thrust, we can also say that the solidification of that thrust as an "actual functional and creative arena" has as much to do with Riley as it did Young. By the early sixties it was clear that the creativity coming from these two composers would serve as a factor to open new options for western art music. Just how much their activity was to affect the mainstream of classical music was to become apparent in the seventies. It is now clear that the music from this thrust has dictated the nature of source transfer (as a factor to extend western art music) as well as the linkage particulars to make transition possible.

As this movement began developing in the middle sixties, it became clear that the spectrum of possibilities for this alternative thrust was limitless. Composers like Steve Reich and Philip Glass

335

developed their languages from this continuum and went on to extend this thrust in the seventies. Many of the composers who had long been associated with the post-Cage movement were also deeply affected by this movement. The later works of Frederic Rzewski are a good example of this—even the move by Stockhausen into his "intuitive music" stage showed an awareness, on some level, that other options had opened up for the contemporary creative musician/composer. It is also interesting that, in this period anyway, so little is known about La Monte Young, as opposed to the people who have learned from his work (whose activity has slowly become available to the general public). Nevertheless, the work which has been taking place from this school of musicians constitutes an alternative creative thrust and direction. Any attempt to understand the actual situation in contemporary western art music today would imply that some effort is made to experience the work from this continuum.

Among the important composers from this continuum I especially would like to cite are:

Philip Glass—the dynamics of Glass's creativity transcend any one criterion and have gone on to profoundly affect the composite continuum of creative music in the seventies. The thrust of his output to date scans the spectrum of creative music—from solo compositions to orchestra music. Glass has even completed two large operas—and the realness of these works has given new insight into extended functionalism and dynamic world music. To view the realness of this composer's activity is to see a continuum that has solidified its own reality particulars, and as such, Glass's work cannot simply be isolated as a La Monte Young derivative. His work will play an important role in the direction creativity will take during the eighties—and nineties.

Steve Reich—the solidification of Reich as an important composer took place in the early seventies. Since that time Reich has gone on to produce a dynamic body of works, and today, along with Glass, is considered one of the most important new composers from America. The spectrum of his works has encompassed tape music to orchestra compositions, and I believe the significance of this composer will continually increase with each new output. If La Monte Young and Terry Riley were the first American composers to utilize the dynamics of repetition functionalism, then it is also clear that Reich and Glass were among the first of the new wave composers to actualize that functionalism as a dynamic thrust continuum. The work of Steve Reich has helped to open up a new continuum for eighties participation, and he must be given credit for what this achievement implies.

There have also been many attempts in the sixties to solidify a world music community, but to my knowledge most of these efforts have been somewhat sporadic. We are now living in a period where every possible transfer cycle is being attempted: there is the movement which seeks to unite eastern and western forms—there is the drive to unite creative music from the black aesthetic and creative music from the white aesthetic—fusion rock—the move to join creative black music in America with creative black music in South America, etc. (and all of these attempted fusions indicate a growing awareness of both the dynamics of earth creativity and the realness that people are able to relate to "composite creativity"). The acceleration of world music as a transformation factor is directly related to the amount of people who are exposed to composite music—which is to say, very few people, when given the chance, are not attracted to some region of composite earth creativity. The reality of our present educational system is directly related to the problems of its information scan. Only a few schools devote any time for the study of non-western music—moreso, only a small number of schools have the facility to even comment about non-western music. Given the present situation regarding our school system, I am surprised at the gains which have been made in America involving both the appreciation of world music and the attempts to become involved in "composite aesthetic."

Fortunately some changes have been made in America's educational system in the last twenty years, and there are several outlets where one can learn about non-western music in an accredited school. An institution like Wesleyan University in Connecticut is a good example of an alternative school that specializes in teaching world music, and there are several other schools scattered throughout America which are involved in expanded musical curriculums. It is clear that the move towards "composite aesthetic" is directly related to the realness of transformation on the physical universe and vibrational plane. The events of the last ten years seem to suggest that this phenomenon has accelerated, and if I am correct, the next cycle will be very interesting for what it reveals about world creativity. It is also clear that this phenomenon will develop whether or not our educational institutions provide adequate outlets for research and study. The more we are able to learn about world creativity, the more we can begin to see the real similarities that every culture and vibrational group has to the "composite whole"—which is to say, the more we can begin to think of ourselves as a collected family and get on with the actual "planet business" that awaits us. In the final analysis, our ability to survive the next cycle—and coming cycles—depends on whether or not we have moved towards establishing a more harmonic vibrational arena for composite existence—having not only to do with the acknowledgement of all humanity, but also moving to gain insight as to the whole of our position with respect to the cosmos (or heavens).

IF.ST.DY.------C.CONT.

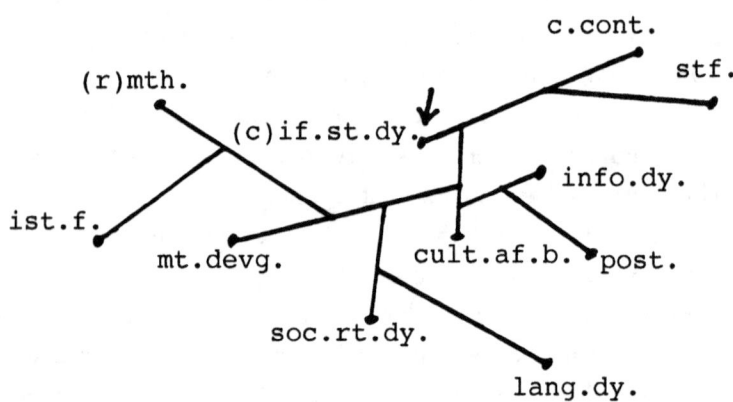

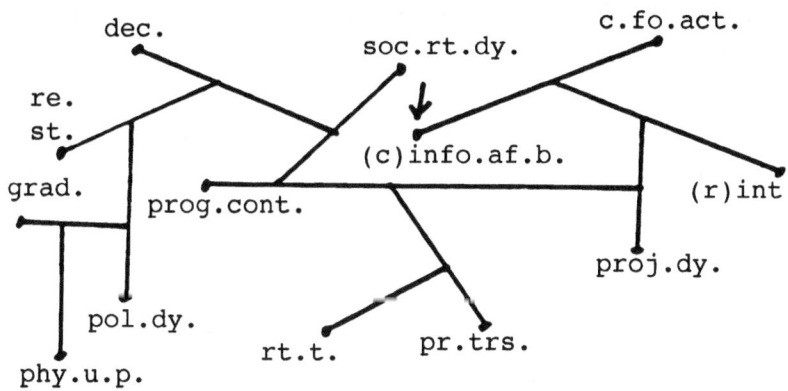

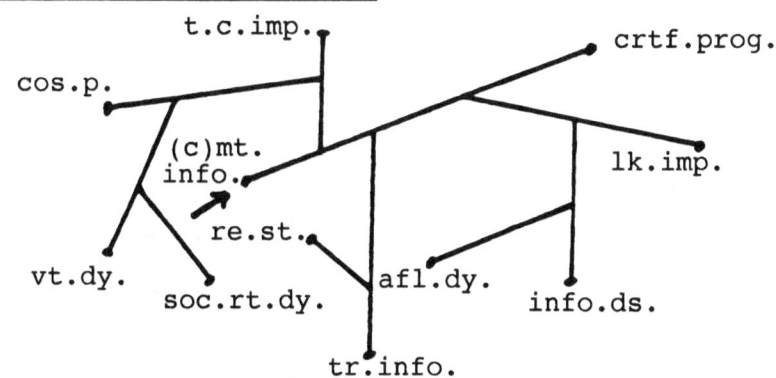

The dynamics of transition in so-called popular music can also be viewed as a factor that has altered the reality position (and direction) of western and world culture. In other words, the concept of transition is not relegated to only certain sectors of the creative community, but instead permeates the whole of earth life. It is important that we as a collective people are not afraid of what this means, for the progressional implications of this phenomenon seem to suggest that the forming transition will be of composite significance—that is, will affect the dynamics of all earth life. For this reason, I have stressed the interconnection of earth multi-information, because the nature of a given transition is not outside of what is "natural"—for its particular state. In other words, the reality of a given change cycle is not outside of what is supposed to happen. Moreover, the nature of a given so-called fusion only sheds light on the meta-implications of its composite information line (or projection). This is so because a given expansion and/or fusion moves towards what is real to its reality and vibrational pull (affinity dynamics). As such, the reality of a given transition can tell us about the multi-dimensional implications of a "principle state"—that is, what a given projectional line "really" is. This is not to say that any given principle state is not "what it is" as it "is" in a given time zone (obviously "something" is as it is when it "is")—rather, the dynamic implications of transition move to give an expanded understanding of "principle state"—which is to say, this concept moves to view a principle state with respect to "what it was and what it is and what it could be in its natural extended context"—this distinction is important.

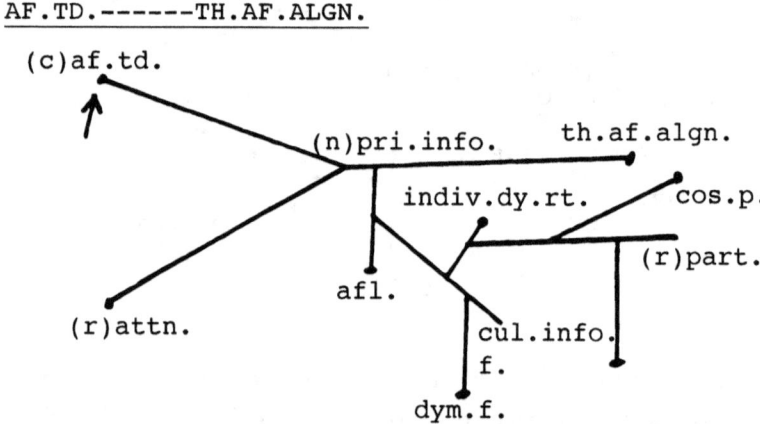

The concept of transition can also be viewed with respect to its linkage implications. This can be understood by examining the nature of progressional continuance—or at least the nature of a progressional continuance. For the affinity continuum that traveled from Africa on through to South America (and the Caribbeans) and now in fusion form to America can be viewed on several levels relative to this concept.

PCC–25

The concept of linkage in this context would have to do with the meta-reality focus or refocus of a given information line with respect to the changes that line has undergone. As such, the implications of a particular projection are not separate from the source-transfer re-implementation of that projection. To view the realness of what this means is to see the resolidification of principle information lines, and this phenomenon must be viewed in dynamic terms.

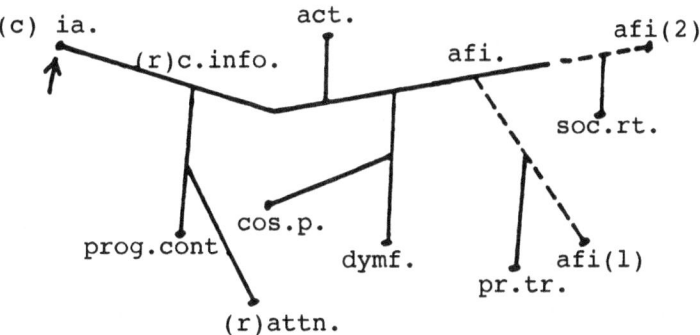

BIA.------AFI.

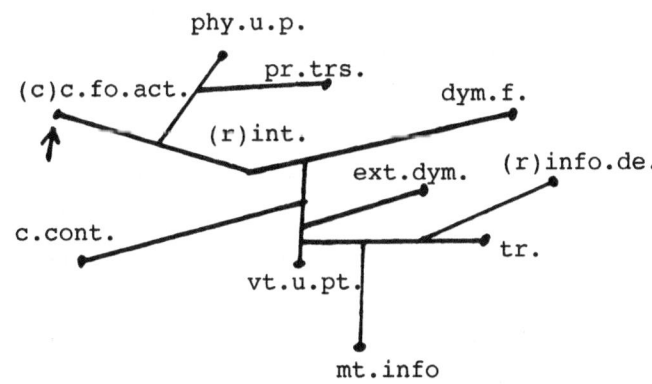

C.FO.ACT.------DYM.F.

PCC-26

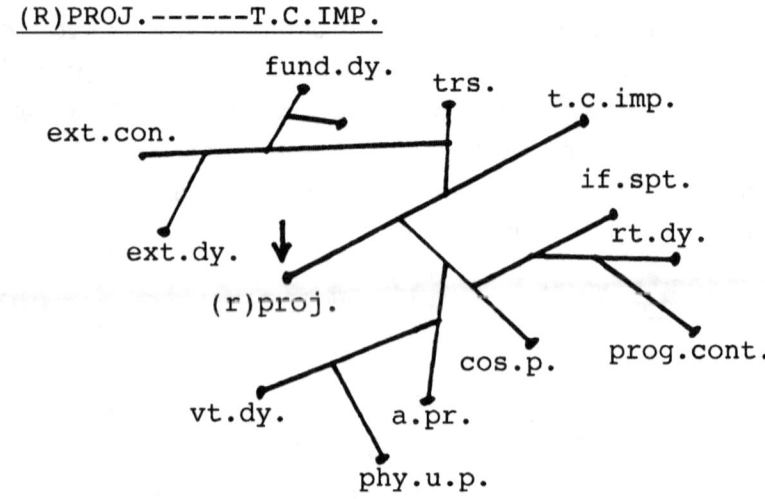

The use of transition as a clarification factor for source initiation can be understood by tracing the reality position of a given projection. For the reality of a particular transition can bring into focus the progressional dynamics of its—or a—given culture. The fact is, a given transition clearly denotes the nature of its related change cycle—in both its physical universe sense as well as its vibrational sense—and in doing so affirms the dynamic implications of its new "ingredients." For example, to view the reality of dance in America for the past fifty years would reveal how this consideration was viewed both before and after the source-transfer adaptation of black American dance. This is so because the dynamic source-transfer adaptation of black American dance (and style dynamics) has moved to totally reshape composite western dance—i.e., how this consideration is now viewed. As such, we can look at the nature of this difference and gain some insight into the reality significance of black American dance with respect to its source-initiation implications. That being: how a given consideration seems to work and what it seems to do—in both vibrational and actual terms, and what this phenomenon might mean with respect to its actual "function." Thus the reality of transition can better help us to understand the nature of expansion on several different levels. For the dynamics of transition are not mono-dimensional but extend throughout the composite

PCC-27

range of its vibrational and physical universe context. The thrust of a given transition moves to give insight into (1) the direction of a given projection, (2) the underlying nature of source initiated information (or at least the total reality position of the projections that are to be co-opted), and (3) the implications of that projection to the dynamics of source transfer. Thus to really deal with the concept of transition, it is important that the multi-implications of this subject are understood (although whether it is or not is irrelevant, because these operatives are activated naturally whenever a given transition takes place).

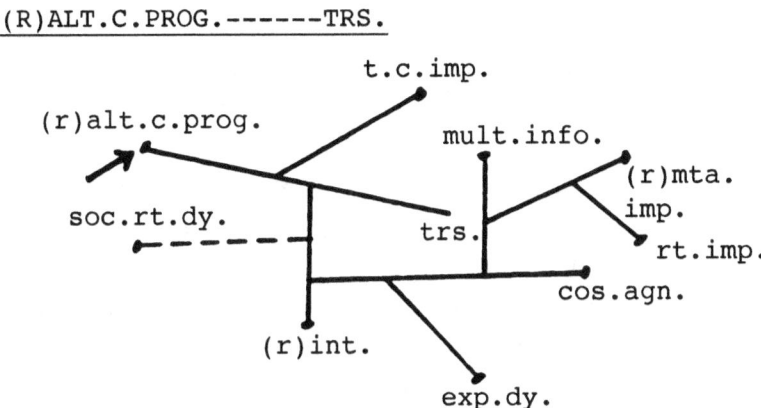

The example of black American dance as a dynamic transition factor can be viewed on several different levels. For not only does the nature of a given transition reveal the dynamics of "particular change" but this same consideration moves to clarify the total hierarchy of its information reality. In other words, not only does the integration of black American dance give some understanding about the nature of the direction (and affinity attraction) of western culture, but this same phenomenon moves to clarify the meta-implication of the material being transformed. In other words, as the progressional use of black American dance continues to reshape the dynamics of western culture, this same phenomenon moves to give insight into the real reality of black American dance—that being, its position as a source-transfer extension of African dance (with the resulting vibrational dictates related to what function it—dance—had in its original "state").

PCC-28

Thus the reality of a given transition moves to totally clarify the composite basis which established its "nature"—and this is exactly what is happening in this time period.

It is important to restate what I have meant throughout this book concerning the concept of transition. I have not meant transition as a term that signified a move towards something that wasn't there before, nor have I meant to imply a condition that once solidified cannot ever be changed. Rather the concept of transition has to do with the nature of how given vibrational and actual solidifications are extended as a means to correspond with physical and cosmic universe "change." But the nature of a given attraction should not be viewed as an isolated factor that has no significance, because this is not true. For the reality of a given attraction sheds light on the "principle zone" of a given phenomenon—which is to say, the transition of a given phenomenon moves from "what it is" (and has always been) to "what it is" (and has always been). In other words "something" is as it always was but changes to correspond with the reality of its "trip." Thus the nature of a given transition moves to give insight into the route a given phenomenon has either chosen to take, or was chosen to take (probably both of these variables are "real" on some level—but I am not qualified to comment about this region).

To understand the concept of transition is to begin viewing the composite inter-relationship of particular information lines with respect to both the concept of principle information and affinity dynamic attraction. The realness of what this means can hopefully move to clarify the composite reality position of planet earth. Because the nature underlying how a given projectional continuum naturally expands has nothing to do with any false concepts concerning either racial or national superiority, but instead comments on the greater dynamics underlying how real change is actualized (from the particulars of its "route"). Thus the realness of what is now called "fusion activity" must be viewed from what this concept poses as a composite observation basis, because there is no form on the planet whose meta-implications are not connected to the greater reality position of composite earth. In other words, the "point of activation" that determines which projections (forms) are to be utilized

PCC-29

only sheds light on the particular focus of that time zone—having to do with "how" a given expansion is to be actualized, and nothing more. Thus the particular forms that are perceived as necessarily relevant to the nature of a given change cycle have more to do with their relationship to the cosmic implications of change—which is to say, the real use of a given projection has to do with that projection's relationship to principle information (in its cosmic position). This is so because the actualness of a given change cycle—in its most real manifestation—is not about how, but rather concerns the cosmic implications of either "grand design" or particular dynamics. As such the reality of a given information continuum is not separate from its cosmic use—or its vibrational affinity position.

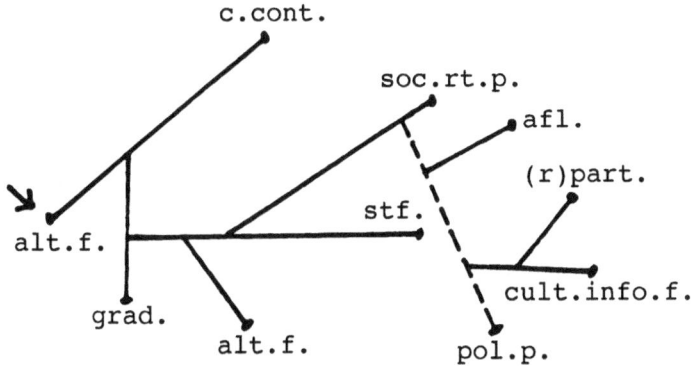

The actual particulars of transition in popular music can be viewed on several levels. There are the fusion developments which have united so-called jazz with later forms, there is the source-transfer solidification of country and western and rhythm and blues and/or rock (which itself is a source-transfer projection from black creativity)—there is the source-transfer solidification of rock with what is now called reggae—there is the redefinition continuance of rock extension (that is really rhythm and blues extension) that was solidified into what is now called disco music, etc., etc., etc. My point in mentioning all of these various levels of integrations is only to comment on the dynamic level of source-transfer expansion in this time cycle, as a means to have us view this phenomenon

345

PCC–30

as something indicative of the composite nature of this time period—rather than isolated acts which have no greater meaning. Furthermore, I have commented on these developments as a means to comment on the greater implications surrounding the reality position of particular projections—my point being: there is no such thing as a projection that has solidified separately from the greater world community, because every projection is related on a multitude of levels. Moreover, the reality of a given expansion must be viewed for what it signifies about the real assignment of its related projections—for the nature underlying how a given projection solidifies has to do with both the reality of its attraction as well as its cosmic destiny. If we are to ever come to terms with the dynamics of world creativity then this phenomenon must be understood—on some level.

(Level Three)

1. Ultimately, how would you assess the activity of the John Cage school?

I believe that the John Cage continuum of western art music will be viewed as important for what it has posed to affinity dynamics and transitional functionalism. The thrust of this school can be cited as an important stimulant factor in western art music, after the initiations of Schoenberg and Webern. I believe Cage's understanding of alternative functionalism (i.e., indeterminism) will prove—and already has, to some extent—to be as significant (or more) as the serialist movement. The advances of the John Cage school must be viewed with respect to what they raise about thrust continuance, because the solidification of this movement has provided the strongest alternative to the strict reality of European postulation and affinity dynamics. What this phenomenon means is clear: the progressional continuance of that which has been viewed as European art music has now clearly moved into its source-transfer alignment position. There can no longer be any doubt that America has, in the John Cage continuum, solidified a unique path to alternative functionalism—and hopefully to culture and art (which, of course, cannot be separated). This is not to say everything about the Cage continuum is positive—because it isn't—rather, the thrust of the Cage movement—whatever its problems—has been the strongest factor to liberate the affinity dynamic position of both the western art music interpreter and composer. My point is that this means something.

2. What significance do you attach to electronic music?

I feel the solidification of electronic music has given the creative person another wonderful area to work in—and as such, another possibility for growth and achievement. I do not feel electronic music is the answer to everything in creative music, nor do I accept the many arguments which somehow attempt to view this medium (electronics) as not being "natural." I believe the reality of electronics has opened many new areas of investigation and for this reason I am extremely excited about the possibilities this medium has for the future. There is so much more to be done—this is true for both electronics and acoustic instruments. I believe that the dynamic implications of this medium have only just been tapped. Electronic music and extended technology promises to be an exciting area for creative involvement, and I for one plan to be as much a part of that involvement as possible. This is not to underrate acoustic instruments, because electronic music will never replace acoustic instruments—nor does there necessarily have to be any conflict between any area of postulation. There is the reality dynamics of electronic music and there is the reality dynamics of acoustic music—and both factors will shape the future of creativity. In the final analysis, it is not about the tools, but rather the individual behind the tools . . . (or it is "not the car but the driver behind the wheel" . . . ?).

3. *What is the nature of your relationship with contemporary music from the western, so-called European strain, and how has this relationship affected your own activity?*

My involvement with western art music is related to my interest in world creativity and world culture. I have found that—for me—every culture has contributed something of great beauty and value, and this is what I want to learn about. My interest in contemporary western art music solidified in the Army and accelerated after the death of John Coltrane. The anguish I experienced after Coltrane's death made it very difficult to continue focusing on only one area of world music—for, to me anyway, the essence of Coltrane's music seems to be opening up the composite dynamics of world music and pointing to world unification. There was also the impact of Arnold Schoenberg's activity—which took place somewhere in this same time cycle in my life. The combination of all of these factors helped me to understand the route my own creativity would take—and that both improvised and notated methodology would play an important role in my future growth. I see the reality of my work in creativity as an affirmation of all that I am—that being, an affirmation of what I have learned in so-called jazz, so-called western art music and world music. I refuse to accept the impositions of the western critical and defining community and their attempts to separate world musics and natural life experiences. I am grateful to have the opportunity to learn and experience world creativity.

4. *Boulez, Stockhausen, and the post-Western school all believe that through the extremities of analysis it is possible to instigate new realities—hence new music. Do you agree?*

NO. Certainly I recognize that the extremities of a given analysis can reveal different aspects of how to view a particular essence, and certainly I accept the notion that the extremities of analysis can help differentiate the dynamics of what procedures can be understood and utilized, but I disagree as to what this phenomenon ultimately means. My point is this: there can be no new music unless there is a new reality, and unless there is also a new vibrational and spiritual basis from which investigation can be made not only to express the empirical surface laws, surrounding how a given phenomenon seems to work, but also including the spiritual position of that phenomenon. In this period we have wrongly applied the word "new" to every so-called observation or reinterpretation that deals with applied investigation. We have used the word "new" even though the basis underlying how a given "new interpretation" is formulated has nothing to do with "a change in procedure"—let alone a "different way of looking at things." The reality of investigation in this time zone has moved to solidify only a very limited spectrum of observation possibilities—and none of these possibilities have anything to do with new. This is not to say no areas of investigation are being uncovered in contemporary science—regardless of region—because of course every day a so-called new information line is uncovered. Rather the spirit that underlines how these areas are viewed and approached is not new—and not transformational. For this reason I believe "we do not even know the things we think we know, let alone the things we think we don't know." I believe that "real" knowing is "about something else."

5. *Do you feel that the art of interpretation is necessarily less creative than improvisation?*

NO. I feel that one of the most basic problems people seem to have on this planet is respecting each other for what we can collectively do. It is very fashionable in this time period to talk of improvisation as the most advanced state of being for the creative person, while the art of the interpreter is frowned upon as representing a less vital area of postulation. This is nonsense and nothing more. I believe one of the best things about living—and this planet's history—is the diversity that has come about through creativity. Every form of creativity has its own challenges and rewards—not to mention every area is equally dynamic. Without doubt the present disrespect for the interpreter is related to the strange concepts we have in this time zone concerning the word "freedom." For the vibrational use of "freedom" in this time zone—especially in the so-called jazz community—has come to be viewed as the only desirable state for the creative person. The seriousness of this misconception was also accelerated in the post-Coltrane juncture of the music, because the dynamics of Coltrane's activity especially focused on extended improvisation—both as a soloist and composer. Many of the musicians who were affected by this music would come to view the significance of any creative music with respect to how close a given participation approximated Coltrane's dynamics. For this reason much of the so-called avant-garde jazz from the sixties on utilized extended solos—even when the musicians had run out of ideas after the first three minutes. It is important to respect the composite thrust of world music—as well as its multi-dynamics. The reality of the interpreter is as necessary and challenging as any other area in creativity, and it is time this is understood.

6. *Improvised music from the black aesthetic is usually considered the only "art form" to have emerged in America. However in the last ten years, many critics and composers are saying that the American composers' tradition represents another original art form, and, as such, "jazz" can no longer be considered the only significant art form developed in America. What is your opinion?*

TR(III)–5

To me this is a very complex question because it assumes many considerations that might not necessarily stand as a valid basis for commentary—let alone true observation. First and foremost of those considerations is the concept of "art form" as used in arguments of this type. The fact is, there is no art in this period, regardless of projection, because there is no culture in the west—which is to say, I immediately disagree with the total reality of the question. But the dynamic implications of this question are related to many other considerations and cannot easily be dismissed. Certainly the composite continuance of black creativity from America has produced a most unique music, and it is also clear there has been nothing comparable to this music—in terms of language dynamics, rhythmic dynamics, and vibrational dynamics—from the American composer's tradition. The thrust of the music has provided the strongest alternative sensibility to the position of western art music in western culture, and no amount of language construction can change this most basic fact. But the meta-reality implications underlying what black creativity really is have nothing to do with "who is the best" but instead move to re-clarify the real position that information—and participation—really has. In other words, to really understand what black creativity—as actualized in America—has posed, is to understand that creativity cannot be used as a tool for lambasting any focus—or "thing"—because of some perceived notion of "isolated differences." Because at the bottom of questions like this can be sensed the concept of "one music being better than another music"—and this idea is false—on every level. Finally, it is true that the American composer's tradition does represent a dynamic creative continuance, and it is also true that recent developments have seen this continuance steadily evolve its own sensibility—as separate from Europe (especially after the initiations of the post-Cage continuum)—but in no way can the specifics of this continuum be completely separated from the greater reality of western dynamics and its related information positions (although again—the post-Cageian movement does have world implications—which is to say, extended dynamics). In the final analysis, every continuum is evolving in accordance to the nature of its route and its cosmic destiny. Every route is equally important and necessary. Yet there is still one more factor related to this subject that should be discussed. For the thrust of this argument has really solidified in Europe—which is to say, factors that have motivated Europe to elevate black creativity while putting down composite American creativity. I believe at the heart of this argument is the legacy of European nationalism—because Europe has never been able to accept the composite dynamics of American creativity—whatever focus. What has happened is that Europe has embraced so-called jazz as an exotic music because she has always been fascinated by black people—and rejected the American composers' tradition—because she cannot deal with what non-Europeans are thinking.

7. *What are the new demands which have been placed on the interpretive musician and what function will interpretation have in the future?*

The last thirty years have seen many new areas for the creative interpreter and I expect this to continue. It is becoming increasingly clear that any person interested in creative interpretation will have to become more involved in the composite music, from many different standpoints. More and more, compositions are utilizing improvisation and this consideration alone promises to have a profound impact on extended creative interpretation. I believe the challenge of interpretation will eventually move to encompass the total dynamics of "the ritual." Which is to say, the creative interpreting musician of the future will be involved in music, dance, theatre, etc. (actually, I do not see much difference between the creative interpretive musician of the future and the creative improvisational musician of the future). I believe the future of the interpreter is very exciting, and will continue to play an important role in creative music—dance, etc.

8. *What is the reality position of the composer after the post-Webern period in Western art music?*

There has been a great change in how the public has come to view the composer in the past forty years. This is not to say the composer isn't respected or highly viewed as a social consideration—because he (or she) is. But the composer is no longer viewed as god but rather as a human being—like the rest of us. Of course there are exceptions (e.g., Cage and Stockhausen), but I believe the historical position of the composer has been permanently altered. The composer still functions as a dominant force in the music and probably this position will not change too much—for the reality particulars of notation necessitate that there be someone to make the necessary decisions as to what a given piece is to be about. Certainly the changes in contemporary music have broadened the interpretational possibilities of a given piece, and as such a given performance of a musical work need not only reflect the basic viewpoint of only the composer but can also include the conductor as well as musicians. I believe this area of compositional direction will continue to be important—both for the composer and the composite music. But the role of the composer after Webern has not diminished—if anything it has increased. This is true even though the reality continuance of this time period has placed a great deal of emphasis on so-called freedom—or even extended functionalism. Probably because before anything can be extended, there must first be a "point of departure" or "reality of methodology"—which is what composition really is—that is, "a point of agreement" and vibrational region for participation.

9. What restrictions does conventional notation place on the potential for what is implied in creativity today?

This is a rather difficult question for it would depend on the musicians as well as the sophistication of the composer. I don't believe anything which is considered "conventional" necessarily places any restrictions on anything especially when it doesn't have to be used. There are definite situations where it is impossible to utilize conventional notation (e.g., conceptual sound environments) and there are definite situations where notation can be a great asset. As we enter the late seventies, many approaches have been developed in regards to creative-notated music both from the western consideration and from the black aesthetic, which puts conventional notation in a different position with regards to the availability of functional systems. The restrictions of conventional notation are obvious, and yet it must be understood that there are restrictions attached to every functional approach (i.e., things you can or can't do). It really becomes a question of each person moving in accordance with what is real to that person and employing the process which best suits the desired goal. Conventional notation is merely one of many functional systems that musicians can utilize—nothing more . . . or less.

10. Can a meaningful integration develop between aesthetic realities from so-called different vibrational alignments such as western art music and black music—or popular music, etc.?

Yes. I believe the forming of a world music is inevitable—and this is true regardless of focus. All of the so-called fusion forms must be viewed as a signal as to how the next transformation will form—that being, the path a given convergence has taken. There have been many attempts to keep this phenomenon from happening—and this is especially true of the journalistic community—but I believe, in the final analysis, that world unification cannot be stopped. This is true whether one is referring to the phenomenon of third stream music in the late fifties, fusion rock, Indian music/jazz fusion, classical music/rock, etc., etc., etc. All of these paths express the dynamics of earth creativity and individual sensibility zones—which is to say there are individuals whose life experience moves towards the participation of one of these areas of so-called fusion as a "natural" means to express their creativity. Each successive fusion moves to bring the composite unification of earth creativity closer. There should no longer be questions as to whether or not a given integration of forms can work; rather, the progressional realness of the last thirty years seems to imply that everything can and will work—because "it is of the same stuff anyway." The challenge for the next cycle is to stop fighting something that is "not about fighting" and to instead move towards creating a dynamic alternative platform that embraces all creativity.

11. What relationship does musical technique have to creativity?

The consideration of technique can best be viewed as "the way a person does what he or she does" on the first level, and the second level of this consideration (technique) has to do with the "proficiency required to execute the methodological specifics of a functionalism." The value, then, of a given musical technique would lie in its ability to best bring about the execution desired. I prefer to view technique in this light as opposed to the concept of unabashed pyrotechnical displays that over-accent the value of real technique. As such, it is somewhat difficult to comment on the real reality position of musical technique. For instance, Thelonious Monk has long been put down because certain sectors of the western critical and defining community decided he had no technique—but in fact, his work has always adhered to the real reality of creative music (and no one could dispute that). For me, there is no such thing as technique in a vacuum—that is, the consideration of technique is interesting as long as it doesn't interfere with the music. The meta-implications of this consideration seem to imply that the weight—or net significance—of a given tool is directly proportioned to whether or not its function is not greater than its end product. In other words, if a given technique best actualizes a particular way of doing things, then that technique can be viewed as positive. Finally, the world culture implications of technique seem to imply that a function must both respect the reality specifics of its discipline as well as its historically handed-down ritual position (with its extra meta-significances—or multi-implications). Which is to say—in that context, a technique is valued as long as it transcends its "doing" and becomes spiritual.

12. *What is the significance of some of the more recent developments in electronic music—especially concerning the development of electronic instruments for creative music?*

The significance of this phenomenon would have to do with how it aids alternative functionalism—and in what direction. For instance, the development of the synthesizer has profoundly altered the dynamics of contemporary music and, likewise, the emergence of the electric piano has altered popular music. I believe we are only at the beginning of this phenomenon. The next fifty years will undoubtedly be one of the most creative periods in this time cycle. Already the past ten years have seen the acceleration of computer music—and this avenue promises to have a profound affect on progressional continuance. However, I would like to hope that the emergence of new technology will not lessen interest in acoustic instruments or cause us—as a collective people—to discard any area of creativity already solidified—as a composite statement about this planet. I personally believe there is room for new and old instruments.

13. Has creative music from the black aesthetic and western art music reached the next composite period for transition?

Yes. I believe the projectional continuum of both creative music from the black aesthetic and western art music have reached a juncture that signals more than simple extension—but carries instead the clear implication of real transition and/or transformation. This is not to say every projectional continuum of black creativity or western art music must necessarily point to dynamic change—or necessarily point to source-transfer resolidification, because it doesn't. But the progressional expansion of contemporary creativity is slowly coming to a point where our present definitions can no longer accurately comment on its reality path or identity alignment. What this means is that the nature of extension permeating contemporary creativity has already moved into its source-transfer stage; which is to say: I believe that the next twenty years will see a distinct creative position—a new all-encompassing information tenet structure—arrive that has nothing to do with regional or national sentiments, but instead views itself as a necessary part of world music.

14. What is the future of notated methodology as practiced in western art music?

It is somewhat difficult to answer this question, for in reality, the future of a form (or methodology) has to do with whether or not that form addresses itself to the needs of its culture—on some level. There is really no reason why notation should ever not be with us as far as I can understand. I reject completely the notion that reading music somehow lessens a person's involvement with creativity—even though it is clear that the discipline of interpretation (as an exclusive participation) is not about the discovery of one's own special affinity dynamics (on an extended plane). In the final analysis, each of us must make the decision as to what route is best for one's own needs—and the reality of those decisions will touch on many different factors. But the solidification of notation (as a function) is not a vibrational continuum but instead a methodology that can be used or not used—in any number of ways. The progressional continuance of this methodology has never been limited to only one use, and in today's creativity there are as many different kinds of notations as there are approaches. The future of what we now call traditional notation promises to also be part of extended creativity as well—and why shouldn't this be so. The good thing about the solidification of a given information line is that it doesn't have to be utilized unless appropriate. This is true for any initiation—including traditional notation.

15. Do you see a period of re-evaluation in contemporary notated music on the significance of Cage and/or Stockhausen?

Yes—in fact, to some extent we have already begun to re-examine the work of these two most important composers. However, the real examination will probably take place in around twenty to thirty years—if for no other reason than the fact that most of their work is not readily available, in America especially. It is very fashionable in contemporary music circles to like one of these composers—but not both. Stockhausen is usually put down because of the enormous success he has had in his career and also because he is documented as not being a "nice guy" (as if the history of western art music—or any continuum for that matter—is a history of "nice guys"). Cage is usually viewed as something akin to a joke—even though the thrust of his work has affected the composite creative music scene. I believe that sooner or later both of these composers will come to be accepted for the dynamic creative people they really are. There can be no doubt both composers have greatly contributed to the wellspring of earth creativity—and in the end, this is what they will be evaluated from.

16. What is the significance of documentation in relationship to people's perception of creative music?

I believe the reality of documentation is extremely important if one is to have the proper overview of both progressional continuance and historical objective. This is true whether the subject is creativity, science, culture contributions, etc. The reality of proper documentation can help to bring a composite picture of earth into focus, because no one culture has brought us to this point in time on its own. The move to restore composite information is also related to the dynamics of documentation, for the last two thousand years has seen a concerted effort by western culture to either dismiss or ignore any contribution offered by non-white people as well as women. As such, the reality of documentation in this time period has been used as a weapon for both national and racial objectives. Hopefully, as we near the year 2000, this phenomenon will change—but it will not be easy. One of the problems with documentation in the west—as it is practiced in this time zone—is that the affinity dynamics of western culture have moved to create dynamic separation as a basis for motivation, rather than dynamic cultural interaction. As such, the emphasis for "doing" in an existential society falls on those individuals who are lucky enough to somehow "want to be creative"—or who were lucky enough to "remember" creativity. Thus the reality of documentation in this context is the recording of one's own achievements—and this can be both positive and negative—mostly negative. Because documentation in this context overly accents "what a person has done" in competitive terms as opposed to "cultural service" terms—yet this kind of documentation will be needed in the near future (to offset what is already established). For to not properly document one's activity is to be at the mercy of the collected forces of western culture interpretations—and nothing can be worse than this. Ultimately, documentation should be a cultural challenge—that being, the recording of what relevant information has solidified in a culture as a means to give it to future civilizations—and hopefully advance the state of humanity—or to have it ready for new civilizations, for positive assistance. In this period, documentation is big business.

17. In the progressional continuance of western art music, what does the repetition school (e.g., La Monte Young) represent with regards to the lifeblood of its aesthetic?

TR(III)–13

I believe the La Monte Young school (i.e., Riley, Reich, and Glass, etc.) represents the nature of source-transfer extensionalism in western art music—for this time period. Which is to say, I believe their work gives insight into what changes are occurring in the affinity dynamic reality of western continuance. In other words, this is the group whose activity will define on what terms the next information transference— from world culture to western culture—will actualize. The thrust of this movement will undoubtedly re-establish the composite nature of western creative functionalism—that being, how a given consideration (e.g., rhythm, harmony) is to be utilized and on what terms. To really view this school of music is to understand its position in the chain of progressional continuance. For the thrust of the La Monte Young movement has in effect rejected the methodological precepts of the post-Webern school as well as the John Cage school, and instead, has reinvestigated world music as a basis for their involvement. The seriousness of this rejection has helped to solidify another attitude in their work—and this difference has also underlined their relationship to continuance.

18. How do you see the many composers who never leave the academic school situation?

In my opinion, western culture is long on technocrats but short on creativity. I believe the reality of creative music could greatly benefit from a change in both how it is taught and who does the teaching. It seems to me that the first prerequisite to establish is simple: before any person is allowed to assume a teaching post, that person must first establish some creative works on his or her own. In other words, a teacher should be someone who has really participated in some aspect of what he or she is teaching—rather than a person who has merely completed the right courses for attaining a degree. Many of the composers who are attached to the university life card are in fact really hiding under "the false cloak of respectability" that this reality affords—and I believe the vibration surrounding their inability to really participate in dynamic creativity is also communicated in what they teach (or don't teach). This is not to say a person's four-part harmony teacher has to have credentials showing a performance with the New York

Philharmonic, nor would a teacher giving classes in ear training have to prove membership in the Metropolitan Opera Company. My point is only that if we are to have better qualified and dedicated artists in the future then we must provide our young people with the opportunity to learn not only from theoreticians but also people who have really "participated" in what they are teaching. Probably the healthiest way to improve education would be for a two-years-on, one- or two-years-off basis. That being, two years of teaching, one or two years of life.

19. Is there a difference between aleatory music and improvisation?

Not really. Aleatory music is nothing more than another form that utilizes improvisation in some capacity (to what extent depends on the composition). In the fifties and sixties, the Euro-American and European western art music community tried to advance aleatory process as a new compositional technique that has nothing to do with improvisation—which is ridiculous. Both aleatory and indeterminism are words which have been coined for several important purposes—(1) to bypass the word improvisation and as such the influence of any non-white sensibility (because any association with black people and/or culture is not tolerated—on any level—by the contemporary western art music community), and (2) the coining of one's own phrases also clarifies the documentation of that initiation. There are, however, problems with both terms that cannot be simply ignored, because in every case, the composite community of western contemporary music wrongly justifies the use of applied definitions as a means to not deal with the already-documented dynamics of black creativity and world methodology. This is so because the composite thrust of black creativity has never utilized only one form of improvisation, but instead a total spectrum of improvisational approaches—and possibilities. The coining of indeterminism and aleatory music somehow moves to create the impression that variable-form techniques had never happened before—and this is false. Every form—and time zone—of black creativity, Indian creativity, Asian creativity, etc. has utilized a more elastic relationship to form than western art music. The use of extended functionalism is not new, only the claim to have invented it is.

20. *Can the activity from the Euro-American tradition be viewed in the same light as creative black music?*

There have been many articles on creative music that attempt to equate the Euro-American tradition—and its related progressionalism—as similar to the position of creative music from the black aesthetic (in the sense that both musics are an outgrowth of source transfer—one from Europe and the other from Africa). I disagree with this view completely, for there are other factors which must be dealt with if one truly wants to understand the "actual significance" of these two musics—and what each music affirms. The most basic difference of Euro-American art music from creative black music is the fact that the Euro-American tradition is directly related to—and defined from—its European counterpart. This is not to say nothing of substance has come from the Euro-American tradition, for this is not true—my point is that the activity "ised" through the Euro-American tradition is directly housed in the European aesthetic. It is not just a question of American composers borrowing materials from Europe; instead it is the realness that the vibrational-philosophical-functional and aesthetic position of European art music has also been adopted by the American school. The Euro-American art music community is no more separated from the western art music aesthetic than the French school is separated from the German school. In short, it is only a question of style. What is referred to as the Euro-African synthesis cannot by any stretch of the imagination be viewed in this context. For while the physical universe social situation has dictated the use of certain functional elements of western art music, the actual creativity that solidified from black music completely transcends the western art music vibrational arena. In reality there is no Euro-African tradition, nor is there a Euro-African aesthetic.

21. *Do you view the progressional continuum of the opera medium as a relevant continuum for the next cycle?*

Yes. I believe the opera continuum is one of the most exciting mediums in creative music—regardless of focus or style. The dynamics of this medium will continue to exert a profound influence on extended functionalism—this is true for the emergence of new opera compositions as well as the traditional repertoire. I believe the next cycle of creative music will see more involvement in dynamic theatre productions, and this involvement will be a positive tool for bringing about cultural awakening and unification. The reality of the opera is important because it creates the same dynamic involvement (and spectrum) as the festival phenomenon—having to do with securing the participation of a dynamic spectrum of the creative community for both the production of a given opera and its execution. The realness of this phenomenon also calls for the cross-involvement of its greater community for vibrational and financial support. The dictates of the eighties seem to forecast many different challenges for western culture—and this is particularly true for America. I believe the dynamics of extended creative involvement will be beneficial to the whole of this time period. For the realness of creativity can supply the necessary vibrational balance to help composite continuance. This is especially true for those spectacle forms and mediums, and as such I view the emerging support for opera as only the beginning of an expanded community effort to initiate more involvement to advance unification and eventually the total culture.

22. Is there a difference in the reality of participation in black creativity as opposed to western art music, and what does this mean?

Yes. There is a profound difference in the reality of participation in black creativity, as opposed to western art music, and this is true on several levels. For when the first Europeans first came into Africa they were welcomed and allowed to experience and participate in the total realness of black culture. All of the early Greek students of philosophy were allowed to come into Egypt to study—in what is documented as the first universities of recorded history. As such, the Europeans were taught all about African music in that period—and nothing has changed to this day. Throughout the history of so-called jazz, one can view the participation of white Americans. Practically every major improvising creative musician has employed the white improvisor at some point in his or her career—which is to say, the reality of penetration in black creative music has always been open to any person who wanted to participate. This practice has always been in keeping with the dictates of black creativity—that being, the music is not about division or exclusion but rather a platform for positive vibrational and spiritual involvement—for anyone who wants to participate. Contrast this attitude with the reality of the black composer or instrumentalist in western art music. How many black people have been allowed in any of the major orchestras in America?—how many opportunities does the black conductor have? Only a token handful of black people can gain access to the upper echelon of western art music, and even those positions are without real power.

(Level One) THE NEW YORK MOVEMENT

THE PROGRESSIONAL DYNAMICS OF CREATIVE BLACK MUSIC in the post-Ayler junction of the sixties can best be viewed by tracing the activity of the New York School, because this group would represent the first consolidated effort to deal with the implications of Coltrane's, Taylor's, and Ayler's activity. To understand what this group would signify is to deal with the aesthetical position of creative black music with regards to its practical implications as well as its social position. For the changes reshaping black music in the sixties were not universally embraced by either the creative community or composite western defining community. Any attempt to deal with the realness of what I now call the New York School would thus necessitate outlining the special problems this group would confront—either collectively or individually. That this group could exist at all is nothing short of amazing, for not only would the New York School be the first contingent of new creative musicians to feel the blunt opposition that was to characterize how post-Ayler creativity was to be greeted even until the present (1977), but this group would also be the first to feel what this rejection would be in naked economic terms. Nevertheless, under the severest conditions imaginable, the New York School collected musicians' community would elaborate on the implications of post-Ayler functionalism and in doing so establish the realness that another creative projection from the black aesthetic had been actualized. The progressional continuance of the activity that was to solidify in this time zone would see the forming of one of the most exciting periods in creativity since bebop. And the intensity of the work generated through the collected New York musicians' community would detail the progressional expansion of black creativity throughout the whole of the sixties. Any attempt to really understand creative music from the black aesthetic would imply that the collected offerings of this group are examined. It is important to understand that the realness of any initiation is directly related to whether or not it is substantiated, integrated, or practiced—on whatever level. The significance of the New York School of creative musicians in the sixties is directly related to how this challenge was met (as well as the actual creativity that resulted from their decision to participate). The composite thrust of their activity would provide a bridge for all future development in the post-Ayler creative continuum, and the strength and beauty of the actual creativity produced in this period would provide the catalysts to reshape the projectional continuum of creative music from the black aesthetic—on a multitude of levels.

If the basic structure of American culture is taken into account, it should come as no surprise that the post-Ayler junction of creativity was greeted with such hostility. For the progressional hierarchy of American culture must be viewed with regards to the realness that more factors than many Americans would like to admit are controlled according to set structure. And while it is fashionable to believe that any alternative form of creativity must naturally be met with hostility—because of being a new form—to view the progressional continuum of creative black music in the sixties is to see what could only be termed "special treatment." Thus the integration of post-Ayler creativity into the general creative arena would fall to the New York School, and the nature underlying how this integration would be approached also characterizes the time zone of the sixties. For this group would begin elaborating on the conceptual implications of post-Ayler functionalism while being forced to also deal with the commercial implications underlying its dissemination. The most basic problems this group would confront could best be understood in simple terms—survival. As such, to attempt evaluating the realness of this period in creative music without dealing with the peculiar social reality particulars related to how the music was actualized is to completely not understand the subject. For while the actualness of creativity can only be experienced in real terms, the composite underlying significance of post-Ayler creativity transcends the concept of isolated participation. In other words, the projectional realness of post-Ayler creativity must be viewed in composite terms—both with regards to the actual creativity as well as the physical and vibrational universe factors that surrounded the music.

NYM-3

ALT.F.------MT.INFO.

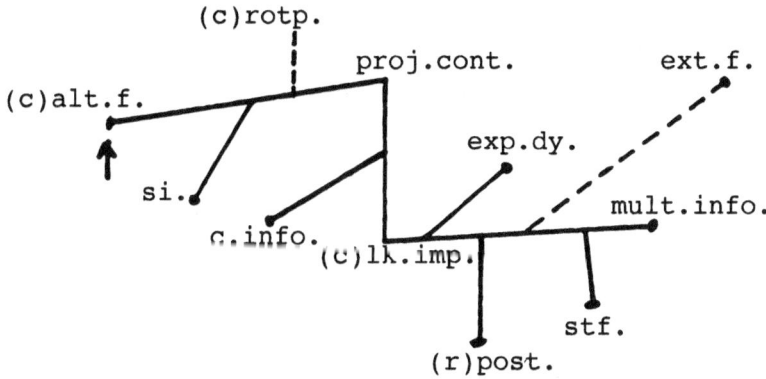

The realness of the transition cycle in creative black music during the sixties can be viewed by the impact it was to have on the creative musicians' community as well as the number of musicians it would attract. In a time zone of three to five years a whole new community of musicians would solidify as a response to post-Ayler creativity, and the collective impact of this development would accelerate the vibrational voltage and spirit reshaping composite black creativity. Many young musicians would thus migrate to New York in this period, and a cross-sectional view of the music scene by 1963 would reveal a whole new school of development—whether with regards to given instruments (e.g., the changes reshaping saxophone playing) or the consideration of composition (form). And by the middle sixties it was also clear that the post-Ayler juncture of creative music was not simply a passing fad, but rather a projectional extension of black creativity.

By New York School, in this section of the book, I am referring to the composite activity that took place in New York City during the sixties concerning how post-Ayler projectional implications were practiced. However, I have not meant to apply this term only to musicians who were born in the New York or greater New York area, but rather my definition of the New York musicians' school would have to do with the collective work that was done in this period—regardless of where given individuals came from—in New York City. The extent of the migration that happened in this period would be as significant as the restructuralist cycle surrounding bebop—in its early period—at clubs like Minton's. Yet the thrust development of the New York School could best be characterized as a stylistic transition in the sense that its basic thrust alignment would address itself to what had already been "ised" through the collected thrust of post-Ayler methodology (as opposed to Minton's, which functions as an outlet for dynamic restructuralism). The progressional expansion of this school would move to reveal the changes reshaping black creativity in its early period, and the spread of this movement would detail the implications underlying what those changes would mean in actual terms. The New York School would thus establish the seriousness of the coming changes in black creativity, and through musicians like Archie Shepp, Marion Brown, Dave Burrell, etc., the dynamic spectrum of post-Ayler progressionalism would move towards transition. The composite realness of this period could best be viewed as the beginning of the next vibrational shift in American culture.

The ramifications of the New York School would affect the reality aspects of creative music on a number of levels, for the solidification of this movement would establish the realness that a profound split had developed in the creative musicians' community. The seriousness of this split would be an important factor shaping the reality of the trans-African creativity throughout the sixties. For the solidification of the post-Ayler creative community would move to establish an alternative pecking order in the musicians inter-community, and in doing so, bypass the traditional creative route reserved for newcomers. The net effect of this alternative route would only make the division between traditional and younger musicians more apparent, and in doing so help sustain an already bad situation (ripe for outside controlling forces to suppress all black creativity). By the middle sixties, the end result of this state would see the rise of many musicians into prominence who had served little—if any—time in the established musicians' community—and there were many reasons for this. Because by the end of the fifties, it had become clear that many of the changes reshaping black creativity were unacceptable to the majority of traditional musicians, and as such, young players were forced to research and practice their creativity away from the established session and social outlets. And when a handful of musicians were able to eventually attract some attention to their activity from the New York critical community, this attraction resulted in resentment throughout the overall music community. All of these factors are related to the solidification of the post-Ayler juncture in trans-African creativity, for the progressional development of this projection was actualized in isolation from the mainstream musicians' community (yet I do not mean isolation with regards to the spirit and vibrational realness of the music, because in fact the composite thrust of black creativity represents one reality; the isolation I am referring to in this context is that the post-Ayler continuum was not able to have its activity necessarily received as being a part of the composite whole, and as such was forced to function separately from the composite musicians' community).

(R)INFO.INTR.------TRS.

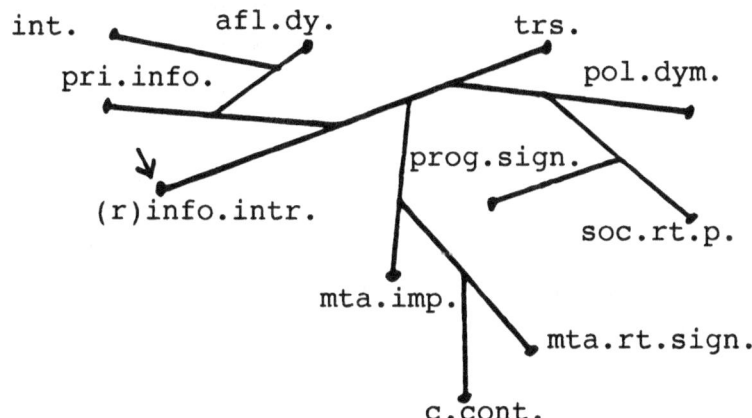

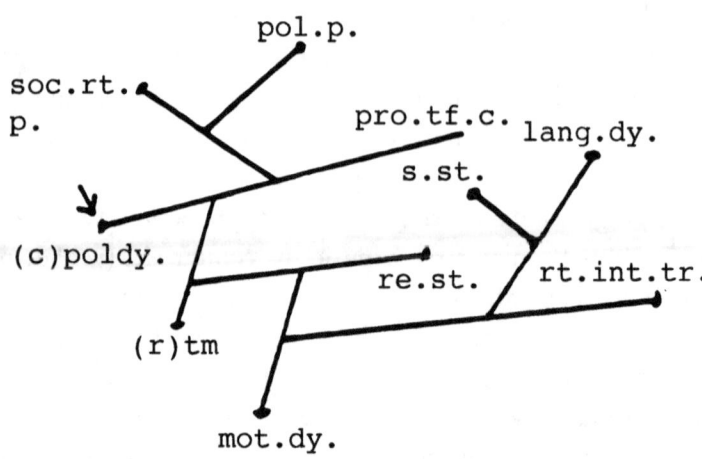

Any attempt to deal with the progressional realness of the New York School would imply some understanding of the environment that housed this collective activity. For the environment surrounding a given projection has to be taken into consideration, especially in the case of the post-Ayler junction—because the vibrational atmosphere of the sixties, and the position of New York City in American culture, is not separate from the nature of what transpired in the music. **The fact that the post-Ayler junction of black creativity was based in New York and solidified in a time zone of three to five years (while the major forces of the late fifties and sixties were themselves still reshaping the music) would be an important factor related to how the thrust expansion of the movement took place.** To really understand what this means is to have some understanding of New York City itself.

Quite possibly New York City is the most interesting city on the planet—certainly it is the most interesting in America—and there is no way to avoid dealing with this city if one has any idea of becoming a professional creative person. The fact is, musicians from all over America are forced to come to this city as a means to establish a political base—on whatever level—and in this regard the post-Ayler musicians were no exception.

To understand this phenomenon is to view the dynamics of New York City as a commercial necessity, for this one city alone has practically three-fourths of the communications industry. Moreover, New York City houses practically all of the creative happenings in America—with regards to not only music but also theatre, sculpture, painting, etc. And to make matters worse, New York City also houses the recording industry—which is to say, any musician who hopes to have his or her activity recorded—as a means to disseminate their activity and thus hopefully secure a position to both be creative and not starve while doing so—must also deal with New York on some level.

The realness of New York City's position with regards to big business should not be viewed lightly. For the effect of the recording industry is much greater than one might normally think. Moreover, that many of these facilities are only available to selected groups of people promotes a definite vibrational platform as well. Thus to deal with the realness of New York City would imply that the business implications of this subject be examined, for a musician's ability to successfully understand the progressional continuance of business can, in many instances, be more valuable than his understanding of creativity. Moreover, the seriousness of the business consideration is directly related to how the disunification of creative people—especially musicians—is maintained. The structural design underlying this consideration promotes a certain kind of competition that is not necessarily beneficial to the totalness of creativity. And as this situation is developed, it is possible to view the composite actualness of New York City as a kind of survival test among creative people. That is, a struggle to gain access to the benefits of both the power structure as well as economic security (and I have not meant to imply that survival in itself is negative—rather, the designed business structure surrounding creativity in the west can be viewed as something extra, added to survival). The nature of the challenge surrounding business in New York can be viewed in terms of a struggle to maintain artistic integrity, while sustaining one's life at the same time (and this is not an easy task).

Compared to most cities in America, the element of control and manipulation is also much greater in New York—especially in the creative arts, and one would be quite naive to not realize that the progressional continuance of creative music is also affected by these same factors. For New York is also the home of the eastern intellectual music-defining community (I use this term even though it might sound somewhat Nixonist—because in fact the controlling and defining community that exists in New York does constitute a bloc of sorts—and certainly functions as one in any case). New York is undoubtedly the most political city, with regards to creativity, in America, and as such the vibrational arena that surrounds the creative community is directly affected by what this control means. Many talented people are simply dismissed or denied the opportunity to have their activity disseminated on political grounds alone. The neglect of a musician like Herbie Nichols was not unique by any means, for in every period there are surely ten musicians of importance for every one who makes it. This was true before the time zone of the sixties and this is also true for the present. The dynamic realness of New York City political decisions poses as a real criterion that has shaped the nature and direction of creative music. The progressional continuance of the post-Ayler school would then be the first of the transitional projections of the sixties to experience what this manipulation would mean in actual terms.

I have not meant to imply that the controlling forces dictating American culture are only preoccupied with the progressional particulars of creative black music, because this is not true. The sophistication that surrounds how events are controlled in this cycle extends to every information area—especially with regards to creativity. The manipulation of big business can be viewed in every sector of the creative community, from decisions in opera to what given artists are to be successful. The realness of business and control is simply a part of what New York City seems to be about—and I am not implying that this phenomenon is inherently negative on every level. My point is only that to view the solidification of the post-Ayler junction in creative black music is to look at many factors, and moreover, many of these factors (from both inside and outside the actual music) helped determine what actually happened in that period. To understand what this means is to look at the effects of being in New York City as well as the effect of the vibrational shift of the sixties, because all of these considerations helped to shape the meta-reality of the post-Ayler creative projection as it solidified in New York City—especially with regards to the economic actualness of survival. To view the realness of the situation that helped solidify the post-Ayler projection is to be aware of both the situation of creative musicians and their potential audiences. In other words, the intensity of the composite sixties economic reality alone would make participation in creative music almost unbearable (in survival terms) and by doing so, this phenomenon also impeded the reality of its contributions. For without an economic base, to expand even potential performing possibilities would be affected—because all of these things cost money—and finally, to be denied the possibility of decent performing outlets also lessens the possibility of developing a cross-sectional listening audience. The end result of this condition would exclude new musicians from being considered candidates for one of the major recording companies. Which is to say: the post-Ayler musicians' movement could be viewed as under the underground. For without a solid economic and political base, the progressional continuance of this movement both began and remained at the mercy of the east coast defining and critical community.

The realness of the economic forces shaping the vibrational arena of the sixties can better be viewed if the composite realness of this period is taken into account. For it must be understood that the New York School was not the only composite thrust to emerge in the time zone of the early sixties, but rather one thrust among several. This would also be the time zone that would see the cross-transfer shift in American popular music and the emergence of white rock music as a new social form. The reality implications of the post-Ayler movement can better be viewed if this thrust is taken into account, for the solidification of white rock would transform the total business arena surrounding every sector of the communications and recording medium. By the time groups like the Beatles and Rolling Stones actualized, it was clear that rock was revolutionizing the American business community, and as such would become the sole focus of composite business strategy in the sixties.

To understand the machinery that rock music would set into motion is to have some idea of the transition American big business underwent in the sixties. The solidification of rock music would establish sales on an unprecedented level in this period, and the effect of these profits would help issue in the next business and controlling hierarchy. The realness of this transition could be seen in the emergence of a new counter-business culture—creating new recording companies, new magazines, etc., and as such securing the potential of what this transition implied economically. Nor would the projectional influence of rock stop at this point; this was only the beginning. For the momentum of this form would also establish new performing outlets throughout the country, and the business community would utilize advertising on a new level, for maximum effectiveness. Nothing was spared. Thus a given tour of the Who would have advertising specialists promoting their concerts in every conceivable medium (i.e., television, whole pages in the *New York Times*, magazines, etc.). Even on billboards (I recall seeing in Times Square for a period of three months to a year—it seemed—a giant billboard poster saying "Grand Funk is coming"). In other words, rock music would gain all of the benefits that the American business community could give—that western culture could give. Because in the final analysis, we are talking of a form that (in this period especially) was about white people and for white people—no matter that it was built on black music. By the middle of the sixties, practically every white musician that participated in the early thrust of rock music could be viewed as a millionaire, or multi-millionaire. Moreover, the success of the recording industry was directly related to whether or not a given company had made the move to rock in its early period. By the middle sixties a new empire had solidified, but what does all of this mean with regards to the post-Ayler creative projection?

The fact is, the emergence of rock and the transition of the defining intellectual community would isolate the New York post-Ayler school even more. For if this movement could be viewed as a narrow projection, in its original state anyway—only appealing to esoteric groups that followed creative music—the progressional realness of rock could practically crush every sector of its reality options. Here then was a group of musicians dedicated to advancing a music that very few people really wanted. Moreover, the thrust realness of rock music would make their reality even more ridiculous—in the sense that given musicians would be forced to compete for jobs that paid maybe ten dollars a week (from the door), while a group like Frank Zappa's could command thousands of dollars a night. To understand the progressional realness of the New York post-Ayler school is to deal with what this separation really means. For the emergence of rock would affect the basic reality options of post-Ayler progressionalism.

RT.ALGN.------CULT.INFO.DY.

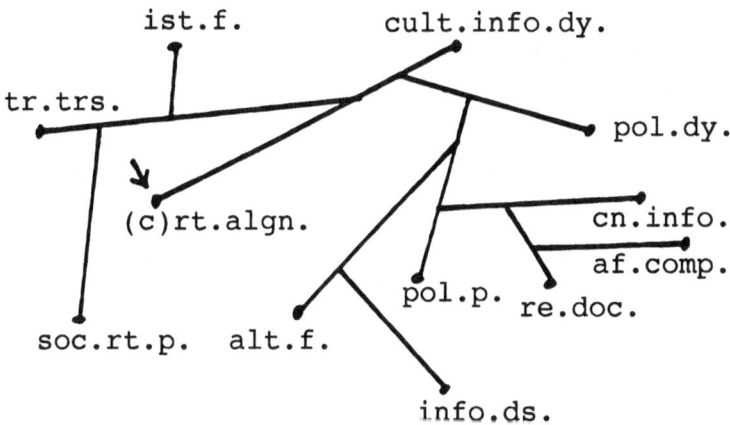

RT.OP.------POL.DY.

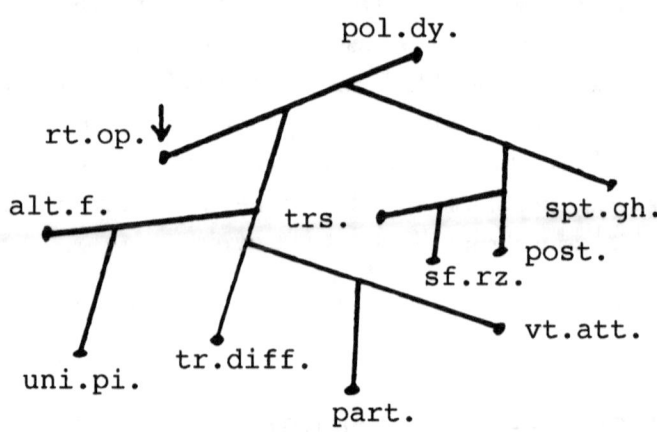

To really understand the reality of the New York School is to view this subject with regards to the progressional implications surrounding how manipulation is utilized in American culture. For while the emergence of rock in the sixties certainly accented the limitations of the creative black musicians' community—as a transformational tool in its own right—it would be wrong to over-emphasize this impact. In actual fact, the functional limitations surrounding black creativity were established long before the time zone of the sixties. The glorification of rock would only accent the realness of this phenomenon, for the progressional reality of creative music from the black aesthetic was determined—and controlled—by the late forties—after the emergence of Charlie Parker's activity and the solidification of extended functionalism. To understand the reality actualness of black creative music is to view how the basic thrust of its path has traditionally been separated from the black community and utilized as "spectacle" (with regards to the "needs" of a given period). By the time rock music appeared on the scene—in the sixties—black creativity had already been systematically defined by the controlling forces from the white community and discarded. **In other words, by separating the music from the black community, the net effect of this control would find black musicians having to rely on the whims of the**

western defining and controlling community for survival—and that is exactly what happened. Thus to view the progressional continuance of creative black music in the fifties is to have some idea of which musicians were allowed to become successful (yet I am not saying that any given individual's activity did not merit some attention)—as opposed to the actual music. The functional and political reality of creative black music in the fifties was totally controlled by the white power structure—which is to say, everything that took place in this period can be viewed with respect to what this control would mean. There are many factors related to how this phenomenon was to occur—and practically all of those factors would have something to do with the economic realness (and social and racial actualness) of American culture. The end result of this phenomenon would promote disunification among the musicians (and yet this disunification has always been there as well) and an even greater dependence on the established power structure. By the time Coleman's, Coltrane's, and Taylor's activity began to reshape creative black music, and thus activate the next area of research for the next generation of musicians, the disunity among musicians was in itself nothing new. Nevertheless, this condition must be viewed as an important factor related to the progressional continuum of the post-Ayler school. For the great percentage of these musicians were young and without the necessary political and social contacts to help them successfully deal with the actualness of their situation. The disunification of the creative musicians' community in the middle sixties would thus isolate what options these musicians would have (i.e., what to do to combat the sophistication of the controlling forces surrounding the music).

By disunity among musicians, I do not mean to imply only one type of separation, nor do I mean to utilize this concept in one-dimensional terms. For the dynamics of separation in the creative musicians' community transcends only one use of the word. Certainly it is true that economics can be viewed as a major factor related to one area of separation in the musicians' community, but this is only the beginning. Because the vibrational realness of disunity between creative people goes much deeper than whether one survives or not. I am commenting on differences between how given musicians relate to the consideration of style (whether or not a given form is perceived as hip or not)—differences extending to how a given individual leads his—or her—band (whether his [her] choice of musicians was good or not)—differences as to the racial mix of a given group (did he [or she] have white musicians—or black—in their band)—differences over how a given individual takes care of his (her) business (did they engage in a business deal that someone felt they shouldn't have)—and it goes on and on. Disunity is also a factor that comes into play when given individuals measure their success against people they feel are "less" than they are—and the vibration that surrounds the music scene can be understood if one can perceive of decades and decades of individual musicians putting each other up or down, and years of people talking behind other people's backs. To view the realness of this phenomenon is very interesting, yet it would be wrong to write that only musicians engage in this type of activity, because what I am describing in this paragraph could apply to practically any area of western—and maybe earth—culture. Nevertheless, while this level of behavior can be viewed in any business group, there is still the need to understand that black people might not necessarily be able to afford this kind of disunity. **The fact is, while the creative musicians' community continually fights each other, the collected forces of western culture progressively secure more and more of its hold on the planet. In other words, somebody is not fighting among themselves—or at least, the fighting of the western controlling circles does not seem to get in the way of business as usual.** The disunity of the musicians' community—especially in the fifties—is directly related to the inability of the creative process to assist in shaping dynamic functional change in western culture. The realness of this phenomenon would thus be a major factor affecting the reality initiative of the post-Ayler thrust—with regards to the nature of its position in the sixties. However, I have not meant to imply that the progressional continuum of creative music—or creative black music—has not functioned as a positive alternative tool, nor have I meant to imply that nothing positive has happened as a result of the music. To do so would be both ridiculous and untrue. But however the progressional continuum of this subject is viewed, my point is that the realness of disunification must be viewed as a factor that has lessened the impact—and potential—of everything it touches. As such, the progressional continuum of creative music from the black aesthetic must also be viewed with regards to what this lessening implies.

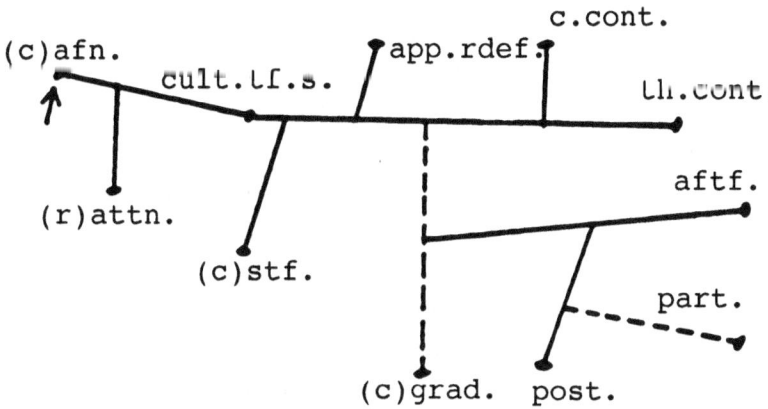

With the separation of creative black music established long ago, and with the economic reality surrounding the musicians' community at a critical point, the real reality of the post-Ayler junction can then be viewed. Because by the time zone of the late fifties, the composite thrust of black creative music had become a whim of the western intellectual community—and as such a subject that could be "talked about" and "written on." The realness of this relationship could be understood by viewing what effect the abandonment of the critical defining community to rock in the sixties would have on creative black music. For before the solidification of rock and the Coleman-Taylor junction, the critical defining community would endorse creative music as a very significant and relevant creative form. And even though only a handful of musicians (e.g., Miles Davis or Sonny Rollins) would be able to benefit from their creativity in economic terms, there was a surface cultural respect for bebop (as a form that took a while to be accepted but when achieved was understood as corresponding to what white people believed black people should be doing) and the power structure would on occasion pretend that the music did exist. But all this would change with the coming of rock music and the post-Ayler thrust. For not only had gradualism established the necessary tools to bring about manipulation, but rock music would also be perceived as a form that carried the same—if not better—meta-implications as black music (with regards to its conceptual realness) and while doing so, also function as a real economic force. On the other side of the fence, the post-Ayler thrust would be perceived as another group of niggers who didn't know their own roots—whose activity was not very pleasant to experience (not to mention that the establishment did not necessarily like them anyway). By 1965, rock would thus be perceived as an intellectual and aesthetic force—moreover, an intellectual and aesthetic force quite separate from black creativity (or people—or culture), and this was done through the collective efforts of the white defining and controlling community. My reason for mentioning this phenomenon is only to comment on the position of the post-Ayler school of musicians and the general state of black creativity in this period. For the functional realness of the black creative community's position relied on the liberal acknowledgement of the western defining community as a means to work (and of course, with the political situation of American culture taken into account, this relationship made sense) and as a means to validate their creativity. Thus when, for the 500th time, the critical community declared "JAZZ IS DEAD," after sensing the magnitude of the coming rock transition, the black musicians' community would be faced with very few prospects for support of their activity. Moreover, if this was true for the bebop musicians (and it was) then one could only imagine what this abandonment would mean for the post-Ayler thrust.

There are many factors related to the progressional continuance of creative black music in the sixties. For the vibrational realness of this subject corresponds to a multitude of considerations—and this was especially true of the post-Ayler school. The intensity of the sixties would help establish the nature of the forming political and functional awareness that would later characterize new functionalism in the musicians' community. That is, the reality awareness of many musicians from this movement juncture would solidify a broader perspective about the totalness of their position in American culture—and in doing so, this perspective would represent an emerging redefined functionalism quite separate from the reality stance of the bebop movement of the fifties. The significance of this new functionalism can better be understood if the progressional thrust of black creativity—and culture—is taken into account. Because however the post-Ayler movement is now viewed, it is important to understand that the political realness of their position in American culture would establish the first real counter-reaction to the historical manipulation practiced on composite black creativity—and there are many reasons for this. For the time zone of the sixties would establish a vibrationaltory lining affecting the basic tone arena of composite American reality. This would be a period that would see every sector of American society challenged—either with regards to the war, racism, politics, etc., or to creativity. As the forming composite alternative functional groups solidified from various sectors of the country, the progressive continuum of post-Ayler creativity would come to be viewed as related to the vibrational spirit of what these new movements implied—as a composite alternative phenomenon embracing every sector of American society. Thus the post-Ayler movement, by benefit of its perceived relationship with western and/or American alternative functionalism, would solidify its composite identity as a thrust that corresponded to the new dictates of the sixties in aesthetic and functional terms, as well as a thrust that established new responsibilities for the creative musician.

Much has been made of the relationship between creative black music—from the post-Ayler junction—and politics (especially with regards to the over-used word of the sixties, "revolution"), but very little effort has been put into understanding the nature of this relationship. For while it is true that many musicians of that period could be viewed with regards to the pseudo-revolutionary cowboy games being practiced in the sixties, it is also true that the greater percentage of musicians functioning in that period were sincerely trying to be of assistance in changing conditions in American culture. The time zone of the sixties would be the period that would see musicians organizing as a means to be of positive assistance to the community as well as to themselves—and the music. Moreover, any attempt to understand the significance of the New York post-Ayler school must also take into account that this movement would represent the first such attempt at composite unification in this time cycle. The progressional thrust of the post-Ayler school would move to reshape the creative musician's perception of his (her) position with regards to alternative functionalism, and the net effect of the work done in this period would secure the projectional expansion of post-Ayler creativity through one of the most difficult periods in this cycle.

The solidification of post-Ayler creativity as a political thrust should not be taken out of context, but rather understood. For if the position of black creativity in American culture is really taken into account—especially in the time zone of the fifties—it would be clear that no other route was available to pursue. Yet I am not apologizing for the political consciousness that was to permeate the creativity in the sixties—because in fact this consciousness was needed—but rather, the progressional spread of the post-Ayler junction of black creativity should be better understood. It is necessary to understand that the basic political and social situation of American culture had produced an intolerable situation on non-white and poor people especially. That being, the basic thrust alignment of western culture is not designed with regards for allowing certain sectors of the community to participate in shaping their own lives. To view the reality of business as it relates to black creativity is to see how little control black people had over their creativity—in terms of either how it is distributed or defined. **The time zone of the sixties would see the first efforts by black creative musicians (from the fifties/sixties post-bebop time cycle) to deal with the seriousness of unification as a means to deal with extended questions.** For it was clear that whatever changes needed to be made would have to come from the musicians' community rather than the business community—because the establishment obviously was not unhappy with their business relationship with creative musicians. The politicalization of the post-Ayler junction must be viewed with this context in mind, for not only would the realness of unification serve as a necessary step towards redesigning the business implications of creative music (i.e., the economic reality of clubs or concert performances), but unification in this context would also help maintain the creative purity of the actual music (for it must be understood that there were many outside pressures on the post-Ayler school to change their activity to more commercial forms as a means to become "famous" or simply to have access to more money; later on, because of intense pressure, many musicians would in fact "compromise" their activity—and who could blame them). But the unification of creative musicians in the sixties would have a profound impact on the progressional continuum of creative music. And while the functional implications of unification would reshape the meta-reality of creative music, the perceived relationship of the post-Ayler school to the alternative political forces in the sixties would also affect the total image creative music would secure in the sixties. The end result of this perceived relationship would establish the perception of post-Ayler creativity—as a political and social form, rather than a multi-dynamic continuum related to the total thrust of black creativity. Moreover, many of the people who functioned in alternative politics would use their position to also affect the composite image of black creativity—for whatever purposes. The perceived relationship between the post-Ayler creative movement and the "new left" would establish outlets for a music that would not have been possible otherwise—and this would be positive and negative.

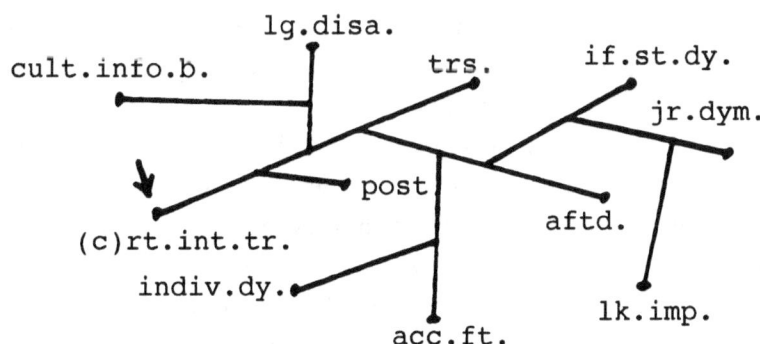

To deal with the realness of the post-Ayler creative movement is to be aware of many factors, for the vibrational realness of this projection corresponded to a multitude of considerations—some having to do with creativity and some not. Which is to say, the reality awareness of many musicians from this juncture would establish a broader perception of their total position in American culture—and in doing so, this awareness did represent an emerging redefined functionalism that was separate from the bebop movement of the fifties. To understand this difference is to have some idea of the progressional effects of the late fifties and early sixties with regards to social and political consciousness. For the sixties would be the time zone where America would experience the first post-Korean responses of its vibrationaltory alignment. As the functional and political movements emerged from various areas of American culture, the progressional continuum of the post-Ayler movement would come to be viewed as related to the composite vibrational spirit—if nothing else—of what this total movement implied. Thus the post-Ayler creative thrust, by benefit of its perceived relationship to the pseudo-intellectual and political games that were being played in the sixties in the white community, could be perceived as being in a better position than even the established bebop musicians' community. For because of this supposed relationship to the "movement," the post-Ayler projectional thrust would gain some access to the media (i.e., hip underground magazines in particular) and thus secure a position that would be advantageous for later growth. By the middle of the sixties the realness of that position would be apparent, for while very few musicians were able to make any money to continue their creativity, there was a noticeable increase in press coverage—and potentially this increase could be viewed in a positive light.

The fact is, the post-Ayler projectional thrust was related to the changes taking place in the sixties on several levels. Certainly one of the distinguishing aspects of this composite movement would be its awareness of alternative functionalism—as a means to deal with the seriousness of life in the black community and what this understanding necessitated in actual policy (and as an unavoidable factor related to how black culture is suppressed). In other words, the move towards alternative functionalism in itself can be viewed as a political position. For no matter how given individuals came to be viewed—with regards to their separate activity (and press) in the middle sixties—the collective thrust of post-Ayler musicians would all be confronted with the same basic "actual life opposition"—that is, "actual life" as designed within and from the western controlling alignment. No single musician could escape this reality, and the dynamics of this situation would also be outside the scope of individual change as well. The political realness of the post-Ayler movement must be viewed from this context, as well as the changing vibrational arena of the sixties—that being, a growing feeling of unrest and intense efforts to establish change, regardless of level. The post-Ayler creative movement was indeed related to this sentiment, and any attempt to deal with the actualness of this period would necessitate that this relationship is understood. For there is a difference between the vibrational reality that shaped options in the black community in the early sixties, and that of the white community, and there is also a difference in how each group would perceive functionalism. The fact that the eastern pseudo-radical diversion movement would champion post-Ayler creativity must be viewed from this context. **For the essence realness of post-Ayler creativity would come to be viewed more as a political thrust—as defined through the western affinity alignment (with respect to what particulars were moving towards "popular" in the early to middle sixties)—rather than an all-inclusive projection related and designed from the actual lining of black culture. From this context, the political implications of black music would come to be viewed as more significant than the vibrational composite realness of the music—and as such, the relationship between post-Ayler creativity's public perception and the pseudo-eastern political movement's use of the music must be viewed as extremely interesting (to say the least).** I have not meant to imply that some sort of conscious conspiracy was directed against the music, because this is not what I believe. Rather, the embracing of post-Ayler creativity by forming political groups in the sixties must be viewed in a multi-dimensional context—with respect to its positive and negative ramifications.

The New York post-Ayler movement could best be understood as the movement that solidified the dynamic realignment changes that Coltrane's, Taylor's, Sun Ra's, and Coleman's work brought forth. That is to say, the progressional continuum of the creativity brought forth in this cycle would vibrate to the ideas of one of these four musicians. For the most part it is possible to view the post-Ayler movement as a stylistic thrust, rather than a restructured cycle, yet I do not mean this in a negative sense. Rather the New York post-Ayler movement must be viewed with respect to its position in the time-linkage progression of creative black music. For it must be remembered that Coltrane, Taylor, Sun Ra, and Coleman were still actively dominating the changes occurring in the music during this same time cycle—that being, the early sixties. The forming post-Ayler thrust would be in response to the seriousness of their creativity, and it was only natural that in this context the movement would first elaborate on what was being learned from Messieurs Coltrane, Taylor—etc. (the seriousness of what was being raised by these four musicians alone would reshape the entire direction of black creativity on a level as important as Charlie Parker—or any period in black creativity). In this time cycle, every recording released from a musician like Coltrane would inspire a whole avenue for investigation by the forming post-Ayler movement. The seriousness of the changes reshaping black creativity in this period would also signal that something more than just a new form had arrived, but rather that another cycle—having to do with both physical universe as well as vibrational cosmic matters—was now upon us. The fact that the New York post-Ayler movement represented the first composite continuum to deal with the realness of what this change would mean in "actual terms" cannot be lightly acknowledged. All of the subsequent changes that occurred in the music are directly related to the work done in the early to middle sixties by the post-Ayler movement.

Yet it would be wrong to blanketly state that no important restructuralist contributions have come from the New York post-Ayler movement. For while the projectional shape of the creativity produced in this period can be traced to Coleman, Coltrane, etc., with regard to functional design, the vibrational spirit of the composite post-Ayler movement did exert its own separate identity. This would thus be a movement that helped clarify the expanded emotional range of black creativity rather than a scientific restructuralist movement. On the physical universe level, this would also be the movement which moved to integrate the post-Ayler restructuralist gains into the composite arena of black—and American—creativity. To view the composite vibrational dynamics that housed the post-Ayler thrust is to have some basis for understanding what position that activity would have in the progressional continuum of black creativity, for the work which took place in this period was of the utmost importance. The New York post-Ayler movement took place at a very crucial stage in the progressional continuance of creative black music—and this is important to understand. The fact that this juncture cannot be considered a restructuralist cycle should not be viewed as an attempt to not "is" the significance of this continuum, but rather the realness of the post-Ayler juncture of the sixties can better reveal to us the "natural" dynamics of "stylism." For when I wrote that the post-Ayler projectional continuum can best be viewed as a thrust which moved towards heightening the emotional potential of projectional dynamics—rather than a thrust which uniformly embraced the established vibrational and functional dictates concerning what a given individual had to be if he or she was to be creative—it is necessary to understand what this viewpoint really means with regards to the total music. In other words, rather than become more technical on the saxophone or more sophisticated structurally, the New York post-Ayler movement placed more emphasis on what had transpired in the late forties and early sixties, as a means to accent the new projectional lines that had been opened for exploration—as this applied in feeling expansion (with respect to affinity alignment).

STY.------WO.EXT.PRI.

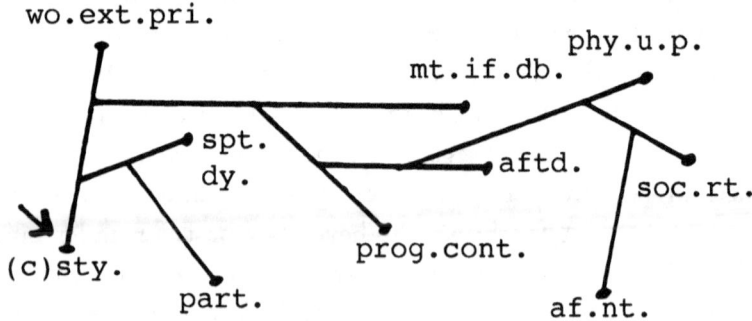

Because I am writing of a movement that solidified only fifteen years—and some—ago, it is somewhat difficult to comment on the significance of its ultimate position—with regards to what particulars have been investigated and adopted—in the composite mainstream. But quite possibly the composite thrust of the New York post-Ayler movement can best be viewed as the junction which re-established the nature of the next transfer cycle with regards to the world community—especially involving the move to non-western cultures. It is with the New York movement that one can view an accelerated affinity move towards African and later composite American affinity alignments, and it is also with the New York post-Ayler movement that one can detect the first responses to the eastern and spiritual pull that Coltrane's activity implied. The New York movement can also be viewed as an important juncture that accelerated the affinity insight principle. By the end of the sixties it was clear that black creativity had completed an important cycle because of the work of this continuum. The composite creativity offered through this movement would forecast a new attitude for black creativity, and the strength and dynamics of this movement would also stimulate a renewed understanding of exploration. But more important, the composite thrust of the New York post-Ayler movement would accent the significance of the affinity insight principle, and in doing so profoundly affect the projectional spread of black creativity for the next decade—and some.

To understand the significance of the post-Ayler composite continuum is to deal with many different factors, for the projectional spread—and dynamics—of this movement are as varied as any thrust alignment. Yet I do not mean to imply that the meta-reality of this junction is impossible to decipher on some level, because there are several factors surrounding the composite arena of post-Ayler creativity that we can view as a means to examine the basic essence realness of its creativity—and it is important that this is done. One factor is this: if Coleman, Coltrane, and Taylor succeeded in advancing their activity to a point where western defining criteria would become more and more irrelevant (as a forum that could meaningfully comment on trans-African exploration and invention dynamics), then the composite thrust of the post-Ayler movement can best be viewed as the projection which solidified what this advancement would be in actual terms—as a unified movement. In other words, if Coleman, Coltrane, and Taylor advanced the realness of the affinity insight principle (as a consideration necessary for retaining the essence focus of black creativity—hence world creativity—hence transformation tool), then the composite thrust of the post-Ayler movement would actualize this sentiment in dynamic terms. In other words, the advancement of the affinity insight principle is ingrained in the very foundation of the New York post-Ayler movement to the degree that the time zone of the sixties can be cited as the beginning of a new cycle for composite black creativity. So real would this affinity alignment be that the progressional continuance of post-Ayler creativity would come to be viewed with respect to its affinity foundation, rather than its functional dynamics. I am writing of a movement whose affinity alignment would move to transcend western definitions to another level—a movement whose most basic vibrational thrust naturally opposed western language, and finally a movement whose progressional continuance would move to resolidify black functionalism on another level. The New York post-Ayler movement would thus be the first composite movement to function from this heightened understanding of affinity alignment, and the subsequent developments which took place in the sixties would reveal the seriousness of what the affinity insight principle really posed as a source-initiation propellant.

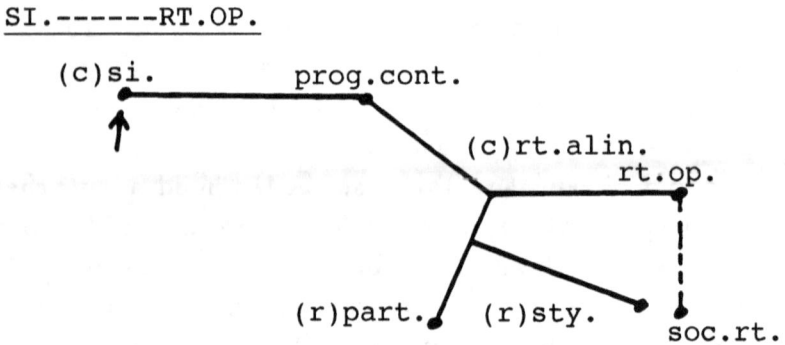

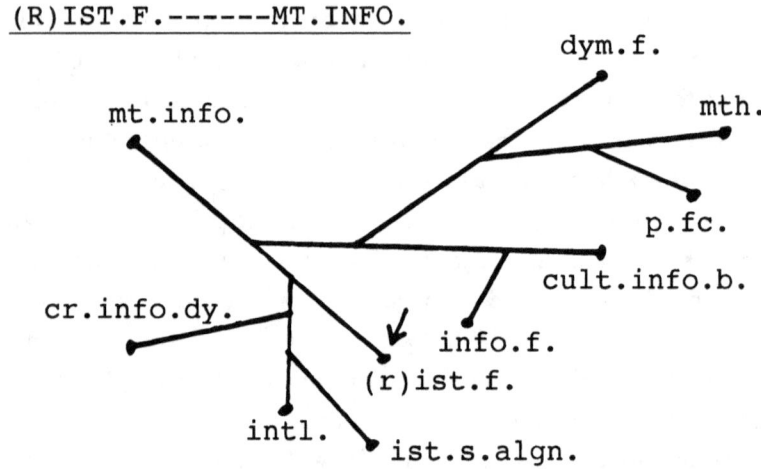

On the physical universe level, the first manifestation of the affinity insight principle could be viewed with respect to the consideration of "definition." For the composite thrust of the post-Ayler movement would move to realign their activity with what was true for each person's individual perception of sound logic (fascination) rather than one prescribed way of being. The time zone of the sixties would see the effects of this realignment in every sector of black culture. Because in the final analysis the move to secure proper definitions for black creativity must be viewed as one of the major goals in this time zone. Only by securing the awareness and power of definitions can a given group solidify their actual reality—and only be establishing composite culture (agreement) can a given culture group expand as a living thrust, with respect to its real potential. The significance of the post-Ayler creative thrust must be viewed with this context in mind, for the composite implications of the work that took place in the sixties would play an important role in helping to establish awareness of the affinity insight principle—both in terms of black creativity expanding into whatever avenue it chose to enter, and in terms of musicians themselves deciding on what the functional requirements of their craft would be. The collective work that took place in this period would forecast a new attitude for black creativity, and the composite implications of the post-Ayler movement would also establish another projectional route for black creativity. To view the creativity actualized in this period would imply that the musician's conception of his (her) own work be respected and studied. The progressional development of post-Ayler composite creativity must thus be viewed in dynamic terms—in its own dynamic terms, that is. We are dealing with a projection that represents a profoundly different cycle in American black creativity, and this must be understood.

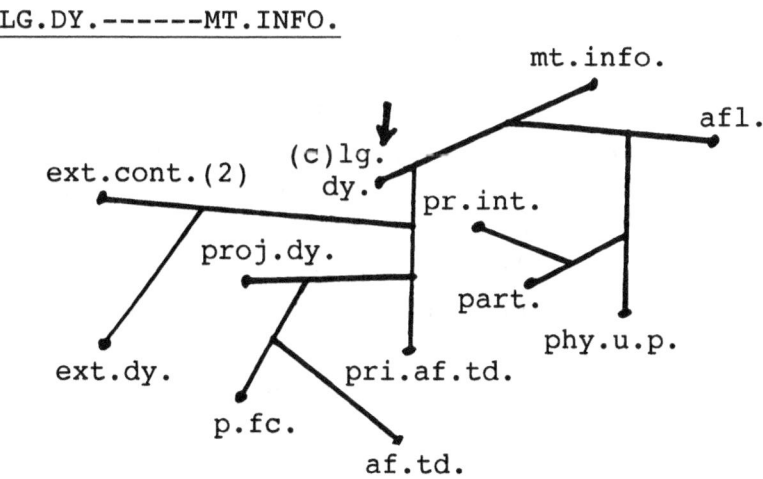

The move towards redefining terms in post-Ayler creativity can better be understood if the work of particular individual musicians is examined. For example, it would be extremely difficult to pigeonhole a saxophonist like Frank Wright in western terms—with respect to what a saxophonist should or shouldn't be about—because the essence of Frank Wright's activity has nothing to do with western considerations. Frank has commented on many occasions that he isn't interested in basic saxophone technique as defined in western methodology, at all. Thus any attempt to view the actualness of his activity would necessitate another way of perceiving the question of technique, or at least, any real attempt to understand the activity of Frank Wright would imply that some effort is brought forth to understand alternative functionalism (as defined by Frank Wright). The question of redefinition in post-Ayler creativity cannot be viewed in mono-dimensional terms if one is to truly understand the meta-reality that actualized the transition of the sixties. In many cases, it must also be understood that western interpretations have served as a distortion to the actual music. Many musicians came to view any attempt by the defining community to reduce their activity to western concepts and words as a move towards distortion—and in every instance this does seem to be the truth. The progressional development of the post-Ayler creative projections served as the strongest example of alternative functionalism in the sixties. The basic thrust alignment of the creativity seemed to suggest that not only would the western analytical microscope have to be discarded, but any reference to the western vibrational and functional sensibility would risk completely missing the actualness of the music. The seriousness of this phenomenon would help solidify the realness of what the affinity insight principle really means—as an expansion factor—and the implications of this phenomenon would help establish the necessary vibrational arena to promote unification in the composite musicians' community (this would be especially true for the activity that would solidify later in the midwest).

I have not meant to advance only one form of alternative functionalism for post-Ayler creativity, because certainly there are many other factors related to this subject. Moreover, I have not meant to imply that every musician from the post-Ayler junction can be viewed in the same context as Frank Wright—or any single musician for that matter—because this is not true either. The composite thrust of post-Ayler creativity represents a cross-section of viewpoints, and as such its related alternative functionalism must be viewed with respect to many different factors. My point, however, is that the thrust alignment of the post-Ayler projection can be viewed as a major continuum with regards to the question (and challenge) of redefinition. My example of Frank Wright must be viewed with this in mind, for while many musicians from the post-Ayler junction might not necessarily feel the same as Frank Wright—about the idea of saxophone technique—on the other hand, practically all of the musicians from this movement would reveal some profound altering (or violation) of the basic creative process as viewed in western terms. In other words, while some musicians might disagree with Frank Wright in a particular sense, every musician would agree with the overall vibrational reasons for redefining creativity. This same spectrum of viewpoint could be experienced by listening to the actual music recorded in this period. For no matter how diverse the post-Ayler projectional thrust might be viewed, the most basic feature of this activity would reveal a pronounced move away from western conceptual and functional pedagogy. This is true for all of the activity associated with the post-Ayler creative thrust. In the final analysis, the composite realness of this movement would move to intensify its understanding of the affinity insight principle—and in doing so secure the vibrational basis for all of the extensions that would develop later.

C.FO.ACT.------SOC.RT.

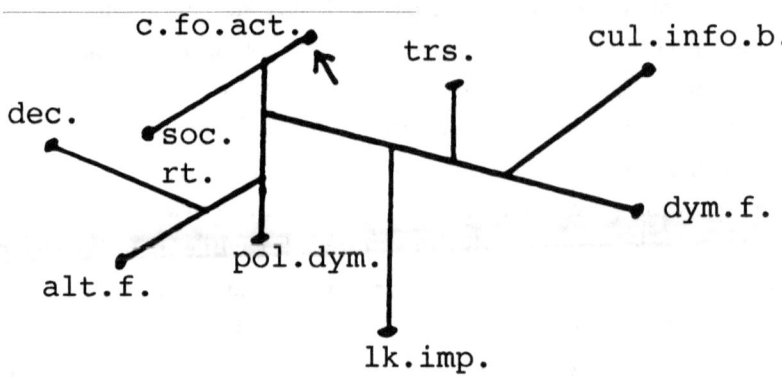

The progressional development of the post-Ayler movement would also affect the actualness of functionalism in physical universe terms. This would thus be the movement that would accelerate efforts to participate in areas normally not associated with creativity, but rather having to do with the community itself. The time zone of the sixties would thus be the cycle when creative musicians would again make real attempts to communicate their activity to the public—using whatever forums necessary. In actual terms, this would be the time period where creative music would begin to make itself heard throughout the neighborhood, as the first step towards communication. Throughout the whole of the sixties, creative musicians could be seen utilizing every outlet available as a means to re-establish some level of communication with the public. The spectrum of this involvement would be instrumental in the developing political consciousness that was also to form in this same period. For the realness of the struggle to communicate alternative creativity to the public would necessitate another level of functionalism—hence involvement. It was the New York post-Ayler school that first began to deal with these extra-musical problems, and any effort to understand the progressional development of creative black music in the time zone of the sixties would imply that this fact is acknowledged on some level. The work which ensued in this period would revolutionize the position of the creative person, and also advance and clarify the next real position of the creative black person in western culture—during this time cycle (the eighties).

The New York post-Ayler movement can also be viewed as the first movement in this time cycle to form non-profit organizations for the purpose of extended functionalism. The Jazz Composers Guild, for instance, represented the next level of unification for creative people, and the work done through this organization would have an important effect on the progressional continuance of creative music. Because of the intensity of the pressure surrounding survival, the Jazz Composers Guild must be viewed as only a brief phenomenon—lasting only a short period of time. But the fact that unification was achieved at all represented a gain of sorts. For the forming of the Jazz Composers Guild would have repercussions throughout the whole of America—eventually resulting in organizations like the AACM. The New York post-Ayler thrust must be credited with setting the example for the next cycle of creative musicians—regardless of area. The fruit of their labor would open up another level of functionalism for the creative musician, and this is important to understand. The significance of this subject is not limited to only the forming of the Jazz Composers Guild, for there is more to the post-Ayler movement than any one aspect.

The progressional thrust of the New York post-Ayler movement in the sixties would show the first composite efforts to form independent recording companies. For until this period, only a handful of musicians had understood the importance of independent recording. Certainly musicians like Sun Ra had long understood the realness of alternative outlets, and I have not meant to give the impression that nothing was ever done in this area before the time zone of the sixties. But the New York post-Ayler movement would be the first composite movement to embrace independent recording, and the New York post-Ayler thrust was also the first movement of its kind to accent the availability of independent recording. The net effect of this activity alone would have a serious effect on the progressional development of creative black music. For it must be understood that the time zone of the sixties saw not only suppression of the music in journalistic terms, but this was also the period which saw the complete neglect of post-Ayler creativity by the major recording companies. The move to establish alternative recording outlets must be viewed as necessary to the basic lifeblood of the music. For without the independent recording that was done in this period, it would have been impossible to consolidate the many different approaches of post-Ayler creativity into a single vibrational movement. Without alternative recording it would have also been difficult to keep abreast of the many changes reshaping black creativity in the sixties.

The dynamics of functionalism also extended into the business of creativity as well. Organizations like the Jazz Composer's Orchestra would create outlets for distributing creative music, and records of alternative creativity would have the possibility to be heard all over the planet. The work done in this period by isolated creative musicians should not be taken for granted if we are to truly view the significance of the post-Ayler movement. The concept of decentralization was actualized from the composite work done in this period, and the realness of alternative functionalism was shown to be both possible and practical as well. In other words, the significance of the New York post-Ayler continuum can be viewed on many different levels because the survival of the music was sustained by collective efforts. Nor have I meant to paint the activity from this time zone in unrealistic terms—certainly there are many factors associated with the advancing post-Ayler thrust that need to be clarified (some of which are positive and some negative), but if we are to gain the perspective necessary for examining an overview of creativity from this time cycle, then it is important to comment on what significance given particulars really have—or have had—to the lifeblood of the music. For that reason it is necessary to view the realness of alternative functionalism in as many contexts as possible. My most basic point is that the post-Ayler movement must be viewed both with respect for what forces it had to function from, as well as what was achieved from its participation. The fact is, the composite thrust of the New York post-Ayler movement laid the basis for all of the extensions that would follow. The collective work done in the early and middle sixties would carry implications that few would have believed at the time—and now. The composite realness of this movement must be dealt with if we are to gain insight into the realness of the next cycle of creative music. For without a meaningful understanding of this juncture of black creativity it will be extremely difficult to view the projections extending from this alignment. **The post-Ayler movement occupies a pivotal position in the transition cycle from what is called bebop—to the forms developing in this period.** Moreover, the realness of this cycle directly relates to the nature of the next transformation in world creativity as well—in other words, the actualness of post-Ayler creativity carries what I call multi-dimensional overtones.

There has been considerable discussion as to the actual ability and level of sophistication of the creative music which emerged in the sixties by the collective forces that control opinion. Any real attempt to view the significance of the post-Ayler thrust would imply that some of these charges are considered and dealt with. The basic thrust of these charges moves to challenge both the validity of post-Ayler creativity—as a projectional alignment relevant to life in the black community—as well as the technical level of those who participated in the music. The consensus of the western defining community for the most part has been that post-Ayler creativity should be viewed as a technically and scientifically less sophisticated projection. Moreover, their view would also extend to the intention factor of the creativity as well, for the most basic view that was perpetrated in the sixties was that only technically inferior players could be attracted to post-Ayler creativity (because this projection was designed for a lower level of invention and/or insight). To understand the seriousness of these charges is to have some idea of what transpired in the sixties, for every expansion of the post-Ayler junction has been accompanied by misinterpretations. Moreover, since the basic weight of these charges would make it practically impossible to respect post-Ayler creativity, it is no wonder that so few people in this time period are able to perceive of post-Ayler creativity as a meaningful projection that possibly carried multi-dimensional overtones (having to do with something positive and/or important). Yet I do not mean to imply that every aspect surrounding post-Ayler creativity can be viewed as adhering to the highest level of spirituality or functionalism, because this does not seem to correspond with what is happening in any projection—and why should post-Ayler creativity be any different in this regard either? It is my opinion that the collective forces which dictate western culture completely missed the point of post-Ayler creativity. In doing so, the composite realness of western functionalism has done a grave dis-service to black creativity. Nevertheless, the collected weight of the charges put on post-Ayler creativity must be looked at and addressed if we are to put it behind us. Because the essence-potential of any form of creativity is directly related to the spirit factor underlying its reception—which is to say, the potential functionality of post-Ayler creativity can be realized only when it is accepted and respected on some level. It is important to understand that the creativity from a given aspect of culture cannot be separated from that which "ised" it. In other words, the essence implications of post-Ayler creativity can be realized only when the distortions which surround it are corrected. The weight of these distortions is seated in almost twenty years of unmitigated negative publicity (and/or wrong conclusions), and this will continue unless challenged.

The fact is, if the post-Ayler creative projection doesn't express a legitimate vibrational actualization of black creativity, then how did it come into existence? For it must be understood we are not discussing a thrust alignment that came into being only because of intellectual considerations (intellectual in the sense of how the word is used in colleges or universities throughout the west—that is, inquiry arrived at through empirical analysis or isolated information gathering), but rather the solidification of post-Ayler creativity must be viewed as a composite response to both the social and vibrational realness of the sixties transfer cycle. Moreover, the thrust actualness of the post-Ayler projection can be viewed in progressional terms—based on real-life considerations. For instance, it is possible to view the progressional development of all of the principal musicians whose activity shaped the post-Ayler thrust and see a consistent continuity underlying their creative growth. Many critics would have us believe that the post-Ayler creative movement suddenly came from nowhere (there was also the "Coltrane has lost his mind" school of critics) to distort the music scene, and the young players who participated in the form were no more than angry racists bent on what *Downbeat* magazine would call "crow Jim." The fact is, the progressional expansion of creative music from the black aesthetic did not suffer from some catastrophic fall when the post-Ayler thrust solidified. The actualization of post-Ayler creativity had been prepared for, and its arrival must be viewed in logical (or unlogical) terms.

To the charges which seek to challenge whether or not post-Ayler creativity is relevant to actual-life consideration—in either the black or white communities—I say the progressional development and actualness of the music—regardless of time zone—speaks for itself. In other words, certainly no one can deny the fact that creative black music (and creative white and Asian music) must be viewed as being in the underground of western culture. Obviously this is so and there are many reasons for this state of being. It must be understood that black people are not in charge of the communications media but rather are the effect of what has been created by these controlling agencies. So real is this one aspect (media sophistication and control) that the position of popular music in this time zone cannot be compared with any non-sanctioned thrust projection in western culture. In other words, the success of popular music in this time period does not invalidate the realness of creative music but only attests to the sophistication of the controlling media that dictates taste to the consumer public.

In actual terms the solidification of post-Ayler creativity can be viewed as a movement formed because of the people—not in spite of the people. Throughout the time zone of the sixties creative musicians could be seen working and functioning in communities throughout America. More than any thrust after World War II, the composite post-Ayler movement must be viewed as a functionally active and community-supportive thrust. This would be a movement whose creativity vibrationally helped actualize and mirror the composite tone level of what was transpiring in the sixties. Yet I do not mean to imply that the relationship between post-Ayler creativity and, say, the black community was perfect in every way—obviously this would not be true (not to mention what do I mean by correct in this instance?). The fact is, to look at a given movement is to deal with a multitude of both people and factors, and it would be impossible to either empirically prove or disprove the validity of post-Ayler creativity based on given notions of which relationships can be called positive or negative, with regards to the "isness" of a community. **One fact, however, is clear: the progressional development of post-Ayler creativity was actualized in the black community and was not transported to America from Russia.** The music was actualized in the black community because it corresponds to the meta-reality of black culture, and the music was actualized in the black community because it solidified a particular projectional affinity— either with regards to given vibrational affinities or emotional affinities, or both. The distortions concerning the validity of post-Ayler creativity must be viewed as a weak response to the arrival of a new dynamic thrust alignment. There should have never been any doubt as to the realness of post-Ayler creativity (and in actual terms I do not believe there *was* really any doubt by the collective forces controlling western culture). The attempts to question the validity of the music must be viewed as moves to limit the potentiality of what the music signified—that being, a move forward towards transformation.

There has also been considerable discussion about the basic sophistication and level of post-Ayler creativity with regards to both its technical brilliance—or lack of brilliance—or its dynamic consequences (that being, the notion that post-Ayler creativity represented a necessarily limited projectional spread rather than a form endowed with the same dynamic possibilities as any other form). Moreover, the general consensus that emerged in the early sixties seems to solidify what this negative response would mean in commercial terms as well, for the most basic idea communicated throughout various publications and articles on the music in the sixties was that the post-Ayler projection must be viewed as a technically less sophisticated thrust than what is considered "acceptable." Musicians like Cecil Taylor and/or John Coltrane were generally spared this level of criticism—yet on occasion it was not even uncommon to read about how the anger of these musicians contributed to their losing perspective on what creativity is really about, etc. On the whole, the lack of respect for post-Ayler creativity was reserved for the younger players who were to take up the challenge of the music in the sixties. For to the critical defining community, many of these new musicians had not properly demonstrated their ability to play bebop and as such were "open game" for attack. So real was the extent of these charges that many players found themselves forced to abandon their activity because of lack of work and fatigue from the pressure of reviews and politics. By the end of the sixties, the critical defining community had achieved its aim—that being, the implanting of negative connotations surrounding how post-Ayler creativity was perceived by the public—and the end result of this implantation would help solidify the growing spread of what is now called jazz-rock as well as diminish the functional potential of post-Ayler creativity. Moreover, the extent of the move to discredit post-Ayler creativity would also accelerate the nature of the next cycle of separation between musicians as well—for the collected journalism surrounding creative music in the sixties would produce a situation which separated post-Ayler creativity from the composite thrust of creative music—and in so doing, promote discontent in the musicians' community (and this is exactly what happened). Any attempt to deal with the actualness of post-Ayler creativity would thus focus on the seriousness of what these attacks really meant. For the question of technical proficiency and sophistication in post-Ayler creativity must be looked at if one is to have some real understanding of the creative transition that took place in the sixties. Moreover, an examination of this question can also give us some basis for viewing what route the collected defining and controlling forces took to discredit post-Ayler creativity, and this information can be useful in helping to really understand what took place in this juncture. For it is my belief that the critical defining community completely missed the boat in trying to understand the composite realness of post-Ayler creativity.

My point is this: any real understanding of post-Ayler creativity would have to take into account the reality dynamics (particulars) of the musicians participating in the form—and what really transpired in the social and vibrational hierarchy surrounding the music. Because for the most part, it is true that many of the players who participated in the solidifying post-Ayler junction didn't correspond to the concept of "technician" as viewed in strict western terms (that being, a person who has attained a working knowledge of western theoretical and functional knowledge—either with regards to the science of western music as applied to system [as perceived in western terms] or manipulation [ability to function from what is understood—or practiced]—i.e., reading music or understanding chord changes)—but in the final analysis none of this really mattered. The changes that reshaped black creativity could not have come from any other sector of the musicians' community, and this is what is important. Moreover, the fact that many of the musicians participating in post-Ayler creativity didn't technically measure up to the reality of bebop or classical musicians can be viewed as advantageous to what the challenge of the next cycle would necessitate—on some level. Because to deal with the transitional realness of creative black music in the sixties is to have some awareness of the profound separation that exists in the creative musicians' community. The technical reality of post-Ayler creativity in its early stage is directly related to this phenomenon. This can better be understood by viewing the transitional realness of creative music.

In the early sixties, after the realness of Coleman's, Taylor's, etc., work became apparent, a rather unusual situation could be seen forming in the creative musicians' community. That situation was this: rather than taking the lead in trying to deal with the challenge of post-Ayler creativity—as far as redesigning the science of creative music to incorporate the expanded conceptual and emotional range happening in the then-changing creative area—the established technically advanced musicians instead preferred to focus on contributing to forms that were already secured as a means to participate in mediums that adhered to what they had come to view as suitable outlets for their talents. And in the final analysis, this sentiment had to be respected and understood, for many of these people had worked long and hard to develop themselves to participate in whatever their desired mediums were—not to mention the music we refer to as bebop is still a young music anyway; there is still much to be learned and contributed through this form. Thus a musician like Tony Williams, who technically in the western sense of the word is second to no one, can be viewed with respect for what he has contributed in the progressional development of percussion—as actualized through the creative context of what we call bebop on through to progressive jazz—to more open forms of modern or atonal bebop (extending to the methodological and conceptional brilliance of musicians like Max Roach, Art Blakey, and Elvin Jones), and as such his work can be viewed as a stylistic expansion of that lineage. But as the dynamic continuance of creative music from the black aesthetic began to vibrate to the demands of the post-Ayler projection, the conceptual and dynamic challenge of this projection would find responses from outside the established hierarchy—so radical would this junction be perceived (even though from our vantage point today the post-Ayler continuum is not radical at all and was a legitimate route for black creativity to take)—and the musicians who would supply the next directions—in actual terms—would come from outside the secured reality boundaries of the bebop continuum. For this reason, the conceptual and vibrational realness of post-Ayler percussion would be supplied by Sonny Murray and Milford Graves, rather than Tony Williams. This is not to discredit any given individual or period of music, because I have emphasized throughout the whole of this book that every projection (regardless of thrust alignment) is both necessary and equally brilliant, but rather to better understand the source transfer realness of post-Ayler creativity. That being: the solidification of post-Ayler activity would open up a whole new chapter in the progressional continuance of creative music, affecting both the essence factor of the music, as well as the physical universe hierarchy surrounding participation (affecting a multitude of levels).

(Level One)
THE MIDWEST (AND WEST COAST) CONTINUUM

THE MIDWESTERN SECTION OF AMERICA has long been an important area for creative music—and this is true regardless of period. It is important to view the uniqueness of this region because the dynamics of creative music have never been limited to only certain sectors of the planet—or given countries. To understand the composite reality of creative music is to have some idea of the dynamic spectrum of factors that dictate how given creative lines are to expand. This is true on many different levels, for the spectrum of a given projection sheds light on what that projection poses in both vibrational and meta-reality terms. All of this information is directly related to possible transformation, because the reality of a given continuum has to do with cross-sectional as well as particular progressionalism. From this information we can move to better understand and appreciate the composite realness of earth creativity. Because by viewing the total theatre of events surrounding a given thrust initiation, we can better come to terms with what that initiation really poses as a dynamic continuance—as opposed to applying narrow interpretations that seek to over-accent particular aspects of projectional specifics (which has been the case with music journalism in the past hundred years). The realness of this information can help us see there are no heroes as such in the music (or in the creativity), but instead a multi-influence of interrelated events that determine (and shape) the composite platform of its given time cycle. The realness of this information might hopefully move to clarify the reality and meta-reality realness of creative music—and earth progressionalism; because this is what is needed.

By focusing on the particulars of midwest continuance it might be possible to better understand the nature of progressionalism as this concept relates to the reality implications of contemporary information feeding (and/or transference). For many of us have come to view New

MID-W-2

York City as the only space in America where creative music is happening, and it is important that this viewpoint is examined on some level. Because obviously, in this time period, New York City does function on a much higher level than most other cities in America, but there are other factors that must be looked at, if we are to understand what this phenomenon means. The fact is, to really view the dynamics of New York City is to begin understanding the route of contemporary centralism in this time period. This is so because the most basic factor that has sustained New York City is not the uniqueness of its citizens—as a group more advanced than the rest of the country—but rather the realness that this city has been solidified as the center of dynamic functionalism, where creative people throughout the whole country have by necessity had to come. To really view this phenomenon is to understand New York City's position in the progressional rotation cycle that was solidified much earlier in time (having to do with the solidification of America itself, and also having to do with the east coast critical and defining community's lock on both communications and information focus).

If the most basic theme of this book has been that the dynamics of earth creativity are manifested throughout the whole of this planet, then it must also be said that the diversity of creative projections in America can only be experienced by acknowledging the dynamic realness of the greater country—as opposed to only the activity of New Yorkers. This is so because not only have three-fourths of the players now living in New York come from other sections of the country, but there is also another whole group—whose activity was and is just as important—who didn't come (or came in a different way). As such, the challenge of positive redocumentation implies that some effort is made to view the progressional significance of composite creativity—especially with respect to the particulars of regionalism—because in the final analysis New York City, and its resultant creativity, is not only about "New York City," but the composite result of a much greater input. The real diversity of dynamic progressionalism can only be approached by examining the particulars of the midwest, south, southeast, southwest, west, and—northwest? (—?) Nine-tenths of the dynamic projections that have shaped the last hundred and some years in this country (America) can be traced to areas other than New York City. The meta- and projectional implications of this phenomenon imply that some attempt should be made to examine what this means. Yet the realness of an investigation of this type transcends the scope of what is possible for me in this period. As such, in this section I will try to comment only on some aspects of midwest continuance (and hopefully one day I will be able to approach other areas of this subject more thoroughly).

(R)CULT.INFO.B.------AF.DY.

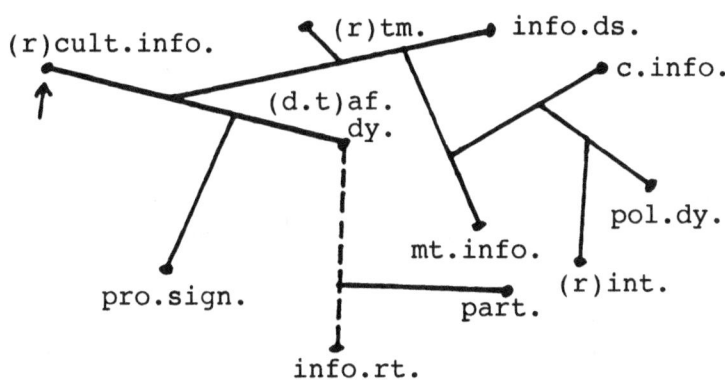

(R)POL.DYM.------TRS.

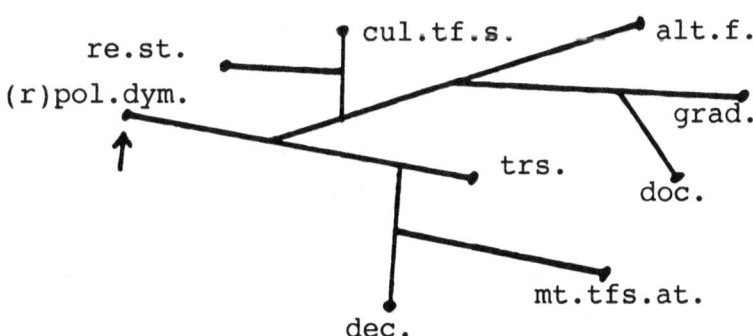

I have chosen in this section to write on the collective activities which shaped the progressionalism of the midwest because of two most basic reasons: (1) because I am from the midwest and as such am familiar (or more familiar) with the reality of this region than most other areas of the country; and (2) because I feel the work that solidified in the midwest during the sixties and seventies has profoundly shaped this time zone. The seriousness of the sixties progressionalism is important for what it implied to the dictates of its own particular region as well as its effect on the greater community of composite creativity. Only in this time period (the end of the seventies) has the realness of the sixties functionalism really been acknowledged by the eastern press (which is the "composite information feed" throughout the country), and in most cases misdocumentation has already started. The seriousness of this time period demands that efforts are made by the musicians themselves to document correctly what has been happening—for I believe that the seeds underlying sixties' functionalism carry dynamic possibilities for world transformation. This is true with respect to the actual music (or creativity) and this is true with respect to the seriousness of alternative functionalism (having to do with world change). It is important that some attempts are made to comment on this most complex cycle of creative progressionalism by the creative community itself. Either artists will write about this subject or another cycle of progressionalism will go "up for grabs" (and the official documentation will credit the Beach Boys with the invention of music in the sixties). Whatever—progressionalism in the midwest is a subject that comments on many different factors—and while I cannot write about the totalness of this subject, I can comment on those aspects that I am aware of—and that I have experienced.

The three basic areas that dealt with the dynamic implications of extended functionalism in the midwest (that I know of anyway) emerged in and around the cities of Detroit, Chicago, and St. Louis. The work that took place in these areas would profoundly affect all of the developments that characterized extended functionalism in the middle sixties on through the seventies (and in doing so, also set the stage for the eighties). This is not to say that every individual associated with these centers was from that particular section of the country (e.g., Leo Smith's activity is generally viewed with respect to the work he has done in the AACM in Chicago, but in actual fact Smith is from the southern part of America—Mississippi, to be exact)—rather, the three cities I have named served as magnet centers for dynamic collectivism. All of these movements could be viewed with respect to what their emergence signified about the dynamic continuance of post-Coltrane, -Coleman, or -Taylor initiations (although the realness of any given intention transcended the particulars of any one individual's—or projection's—reality). Many of the musicians who emerged to prominence in the late seventies can be traced to one of these three centers—so important was the work that took place in this cycle. It is important that attempts are made in this time period to examine each of these areas of functionalism—too much important work has already been either forgotten or misdocumented.

Of the three areas I will write about concerning creativity in the midwest, the work that took place in Detroit is the most unfamiliar to me. Yet everything I have read about this area seems to only accent its value as a positive transformational force for alternative functionalism (the only person I can think of who participated in all three creative centers in the midwest is Joseph Jarman). The basic thrust of the work coming from Detroit can be traced to the Detroit Artists' Workshop and the efforts of the trumpeter Charles Moore. In the middle sixties this organization was extremely effective in helping to reshape both creative music and dynamic functionalism (e.g., dance, poetry). The thrust of this movement would help establish many important musicians—and the work of musicians like Don Moye is directly related to the reality of this movement. For a period of four to six years the Detroit Artists' Workshop helped to establish momentum for alternative investigation, and only when the musicians themselves document the dynamics of this organization will we have the real story of what went on in this most important organization.

The work of the Detroit Artists' Workshop can be viewed as an important stimulus towards the establishment of independent self-help functionalism. Many of the members associated with this group would move on to become very important for the role they played in helping to reshape the reality aspect of creative music. Musicians like Stanley Cowell, after moving to New York, would help to establish many of the alternative attempts to create independent record companies as well as new sources for economic continuance. All of this work was and is very important for what it posed to creative music and progressional continuance. The thrust implications of the Detroit Artists' Workshop would move to expand the reality perspective of independent performing outlets—for by the middle sixties, this organization had already created its own independent performing space. It is unfortunate, to say the least, that no national attention has been focused on the developments of this organization. Even worse, the last ten years have seen many changes take place in this area—as in every other area—so that the initiations of given individuals have in many cases gone on to other things—because, of course, we are all changing. Hopefully, there are recordings that I am not aware of, documenting the music from this juncture. I do recall reading about recordings of the Charles Moore contemporary five or sextet, and hopefully this music is still available. Unlike the AACM or Black Artists' Group of St. Louis, the collective continuum that emerged from Detroit did not seem to stay together (or at least if this organization is together, I have not heard any information as to what it is now doing). Hopefully the original intentions of this collective have passed on to the next generation of creative musicians in this area—because the Detroit creative music community has long been a dynamic region for all forms of creativity. So many great musicians have solidified in this one area of the country that I find it difficult to now believe nothing is presently happening. The real documentation of this movement must be written by someone really familiar with the particulars of sixties functionalism—hopefully that someone will be one of the people who was actually involved.

AACM

The Association for the Advancement of Creative Musicians was founded in Chicago in the early sixties by Muhal Richard Abrams, Steve McCall, Philip Cohran, and Jodie Christian. For more than ten years this organization

MID-W–7

has participated in shaping the direction of creative music from the black aesthetic. The forming of the AACM was a response to the growing awareness that the situation for creative music had become critical in the Chicago area. Chicago has long been a center for creative music—regardless of time zone—but by the middle sixties, a clear pattern had emerged which threatened the growth potential of creative music. This pattern—which was the merging of the black and white musicians' unions—affected both the musicians' chance to earn a living as well as many of the performing outlets for creative music. The end result of this phenomenon was that many musicians were forced to leave Chicago. Musicians like Johnny Griffith and later Sun Ra would make their move in the fifties. In short, Chicago in this period could be looked at as being very similar to Kansas City during Pendergast's reign—that is, the social-political factors underlying the reality of the greater metropolis at some point had become an intolerable burden on the creative community—forcing musicians to migrate.

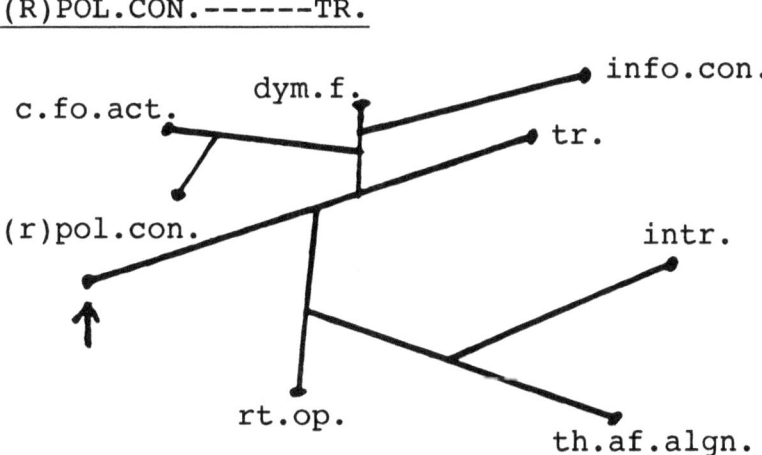

There were also other factors of equal importance directly related to the forming of the AACM. Those factors would be the emergence of the transformation cycle in creative music that occurred during the late fifties/early sixties, and the philosophical and sociological implications that were triggered by this change. In other words, the initiations which personified the next restructured cycle in creative music (the work of

MID-W-8

Coltrane, Coleman, and Taylor) also served as a divisive factor among the musicians themselves. This was the time zone where extended creativity had become a source for heated debates between all musicians. Needless to say, the established defining communities exploited this factor on every level, and by 1962 there was very little unity between musicians with different views about the so-called new music. By 1962, if a young musician chose to build his/her affinity thrust from the activity of a musician like Cecil Taylor, that musician risked being ostracized by a considerable portion of the musicians' community—so great were the hostilities at that time. Whatever the conceptual differences among the early membership of the AACM during its formative period, the strongest basic affinity that tied them together was understanding there was an urgent need to establish outlets to pursue the implications of creative music—in whatever form. It is this understanding which accents the significance of the AACM as a positive functional asset in the drive towards establishing alternative outlets for creative music. The activity of these men and women could best be looked at from this context, as opposed to creativity for its own sake.

RT.OP.------INFO.AF.B.

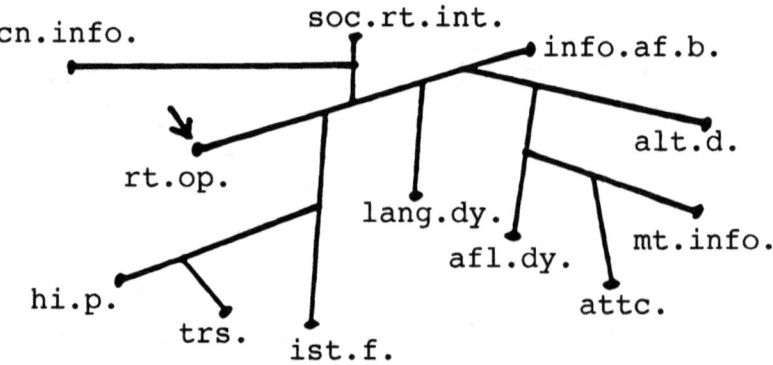

The Association for the Advancement of Creative Musicians is a non-profit collective organization, chartered by the State of Illinois, formed solely for the purpose of creating a more meaningful environment for both the creative musician and the community. Among the priorities the AACM sought to establish in its formative period were: (1) the task of creating an outlet for performing music; (2) the challenge of creating an atmosphere where there could be collective dialogue among creative musicians (both for the music and the realness that unification is a must for any real physical universe attempt to change the existing situation); and (3) to establish a more meaningful relationship to the community—that being, the black community on the south side of Chicago. The significance of the AACM is directly tied to these aims, and the success of the AACM—whatever the context—will be based on how many of these priorities have been met and furthered by future collective organizations.

The move to establish performing outlets for the music during the sixties was extremely difficult; nevertheless, the AACM was able to achieve that goal by renting facilities whenever possible—or utilizing existing facilities at some of the universities on the south side of Chicago (most notably, the University of Chicago). All of the musicians participated in helping a given concert function—that is, the collective membership of the AACM would assist with the publicity of a given concert, help with selling tickets—working lights—curtains, etc. Between 1966 and 1968 the AACM managed to program at least one concert a week at various points throughout the city (although on many occasions there were as many as three or four concerts in a given week). By establishing performing outlets in this manner the AACM provided a situation for people to experience and thus keep in contact with the changing forms of the music, and as such this work was important. For unlike notated music from the western aesthetic, creative improvisational music is a form that depends very much on the contact between the musician and listeners. Which is to say, creative music is an affinity-thrust aesthetic that developed directly through the process itself—by actually playing to a given audience, as opposed to a strict theoretical situation. Every musician in the AACM profited from the collective assistance during this period, for it has always been difficult to organize a concert without help (not to mention very few of the musicians in this period could afford to even produce their own concerts). None of the gains that were made by given members of the AACM would have been possible without the

MID-W—10

establishment of these performing outlets and the collective assistance of the AACM membership. If 1966 to '68 represented the strongest alternative period for establishing performing outlets for creative music, it can also be said that this same period saw the greatest advances in the music as well—such is the importance of unification.

(R)STY.------PHY.U.P.

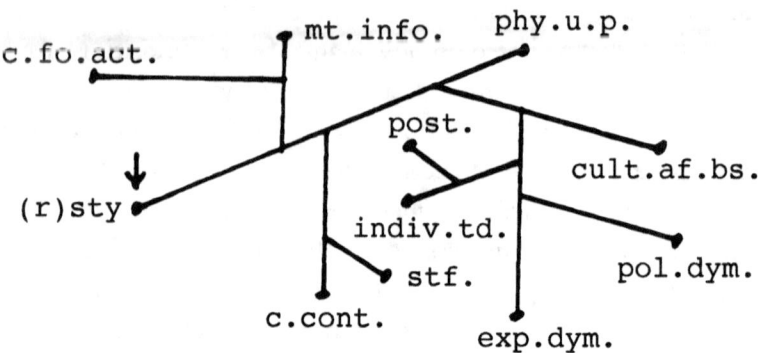

The AACM encouraged unification between the musicians on whatever levels possible. The actual atmosphere in the organization was conducive for communication on every subject pertaining to creative music, and this factor is generally overlooked in present-day documentation about the AACM. All of the changes initiated through the organization were the direct result of its unification rather than its isolated individuals. Yet I do not mean to discredit the work of any given individual either. Many of the changes in the functional dynamics of the music can be traced to a handful of its members, rather than the whole organization. But my point is that the composite vibrational identity of the AACM provided the backdrop which allowed for these changes to happen. This can better be understood if the reality and objective dynamics of the organization and members are taken into account. For a period of three years from 1966 to 1969 the musicians of the AACM pursued—and encouraged each other to pursue—every possible direction in the music. This was the period where great exchanges of ideas took place—concerning the significance of the activity raised in New York, as well as how the gains

MID-W–11

from that region could be extended, on whatever level, for the activity solidifying in Chicago. It is for this reason that the extensions "ised" in Chicago are especially relevant in this time zone (the eighties); for the music that developed through the AACM was a direct manifestation of each individual's work as well as the end product of a composite-affinity agreement (representing the composite organization as well as the community). In this context, the AACM functioned as a platform where a given musician could be exposed to many different schools of thought. It is important to understand that although the level of communication in the organization was high, I have not meant to imply that the AACM promoted a unified approach to the actual music, because this was not the case either. If anything, the opposite was true. My point is this: no musicians—or groups for that matter—employed the same approach to making the music. Instead, the diversity of its composite investigation has been the strength of the organization. The communication and exchanges of ideas that took place in the AACM produced a composite vibrational attitude that transcended any single style. It is this common factor that is experienced when the total activity of the AACM is examined—in other words, the composite vibration of the many different ensembles constituted a "school" of music in itself.

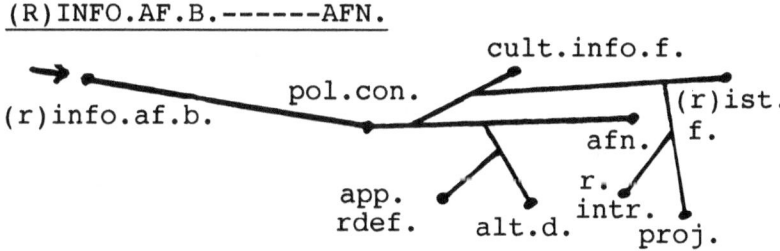

Without doubt one of the most important projects of the AACM was the initiation of programs to bring the community in closer contact with creative music. This is so because the present-day reality of creative music has long been outside the awareness (or even interest) of the majority of people in the greater culture, and this separation can be attributed to many sources. There is also the realness that as long as black people continue

417

MID-W–12

to let present-day sources of western information manipulation dictate and interpret black creative music, this separation will increase; for not only is the present-day reality continuum of western culture designed for the exclusive advantage of those white people in its defining class, but this situation also reflects western culture's exclusive affinity dictates. In short, if this situation is to be changed, it will be up to the people who are the victims of its effects. Moreover, the burden of the creative musician is such that he/she has little choice but to direct him/herself towards functioning for possible change, because in the final analysis, the creative artist today has nothing to lose—either move towards activism or face annihilation. Nevertheless, the enormity of attempting to change the developed schism between black creativity and the black community is such that only a unified collective group could possibly be successful (and it is understood that whatever inroads any group might make towards solidifying change in this context—whatever time period—the fact is, it will take years before the actual fruits of this challenge can be successfully achieved). The decision of the AACM to undertake this challenge was and is one of the most important commitments of the organization—as important as the creativity itself.

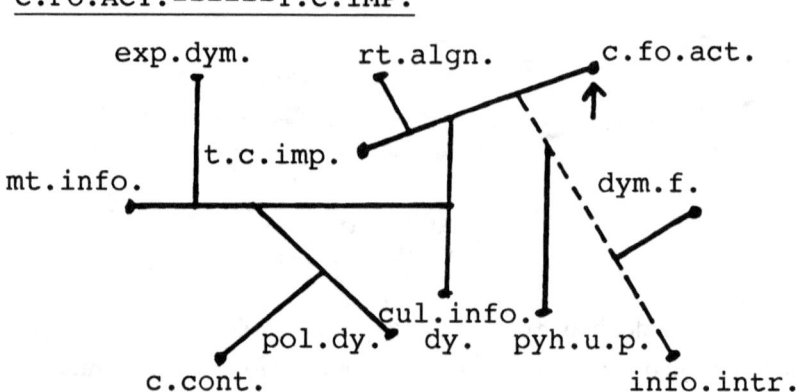

In 1967, the Association for the Advancement of Creative Musicians addressed itself to one of the most important problems facing the black community—that problem being: the lack of programs in the black community for the creative child interested in music. It must be understood that for every young child on the south side of Chicago who gets a chance to study music, there are literally hundreds who never get that chance. Who can say how many Charlie Parkers are lost solely because no one provided an outlet where that child could develop his or her creative interest (not to mention that whether or not a child is another Charlie Parker is, in the end, irrelevant—for the basic fact that must be understood is that everyone needs to have a creative outlet, and everyone is capable of being creative). The program that the AACM initiated was the establishment of a free music program consisting of (1) a music school, and (2) encouraging parents to bring their children to concerts. The work done in this area has clearly been an important beginning towards dynamic involvement. Young children in these programs were given instruments and lessons free of charge (in many cases, AACM musicians would have to also provide transportation to bring students to their lessons), and after two years the realness of this experiment had broken new ground for both the musicians and the community. The music school project represented the first real effort by a musicians' collective in the sixties to meet the people in its neighborhood and work with them. The AACM also gave many free concerts and encouraged the people of the neighborhood to come and experience the music whenever possible. Children were admitted free of charge, and several times a year there were concerts by students in the music schools (a recital) which were designed to attract people in the community as well as the families of the students. My point is that programs of this sort are only possible when there is a level of unification between the creative community and the actual community. Yet I have not meant to imply that everything at the AACM was perfect either—because this is never true, whatever the time zone—but the forming of the AACM clearly did represent a positive step towards alternative functionalism.

(R)INFO.DS.------AFL.

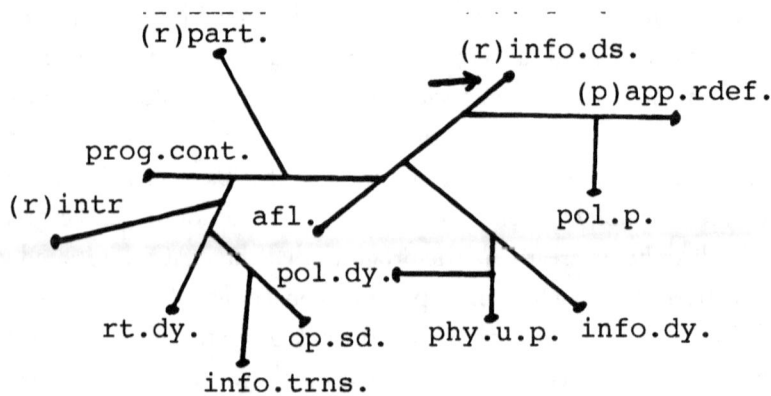

If the Jazz Composers Guild represented the first level of unification—and this does seem to be the case, no matter that this group didn't fully realize all that we had hoped for it—it is possible that the AACM represented the second level of unification for the creative musician. And just as the Jazz Composers Guild was successful only to a point, so too has been the AACM; and there are many improvements which need to be made as the organization moves into its eleventh year (and it is important to not ignore this most obvious fact). But it is also clear that unification is the most important tool the creative musician has. The difference between the Jazz Composers Guild and the AACM can be viewed as degrees of collectivism; which is to say, the factor that best distinguishes the AACM from the Jazz Composers Guild was the degree of each organization's collective participation and unity. Hopefully, the next functional organization in creative music will expand the realness of unification to even greater heights. It is a question of building an organization founded in composite understanding—of both purpose and humanhood, where each individual can function as a part of a collective movement—as opposed to the extraordinary emphasis that this society now places on the individual ego—or separateness. Somehow it seems that each new generation of creative black musicians is more open to examining the dynamics of collectivism than the previous generation. If this is true, then the functional gains of the AACM will be viewed as one of the early steps in this direction, and, like the Jazz Composers Guild, will be improved upon by each succeeding generation—or at least I would like to hope this is true. There are many different factors that must be understood before the seriousness of unification can be realized. For the realness of unification is directly related to how much of an overview one has (or develops)—and the seriousness of unification is directly related to one's perceptions of present-day physical universe multi-progressionalism, with regards to transformation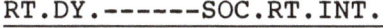.

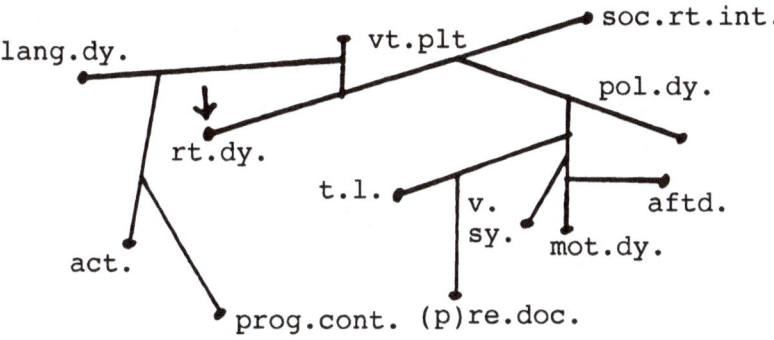

Among the many factors related to the successes of the AACM is the reality of the physical universe situation in the midwest. There is a remarkable difference in the reality particulars of the midwest—and in particular Chicago—from the life tone which permeates New York City, for example. One of the most basic differences between these environments would be that in Chicago there seems to be more time for actual research than is available in New York. That is to say, the vibrational arena of a place like Chicago lends itself more towards preparation than centers like New York. This difference is undoubtedly connected to the political-economic situation of the composite country, because New York City is designed more or less to market creativity—with the accent on exploitation and discovering new talent. Any musician who performs in New York is more vibrationally aware that a given performance has the possibility to make him/her more known—which is to say that New York City is not

MID-W–16

designed for the "on-the-job training" zone, as much as to exploit what has already been developed. I have not meant to imply that it is totally impossible for a musician to develop in the New York environment, but only to point out that there is a marked difference in the reality situation in the midwestern, southern, and western parts of the United States to New York City. Certainly in Chicago a musician must have a deep grasp of his activity if he seriously intends to have his activity received, but it is also clear that the vibrational and social situation in Chicago has more room for the developing student of creative music. The fact that the major recording studios are not in Chicago, or the close scrutiny from the collective and defining community of the western press, gives the creative musician extra room to better prepare him/herself for the challenge of the music. There is also the realness that work possibilities in a place like Chicago are somewhat limited compared to, say, the east coast. The social and physical universe situation in Chicago was perfect for undertaking a project like the AACM, and to a great extent, the gains which solidified through the organization are directly related to the vibrational arena that allowed it to occur.

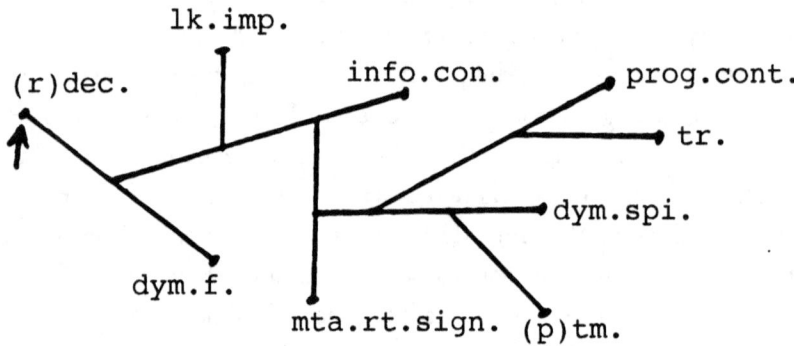

If the New York School that emerged in the early sixties represented the reactions and implications of (the functional dictates underlying) progressive jazz, and if this movement was an extension of the ideas practiced by the first restructuralists of new improvisational

MID-W-17

technique—Coleman, Ayler, Taylor, Coltrane, etc.—then the AACM could best be viewed as the movement which redefined what these new techniques would mean on a practical structural level (i.e., the actual music, and playing the music) and on a conceptual level as well. If we can talk of the New York School as the movement which dictated how the emotional implications of creative music would flow in a given time zone, we can also view the AACM as the movement which dictated what this new emotionalism would mean on a functional level. In other words, if the New York School could be characterized as the movement which spiritually and explosively met the challenge of creative music after the transformation in the sixties, then the AACM could be understood as the movement which scientifically met the dynamics that this transformation implied.

The multitude of ideas which have come out of the AACM experience is directly related to the communication and interchange that took place in the organization from its beginning period. It is this factor which accounts for the great diversity of ideas that are now documented on record (in both early and later recordings). By 1967, the AACM held composers' forums where every aspect of composition—from traditional to avant-garde techniques in western art music, to the complete tradition of trans-African music—was examined. These forums were extremely important for the information that was shared by the collective membership, and are directly related to the architectural concepts which later emerged through the organization. It is possible to trace all of the developments of the AACM back to this period—so great was the interchange of ideas. Moreover, while the AACM functioned as the central foundation of this interchange, each individual musician contributed his or her own research to the collective group (where the potential weight of a given direction could be evaluated or critically examined by the composite organization). That is to say, while Roscoe Mitchell and Lester Bowie studied some of the concepts from the black minstrel groups, Joseph Jarman and Malachi Favors were researching into the history of black music in Africa (or Egypt). Muhal Richard Abrams researched the spiritual implications of the black aesthetic—Leo Smith and I focused on the reality of alternative scientific functionalism for structure (composition)—etc., etc. The AACM produced an atmosphere where the different interests of each individual musician could be expressed and shared with the total group—in short, there was much interchange (I do not mean simply borrowing another person's ideas, because this was not the case). Among the concepts solidified in this period were: the utilization of the spectrum of sound as a legitimate concern of the creative musician—the expansion of the functional creative ensemble (no longer would a musician need to function from only one instrumental concept)—the study of timbre implications with regards to composition—research into the language implications of creative music—and finally, a refocusing of the composite meta-reality of creative music from the black aesthetic.

The AACM also played a major role in the expansion of contemporary percussion concepts, but this area of involvement is not generally known. For musicians like Airto Moreira (who is from South America) are generally given credit for employing percussive sounds and, in general, expanding the tools of the creative percussionist. But as early as 1966, the AACM had developed alternative concepts that dictated new roles for every family of instruments—including percussion. The concept of "Little Instruments" or "Sound Tools" was an accepted part of the musical scene in Chicago by the time Airto arrived in America. (I say this not to take anything away from Airto, because obviously he came with his own approach to creative music as well; my point is that the AACM has developed many areas of the music which are to this day not really recognized.)

Without doubt the greatest service that the AACM instigated would be the re-examination of black music in all of its different permutations. The AACM was the first organization in its time period to emphasize the significance of composite black music. I do not mean to imply that no creative musicians—whether in Chicago or New York, etc.—had any knowledge of the early forms of creative music from the black aesthetic. But never before has there been the kind of collective research into the "essence factor" of the music as initiated by the AACM in the sixties. Nor do I mean to imply that every musician from the AACM has a complete knowledge of black music history either. I am only stating that the AACM provided a backdrop for understanding and researching the significance of creative black music—throughout its various time zones—and the knowledge from this research has and will have a profound impact on the direction of creative music—and the total understanding of black culture. The research done in the early sixties is also directly related to the re-adaptation of composite trans-African functionalism, and in that context the musicians from the AACM in the course of the last ten years have been found using Dixieland forms—bebop forms—no forms, as well as their own structural initiations (sometimes in the course of one concert). The work of the AACM will be important for the establishment of a complete "composite aesthetic," and the vibrational consequences of this phenomenon will be extremely important for what it will politically and socially imply in the near future.

The musicians from the AACM have explored the spectrum of creative music, from solo music to electronic music, and the work done through this organization has been extremely important for shaping the dynamics of present-day contemporary creative music. From the very beginning of the AACM formation, the Experimental Band has functioned as an important center factor for large ensemble postulation. This band has been the organization's focal point for practical research on the orchestral medium. Many of the developments which have taken shape in the orchestral context of the AACM's music have not been fully made public (i.e., records) because of the economic problems which surround large projects—but hopefully this aspect of the AACM contribution will be corrected in the future (at present there are only four records of AACM musicians that contain creative orchestra music). The AACM has also extended the art of solo playing, and this was done as early as 1966. All of these aspects of the music, with the exception of the orchestra context, have been well documented, and it is still possible to experience some of this music on record (as this section of the book is being written).

The AACM was not concerned only with creative music at the expense of the total "composite arena" of creativity. During the first ten years of the organization's history one could have experienced many concerts that accented dance, poetry, films, exhibits, plays and theatre, etc. The organization's emphasis on music was only because of the early factors which dictated how the AACM was to be formed, as opposed to an imposed policy that sought to isolate dynamic functionalism. The economic factor also determined whether or not a given creative area could be utilized as desired, and hopefully the next ten-year cycle of the AACM's development will see this problem (economics) harnessed to some extent (although it is clear that alternative organizations like the AACM will continually have this problem on some level).

The AACM was among the first organizations of its kind to bring in outside creative organizations and present their activity to audiences in Chicago. Groups like the Black Artists Group of St. Louis were regularly presenting concerts of their music through the AACM. This is another area of the organization that will hopefully be expanded in the future by other creative groups. **I believe the Association for the Advancement of Creative Musicians represents the next level of commitment for creative music, and as we move towards the eighties, I have no doubt that this opinion will be shared. The work of this organization in the sixties and seventies was among the most significant factors in creative music in that time zone.** Hopefully the realness of the eighties will see serious examination about those particular musicians whose viewpoints and activism underlined the growth of this organization, because the significance of the AACM is not separate from the significance of those individuals. In particular I would like to hope that the challenge of the next cycle will see a greater appreciation of those special individuals whose contributions to creative music profoundly altered the course of present-day creative music—like, for instance:

(1) Muhal Richard Abrams has produced a body of necessarily relevant creativity that must be dealt with in the eighties. The thrust of Abrams's work can be traced back to the time zone of the fifties—from his involvement with hard bop, to the founding of the Experimental Band, to the theatre work he contributed in the sixties, and to the inspiration he provided for all of the musicians in the AACM. Muhal's piano music is like a history of black music—encompassing every area and period of

black music, yet offering something that is uniquely different at the same time. This is a musician who has worked with master musicians in every period of black creativity—from Dexter Gordon to Eddie Harris, from Max Roach to Clifford Jordan. I believe Muhal's contribution to creative music represents one of the significant offerings of the post-Ayler continuum.

(2) The dynamic activity of multi-instrumentalist and composer Leo Smith should also receive the recognition he so richly deserves in the eighties. For the thrust of his work has profoundly contributed to the professional expansion of both creative music and composite alternative functionalism. Smith's activity is one of the few composite visions of creativity in this time cycle, and the realness of his work in the seventies has seen involvement in every area of creative music. This was the first musician from the AACM continuum to form his own record company and also the first musician from the midwest movement to publish books on creative music. By the middle of the seventies, Smith would also become the first musician from the AACM to publish essays on alternative approaches to rhythm in creative music—making him the first real theorist from the post-AACM juncture. In terms of his actual music, Smith has extended the reality dynamics of creative brass—notated and improvisational—music on a level that has no comparison. The thrust of his work can be viewed as representing its own unique space—with its own laws (yet at the same time, all encompassing as well). The net effect of his activity transcends any one context and cannot be termed jazz, or notated music—but instead is a spiritual offering from one of the most significant contributors in this time period.

(3) The Art Ensemble of Chicago must come to be viewed as one of the most dynamic ensembles in creative music—regardless of period. The thrust of their activity has helped to open up every area in creative music—involving the composite reality of black creativity. Since the middle sixties, this ensemble has functioned in every possible context in black creativity, from black church music to hard bop, and the work they have documented should be required listening for any serious student of music. Fortunately, the Art Ensemble is finally beginning to receive the respect their works merit, and the thrust of the eighties will no doubt

see this group leave its mark on the whole of earth creativity. All of the members of this ensemble will hopefully one day come to be viewed for both their individual and collective achievement. For the dynamics of this group are not limited to only the particulars of its collective viewpoint, but instead involve each individual's special musical vision. The work of Roscoe Mitchell, Joseph Jarman, Lester Bowie, Don Moye, and Malachi Favors will undoubtedly come to be viewed as a significant offering to world creativity.

(4) The work of Leroy Jenkins must also be cited as extra-significant for what he has contributed in creative music. For Jenkins, more than any other musician in this time period, has shown the dynamic implications of the violin as a necessary instrument in extended improvisational music. Since the middle sixties, Jenkins has functioned in a variety of contexts as a creative instrumentalist, and many of the ensembles he has worked in helped to shape the reality of the post-AACM functionalism. In groups like the Revolutionary Ensemble, Jenkins's work helped to ignite the whole of creative music, and throughout the seventies his approach could be experienced in groups—and with individuals—like Rahsaan Roland Kirk, Dewey Redman, and Ornette Coleman. The span of Jenkins's activity is documented in every context, from solo music to orchestra, and the time zone of the eighties promises to see this great musician make many more important statements as well. Like most of the musicians from the AACM, Jenkins also functions as a composer and/or multi-instrumentalist.

(5) The dynamic contributions of a musician-composer like George Lewis can also be viewed as another example of extended involvement. The thrust of Lewis's activity encompasses the composite reality of contemporary brass dynamics as well as new advances in electronic music. Hopefully the time zone of the eighties will see more serious focus on this most important musician. Lewis is one of the first musicians from the AACM to really move into the dynamic world of composite electronic music—from computer music to building his own source-generating devices—and the weight of his encounter with extended technology has already opened up new areas of exploration for the creative restructuralist. As an instrumentalist, Lewis is recognized as

one of the most important instrumentalists in the time zone, and I have no doubt that the eighties, nineties, etc., will continue to see necessary contributions from this great musician.

(6) Air—The ensemble Air has emerged to become one of the most impressive groups in the seventies, and undoubtedly the future will see many more contributions from this collective. Air is able to effectively participate in the composite spectrum of the music—from the early forms to the present—and in each case, extract necessary and dynamic invention for the composite music. Any attempt to deal with the reality dynamics of creative music, as we move into the eighties, will necessitate that the music of Henry Threadgill, Fred Hopkins, and Steve McCall be examined—in every context.

(7) Roscoe Mitchell—The reality implications of Roscoe Mitchell's activity will undoubtedly come to be viewed as a factor in the restructural dynamics of creative music. For over twenty years, this one musician has continually found dynamic solutions to the challenge of transformational creativity. The thrust of Mitchell's music has given us new insight into (1) musical language, (2) composition dynamics, and (3) composite integration. As an instrumentalist, Mitchell has helped to transform those participation dynamics of creative music by establishing new insight into the role of extended multi-instrumentalism and conceptual focus. As a visionary, Mitchell has shown us dynamic possibilities for the future—and this is true in every area (or focus). The thrust of his efforts in the past fifteen years qualifies him to be considered as a master musician.

By citing these particular individuals I have not meant to imply that only these musicians have contributed to creative music—for to do so would be both wrong and detrimental to what the AACM stands for. To really view the AACM is to experience the composite work that has come through this organization—from individuals like Fred Anderson to Kahil El'Zabar. Contrary to popular belief, the AACM has no one musical viewpoint or criterion, but instead represents a composite cross-section of various approaches and beliefs. To me this is the strength of the organization. Because in the final analysis, the most basic factor that stimulated the formation of the AACM was its open attitude about letting each individual pursue his or her natural attraction in creativity. I have mentioned the musicians in this section only as an example of the spectrum of the organization—because each musician outlined in this section represents a totally different musical viewpoint. The challenge of dynamic alternative functionalism must involve the same respect for individual affinity dynamics. I believe the AACM represents a positive contribution for advancing world creativity—regardless of region or focus—and this is important.

St. Louis Movement

Only in the middle seventies did the collective forces of western media become aware of the dynamic activity that solidified in St. Louis. For the physical universe position of St. Louis is even more isolated from the main information feed of America than Chicago—not to mention that many of the musicians who formed the backbone of the St. Louis movement were reluctant to travel on a composite level until the middle seventies. Nevertheless, the arrival of the musicians from St. Louis would have a dynamic impact on the composite scene—for these musicians had done their homework many years earlier (which is to say, the continuum that arrived in New York during the middle seventies was prepared in every way to participate in the music). It is important that some attempt is made to better understand the activity of this group of musicians. One thing is clear: the collective realness of the St. Louis movement will be an important factor shaping the creativity of the eighties. The music we have experienced from this sector (in the late seventies) seems to forecast even greater challenges for creative music in the next cycle. Hopefully the emergence of the St. Louis movement will be the beginning of an increased information feed from the greater community of American society—for the realness of both this group and the AACM might hopefully serve as the beginning of decentralization. The realness of composite information feeding would undoubtedly change the whole reality position of alternative functionalism in western society, on every level. As such, it is important that the dynamic implication of the creativity from St. Louis is received and understood.

MID-W-25

The historical progressions surrounding the solidification of the St. Louis movement can be traced back into the middle to late sixties. For the St. Louis movement in many ways can be viewed as inspired by the solidification of the AACM. Many of the musicians associated with the creative music scene in St. Louis were also connected to the scene in Chicago—and there has always been much communication between these two groups as well. Certainly the reality of creative music in St. Louis was not very different from the situation in Chicago, and as such all of the musicians interested in extended functionalism were dealing with the same pressures—both socially and politically. Because, like the AACM, the creative movement in St. Louis was concerned with understanding the dynamic implications of post-Ayler initiations—and what this implied for future postulation—and there is more. The seriousness of post-Ayler activity would raise the same questions in St. Louis that it posed to the greater Chicago community—for without doubt the most basic factor that determined why both organizations were formed in the first place had to do with what the accelerated continuum of post-Ayler creativity posed for dynamic collectivism as well as community organization. Thus by the late sixties, the Black Artists Group of St. Louis (BAG) formed as a means to deal with the challenge of extended functionalism, and reinvestigation. The solidification of this organization would expand the midwestern creative network and provide a necessary link for the composite community of creative people in that region.

By the late sixties it was not uncommon to experience activity of the Black Artists Group of St. Louis in Chicago, or the AACM in St. Louis, for there has long been many levels of interchange between these two organizations. For a period of three years, musician-composers like Julius Hemphill and Roscoe Mitchell could be heard in both cities, in several different contexts—with large ensembles from their own respective groups, or as guests in each other's groups. This kind of interchange would be quite common until the changes that affected both groups in the late sixties—1969–70 represented a kind of migration period for both organizations (the AACM first went to Europe and later New York, and this same cycle would actualize in St. Louis in the early seventies). The

431

closeness between BAG and the AACM should not only be viewed as the logical results of their physical proximity (the distance between the cities and the vibrational particulars of the midwest) but instead indicative of the total fabric that dictated alternative functionalism in the sixties. Several of the primary musicians of the AACM—whose activity had a profound influence on the overall vibrational tone of the music—had actually come from St. Louis. Musicians like Lester Bowie—known for his work in the AACM and the Art Ensemble of Chicago—was in fact born in St. Louis and developed many of his ideas in that region. To say his work has influenced the composite dynamics of the AACM would be an understatement (for Bowie was one of the first musicians to speak of the composite spectrum of black creativity). In fact there was a period where half of the Art Ensemble of Chicago membership was from St. Louis (at the time the Art Ensemble was called the Roscoe Mitchell Quartet and its membership included Bowie on trumpet, Phillip Wilson and/or Leonard Smith on percussion—all of whom were from St. Louis). To really understand this is to have some idea of the multi-complexual factors related to post-Ayler progressionalism (as it relates to the cycle of creativity that solidified from the midwest).

In many ways the Black Artists Group of St. Louis was even more successful than the AACM in establishing a working platform for alternative functionalism. For the most basic factor that affects the reality option of any functioning organization is the consideration of economics and political support; and in this avenue, BAG achieved tremendous breakthroughs on every level. Because while the AACM was never able to gain financial assistance from the political machinery in Chicago (or from the federal government) in its early period—from the middle sixties until the late seventies—BAG was much more successful. The functionalism which developed in Chicago was much more strenuous than that in St. Louis. Because without federal support it was very difficult to advance the music school of the AACM, and it was also very difficult to develop the kind of vibrational atmosphere that the AACM postulated for the greater community. This is not to say that any objectives were necessarily not realized at the AACM—because there have been many gains in every avenue—rather, the lack of state and federal support did affect what level a given function could operate from. But this was not the case for the Black Artists Group of St. Louis, because BAG had been very successful in attracting greater public support—involving both state and federal support. Undoubtedly the success of BAG dynamic functionalism is related to the reasons that its members chose to stay in St. Louis for as long as they did—rather than risk traveling to unknown or untested areas. The dynamic solidification of BAG's business structure created a situation where each member was able to teach music in the community—and give concerts, and also get paid enough money to continue their lives. The solidification of this machinery represented the next level of alternative functionalism—for the realness of financial support created a situation where BAG was even able to have its own creative center—with enough economic support to keep it running.

The progressional expansion of the Black Artists Group of St. Louis could be viewed forming around 1973—as a composite phenomenon. Many of the musicians in this period came to realize that the actual continuum of the music could no longer be contained to any one section of the planet—let alone region in the midwest. Plus, the successes of the AACM clearly showed that it was possible to survive outside of the midwest and still be involved in creative music. By the end of '73 one would be able to experience the music of BAG throughout the whole of the planet. Musicians like Oliver Lake and Baikida E. J. Carroll would migrate first to Paris and later New York City as a means to establish the realness of their activity—and it would be possible to experience the work of Julius Hemphill in places like San Francisco or Sweden Hamiet Bluiett moved to New York and began performing his own music as well as working with musicians like Charles Mingus. In a time period of two years, the collective membership of the Black Artists Group of St. Louis would move to establish themselves as a powerful continuum of creative music.

It is important that the emphasis I have put on the activity in Detroit, Chicago, and St. Louis is not taken out of context. For the dynamics of creativity in the midwest is not limited to only three given regions but involves all of the factors taking place in that area. I have written on the

Detroit Artists' Workshop, AACM, and BAG because it is really all I am aware of in this period—but obviously there is much more to be written about. Hopefully the eighties will see more alternative documentation about the whole of progressional continuance. I for one would like to learn about the work which took place in such cities as Philadelphia or Cleveland—or areas like Washington, D.C., or Baltimore. It may not be fashionable in this period to write of all of these areas as creative centers, but I have no doubt that many exciting contributions have taken and are taking place in all of these areas—and more. **My point is simply this: no area has a monopoly on creativity, and if we are to really view the realness of creativity as a transformational tool, then it is important that some effort is made to learn about the composite spectrum of this most important subject—regardless of so-called area.** The real story of the midwest will have to wait until the musicians themselves document the last ten to twenty (to one hundred and some) years. The challenge of the next cycle calls for this and nothing less. We cannot wait for the collective forces of western culture to make the decision that a given area's creativity is "worthy of examination." Instead, some efforts must now be put forth to establish what has happened and is really happening in this country (America)—and later this planet. There are more positive things happening in this period than most of us would believe—and the work shaping creativity in the midwest is necessarily connected to even greater considerations. To delay too long in properly documenting a given progression and/or projection is to risk having that phenomenon not documented correctly. Now is the time to function and not later (but then again, later is better than not at all).

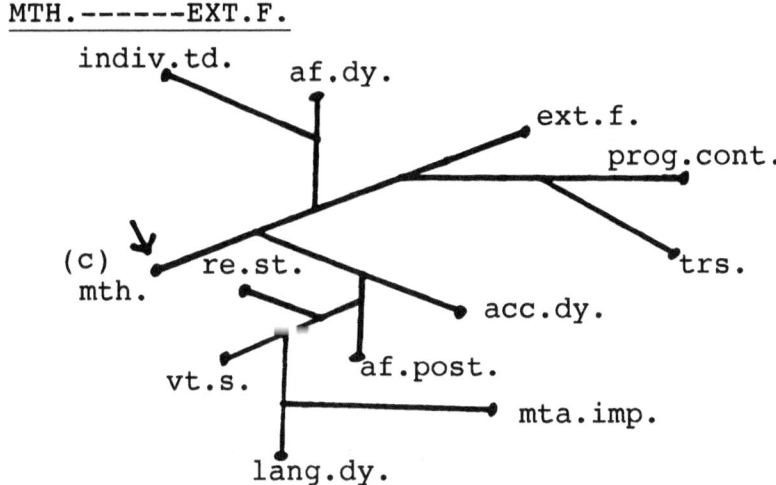

West Coast

The reality particulars of alternative functionalism from the western sector of America involve many different factors. For there have been many important contributions from the west coast—more than is generally recognized. Somehow the west coast has come to be viewed as culturally and dynamically barren—but in actual fact this viewpoint does not correspond to documented history. Still, most of us have come to view the west coast only with respect to the activity that solidified in the early fifties under what was then called "west coast jazz"—involving musicians like Bob Cooper or Shorty Rogers, etc. To really examine the vibrational attitudes that have surfaced in the last seventy years is to come to terms with the progressional arrogance of the east coast defining and controlling community—for in the final analysis, many of our present misconceptions about the west coast have actualized as a result of the superiority complex that has long characterized the so-called cultural center of America. Nevertheless there have been many important musicians from the western half of America, and more important, there have been many important contributions in alternative creativity and/or functionalism from this sector. As such if we are to understand the reality position of alternative participation, then it is important that some attempt is made to view the dynamics of composite functionalism.

The realness of the post-Ayler junction of the music is not separate from what was inspired from the post-Coleman progressionalism that altered the late fifties and sixties. To understand this, however, is to recognize that neither Ornette Coleman nor his musicians per se were from New York—but rather from Texas and the west coast. For there has long been a dynamic continuum of creative music from this sector of the planet—and this should not be viewed lightly. The challenge of Ornette Coleman's activity can be viewed as one example of the special "affinity posture" of west coast creativity—and his approach is not alone in that regard. Musicians like Charles Moffett and Dewey Redman can also be viewed with respect to that special "something" which permeates Texas's creativity. All of this music is and will be important as we move into the eighties.

But Texas is not the only creative platform producing relevant music for the next cycle. To view the realness of Los Angeles is to be confronted by one of the most interesting cities in this time period. I say interesting because there has always been several reality degrees in this most complex city. Los Angeles has long been the home of Hollywood and, since the early fifties, the haven for studio interpretative musicians—while on the other side, this same city has functioned as the learning tank of musicians like Charles Mingus, Eric Dolphy, Sonny Criss, and Gerald Wilson among others. There has never been a shortage of creative musicians from this area, and it's time that the image of so-called west coast jazz is either discarded or revamped. There is no way that creative music could have developed its present dynamism without the collected participation of musicians from the west coast. This is true when viewing creative progressionalism from the early periods of the music as well as the present.

If the work of Ornette Coleman characterized a primary zone of functionalism, and in so doing helped transport alternative creativity to the next cycle, then it is possible to view the activity of musicians like John Carter and Bobby Bradford as necessarily important to this same continuum. Both of these musicians have long functioned in Los Angeles—on every level. Hopefully the realness of their activity will become available on a national level in the eighties. Carter and Bradford together have been instrumental in helping to advance the composite scene in Los Angeles, and both musicians deserve credit for years of dedicated activism. Hopefully the next cycle will provide proper documentation about this region, because at present there is no literature on west coast progressionalism from the fifties and sixties—until now (end of seventies). It is clear however that when the proper documentation arrives it will focus on the work of musicians like Horace Tapscott, whose dynamic activity has shaped a whole region of alternative functionalism. From what I have read, Tapscott's activity seems to be akin to that of musicians like Muhal Richard Abrams and Sun Ra in the sense of both its scope and his dedication. Tapscott has been functioning for years as both teacher and bandleader (with both small and large groups), and many of the musicians who have worked with him have gone on to become important musicians in their own right (e.g., Arthur Blythe).

To lightly view the progressional continuance of California functionalism from the late fifties until today is to deal with many factors. For Los Angeles is not the only large city in this area that has brought forth dynamic creativity. To really view the collected offerings from cities like San Francisco is to have awareness of extended progressionalism regardless of level. The solidification of the post-Coleman continuum would help shed focus on a whole new school of unacknowledged masters of creative music. The work of Prince Lasha and Sonny Simmons and Barbara Donald must be experienced to really understand where musicians like Eric Dolphy came from (for it is important to understand that all of these people—Dolphy, Coleman, Wilson—did not come up alone, but rather worked on their craft and performed with other musicians of like sympathy). I write this not to discredit Dolphy (because obviously he was a great musician), but it is important to establish a broader understanding about the reality of creativity. The realness of San Francisco has seen contributions from musicians like Smiley Winters, John Handy, Paul Desmond, etc. It is important that efforts are made to keep abreast of the work from this region—because the realness of composite creativity is not only about a particular period but also encompasses the whole of what a given information line really is. Obviously my comments on this subject are only the tip of the iceberg—but I have at least attempted to include this aspect as a means to comment on the broader realness of earth creativity and dynamic progressionalism. I wait, like all of us, for the real documentation about this area.

As we enter into the eighties, there is now a whole new generation of musicians from this region, and there can be no doubt that the collective imprint of their work will be a factor in shaping the next cycle of the music. Musicians like Roland Young from San Francisco as well as the Rova Saxophone Quartet (Jon Raskin, Larry Ochs, Andrew Voigt, and Bruce Ackley) are among the new musicians who have begun reshaping alternative functionalism—and of course there are many other musicians (it would take a year to list all of the individuals whose work I have come across—not to mention the work I haven't heard). In Los Angeles, the late seventies saw many important attempts towards broadening the circulation of the composite creative scene. As the eighties continue, I have no doubt that we will be hearing from many of the new musicians who have solidified their activity in the west coast. Musicians like James Newton had already begun to attract attention in the late seventies (and based on his recordings, which number between three and five, there appears to be no end of his talents), and this is also true for the multi-instrumentalist Vinnie Golia. My point is only that the dynamic continuum of creative music seems to be in great shape. This is true no matter what section of the country—or planet—we choose to focus on. Hopefully the realness of the eighties will find a level of commentary that matches the work that all of these musicians have put into their craft.

(Level Two)

THE PROJECTIONAL SPREAD OF BLACK CREATIVITY can best be understood by examining the composite activity that took place in the sixties and seventies. For the dynamic expansion of black music has never been dependent on any one area of the planet or region—regardless of focus. To understand the state of black creativity as we approach the time zone of the eighties is to be aware of the significance of what was raised in the sixties and seventies—not only with regards to the activity centered around New York or Chicago, but the total context of the music. Moreover, it would not necessarily be correct to assume that only the post-Ayler or AACM developments are important—at the expense of the composite whole of the music, because there were many other developments taking place in creative music as well. The fact is, no one projection has determined the actualness of creative music from the black aesthetic—either in this period or any other period, and if one is to understand the reality of creative music as we approach the 1980s, it is important to view the composite forces shaping the music—regardless of what region a given thrust solidified in.

The reality of creative music in the late seventies is both dynamic and complex. Dynamic in the sense that many factors have participated in shaping the composite reality of the creativity, and complex in the sense that it is somewhat difficult to isolate particular projections as a means to accurately comment on a given participation. This is undoubtedly because of what transpired in the seventies—on both the physical and vibrational universe level. For if the sixties was the time zone which saw the dynamic exploitation of revolution and expansion, then the seventies was the period which felt the first institutionalized response to that cycle. Not only would this be the period that would see the end of America's misinvolvement with Vietnam, but this would also be the cycle that would see the results of the next level of media indoctrination (i.e., gradualism and political containment) and withdrawal of social awareness and responsibility. The

EXT. F (II) –2

reality awareness of creative music is directly related to these physical universe developments and more. For the vibrational tone level surrounding how creativity is to be perceived is not separate from what is happening in actual terms on the physical universe level. Any attempt to understand the progressional continuance of creative black music in the late seventies would necessitate examining the cross-sectional realness of what transpired in the last twenty years—involving both the spectrum of the music as well as how that approach was perceived by the public—and what this viewpoint would mean in progressional terms.

The time zone of the seventies will one day come to be viewed as a major integrating period for the solidification of alternative—or progressive—creativity. It would be in this time zone where one could see the composite linkage of world creativity begin to take shape (or at least the forces which seem to be moving towards unification would manifest as an actuality in this cycle), and as such, the progressional continuum of the seventies must be viewed as significant with regards to transformation. So pronounced is the emergence of cross-transfer creativity in this period that no one thrust can claim "purity" or separateness. Because the realness of this period was connected to a new spirit with regards to traditional values in creativity as well as the emergence of new forms. This new spirit can be experienced in practically every creative thrust in that period from "jazz" to "classical" to "rock." In other words, what we now call fusion music is in fact the emergence of the next attitude with regards to investigation—that being, the progressional realness of the seventies seemed to invite a resurgence of cross-sectional exploration. Moreover, the realness of this phenomenon is reshaping earth music, for if in the beginning jazz-rock, as an actualness, was frowned upon by purists in its early inception—towards the end of the seventies practically three-fourths of the "jazz" community would find themselves participating almost exclusively in jazz-rock. The seventies would also be the time zone that would again see audience support for the more commercial forms of creative music and in doing so reverse the trend of the sixties. This would be the time zone where many creative musicians would attain commercial success on an unprecedented level because of their involvement with jazz-rock—(and of

EXT. F (II) –3

course because of the music they were able to create within that medium). Musicians like Herbie Hancock would secure very important positions in the commercial hierarchy surrounding the business of creative music as well, and by the end of the seventies he could justifiably boast of reaching millions of people through both his performance schedule—in a given period—as well as record sales. The momentum of jazz-rock would also be an important factor for the whole of creative music—for at the heart of this projection was the realness that both the public and musicians desired more emphasis on what they perceived to be the essence realness of the music, rather than the "antics" of the sixties. The emergence of jazz-rock signaled a move back to composite culture awareness—or at least the arrival of this form would help bring an appreciation of advanced music techniques on the part of the greater sophisticated music community.

The dynamics of creative music in the late seventies is directly related to the multiplicity of projections actualized from the spectrum of the music during the middle and late sixties. Not only would the post-Ayler continuum carry multi-complexual implications as a vehicle for extension, but the time zone of the late sixties (and early seventies) would also provide the setting for a similar revolution in rhythm and blues. In other words, the composite realness of the seventies is related to the projectional spread underlying what really actualized in the sixties. The progressional continuum of this period would affect the post-Ayler reality, as well as the nature of the source-transfer movements of the seventies. Moreover, while the solidification of the post-Ayler projection would make possible the developments which actualized in Chicago and the midwest—at the same time the progressional continuance of post-Ayler creativity would continue to function as a separate entity in itself (and thus serve as an extended source of inspiration for its given vibrational viewpoint). That is—even though the AACM formed as a response to what had actualized in New York (i.e., the activity of Coleman, Taylor, etc.), the music that developed from that response would imply its own set of variables—and in doing so, affect the nature of options surrounding creative black music (towards expansion). By the end of the sixties both the post-Ayler and AACM continuums could be viewed as two independent routes available for the

EXT. F (II) —4

creative musician, and by the same token the progressional route solidified by musicians like Stevie Wonder or groups like Earth, Wind & Fire would actualize another important viewpoint for the composite realness of the music. To view the progressional continuity of the seventies is to have some awareness of what transpired from the composite developments of these various projectional routes and variants.

Before an investigation of creativity in the seventies can take place it is necessary to first comment on the multiplicity of forms actualized in the closing period of the sixties. This is necessary as a means to establish a basis for viewing the composite actualness of the seventies. For if I have directed the focus of this section on the dynamics of post-Ayler creativity, as well as the AACM, it is important to also balance this information—for I have not meant to imply that only these two thrusts are relevant, at the expense of the total music. Certainly the post-Ayler and AACM junctions are necessarily important—because of their relationship with restructuralism (that is—because both of these thrusts have helped to redesign alternative projectional routes for creativity of the affinity insight [1] principle)—but the composite realness of the seventies is not limited to only the significance of restructuralism (not to mention, no continuum has a monopoly on restructuralism either). The composite solidification of what would transpire in the seventies transcends both regionalism as well as conceptualism. By the end of the seventies it became clear that many other factors were also profoundly shaping the composite creativity of that time period. In other words, to view the realness of black creativity in the seventies is to deal with a multitude of connecting and interconnecting considerations—determining the course creativity would take as well as the spirit underlining its utilization.

The projectional spread of post-Ayler creativity can best be understood by examining the composite specifics that took place in the sixties and seventies. For while it is clear that a city like New York houses practically three-fourths of the musicians who make their living from creative music—especially creative improvised music—it is also clear that many of those individual musicians came from various sections of the country. In other words, no one section of the country (or planet) has a monopoly on being creative. The fact is, every area of the country can be viewed with respect to the uniqueness of its vibrational hue, and what this uniqueness means for creativity. To view the solidification of the post-Ayler projectional thrust is to have some awareness of what transpired in both vibrational and regional terms during the time cycle of the sixties. Because to gain insight about the present cycle we are now in (the seventies), it will be necessary to first solidify some progressional basis that can serve as a relevant overview to the composite dictates of this time cycle. For the solidification of post-Ayler progressionalism was not the work of any given group—or the intention of any given individuals—but rather the end result of a multitude of factors. The New York post-Ayler thrust on its own could not have survived unless perceived as relevant to what the composite vibrational arena of black creativity signified—and this is also true for the work done in the midwest (i.e., AACM or BAG). In other words, no one group or section of the planet can really determine the particulars of a given thrust continuum unless its participation relates to the reality of the composite community it addresses itself to (and this is especially true of creative music as opposed to commercial music—because of the sophistication surrounding present-day information control). The seriousness of the post-Ayler junction can be understood by the fact that it survived, and the reason it survived had to do with both the persistence of the musicians and the fact that it was recognized as relevant by the greater world community and accepted. This is true even though the form had been—and still is—subjected to an extraordinary degree of both distortion and suppression. The projectional spread of creative music must then be viewed from its position in western culture, and the cross-sectional realness of post-Ayler creativity must be viewed as the dynamic factor responsible for extended functionalism in the sixties. To view the progressional continuance of creative music through this period is to gain insight into the nature of the next transformation cycle and how it seems to be forming.

EXT. F (II) –6

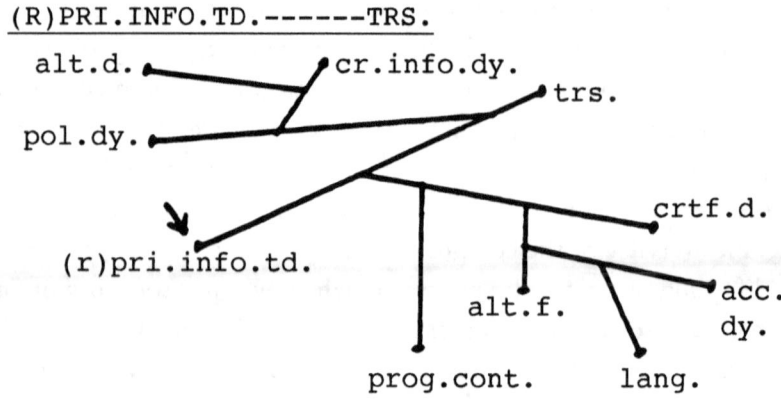

The time zone of the seventies can also be viewed with regards to the concept of decentralization. For while the projectional continuance of the post-Ayler creative thrust (as it actualized in New York) would move to establish a new alternative projection in creativity, the composite forming of this development was not limited to any one area. The realness of what this phenomenon means would help to establish the composite vibrational tone of the early seventies. For if the AACM can be viewed with regards to the separateness of its position from New York—both vibrationally (what actually happened in the music) and regionally—as a means to examine the dynamic spectrum of the music—then the significance of decentralization would reveal the true developments

EXT. F (II) –7

occurring in the music on a national and international level. It would be in the period of the early seventies where the realness of this consideration would surface to the greater public. For the progressional continuance of this time period would see the solidification of creative music from many different quarters. An example of this phenomenon would be the developments taking place in Iowa in the sixties (in conjunction with the Center for New Music) or the emergence of the west coast post-Ayler movement. All of this activity would help advance the affinity-insight principle and in doing so also help accelerate the composite vibrational lining surrounding creativity and creative projections in this cycle. I have not meant to comment only on the continuance of post-Ayler (or in some cases, post-Cageian) progressionalism at the expense of composite activity, because many different factors affected the vibrational tone of American and Western culture.

The seventies would also be the time cycle that would see rock music return to the composite continuum of popular music—as opposed to the elevated status it enjoyed in the sixties. By the middle seventies it was clear that no new group would command the same stature of ensembles like the Beatles and Rolling Stones in the sixties, and this awareness would help to normalize how the commercial arena of the form would be perceived. I do not mean to imply that the spectacle implications of rock had exhausted itself, because this is not true—rather, by the end of the seventies the dynamic newness and brilliance of rock would come to be viewed in human rather than godly terms. Certainly the spectacle expansion of rock had not run its course in the seventies, for this would be the time cycle where punk rock and funky music would establish new attitudes with regards to both presentation (i.e., theatre) as well as dynamics (focused manipulation for a wider composite image affinity pull—from Olivia Newton-John or Peter Frampton representing a kind of all-American wholesome look, to the macabre ensembles practicing punk rock—i.e., Alice Cooper). The composite realness of popular music by the late seventies would profoundly affect the tone level of western culture, and dynamics of this effect could be viewed in both positive and negative terms. Whatever, the effect of rock's new position in the seventies would

445

help create new interest in world creativity—and by the middle of the seventies many journalists would begin to write about the resurgence of interest in "jazz" (although it must be said that in practically every case the word "jazz" in this period meant rock—or jazz-rock).

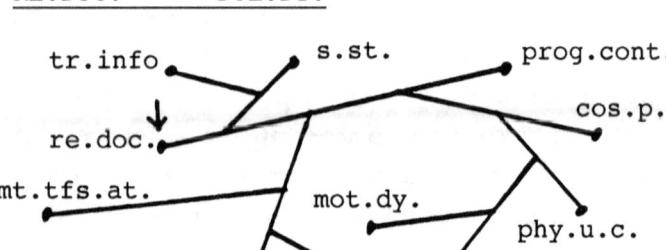

```
RE.DOC.------POL.DY.
```

The composite thrust of creativity in the seventies would also experience a breathing period in the public's perceptions of new initiations. This period would see many of the gains of the post-Coltrane projection appear on the total scene. Practically every saxophonist who surfaced in this period would display some aspect of Coltrane's music—and this is true in popular music as well. The cross-sectional realness of the seventies would even reveal to what extent rock musicians listened to creative improvised music as a means to expand. The projectional realness of this period would also be beneficial to many of the musicians who had worked with Coltrane (e.g., Archie Shepp and Pharoah Sanders would move into prominence in this cycle). The basic vibrational platform of the seventies would be helpful for re-evaluating the composite thrust of creative music—not only the post-Ayler thrust but also the traditional continuance of the music (and to a great extent we are still in this cycle). The seriousness of this development should not be underestimated, for the progressional spread of the seventies would move to provide a vibrational platform conducive for dynamic transition. Moreover, the solidification of this affinity state would have a direct bearing on the coming eighties. For if the position

EXT. F (II) –9

of composite creativity in western culture during the seventies is directly related to the programmed patterns developed in the forties, then the significance of the seventies might well have to do with what changes transpired in the vibrational lining of western culture after the sixties, as well as how those changes helped to establish new options—for both functional considerations as well as creativity. By 1977 it was clear that the vibrationaltory lining of American culture had completed a cycle with regards to the media's suppression of creative music. In this period many different attempts would be made to recognize the existence of forms of creativity—and as such the realness of post-Webern/post-Cage activity, or post-Coleman/post-AACM activity would experience limited media focus. Yet I do not mean to imply that any real attempt was made to actually bring alternative creativity to public awareness as compared to popular music—to imply such would be an exaggeration to the twelfth power—but compared to what had transpired in the sixties, one could detect a change in the various critical and defining controlling centers' (i.e., the press) treatment of the music.

The peripheral interest in alternative creativity which emerged in the seventies can best be understood by viewing the composite whole of creativity—especially with regards to popular music. For it must be understood that by the middle seventies rock music had reached a saturation level in commodity terms—that is, rock music had absorbed every commercial possibility available. **In other words, the new-found interest in alternative creativity that emerged in the middle seventies must be viewed with regards to the total economic realness of its emergence.** This is not to make light of the positive interest shown in alternative creativity by the collective forces of western culture, but only to keep a clear perspective of the composite factors surrounding why particular decisions are made. For if the time zone of the seventies can be viewed as the first period after the forties to acknowledge the existence of creative music—especially creative black music—then it is important that the particulars surrounding that concern be understood. For while it is true musicians like Herbie Hancock could rightly claim record sales in the millions—as a means to state that the public response and support

447

EXT. F (II) –10

of creative music had changed—this was not the norm for the creative music community by any means. What's more, the progressional thrust of the seventies would be the same time zone where even the word "jazz" would not really mean "jazz" anyway. In other words, the new-found so-called interest in creative music by the collected forces of western culture was not necessarily related to the post-Ayler or Cage developments, but really involved commercial forms of improvised music. At the same time, the progressional development of rock music in this same period would see the solidification of greater and greater functional outlets. For by the middle seventies, rock music would command the use of even network television (either in the context of what is now called "specials" or special programming, or weekly programs) and also the best performing outlets developed in this time zone. The emergence of creative music in the seventies to the greater public must be viewed in this context—or at least, the emergence of alternative forms of creativity should not be taken out of context to what actually happened.

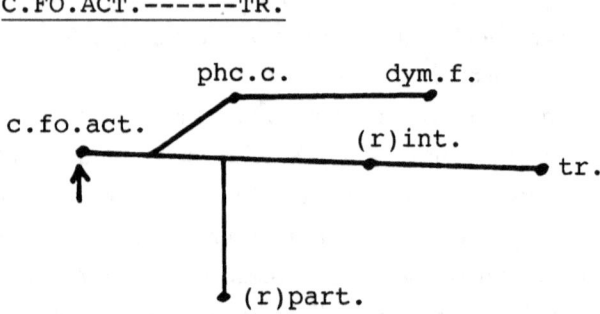

The basic thrust alignment of the seventies would provide limited exposure for a cross-section of alternative creativity—regardless of time zone—even the progressional solidification of bebop would again find an audience. The continuum of this period would see interest focused on musicians from earlier periods who had never really gained the attention and audience support their work merited. By the end of the seventies, musicians like Dexter Gordon would find an increased awareness of their activity in America—even Warne Marsh's name would become familiar to

EXT. F (II) –11

readers of *Downbeat* magazine, and the vibrational realness of these changes would help promote a broader understanding of composite creativity. The net effect of these changes would play an important role in affecting how the next progressional continuance of creativity would function—either in world terms or with regards to western culture exclusively.

The progressional expansion of creative music in the seventies would manifest itself in many different contexts. This would be the time zone which established attempts to create alternative outlets for expansion, and this would also be the period that solidified the progressional implications of post-Ayler creativity. To understand this period in American culture is to be aware of many divergent forces reacting to the thrust development of creative music. Moreover, the extent of the sixties and seventies repression would affect the progressional development and spread of creative music. The most basic response to what this phenomenon would mean could be seen by examining the late sixties' musicians' migration to Europe. For the early seventies would see practically three-fourths of the creative musicians' community settled and functioning in Europe. Many of these musicians would choose to base their activity in Paris—or at least Paris in this cycle would become a dominant outlet for the music. Some of the most important work in creative improvised music would actualize in that period, for not only was the music in a fresh cycle—in terms of spirit or vibrational dynamics—but the climate of Paris would also be conducive for better communications between the musicians themselves, and this would especially be true for the New York musicians' movement. The progressional spread of the composite musicians' creative community in Paris would find musicians of the caliber of Archie Shepp, for example. To experience only the breadth of his activity in that period alone would help clarify one's perception of the dynamic potential of post-Ayler creativity—but this was only the beginning. For the repression of the sixties would create intolerable pressures on every segment of the creative musicians' community—regardless of region.

The arrival of the New York post-Ayler movement in Europe was not an isolated development but rather the first composite response towards re-establishing functionalism. For if the New York musicians'

449

EXT. F (II) –12

movement could be seen practicing their craft in Paris during the middle and end of the sixties (as a separate block from the composite musicians' community), it would not be long before musicians from Philadelphia and Chicago would also follow. Moreover, Paris in the early seventies would house the first real meeting between post-Ayler musicians from the eastern and midwestern parts of America. The intensity of that meeting would help establish Paris as an important center in creative music for the whole of the seventies, and the creative output generated from that meeting would solidify the realness of alternative creative music at the end of the seventies. In a way, the cross-sectional activity generated in Paris during the late sixties and early seventies can be viewed as a definite pivotal point for the survival of post-Ayler creativity. The work that took place in Paris during that period would solidify the composite musicians' awareness of what had transpired during the sixties. For it must be understood that many of the musicians in New York had no idea of what had been developing in the midwest—and by the same token, very few musicians from the midwest had actually experienced the realness of the New York musicians' movement live.

By the early seventies it would be possible to view the gains of the composite activity which had taken place in Paris. This would be a period where musicians like Lester Bowie performed with musicians like Archie Shepp, or the Art Ensemble of Chicago would perform and record with Julio Finn and Chicago Beau. It would also be in this period where one could experience the activity of a musician like Steve McCall in a variety of contexts—from his work with Don Byas to the Creative Construction Company to Gunter Hampel's various ensembles. The large number of musicians in Paris during this cycle would also make orchestral realizations more possible, and musicians like Alan Silva would concertize in various combinations. Very few people in America would be aware of the intenseness of the creative scene in Paris during this period—and it is easy to understand why. Because in America during this same period practically all of the outlets for creative music had been cut off. From the time zone of 1968 to 1973 practically every musician involved with creative music would appear in Paris—and

EXT. F (II) –13

participate in the scene as well. The spectrum of musicians that would affect the scene in Paris during this cycle would include both Ornette Coleman and Cecil Taylor, Charles Mingus, Leo Smith, as well as the progressional thrust of post-Webern practitioners—e.g., Stockhausen, Cage, and Xenakis. The composite spectrum of activity in this cycle would also see contemporary dance (e.g., Merce Cunningham—even though by 1969 one could not really talk of Cunningham as being in the vanguard of new dancers on the scene, but rather, simply a wonderfully creative and brilliant dancer). All of this activity would make Paris an ideal place for the transported creative music community, and for a period of three to five years many important changes would clarify the projectional development and path of post-Ayler creativity.

Nor have I meant to only focus on the initiations offered by American musicians at the expense of the world group. For as the thrust expansion of post-Ayler creativity began to spread in Europe, many important European musicians would begin contributing to the composite solidification of the music as well. Musicians like J. F. Jenny-Clark could be seen working with a wide variety of contexts, and the sixties would also be in the cycle where Willem Breuker would emerge as a new force in creative music. The invasion of post-Ayler creativity in Europe would have an impact equal to the landing of bebop in the late forties, and the implications of this spread cannot be viewed in one-dimensional terms. For the composite work completed in this cycle would substantiate post-Ayler creativity as a legitimate creative projection for both transition and transformation. Moreover, the activity which took place in Europe would be an important factor related to how the majority of creative musicians were able to survive as well. For by the early seventies many performing outlets for post-Ayler creativity had been created. By the middle seventies work possibilities in Europe could be viewed with regards to the concept of alternative outlets—not limited to only one area or country. And if in the beginning France functioned as a major center for creative music—or at least creative music from the post-Ayler American contingency—by the middle of the seventies the whole of Europe would have work possibilities. The realness of these

EXT. F (II) –14

outlets cannot be under-valued, for not only would Europe provide economic hope for post-Ayler musicians, but Europe would also provide an audience to play for.

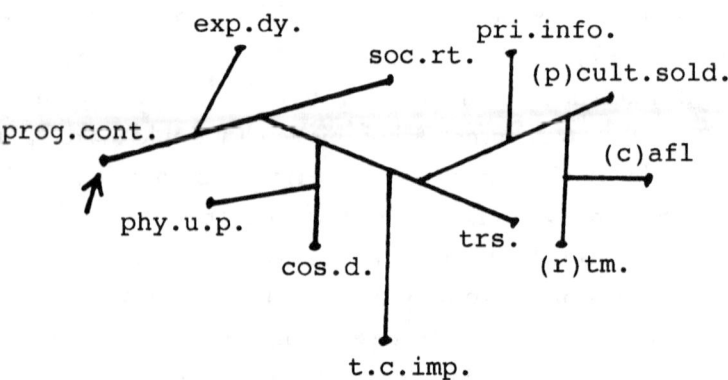

The composite move of creative musicians back to America solidified by the middle of the seventies, and this phenomenon would also represent another cycle for post-Ayler creativity. Moreover, while many musicians from this continuum had established themselves as commercially marketable in Europe during the previous cycle, none of this marketability would matter in America. For the interim between the late sixties and early seventies in America had produced little or no change in the reality particulars surrounding post-Ayler creativity. In actual terms, this meant either the arriving musicians would be forced to again re-establish their names in the same manner attempted in Europe (and by "again" in this context I am commenting on the totality of the struggle one has to endure to participate in alternative creativity) or remain in Europe as expatriates. Many musicians would actually make the decision to return to Europe rather than endure the hopelessness of struggling in America, while another segment of musicians would decide to resettle and fight. The nature of the struggle both groups would endure is directly related to what transpired in the late seventies—with regards to creative functionalism. **For the arrival en masse of the post-Ayler continuum in America would totally reshape**

EXT. F (II) –15

the music scene in New York and define the next level of functionalism at the same time. Yet I have not meant to imply that any one movement can completely reshape how creativity is perceived in America, because obviously the vibrational reality of American culture transcends the effectiveness of any single movement. The composite thrust of post-Ayler creativity must instead be viewed with respect to the spectrum of factors that are simultaneously affecting western culture—which is to say, the gains of creative music in the seventies must be viewed with respect to the total theatre of composite western culture. For it must be understood that the controlling forces which dictate culture in America did not greet the post-Ayler continuum with open arms. Instead the work that was begun in the early sixties would necessarily be restarted—because there was no other course available for post-Ayler creativity. Any attempt to view the last part of the seventies would necessitate focusing on some aspect of specific functionalism as it applied to rebuilding outlets for expansion. Because the challenge surrounding how this goal was pursued directly sheds light on the present reality of post-Ayler creativity—and this is what I am interested in.

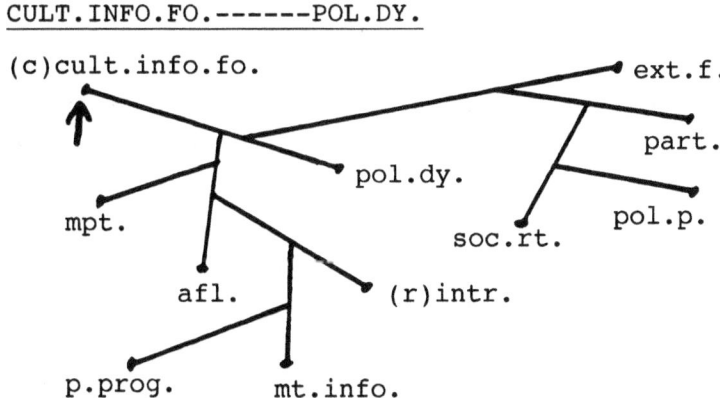

To write of the present cycle of creative music (late seventies) is to deal with many factors. For by 1977 the progressional spread of post-Ayler creativity—and the movements which sprang from its projection—would transcend any one definition or category. That is,

EXT. F (II) –16

the dynamic spectrum of alternative creativity would find extensions into practically every area of creative music. Moreover, not only had the music survived in seclusion from America, but in several instances it was possible to view an expanded interest in creative music throughout the country. The late seventies would then be the cycle where attempts would be made by the press to recognize the existence of creative music on one level or another. Even a paper like *The New York Times* would acknowledge given performances of alternative activity, and after a while given musicians would begin to finally establish limited commercial momentum. Moreover, as the information focus of western journalism began to take notice, magazines like *New Times* and *Newsweek* would even have articles on the music—which is to say, the time zone of the late seventies would also be important because of its position in cyclic western information transference. So real would this change of position be that the middle to late seventies could be viewed as the time zone which saw the "apparent" gradual acceptance of alternative creativity (yet I do not mean to imply that any of the articles written on the music in this period had anything to do with correctly interpreting the music— but rather, the fact that attempts were even made to write at all on the music [in positive terms] did in itself represent a change of position) in America. Even forums like *Downbeat* magazine would make an effort to view the music in a somewhat more balanced manner, and while many musicians might find this statement a bit hard to take (for *Downbeat* has long been recognized as an outlet detrimental to creative music—as if the other magazines are not detrimental), in actual fact, something in America was changing with regards to creativity.

The gradual acknowledgment of alternative creativity by the press in the middle to late seventies would also be a factor related to the support of creative music by the public. By 1976, many musicians would comment on what seemed to be a growing support of the music—either with regards to concert and club performances, or recordings. This would be especially true in the large cities, and in places like New York, San Francisco, or Chicago one could notice this change immediately. Yet I do not mean to imply that any given performance of creative music would find twenty thousand people attending—because this would not be correct. But rather—creativity from the post-Ayler continuum would enjoy in the late seventies a respectable amount of people for a given performance (respectable meaning more than one or two people—and this difference must be viewed as a great improvement). In many cases, a given performance might even find itself sold out—although this was more true for the jazz-rock continuum than for the post-Ayler movement—or at least well attended.

The middle to late seventies would also be the time zone where the composite realness of the AACM emerged as a recognized force in creative music. This period would move to focus attention on groups like the Art Ensemble of Chicago, myself, or musicians like Richard Abrams, and towards the end of the seventies no one could deny the impact of this organization. Moreover, by the end of the seventies another whole generation of musicians from the AACM had emerged. Musicians like Douglas Ewart and George Lewis would make a deep impression on the music scene in this period, and the composite implications of the next cycle seem to forecast even greater impact in the not-too-distant future. For if the first wave of the AACM signified a new attitude with regards to creativity and extension—and in so doing establish the momentum of a definite thrust alignment—then the second wave of musicians from this continuum could be viewed as the first recipients of what that alignment would forecast in future terms. Whatever, the late seventies would be the time zone where the next projectional spread of the AACM could be viewed—and this is true on more than one level. That is, the period of the late seventies would see the first wave of musicians from the AACM recognized as contributing to the music—because of the ten years (and some) of struggles in the sixties and seventies (for it must be understood that however one perceives of the activity from the AACM—with regards to what particular area of music one has experienced or from what given musician—many areas of exploration were necessarily not continued in the travels undertaken during the late sixties because of financial considerations: which is to say, very few people have really had the chance to experience the total

EXT. F (II) –18

dynamics of the activity actualized in Chicago from the late sixties—let alone what has really developed in the decade that followed)—while the second level of the AACM would emerge with their own separate implications to be dealt with.

Moreover, the middle to late seventies would also be the time zone of the second extensional thrust of the composite AACM. The realness of this cyclic phenomenon would see musicians from the AACM resettling in other areas outside of Chicago. This expansion would help to make the organization more all-inclusive rather than a regional fixation (yet I have not meant to imply that the base of the organization has been transferred outside of Chicago because it hasn't). The progressional spread of the AACM membership must be viewed with regards to what its expansion signifies about the challenge of decentralization as a composite functional objective for the next time cycle. For if the first movement from the AACM moved to investigate the dynamic arena of world culture as a means to view the multi-dimensional realness of the total music scene (and in doing so establish basis for developing an audience and surviving), then the challenge of the second composite thrust of the AACM would have to do with securing what this expansion means in functional and actual terms—for both the individual and the collective. The time cycle of the late seventies would then be the junction where this phase of AACM related moves would actualize.

By 1976 the progressional reformation of creative music in America could be seen in several centers across the country. The dynamics of this realignment could be viewed in the spectrum of new migrations that solidified in this cycle. For the progressional spread of the AACM was not unique but rather in accordance with the general vibrational climate of the late seventies. In this same time period many other groups of creative people would make the same functional moves—and as a result, a city like New York would again become host to forming transitional activism. To view the significance then of the composite creative music scene in America during the late seventies is to have some idea of the dynamic forces that settled or resettled in this region. Because the spectrum of forces that personified the creative vibrational arena in New York City during the late seventies

EXT. F (II) –19

would have great bearing on both how the vibrationaltory lining of post-Ayler creativity would be perceived (in general and specific terms)—as well as how the nature of the composite extension of the music would be perceived (i.e., whether or not a given projection would be recognized as being relevant to the composite realness of the music, etc.). The importance of the progressional developments surrounding creative music in the late seventies cannot be over-estimated if we are to understand the position and potential of alternative creativity in western culture—during this cycle. For while it is certainly too early to comment on the ultimate ramifications of alternative post-Ayler-AACM creativity—with regards to particulars— (because it is still happening while this book is being written), it is possible to comment on the seriousness of the position creativity—and in particular, creative music—is now in. The fact is, if the late seventies is the time zone which promised to integrate the composite thrust of post-Ayler creativity into the mainstream of American culture, then the developments that took place in various creative musicians' communities in this same time period must be viewed as especially important. The progressional spread of creative music in the late seventies is relevant because of what it signifies for the next cycle of creativity. To view the composite realignment of developments in New York City during this cycle is to have some idea as to how this expansion was perceived—and in what terms. It is not simply a question of whether any one given movement provided the direction—or projectional alignment—for the composite thrust of the music, it is more a question of understanding how the composite forces of the pre-eighties time zone functioned—with regards to the total challenge of the music and extended functionalism. To view the seriousness of the late seventies is to have some understanding of these questions—both with regards for what was completed as well as what was abandoned (and why).

The composite arena that formed in the late seventies in New York would see musicians from the AACM projectional thrust from Chicago, as well as musicians from the St. Louis School (who had also spent time in Europe by the final cycle of cross-sectional activity—around the early seventies) and finally musicians from the West Coast (e.g., Frank Lowe or David Murray). The solidification of this composite arena would also

457

EXT. F (II) −20

find musicians from many other divergent sources (e.g., the east coast developments from outside New York City, in places like New Haven, Connecticut, and Boston—bringing forth new musicians like Anthony Davis, Michael Gregory Jackson, or Bobby Naughton)—as well as the late sixties' movement. The spectrum of creativity actualized from this new expanded community would reveal a broader dynamic scope for alternative music, and the progressional thrust of this activity would extend into many other forms as well (e.g., Sousa music or post-Stockhausen and -Cage extensions). This would then be the time cycle that would manifest many of the gains solidified through the AACM continuum with regards to timbre implications, instrumentation, and rhythm (i.e., extended rhythmic forms or the use of various spatial forms), and this would also be the cycle that would see the extended development of post-Ayler creativity—as a separate projection in its own right. By 1976, the various creative movements could be broken down into two basic categories: those being the post-Ayler projectional movement which expanded as a means to fulfill the dynamic potential of what had been raised from the transition cycle of the sixties—and for the most part this movement would have limited use for structuralism as a functional tool, but instead vibrate more to improvisation and energy as a dynamic vehicle for expression—and the post-AACM thrust, which functioned with respect to scientific investigation as it pertained to both expansion and invention, having more to do with the postulation of whatever seemed interesting as a vehicle for exploration (this movement would also make use of notation and composition in every possible context—and the thrust of these approaches would be the most extensive use of notation of any movement). The combination of these two movements would provide a dynamic cross-section for creative improvised music in the late seventies, and the progressional development of creative music from this mixture can also be viewed as an important realignment factor for the vibrational complexion of present-day creative music. There is already a substantial body of creative music actualized from the middle seventies that is essential to the composite whole of creative improvised (and notated) music (the problem, of course, is to be able to find it).

EXT. F (II) –21

The expanded interest that seemed directed towards creative music in the middle to late seventies should not be over-accented or distorted. For while it is true that numerous articles could be cited that attempted to acquaint people with some area—or aspect—of the music, in actual fact, the progressional economic hierarchy surrounding creative music has not changed at all. In other words, very little of the publicity that centered on the music resulted in actual work possibilities for the greater segment of the musicians' community. The basic reality surrounding participation in creative music has not really changed since the time zone of 1945. Not only that, but the basic thrust of publicity in the late seventies would focus on only a limited segment of the composite music scene (which is to say, the projected stream of so-called information in this period would be no different from any other period of journalism) and as such the picture of the music that would finally emerge would be somewhat slanted—at best. If the composite press could be cited as focusing on the progressional continuance of post-Ayler creativity in the late sixties and early seventies as a means to gain surface insight into the new projections being developed in that period, then the same could be said of its treatment of the initiations that emerged from the jazz-rock continuum (and the AACM solidification) in the late seventies. My point however is that this limited focus—however much appreciated and needed—cannot be perceived as fulfilling any kind of real commitment to the music—as compared to what could necessarily educate people about creative music. My point is also that the so-called resurgence of interest in creative music by American journalism in the seventies has yet to solidify any real information and/or interpretations to balance the neglect that characterized how this same sector dealt with the music in the sixties. For it must be understood that journalism—especially American journalism—has long played a significant role in helping to create and maintain the vibrational context from which creative music—and composite information in general—is perceived. So real is this involvement that one might rightly assume that some form of reconstituted treatment of extended information is owed to the greater public—by the composite wing of American journalism. Whatever, when I wrote that the middle to late seventies time period

EXT. F (II) –22

experienced a degree of acknowledgment by the collective forces of western culture, I did not mean that this acknowledgment can be viewed as being in the same context as that given to popular music—or on the level where it might possibly affect the "awareness scan" of American culture (because to the greater public, alternative creativity doesn't even exist)—but rather this so-called renewed interest can be viewed as greater than what transpired in the sixties.

IST.PT.------WO.EXT.PRI.

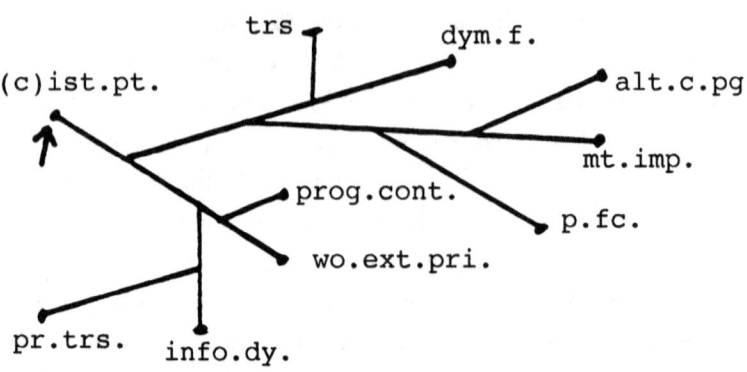

Another example of the actual reality of the seventies is the situation surrounding the recording of creative music. For the sole exception of myself (and the Art Ensemble of Chicago for a brief period), practically none of the activity that took place in creative improvised music from the post-Ayler/AACM junction was documented and made available on a major label. In other words, the composite thrust of the American recording industry has demonstrated no desire to deal with post-Ayler creativity, nor has it felt any responsibility to give the American audience a greater spectrum of music to experience. In fact, the opposite seems to be the case, for the last three years have seen a withdrawal of commitment to alternative creativity—regardless of focus. The total realness of this rejection must be understood, for I am not commenting on any one company or outlet dealing with recording and distributing music; I am commenting on the composite solidification of the American recording industry. In other words, the suppression of post-Ayler creativity by

EXT. F (II) –23

the major recording companies in American must be viewed in terms of many different factors.

By the middle of the seventies another phenomenon could be viewed in creative musicians' communities across America—that being, the emergence of new underground performing outlets. In New York City the impact of this development would have a great affect on the progressional continuance of alternative creativity. For by the middle sixties many of the established clubs and theatres that employed creative improvised music had either closed or excluded post Ayler creativity as a form to consider hiring. The new alternative performing outlets would thus move to fill this vacuum, and by 1976 the impact of this phenomenon would greatly help the position of creative improvising musicians. The alternative performing outlets would help provide the necessary momentum for creative music to both expand and attract listeners in this period, and as such the dynamic realness of New York City would thus find itself again host to a multitude of creative happenings (and in a given weekend one could experience the complete time spectrum of creative music—from Dexter Gordon to Henry Threadgill). The solidification of alternative performing outlets in this context must be viewed as a positive asset in the seventies. This phenomenon would help musicians to both expand their art, and also survive at the same time.

The solidification of alternative performing outlets in the late seventies would also give the media basis for "spectaclizing" creative music. For the resurgence of creativity in this cycle would be perceived by the press as a new form of music that could be exploited in accordance to the spectacle diversion syndrome, rather than activity related to the composite whole of what was happening in creativity. The use of the term "loft jazz" can be viewed as vibrating to the late sixties concept of "free jazz"—which is to say, the phraseology surrounding how given projections are commented on in many cases serves as a distortion to the essence foundation of the music. For by the late seventies the media's use of the phrase "loft jazz" would seek to give the impression that a new form of music has been actualized that was about "lofts," rather than a form of creativity conceived to be performed any place on the planet

461

but which was regulated to alternative spaces because of the social and political forces dictating western creativity. The use of the term "loft jazz" would have multi-complexual implications in other contexts as well, for the vibrational mentality surrounding this concept would also affect how economic transactions in alternative creativity would be perceived—that being, the collected thrust of western business would perceive of "loft jazz" as a form that could necessarily be paid "less" (because why pay a musician who plays in lofts more money than what he or she is used to?). Not to mention, no one functioning in creativity needed another new "catch-all title." The accented use of the term "loft jazz" in the late seventies could be viewed as a journalistic tool to provide a slogan for creative music—and in doing so establish a basis to write about current activity as well as define the music (because in actual fact, to view the progressional continuity of imposed titles on black creative music is to see how western culture has semantically found ways to keep black music in an inferior position—for if one can define the "isness" of a given creative reality, then one can establish the significance underlying how that reality is to be both interpreted and valued). Nevertheless, the late seventies would see the resolidification of creative music into the composite community of trans-African functionalism and continuance—which is to say, the late seventies would see the composite suppression of alternative creativity without showing any favors. I do not mean to imply that no musicians were able to see their activity advanced in this period, because this is not true. Many musicians would establish the realness of their activity in the seventies. But the composite thrust of creative music—what this subject means with regards to the spectrum of musicians participating in alternative creativity (with regards to what the solidification of alternative creativity really poses—to the propagation of culture and life)—would remain a closely kept secret.

The actualness of limited performing outlets in the late seventies would not help social relationships between musicians either. And to view the realness of creative musicians' community in the seventies is to see the same diversions that characterized the sixties—and this is especially true with regards to the phenomenon of race relations. For this reason

EXT. F (II) –25

musicians like Perry Robinson or Gunter Hampel could be viewed as separate from the composite music community—which is to say, white musicians would basically function with white musicians (and of course there are many other factors related to this development, for the musician's creative universe is indicative of many different considerations—including what is and isn't happening on the physical universe level). But in the final analysis, the composite implication of earth creativity is directly related to whether or not people can rise above prejudice and isolation—and move together with regards to both humanity and God for positive change. With that in mind, the social reality surrounding creative music in the seventies must be viewed as not conducive for composite expansion. Nor have I meant to over-emphasize the racial particulars of the scene in the seventies. Because in fact, very little change has occurred in the musicians' community—in terms of social relationships and business—since the forties. The music scene can be broken into several different cult-like movements, and few groups seem to have any respect or affinity for what is perceived to be outside initiations. This was the state of alternative creativity in the seventies—that is, if New York City is indicative of more than itself (and of course, if my observations are correct). And yet I have not meant to paint a negative picture about any given musician's community.

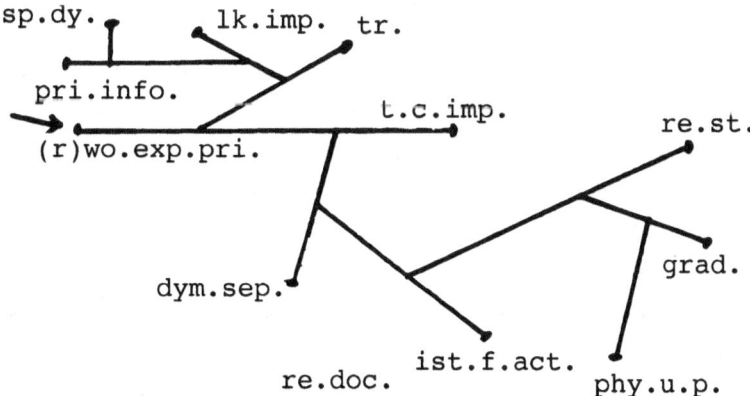

463

EXT. F (II) –26

The time zone of the late seventies would also have many positive attributes. This would be the cycle where the vibrationaltory lining of the sixties would move into its natural/unnatural completion. In actual terms, this period would be perceived by many people as a time of hope and preparation for the future. Many musicians would see this cycle as one of the few uplifting periods since the fifties, and there was also a general feeling that the negative vibrations of the sixties was over. In cities like New York one could not help but notice that creative activity was generally gaining momentum. And while no one got rich from their involvement with creative music in that cycle, all of the musicians were able to survive. The time zone of the late seventies was a period of preparation and anticipation for the future. This would be a cycle for furthering different areas of research, and contemplating one's position in his or her own separate work. This period would also see moves toward redefining the next level of functionalism—with regards to either a given individual's growth, or the composite functionalism of organizations. The reformation of the AACM as a multi-dynamic organization represented only one example of this new spirit. This same attitude can be sited throughout the whole of America.

Among the many individuals whose creativity helped to shape this period, I would like to especially single out:

Steve Lacy—I believe that Steve Lacy must be viewed as a dynamically important musician whose activity represents what the reality of creative music is all about. The thrust of his work has proceeded on its own terms, without regard for what is considered in or out, and in doing so, he has created a dynamic body of relevant creativity. As both an instrumentalist and composer, Steve Lacy has helped to open new avenues of creative postulation, and it is past time that his contributions are recognized. The spectrum of Lacy's work involves his solo music to various other projects—including his quintet and his involvement with "open" improvisation. To all of these areas of involvement Lacy brings what can only be called integrity and invention.

Andrew White—In my opinion, Andrew White must be considered one of the most important single forces to emerge in the post-Coltrane continuum of the music. In many ways his activity will come to be viewed as the yardstick of extended participation dynamics. This is so because as an instrumentalist White has redefined the execution dynamics of the woodwind family (i.e., increased what was considered possible) and as a scholar he has given us a whole new look at the music. White was among the first (if not the first) to begin the process of notating solos of Coltrane's music (and his efforts in this one area alone would have made his activity essential). Andrew White was also among the first musicians of the post-Ayler generation to recognize the value of independent recording. His work in this area has set the standard of excellence for future generations. As this section of the book is being written, it is clear that Andrew White, if he does nothing else as of now (1978), has profoundly affected the path of earth music. I find it especially curious that his efforts are so neglected in the light of this new interest in bebop. It's almost as if everyone is afraid to mention his name (maybe he'll go away and not frighten us). I believe Andrew White must be considered among our most gifted musicians.

Dave Holland—When the haze of the sixties and seventies time period is understood, I have no doubt that the work of Dave Holland will be viewed as representing what is best about creative music and total commitment. Holland has demonstrated a musical viewpoint that has extended the execution and conceptual nature of contemporary bass playing—regardless of style or content. The strength of his work must be considered and received in any serious attempt to understand creative music progressionalism in the eighties.

Anthony Davis—The emergence of Anthony Davis in the middle seventies has signaled the arrival of an important new musician. I have no doubt that his activity will be an important factor in the continuum of creative music—as we move into the next cycle. Already Davis has established himself as an instrumentalist and composer, and the depths of his initiations reveal a vital and extended awareness of transformational participation. Davis, in my opinion, is one of the most impressive, and complete musicians to emerge in the seventies.

Gunter Hampel and Jeanne Lee—The work of Gunter Hampel and Jeanne Lee represents what is best about creative music and creative

EXT. F (II) –28

thinking. These are dedicated artists who have established a necessary body of music that will outlive all of the pseudo fashions and surface commitments that characterize present-day so-called involvement. As we enter the eighties these artists have already established fifteen and some years of documented music, and I look forward to experiencing more of their work in the future.

Warne Marsh—There is no way I could allow myself to cite individual creative musicians without including a mention of this most special instrumentalist (person). Warne Marsh represents to me what a creative instrumentalist is all about. No nonsense, vision and dedication. From the early work in the late forties with Lennie Tristano, until the present (i.e., 1984—with master instrumentalist Hank Jones), this musician has offered a unique and personal music that is the personification of creativity. Even more amazing is the fact that so little real appreciation and understanding has been given to this master musician by the jazz press. I can write this: the direction of my life would not have been possible were it not for the strength and dedication of instrumentalists (and thinkers) like John Coltrane and Warne Marsh. I enter his name in this book as part of my responsibility to creative music.

Keith Jarrett—There can be no separate emphasis on creative musicians in the time zone of the seventies to eighties without including the activity of Keith Jarrett. For the activity of this most special musician has had a profound impact on the affinity dynamic nature of creative music during the transition period of the seventies. Jarrett, to me, represents a source of commitment and integrity. This is a musician whose creative path has been consistent and dynamic—on every level. It is also important to note that the public acceptance of this great musician was not attained by any deviation or gamery. Rather, Jarrett was able to forge his original music to the greater public without compromise—in a period where commercial machinery was set up to help musicians sell out. Furthermore, Jarrett was the first musician from his generation to take up the challenge of solo music (before it became re-fashionable) and he was also among the first to take up the challenge of performing traditional classical works (on the piano). He is also a gifted composer.

EXT. F (II) –29

James Newton—Represents what is best about the generation of musicians who emerged in the late seventies. He is a musician of impeccable stature and character, and also a gifted composer. To experience the dynamics of his work is to have real hope for the future of creativity. Newton can function and contribute to any area of the music, from open improvisational approaches to early blues. At present his recordings include offerings for the solo music context on through to chamber ensemble works. The dynamics of this musician will be an important factor in the next cycle of the music, and I for one am eager to learn from his vision.

In many ways the social reality position of post-Ayler/AACM creativity could be viewed as more stable in the late seventies than in its solidification during the early sixties. For the progressional activity which characterized the sixties not only substantiated post-Ayler creativity—as a meaningful projection in its own right—but the realness of that establishment signified its continuum was not simply an abbreviated spectacle but rather a legitimate extension of creative music (and as such, a projection that wasn't going to simply disappear). The realness of post-Ayler creativity in the seventies reflected this understanding coupled with the weariness of the sixties struggle. For if in the beginning many musicians felt their activity could change the world, the subsequent progressions of the sixties revealed that change was not just dependent on noble intentions. Not to mention, many of the concepts propagated in the sixties were ill-conceived and detrimental to positive transformation anyway. Many of the ideas surrounding alternative creativity in the early sixties did not take into account the actual realness of life on earth. As such the seventies would see a new-found respect for the composite tradition of creative music, and this period would be the time zone that brought forth the postulation of realistic goals (that being, postulation with respect to what might really be possible). The changes that reshaped creative musicians in the late seventies were based on actual life experiences learned in the sixties and seventies, and hopefully the insight gathered from those experiences as well.

It must be remembered that many of the musicians who aligned their activity with the post-Ayler projectional continuum in the early sixties were young musicians. The average age of this group would be under thirty

EXT. F (II) –30

(there I am speculating) and many of the functional moves this group made would be colored by their lack of experience. It was in fact the youthfulness of this group that would shape the dynamic brilliance and power of post-Ayler creativity. One has only to play recordings from that period to experience the emotional dynamics permeating the composite activity from that time cycle. The youthfulness of the early post-Ayler movement must be viewed as necessarily relevant to the composite physical universe particulars surrounding what and how the music came to be. For the dynamic challenge of Ornette Coleman's, Cecil Taylor's, and John Coltrane's activity necessitated a new spirit and commitment to creative music. **The multi-complexual challenge of restructuralism in the sixties could only have been successfully carried out by a contingent of musicians who were either not afraid of what risks the music posed or had nothing to lose (and were either too young or naive to deal with the question of consequence).** Thus the dynamic challenge of creative music would be characterized by a robust and often ill-conceived rhetoric that could only come from young musicians. However that early period is now viewed, my point is that the development and expansion of creative music was successfully carried out through their efforts—and in the final analysis they did advance the music. By the time the projectional realness of the music solidified in the late seventies, many of the musicians responsible for that solidification had moved passed thirty.

The progressional struggle to participate in alternative creative music, from the time zone of the sixties to the late seventies, had also produced another natural phenomenon. For, if in the beginning many musicians of the post-Ayler movement could be viewed as simply jumping on the bandwagon of a form that might be perceived as "hip"—and in fact, post-Ayler creativity in its early cycle was perceived as "hip" or revolutionary, etc.—later this perception of the music would change in the actual realness of "life changes"—through a lengthening time continuum. In other words, both the pressure surrounding one's participation in alternative creativity, as well as the time realness of that participation in progressional terms, would serve as a weeding-out factor for who was or wasn't serious about the music. If in the beginning one hundred musicians could be cited as

EXT. F (II) –31

totally involved in post-Ayler creativity—as a commitment having to do with maintaining the ethical and spiritual integrity of what that creativity signified—by the late seventies there were only forty musicians left. For the progressional struggle surrounding post-Ayler creativity would move to separate those musicians who were not serious about their commitment— or those who did not fully understand what they had gotten themselves in. The transfer-shift awareness of this phenomenon could especially be seen in the early seventies where many musicians suddenly moved to abandon any kind of struggle towards alternative invention and instead gravitated to more commercial forms—as a means to not deal with the pressure of non-accepted creativity (yet I do not mean to imply that this example is the only factor related to why given individuals moved towards commercial music, because there were many other factors connected with this phenomenon—and it would be detrimental to commercial music as well as the musicians who decided to abandon the music to not clarify this point). Nevertheless, the challenge of participating in alternative creativity in the sixties would prove too much for a great percentage of the musicians who originally helped instigate the solidification of post-Ayler creativity, and as such, by the late seventies many of those musicians would establish themselves in other areas of creative music. To deal with the realness of post-Ayler creativity is to understand the intensity surrounding its advancement—in other words, the survival of the post-Ayler continuum in itself was quite a feat.

The reality options of the creative musician in the late seventies can be viewed with respect to a decade of completed work. For not only did the post-Ayler contingent survive the sixties and early seventies, but by surviving, the musicians also secured the necessary connections to continue their activity. In actual terms, this would have to do with the development of outlets for alternative creativity as well as an expanded awareness of individual initiative. **The composite post-Ayler musician community would be the first contingent of the post-war generation (from the late forties and fifties) to advance and re-establish alternative functionalism—with regards to either the promotion and distribution of recordings, or the establishment of new business connections.** The

EXT. F (II) −32

end result of this understanding would move to spread the performance possibilities of creative music, and in doing so, also secure the actualness of the music—as something that does exist. The work that took place in the last decade would help to clarify the significance of decentralization in actual terms. Nor would the dynamics of this understanding pertain to only certain regions of the planet, but rather, the lessons learned from the last cycle would be relevant on a composite level. That is—the progressional continuance of post-Ayler creativity would come to establish its presence in both America and Europe. (Japan would represent extra problems in terms of distance, and as such, is separate from my point here.) The realness of this establishment would help spread the music on a global level—but this is only the beginning. For the spread of creative music in the seventies would help solidify the next level of composite continuity (or at least this phenomenon is not separate from composite world change and unification). For these reasons I view the progressional realness of post-Ayler creativity as necessarily relevant and important to the music.

(Level Three)

1. *The newer music forms have developed past standard techniques. Is this an important step in the forming of alternative functionalism?*
    Yes, but the realness of this phenomenon is not limited to only the forms we now associate with "being new." Every projectional thrust can be viewed in this same context—that being, "advancement as a phenomenon that moves towards the composite solidification of world culture." It is possible, however, to view the dynamic acceleration of trans-African progressionalism forms as extremely significant for what it has posed for continuance in this time period—on through to the 2000s, I imagine. This is so because the working floor of trans-African affinity dictates supplied the first response to the changing vibrational position of western culture—as it applies to both methodology and spiritualism (and as such to affinity dynamics as well). There can be no proper "standard technique" unless the reality specifics of its culture's alignment are "real"—which is to say, the dynamics of progressionalism in this cycle are important in that they can reveal how change is solidifying—both vibrationally and physically. The realness of a given extension is definitely the first sign of alternative functionalism in the making—because there is a cosmic reason why given movements and/or people are moved to "change the appearance of things." In its most basic realness, this phenomenon signals "motion."

2. *There have been many charges by both black and white academics that bebop is a more restrictive form of music than earlier black creativity and, as such, a form of less relevance when viewed in its composite context. What is your opinion?*
    I feel few of the people who have made these charges are really aware of the "actual" realness of bebop. I write this because I find these charges ridiculous and nothing more. Certainly the functional considerations surrounding bebop were and are of a different nature than the forms

preceding it, but bebop is as relevant and creative as any alignment that has ever existed, regardless of time zone or country. I believe that underneath this viewpoint is a subtle kind of racism, because the heart of this argument moves to evaluate the significance of bebop only in terms of its cross-transfer imposed definitions—as opposed to seeing the form as a natural continuation of its projectional route. Bebop, to many of these people, is viewed as a form that functions from the same vibrational hierarchy as European art music—with its same strengths and weaknesses. To believe that viewpoint is to not really understand the real reality position of black creativity and/or its second encounter with trans-information (i.e., world information)—as interpreted through affinity dynamics attitude.

3. *There are many black academics who feel that bebop is more a European music than black music. What is your opinion?*

I have heard this argument before in certain circles of black academia and quite frankly I am somewhat at a loss as how to respond to this question. I believe the reality and meta-reality implications of bebop have suffered profound misinterpretations by the collective forces of western culture, and probably the misunderstanding of this sector of the black community can be traced to what has resulted from this phenomenon. The misinterpretation I speak of concerns the relationship of bebop to "what is now called" western methodology—concerning the reality of its harmony as well as its form. But to even lightly examine the actualness of bebop is to see the uniqueness of dynamics—in every way. Which is to say, to really view the realness of bebop then one must first come to terms with what each extension has brought forth—with respect to both the actual music and what has transpired in its language. Because any attempt to comment on bebop must include some understanding of what this projection has raised in actual alternative language and language postulation—for a future creative position (and this is also true for its use of rhythm and vibrational attitude)—and there is more. For to really view the realness of bebop is to have some understanding of what this projection has supplied in terms of its cosmic information and/or

EXT. F(III)–3

information transference—in both physical universe terms and vibrational terms. As for the charges that the music is seeded in the affinity dynamic attitude of western culture, then the obvious question would be why didn't bebop solidify in Europe? Why has every projectional extension of bebop been dictated by black musicians? Finally, in the end, I feel charges of this nature really tell more about the black intellectual community's inability to deal with bebop than the music itself.

4. *New York City is considered the most sophisticated city in America as far as its relationship to so-called art is concerned. What is your opinion?*
It is undebatable that New York City has a greater percentage of people who have declared themselves professional artists as compared to the rest of the country, yet there are many reasons for this. The fact is New York has long enjoyed the benefits of both media and financial support. This is true whether we are commenting on the dynamics of music recording or theatre possibilities. As such it is natural that any person aspiring to be "successful"—as this concept is now understood—would sooner or later try New York. But the dynamics of New York's possibilities should not be interpreted as a signal that this one sector of the planet is in any way somehow "more real" than any other place—because it isn't. My own experience has shown that there is nothing special as such about this area—because in the final analysis, New York City is simply another place on the planet. Moreover, if the articles I have read on creativity are indicative of what the New York creative community is thinking about, then quite possibly New York City has even less real understanding about creativity than the rest of America (not to mention the world). If, outside of its business community, New York City has any real advantage over the rest of America, then why hasn't that advantage translated into the dynamics of the actual music from this city—from its so-called artists? Because nine-tenths of the musicians whose activity has altered some basic continuum of the music have not come from New York but rather "to New York." This is not to say no New Yorker has contributed to the music, nor have I meant to imply that no restructuralism (or innovation) has come from New York creative people—obviously people are creative

EXT. F(III)–4

or not creative wherever they come from. My point is only that however one chooses to view New York City, the specialness of its dynamics have not made New Yorkers any more sophisticated—in any real sense—than the rest of the country. This is true for the creative community as well as the critical defining community that misinterprets composite information dynamics—on whatever focus.

5. *Bebop is generally considered to be a completed form of improvised music, especially after the initiations of the post–Coleman, Coltrane, and Ayler continuum. What is your opinion?*

Very few people seem to realize that the music we call bebop is only thirty-five to forty years old—which is to say, young. For that matter even Dixieland music cannot be viewed as an old music, especially if its meta-reality and meta-reality dynamics are understood. No, I do not consider bebop a completed form on any level. I believe there are still many areas to be learned about and explored in this form—which is to say, bebop is still a vital projection. As we move into the eighties the importance of this form will take on added weight, because both Dixieland and bebop are forms realized through the composite affinity-insight-principle implications—as made real from the collective thrust of black creativity and as made real from the composite vibrational particulars of American so-called culture. Moreover, how could the life implications of bebop be decidedly less effective after forty years when, as this book is being written, people are still actively supporting Bach and Beethoven? The inherent life relevance of bebop is no different from any other dynamic projection—and with the profound ingredient of improvisation, the realness of this form should always be adaptable regardless of time zone—regardless of culture. Finally, the most basic thrust of this book has tried to take the viewpoint that the progressional realness of alternative functionalism cannot be viewed in separate contexts but instead as a whole. In other words, bebop is not separate from whatever is viewed as current today (if that something is related to the same progressional lineage). There is really no such thing as new music—in the way we have come to view this concept.

6. *There were many established musicians who dabbled in the so-called avant-garde with the understanding that this continuum represented nothing more than a release of frustration. How do you view this phenomenon?*

If I am correct, this cycle was in full swing around the middle to late sixties. I can recall reading several articles of musicians talking about how frustrated they were in a given period and as a result of this frustration began to play "free" music—to let off steam or something—but later that same musician was now "getting back to serious jazz" and feeling better. I recall, even in that period (the middle to late sixties) thinking "what nonsense"—because everybody knew that three-fourths of the "born-again bebop players" from that juncture had really come to extended music because they were under the wrong impression that "freedom was in", and "playing weird" was compatible with "going Bossa Nova"—that is, the next fad. Many of the musicians who expressed their "change of status" in this period are commonly referred to as "middle-of-the-roaders" (that being, whatever form seems to be in, they will go to that form) and while on the surface there is really nothing wrong with this elasticity—a definite vibrational attitude does result from this phenomenon. I write this because every form is vibrationally important, and every form—if approached with respect to its essence realness—will reveal necessary vibrational information. But the seriousness of this revealing is always lost to that segment of musicians who jump from one fad to another, because musicians of this type bring no real level of sincerity (or awareness) to their participation. What's interesting about this phenomenon is the large number of musicians who made the switch and are still switching, in an attempt to "get a hit." This is not to ignore real change, or growth—and obviously all of us are hopefully trying to grow as well—but the dynamic challenge of making a living in this culture (in this time period) has produced two generations of the most "chicken—" musicians that I have ever seen. In the sixties they all tried "free jazz," in the late sixties (when it was clear that free jazz would never really be profitable) they went to jazz-rock, after that—disco, etc., etc. The only constant about this phenomenon is that few of these musicians will ever make a creative statement (that being something about what could be "the most" of who they are—or could be) whatever form is tampered with. By the same token, some of these individuals might also reply that "at least they had sense enough to make some money"—and this point is not without validity (on some level) either. Not to mention each person must pursue the focus of his/her attraction—in other words, every time I re-read this answer I want to back off more. (I feel as if there are negative feelings in my answer—and who needs this.)

7. Is bebop suffering in audience attendance as a result of a growing interest in so-called newer forms?
I believe this in fact was the case all through the sixties and seventies, but by the late seventies a change became apparent, and now bebop seems to be changing positions with the so-called avant-garde. But in the sixties, the dynamics of media focus somehow moved to view bebop as a less relevant form (i.e., the jazz-is-dead syndrome) than the so-called revolutionary wing of extended functionalism—and of course this was a serious mistake. In the final analysis, probably this phenomenon will continue—that being "one day you're in, one day you're out"—until America (and western culture) moves to solidify a real understanding of creativity—and art. At present the vibrational tone level of American culture moves in accordance to the whims of the spectacle diversion syndrome, and this is unfortunate—to say the least. The seriousness of this problem is compounded when one considers that only a small segment of the greater community supports creative music anyway (creative in this case meaning not commercial)—thus the move to isolate bebop or the so-called avant-garde only intensifies the dilemma of all alternative creativity. Hopefully in the future, education will move to correctly teach about creativity, because the reality and vibrational dynamics of this most important subject are directly related to both world change and consciousness raising. We are thus either in a time period that has no respect for its earlier projections or—when changed—a time period that can only focus on the past as a means to not deal with the present. Either condition is not conducive to positive transformation. The eighties promises to

continue the "return to de great ole days" syndrome—hopefully this time around we might actually hear the music.

8. *What significance do you attach to Albert Ayler's music?*
To me, Albert Ayler's music personified the realness of progressional continuity and creative extension—and the fact that the next vibrational continuum of the music had now been entered into. For Ayler's music can be viewed as a direct extension of Coltrane's, Coleman's, and Taylor's activity, as well as what the implications of those works would mean in a different time context. Ayler's work forecasted directions for saxophonists on several levels—and his exploration of the sonic implications of his instrument has changed the total picture of saxophone technique and dynamics; his language has also underlined the whole of the creative musicians' vocabulary. Ayler's creativity was one of the first of his time period to re-utilize and investigate the composite spectrum of the music, and it was possible to hear everything from Dixieland to church music in his playing. The realness of his activity must be viewed as one of the more important breakthroughs of the sixties. Even more amazing is the relatively brief period that Ayler had on the planet, considering the magnitude of his contribution.

9. *To what degree is specialization desirable in creativity?*
I believe the answer to this question might be different for different people. There have always been individuals whose activity focused on only one area as a means to make, what they would call, a complete statement in the same context—or complete participation to what they perceive as "real." In actual fact, the reality of specialization is really related to the particulars of one's own affinity dynamics, because all of us are necessarily limited in one way or another. For me, specialization is positive as long as it doesn't move to distort the composite reality of what is being specialized. At present, the progressional continuance of contemporary information transference makes it very difficult—if not impossible—to "know everything there is to know" about a given area of information. But the end result of present-day information dynamics also makes it clear

EXT. F(III)–8

that the dynamic effectiveness of specialization has to do with whether or not a given participation understands—and affirms—its vibrational center. This is what interests me.

10. Is there a comparable creative discipline—in the black community—to the reality and vibrational realness of creative music from the black aesthetic?
I have in this series of books tried to stress the significance of creativity—especially music, and even more especially black creativity—because I believe the realness of this subject is profoundly important on every level. But if we are to understand what this consideration really means—with respect to its discipline implications—then it is important to not forget the route black people have had to travel to get to this point in time. Rather than methodological particulars, the most basic factor that has solidified through the composite spectrum of black creativity is vibrational transference and affinity dynamic magic discipline, and this has been constant whether we are referring to music, dance, or painting. The greater effectiveness of black music is related to its position with respect to information dissemination (i.e., it has been put on records, it has been universally packaged, and it has assumed great importance in western culture's business decisions)—but in actual fact, music is only one important discipline among many. The challenge is to make the composite spectrum of black creativity available—whether we are talking of theatre and/or poetry. To say that black music has no comparable discipline in the black community is to say black people are only involved in music—and this is false. This is not to take away from the music—or the power of music; certainly I believe the dynamic implications raised in black creativity have profoundly altered this period in time—and they have. But music is only one avenue of vibrational transference and must not be used to disrespect the composite realness of all creativity.

11. In the past fifty years, the role of the soloist has been prominent in creative music. How has that role changed today?
Although the reality dynamics of creative music has seen many changes in the last twenty years—and especially from the sixties until

EXT. F(III)–9

now—I do not believe that the soloist feature of creative music is in any jeopardy—regardless of context. Yet by the same token, I question whether the role of the soloist can continue without any adjustments in the light of what has transpired in the last twenty years. For the dynamics of musicians like John Coltrane for instance have created a situation where many soloists now regularly extend themselves for four hundred choruses on every solo—and this added feature has opened new avenues as well as problems for the music. Hopefully this aspect of solo invention will undergo change (and in fact to some degree this has already started). It is my hope that the next cycle of creative music will accent the dynamics of the total group as opposed to the soloist—yet I have not meant to imply any disrespect for the solo tradition of the music, because there are many new challenges for the contemporary soloist. For instance, the re-emergence of the complete solo medium during this time cycle will be important for what it will pose for extended functionalism, and the last ten years have seen solo breakthroughs for instruments of every category. In the last five years I have come to view new compositional approaches that involve giving the soloist less actual time for extending but more actual time for "compositional execution"—that being the idea of "improvisational phrases" as opposed to having as much time as one desires. Whatever, I do not believe the solo tradition of the music is in any danger of extinction. Certainly this feature has long been an important addition to the projectional dynamics of creative music, and I expect this will continue in the future as well.

12. How has the emotional dynamics attained in the sixties been channeled into the continuity of creative invention?
    The emotional dynamics and intensity that were generated in the sixties are slowly integrating into the composite nature of extended functionalism. In many ways this development was inevitable, for the post-Ayler thrust at one point only functioned as a fortissimo energy continuum—whose makeup in many ways was even more limited than the forms it proposed to open. Moreover, the last ten years have seen a kind of period of introspection in the general creative music.

EXT. F(III)–10

Many of the musicians who emerged in the sixties, who participated in the post-Ayler thrust of the music, have now advanced into their thirties—and in some cases forties—and this consideration alone has affected the physicality of the music. The combination of all of these factors has moved to produce more mature music—and overall viewpoint for participation—rather than explosive postulation. There is of course more to this question, for the participation of the post-Ayler school has not taken place in a vacuum—which is to say, all of the musicians from this continuum are as open to the "vibrational changes" affecting the composite culture as everyone else. The information focus that refocused on bebop and traditionalism in the seventies has also, to some degree, played an important role in shaping composite creative participation. However, it would not be true to write that no musicians are involved in intense and emotional music, rather the reality of present-day postulation dynamics (in the early eighties) is as diversified as ever.

13. What have been the major changes in creative improvised music after Albert Ayler?

The changes which occurred in creative music after Albert Ayler can be viewed from several different contexts: that being, with respect to region of planet, with respect to functional material, and with respect to conceptual dynamics. In every context the post-Ayler continuum has altered the "central dynamicism" of creative music postulation, as this concept applies to the functional "room and design" of creative music as well as new techniques. The progressional continuum of post-Ayler creativity can also be viewed as a factor that solidified how new material would come to be viewed and applied—whether that material was related to language (i.e., new sound material) or new instrumentation. In short, the dynamics of Albert Ayler's music supplied the second (after Coleman, Taylor, Sun Ra, and Coltrane) response of restructuralism dictates—and in doing so, solidified the transition period of the sixties.

EXT. F(III)–11

14. *What role has tonality taken after the initiations of the post-Ayler period?*
The progressional use and expansion of tonality after the post-Ayler period of creative music is both complex and diverse. Complex in the sense that no one application of transitional harmony has solidified as a composite factor, and diverse in the sense that the realness of this question transcends the reality focus of so-called avant-garde jazz. Because, for the most part, the post-Ayler movement of the music was not a harmonic movement but rather a vibrational and rhythmic extension. This is not to say the dynamics of harmony had no relevance whatsoever to this movement—for the solidification of the post-Ayler continuum would utilize a kind of vibrational sound order approach (and in a sense this ordering could be viewed—and correctly viewed—as an attempt to initiate an alternative vibrational approach to harmony) but the realness of traditional harmony and its so-called logical application and extension was not a regular—or all inclusive—feature of post-Ayler creativity. Instead, the continuation and extension of this area of functionalism (harmony) would involve the work that has long characterized post-bebop investigation as well as the emergence of jazz-rock and extended rock. The dynamic implications of extended harmony would then fall into the hands of those individuals, and movements, whose activity had—in some way—re-synthesized and constructed both new theoretical bases for the music (and its science) as well as new practical points for actual creative participation (which in any case involved the source-transfer adaptation of world music principles in collaboration with western music methodology—e.g., the use of modes). The utilization of extended harmony in popular music would be important for how it would make given harmonic breakthroughs "real" on a composite level—by the greater public. Finally, in the late sixties and seventies the role of tonality has again assumed great importance in the contemporary so-called western art music community. Composers from the post-Young continuum of the music like Philip Glass and Steve Reich have begun to open another approach to harmony and this is also true of the xenharmonic research taking place in places like San Diego in particular. I believe many breakthroughs will occur in harmony as a result of all of this varied activity—somewhere in the late eighties.

EXT. F(III)–12

15. *The drum has played a prominent role in the development of black creativity in every period of the music. Has its role diminished in contemporary music today?*

I do not believe the significance of percussion has diminished in contemporary music—regardless of form. Yet I do believe that the dynamics of contemporary percussion have altered the possibilities surrounding how percussion is to be utilized—on given occasions or compositions. As the progressional continuance of creative music moves into the eighties, it is now clear that no single instrument can be viewed as the center of the music—or the most pivotal factor in the music—and for many percussionists (with today's sentiments being as they are), this variety might be interpreted as a move away from percussion as an important instrument in the music. But this viewpoint is not true. Because percussionists today have never had more room to define what role he or she will have in tomorrow's creativity. I believe that percussion will continue to play a prominent role in creative music—whatever projection. The role of percussion has not really diminished today—it has only changed... like everything else.

16. *How important is personal affinity in group improvised music?*

I imagine the importance of personal affinity differs from musician to musician. For myself I believe the very success of the music is related to the composite affinity of each member in the group. However, this kind of affinity takes time and cannot be forced, because even if given individuals have similar conceptions about the music, this does not always translate into compatibility in the actual playing—or creating. There is also the realness that in many cases a given group—or individual—simply does not have the time or inclination to form a long-term ensemble (and as such establish a "family" vibrational music). In these cases I have opted to pick individuals with whom I can work well and with whom I feel "good" vibrations. I also try to pick musicians who can work well and inter-mix positively with all of the participating members of a given project—but this way of working is not to everyone's taste. For instance, I have been told that Charlie Mingus preferred to have vibrational areas of discord in his various ensembles as a means to "stay on top of the music." Thus to answer this question is somewhat difficult because it depends on what zone each person is in and what zone each person wants to be in, and finally what zone that person "will" be in.

17. *What effect—if any—has the lack of spiritual and economic support by the greater public, as well as the culture, had on creative music?*

The lack of support for creative music has simply made it harder for individuals to work, and as such live—and if any one factor can be singled out, it must be the vibrational implications underlying what this area of struggle has brought about. By the same token, the dynamics of present-day intensities have produced a situation where any individual that really desires participation in alternative creativity is forced to examine the reality of his or her commitment. In other words, the challenge of creative music in this time zone will be taken up by those individuals who have made the decision to really be part of alternative creativity—whatever the rewards or problems—and the realness of this decision will be about "the survivors"—rather than "the fadists" (or those individuals who thought they were interested but later changed their minds when confronted with the dynamic life problems surrounding living from the music). On the physical universe level there are other problems related to the non-support of the music. For the use of large ensemble projects cannot be utilized with any regularity simply because it costs too much—and this is a serious problem. One of the positive features of this same phenomenon has been the move by musicians to become independent of all outside resources—by making their own records and creating independent performing spaces—because in this context, the awareness of non-support has helped to stimulate dynamic functionalism. Certainly the neglect of creative music is directly related to the rush of many gifted musicians towards commercial music—and while this rush helped to separate "those who were serious from those who weren't," by the same token, creative music lost many valuable musicians—people whose contributions could have potentially been very important for the composite realness of alternative functionalism, and this is a shame.

EXT. F(III)–14

Finally, the lack of support for alternative creative music has accelerated the negative competition between musicians in the race for becoming "known." The end result of this phenomenon has seen the continued separation between humanity and resolidification—on every level, and this cannot be viewed as positive.

18. How does the concept of style serve the improvisor? Is this factor positive or negative?

There are two levels of what style really means. First, there is the realness that as people, all of us are born with our own vibrational identity—and this identity permeates everything we attempt to do. In creative music from the black aesthetic—as well as world creativity—this phenomenon has long been recognized and viewed as the ultimate point for one to reach in his or her activity. Because the most basic understanding—and use—of improvisation has always been for the individual to "be as he or she can 'most' be" in their creativity. This concept of style has been the backbone of black creativity, regardless of time zone, and represents to me what is most positive about the reality of "style." But there is also another aspect of style that has to do with how a given individual sees him or herself with respect to the dynamic utilization of some aspect of functionalism—whether or not that functionalism ultimately serves to either further that person's goal creatively (with respect to that person's 'original intention') or whether that functionalism is employed because it is "effective" (even if not honest). Which is to say, as long as a particular style serves the improvisor and not the other way around, then that style can be viewed as useful (meaningful). When a style (or particular use of process) becomes so automatic (or accented) that it becomes an affirmation of the process—rather than the music—then that style can be spoken of as a negative factor.

19. What is your opinion on the concept of "swing and syncopation" with regards to creative music?

I believe the concept of "swing and syncopation" has been greatly distorted. What is really happening in creative music is that Europeans have narrowly defined one aspect of the music as a means to put themselves in the position of being able to evaluate its functionalism. It is foreign to the nature of creative music that one aspect of a person's creativity can be treated in this manner—especially by people who historically have always viewed themselves as outside of the vibrational dictates of the music. I believe if a person is creative and functioning from his or her natural vibrational flow, then that activity must be received as being "ised." There is no one criterion or formula for swinging in fact, there is no form of music—from parade music to Webern, etc.—that doesn't swing; there is no person on this planet whose creativity—when developed—doesn't swing. I believe the whole concept of swing should be re-examined because I think the people who most use this concept (critics and writers) are really writing about something else.

20. *Why have so many creative musicians begun to re-utilize bebop in the seventies?*

I really believe this phenomenon is related to the fact that America as a whole is in a period where much re-evaluation is taking place. In this context, the re-evaluation of bebop can be viewed as a natural response to progressional continuity as well as spectacle diversion information manipulation. For it must be understood that this re-utilization is not separate from the composite manipulation we experience, in every area, from the collected forces of western media in every area. Nevertheless, the move to re-adopt bebop is not without its positive implications because not only has this projection been misunderstood (and misdocumented) by the critical and defining community that controls cultural information, but there is also much valuable music for us to experience from this projection. Moreover, I believe that the reality dynamics of bebop still have many more areas for exploration and as such the present re-focus on bebop must be viewed as positive—especially if some attempt is made to solidify real (correct) information about this most dynamic form.

EXT. F(III)–16

21. Does the concept of multi-instrumentalist today represent innovation?

NO. The concept of multi-instrumentalism is as old as this planet and can be experienced in every area of creativity—in every form and/or time zone (for the most part). It is possible to experience this concept in every extension of black creativity in its resolidification—after being brought to America—and every continuum of the music has utilized some aspect of multi-instrumentalism. As such, to experience the music of Duke Ellington—from his early bands until his death—was to see one use of dynamic multi-instrumentalism, and this is also true for the spread of creative music from Kansas City and the southwest leading into the solidification of bebop. Actually, the realness of bebop would accelerate the coming of the specialist instrumentalist more than any other form, but this period was an exception rather than the rule. I have read many books questioning the sonority implications of black creativity, but in truth, black creativity has always been a diverse music. The re-utilization of multi-instrumentalism would begin to appear in the late fifties and sixties. Certainly the work of Eric Dolphy was a significant factor in casting focus on this area of functionalism—but in fact, Dolphy was never alone in this area (witness the activity of James Moody or Jerome Richardson, for example); rather, the dynamics of his work would tap the alternative functionalism implications of sonorous participation. In other words, Dolphy's work captured the dynamics of his time period. The realness of his activity would provide inspiration for dynamic multi-instrumentalism as practiced by the AACM.

22. Did the forms which developed in the AACM happen by chance?

The forms which were developed through the AACM came about because of the work of those members who were consciously looking for "new" ways to grow and learn. As such, it is impossible to really comment on this question because no one, in the beginning of a given area of research, can forecast exactly what will result from that research. In that context, every discovery is by chance. One thing is clear, however: every so-called route of extended information that solidified from the AACM came about because of the collective unity and dynamic cooperation of the composite

EXT. F(III)–17

membership—as opposed to the idea that one or two particular people developed everything. The AACM, in that period of its growth, represented another level of transitional unification and functionalism.

23. *The Chicago school (movement) is the first school in the last twenty years that placed emphasis on the total progression of creative music from the black aesthetic. Was there a reason for this type of research outside of the natural affinity to earlier forms?*

It was necessary to research the composite scope of black creativity to better understand the juncture creative music had arrived at in the middle sixties. For the fact is, many musicians of my generation—myself included—never had the opportunity to even experience the composite scope of the music or learn about it. There were no books written about the music (or at least, very few that were recommended as having anything to do with accurately commenting on the music) and also no instructions within the established educational system. After John Coltrane's death, many of the musicians in the AACM realized that the only way to extend—and integrate—Coltrane's advances into the composite music was to broaden the total arena that dictated what the reality of his work was about. In other words, the move to review and investigate composite black creativity was essential to have a basis for further investigation—because the total route black creativity has traveled is necessarily relevant to both its past and future. It was from this investigation that the AACM began to understand there is no such thing as "new" music (in the way this concept is now understood) because everything has been done (and in many cases—done better before). It is important to review the past so that we can learn about the future.

GLOSSARY

Accelerated Dynamics: (1) a time period that experiences an increased rate of dynamic particulars; (2) the phenomenon of increased motion and information awareness or exchange; (3) information or dynamic particulars which are occurring at a faster rate than the concept of "progressional continuance" (which is my phrase for the "normal" pulse flow of information and/or affinity dynamics); (4) the phenomenon of moving faster towards affinity insight—or self-realization—than what is otherwise viewed as normal.

Accelerated Functionalism: (1) a "particular" that advances the nature or effectiveness of a given discipline; (2) the phenomenon of a given discipline expanding at what is perceived to be faster or greater than normal.

Activism: (1) the act of participating in a given discipline; (2) the act of participating in a given moment or collective with the intent to making a "particular" result solidify.

Actual Terms: (1) my phrase for "concrete terms"; (2) in the physical universe sense of a given phenomenon act; (3) a term used to bring in a physical universe or "solid" example of a given concept or statement; (4) a term for either clarifying or simplifying the concept being dealt with.

Actual Transformation: (1) the state of "total change" in both the physical and vibrational universe; (2) the arrival of transformation whether or not it was intended; (3) the phenomenon of transformation solidified because the precepts of the phenomenon (or focus) under review adhered to the dictates of what transformation is; (4) the phenomenon of total physical and vibrational universe change.

Affinity Alignment: (1) the way of one's vibrational nature or sensibility; (2) how a given nature is manifested in both doing or perceiving—in terms of its vibrational and actual slant.

Affinity Compression: (1) a move to lessen an individual's vibrational make-up; (2) the reality of isolating affinity dynamics for the purpose of limiting a given individual's vibrational or spiritual realness; (3) the phenomenon of stagnating a culture or individual's ability to gain self-realization or affinity-insight awareness about their lives—or life purpose; (4) the phenomenon of suppressing affinity dynamics.

Affinity Convergence: (1) the phenomenon of different vibrational sensibilities coming together; (2) the solidification of different so-called affinity tendencies; (3) vibrational unification or point of.

Affinity Dictates: (1) the reality of information as it applies to the particulars of a given sensibility; (2) the realness of information or observation tenets as it involves the laws which govern fundamentals and affinity postulation, and what this means for a given vibrational observation or participation; (3) that being, the laws which support a given reality of information and/or information affinity basis; (4) in other words, whatever one does there are fundamental laws that are related to whether or not a given focus can be successfully utilized—this is also true for the nature, or vibrational realness, of those fundamentals.

Affinity Dynamics: (1) vibrational diversity or the spectrum of possibilities related to a given vibrational position; (2) the related vibrational spectrum of a given phenomenon—that being, areas that are related to the vibrational particulars of a given phenomenon; (3) the scope of a person's life options, as related to vibrational attraction and what this phenomenon means with respect to that person's vibrational make-up.

Affinity Insight: (1) the uncovering of necessary information through self-realization; (2) the phenomenon of spiritual awareness as uncovered by an individual tapping his or her "life experiences" and vibrational make-up; (3) the secrets of a given information continuum as made real by affinity dynamic awareness.

Affinity Insight (1): (1) the realization of spiritual and necessary information about the whole of a given route of participation or culture, or cultural group, by or through self-realization; (2) self-realization as a basis to understand the reality of a given phenomenon as that phenomenon pertains to the greater culture or space; (3) the uncovering of spiritual information as to the "composite state of things."

Affinity Insight (2): (1) the use of self-realization as a basis to connect to one's own "life realness"; (2) the phenomenon of individual awareness as developed by the individual to better understand how to live; (3) taking one's spirit and beingness into one's self as a basis to connect with "the IT" as a means to better understand one's life or life purpose—or desired purpose.

Affinity Nature: (1) the reality of a person's feeling and vibrational make-up; (2) the reality of a phenomenon's inherent tendencies; (3) the reality of a given individual's basic feeling and vibrational tendencies.

Affinity Negation: (1) the move to not acknowledge the "way" of a person's vibrational nature; (2) the realness of isolating the reality interpretation of a given phenomenon in a way that doesn't correspond to the composite platform of affinity dynamics; (3) the isolated vibrational focus of a given area of information as a basis to undermine that same information's composite value.

Affinity Postulation: (1) the phenomenon of "reaching" for "understanding" without the information tenets that are accepted as true, but instead "reaching" with respect to what one feels and senses; (2) postulation with respect to affinity dynamics and affinity insight; (3) learning with respect to one's basic nature (or way of doing "things") and/or feeling.

Affinity Tendencies: (1) the nature of principle information that a given individual normally vibrates (or draws) from; (2) a concept which observes that given individuals over a period of time in "normal situations" are attracted to particular aspects of principle information rather than composite information interpretation; (3) the nature of a continuous "attraction" to a particular vibrational focus.

Affinity Transfer: (1) the phenomenon of changing vibrational continuum interpretations; (2) the refocus and interpretation of principle information with respect to its affinity nature—usually taking an extended time period to become solidified; (3) the natural exchange of principle information with respect to its focus particulars and vibrational dynamics.

Agreement: (1) vibrationally conducive to; (2) in accordance with; (3) a phenomenon whose vibrational properties and "way of being"—with respect to interpretation of the reality of procedure—are within the accepted nature and reality position of those individuals or "things" that are dealing with it.

All-Purpose: (1) a term to emphasize that the actual realness of a given phenomenon has to do with cosmic or spiritual matters; (2) a term to stress that even though I have observed a given information line or observation route to the best of my ability, I am also aware that its real "reason to be" goes much further than its surface; (3) a term used to comment on the destiny implications, or greater spiritual purpose, of a given phenomenon.

Alternative Activism: (1) participation that is outside of what is perceived to be in accordance to the "accepted" reality of things; (2) participation that is not viewed as politically conducive to sustaining the "vibrational" or physical universe reality of things; (3) participation that utilized different information tenets or vibrational tenets from what is perceived to be the "accepted" reality of procedure.

Alternative Composite Progressionalism: (1) my term for the time continuum changes which are taking place, involving total information tenets (that being spiritual and empirical)—as those tenets relate to given cultures or movements or vibrational phenomena—that are separate from the cultural manipulated version of "sanctioned progressionalism"—or its interpretation; (2) a term to comment on the dynamics of progressionalism, as a given focus is accented to the degree that it becomes necessary to include the fact that other movements (or focuses) were also happening as well (and the thrusts of some of those focuses were and are in opposition to the dictates of the accented focus mentioned).

Alternative Definitions: (1) definitions that are equally as real but not accepted or realized; (2) definitions that are related to other regions of affinity dynamics; (3) definitions that are related to other areas of its principle information reality and in some cases give a completely opposite interpretation from its other alternative type.

Alternative Functionalism: (1) disciplines that are perceived as not being in alignment to what is accepted as "correct" or "culturally sustaining"; (2) disciplines that are the outgrowth of alternative information and/or affinity positions; (3) disciplines whose "participation intentions" are not perceived or practiced as a means to affirm what is generally believed to be true for only one region of information, but instead participation that is directed towards uncovering other aspects of principle information and information dynamics.

Application Dictates: (1) a term used in the integration schematics to denote the reality of application for its given concept mixture; (2) a term in the integration schematics to clarify that the reality of a given set of ingredients must be calibrated into actual use (as opposed to simply using in any manner or order).

Applied Redefinitions: (1) the move to reinterpret what a given area of information means; (2) the point underlying when a given information interpretation is changed—and for what reason; (3) the move to focus on another aspect of a given definition's vibrational dynamics; (4) the conscious move to change what a given area or focus of information means—or could mean.

Aspect Essence: (1) the phenomenon of focusing on one part of a given area of principle information as a means to proclaim a universal interpretation; (2) a phenomenon that accents the particulars of a given focus on principle information to the degree where it moves to distort what that principle information really means—or could mean; (3) a phenomenon related to information manipulation in the west involving how given areas—and interpretations—of information are kept in perpetual motion as a means to sustain what is considered to be "interesting" at the expense of what is "most spiritual."

Attachment: (1) to be aligned with or the act of aligning with; (2) to be in agreement with and in being so, to come together with; (3) to not be in agreement with but to come together anyway.

Attitude: (1) vibrational persuasion or way of being; (2) having to do with the vibrational state underlying how a given person or composite culture approaches "phenomenon."

Attraction: (1) to be drawn towards a given focus; (2) to naturally be moving towards a given phenomenon because of either interest or not interest or vibrational interest; (3) the coming together of different phenomena because those phenomena were supposed to come together because of cosmic matters.

Basic Science: (1) in this context involves the use of this term in present-day western culture—that being, extended empirical investigation without respect for (or awareness of) spiritual dynamics; (2) extended functionalism that moves to investigate "the reality of things" as that "thing" works but not as that "thing" is.

Bi-aitional: (1) my term for viewing the reality of principle information with respect to the realness of two basic vibrational continuums, that being the masculine and feminine vibrational principle.

Circular Information Dynamics: (1) the phenomenon of changing the focus of a given principle information interpretation to the detriment to its real reality; (2) the phenomenon of continually refocusing on principle information as a basis to accelerate information dynamics.

Collected Forces of Western Culture: (1) by this term I am referring to all of the agencies that have been constructed to perpetuate the reality of western culture—whatever that perpetuation involves. In other words, the western media, and its educators, the so-called right and left wing (and new left), the western scientific community, western politics, western information interpretation and regulation, etc.

Composite Activism: (1) participation that functions with respect to humanity and composite information; (2) participation with respect to physical universe objectives and spiritual dynamics; (3) the realness of different so-called sectors of humanity working towards the same objective; (4) participation with respect to composite information dynamics—thereby having positive relevance to the composite community.

Composite Affinity Alignment: (1) a vibrational relationship to principle information that attempts to respect and reflect the greater dynamics of composite humanity; (2) a vibrational relationship to information that brings together empirical information dictates with spiritual intent or insight; (3) a vibrational relationship to information that seeks to better understand and include composite humanity within the tenets of its particular focus; (4) the bringing together of composite humanity by establishing an all-encompassing information basis for information and information transference.

Composite Continuance: (1) repeated involvement with respect to both composite information and composite humanity; (2) the reality of time progressionalism as it involves composite humanity; (3) the nature of time changes as it involves composite information.

Composite Culture Attitude: (1) the reality of a culture's vibrational sensibility as it concerns all of the different vibrational persuasions in that culture; (2) the state of a given culture's composite vibrational nature and way of being.

Composite Focused Activism: (1) participation directed at a "particular" that also seeks to reflect the composite concerns of humanity; (2) participation by different kinds of people—both vibrationally and socially—on a particular area of interest; (3) composite participation on a given focus as a means to interpret that focus for the greater good of composite society. Composite participation and/or interest in a given area of information or physical universe particulars.

Composite Humanity: (1) all humanity—men, women, and children, regardless of planet sector; (2) with respect to all humanity.

Composite Information: (1) information that gives insight into the physical universe principle reality of a given phenomenon and also its accompanied vibrational or spiritual universe particulars; (2)

information that respects and reveals the multi-dynamic realness of a given phenomenon.

Composite Research: (1) research with respect to the past and present; (2) research with respect to composite information and interpretation; (3) investigation with respect to composite perception dynamics.

Controlled Information: (1) interpretations that have been sanctioned for the greater public to assimilate and believe; (2) interpretations which have consciously been manipulated as a means to suppress affinity dynamics and/or alternative definitions.

Cosmic Assignment: (1) a term to acknowledge that the "particulars" of a given phenomenon really have to do with "the greater forces" or quite simply "GOD," rather than something that can be only "talked about" or "written on"; (2) a term to acknowledge that some phenomena and/or focuses are indicative of the intent of forces that are greater than humanity or "what humanity can do."

Cosmic Dictates: (1) a term to acknowledge that the fundamentals or particulars underlying a given focus transcend the "intentions" of humanity and instead involve "the greater forces" or "GOD"; (2) a term to acknowledge that the reality of a given set of dictates is related to increased "understanding—or not understanding" of the cosmic realness of everything.

Cosmic Particulars: (1) that being, the reality of a given focus has nothing to do with our information dynamics but instead has to do with spiritual matters; (2) the point of a given interpretation or focus that transcends words and moves into the "real."

Criticism: (1) the phenomenon of commenting as to the reality particulars and/or dynamics of another person's participation; (2) the move to isolate a person's participation as a basis to apply value judgments—even if those judgments are outside the actual reality of that person's affinity participation; (3) an existential observation tool that moves to isolate a given phenomenon's "way of being—or participation" as a means to determine the success of that "beingness or participation"; (4) a unique tool of western information dynamics that involves the imposition of observation criteria (without spiritual dictates) as a means to isolate whether or not a given postulation is in accordance to its dictates.

Cross-Transfer Definitions: (1) interpretations which are solidified and applied when a given continuum of information moves into its change (or affinity refocus) cycle; (2) interpretations that are made "real" as a given continuum of information changes its vibrational or physical universe perceived focus; (3) definitions that had no or little meaning (or different meaning) in a given information continuum that are suddenly elevated into prominence because of the change of that information's use (on the physical universe level or political level).

Cross-Transfer Progressionalism: (1) the reality of continuums coming together and moving apart (and while doing so, taking or exchanging information dynamics in the process); (2) the reality of alternative continuums and the point of interchange between their reality or vibrational ingredients.

Cultural Transfer Shift(s): (1) those cycles in time which underline the phenomenon of different cultures changing or exchanging information and/or information dynamics; (2) the phenomenon of a given culture coming to an end while at the same moment another culture is emerging based on the same information or information dynamics—and what this inter-relationship means.

Culture Affinity Basis: (1) the reality of a culture vibrational and postulation make-up and what this phenomenon means for the establishment of that culture's "way of doing things"; (2) the vibrational particulars which underlie a given culture's reality and vibrational way of living.

Culture Information Basis: (1) the reality of a given culture's idea nature and its accompanied dynamics; (2) the affinity dynamic nature of a culture's intellectual "way of being."

Culture Information Dynamics: (1) the natural and unnatural possibilities that are related to a given culture's idea alignment in terms of "participation spectrum" and "vibrational postulation spectrum"; (2) the variety of focuses or "things" that are related to a culture's information reality—or position; (3) the spectrum of "focuses" or "things" that are related to—and the result of—a culture's relationship with its information.

Culture Information Focus: (1) the agreed-upon interpretation of a particular area of information by those individuals responsible for establishing cultural information; (2) the reality of how a given focus of information reflects the dynamic solidification of its culture's idea nature.

Culture Order: (1) the establishment of whatever devices are necessary to insure that a given culture can function in whatever way that culture desires to function; (2) the move to functionally insure that a culture can "work" the way its founders intended; (3) the reality of those devices which have been designed to solidify "how a culture works" with respect to that culture's political reality and/or dynamics.

Culture Solidification: (1) the establishment of the physical universe situation for a way that affirms the collective intent and desire of those individuals in that space, for the purpose of living in accordance to what is perceived to be "most real."

Decentralization: (1) the move to open up the reality dynamics of a given phenomenon as a means to have the greater spectrum of its forces able to equally have both input and relevance; (2) the move to spread the resources of a given phenomenon to all areas of its principle space, and in doing so, opening up the greater dynamics of the composite space.

Definition: (1) meaning of; (2) the reality of.

Despiritualization: (1) the phenomenon of having something viewed in less spiritual or vibrational terms; (2) the move to solidify the reality of a given spiritual phenomenon in terms that adhere to what is now called rational or logical—that being, the reality of "how something is" as opposed to "how something really is"; (3) the move to take away or not acknowledge—or not even be aware of—the magic or spiritual realness of a given focus.

Disintegration of a Culture's Center: (1) the phenomenon of a culture's vibrational and informational tenets moving to complete destruction; (2) the realness of a culture's idea and affinity support structure being overthrown.

Documentation: (1) the recording of information and particulars as a means to have that information available for future study or use.

Dynamic Functionalism: (1) a discipline that is pursued with respect to its number dynamics as well as spiritual dynamics; (2) a discipline that can bring about a spectrum of information awareness because of its ability to tap the system's particulars of a given phenomenon as well as vibrational dynamics related to that same phenomenon; (3) disciplines that are pursued because they are related to advancing the state of composite humanity; (4) disciplines that are pursued because their tenets are from—and moving towards—composite humanity (that is, disciplines that are about positive transformation).

Dynamic Separation: (1) the isolation of information to the degree that its particulars are viewed without respect for the whole of its principle platform and the creation of a dynamic functionalism from those separate focuses; (2) the intense focus of particulars as a means to view its fundamental law as a means to solidify that procedure for "spectrum participation and investigation"—all of this being done separately or not separately from its spiritualism.

Dynamic Spiritualism: (1) a spiritualism that is all-purpose—involving every aspect of one's life and living; (2) a spiritualism that moves to solidify living in accordance to the secrets and intentions of the greater forces; (3) a spiritualism or mystery system that serves to help humanity to come together for positive acts; (4) a spiritualism that moves to "ritualize" the reality of participation.

Economic Dynamics: (1) the reality and multi-particulars that involve how "contractual dynamics" are solidified and in what form.

Establishing High Order: (1) solidifying composite all spiritual and dynamic functional context, in accordance to transformational precepts; (2) solidifying the spiritual and information dynamics of a given state (and its related pedagogy all system); (3) solidifying the "most" spiritual and vibrational platform with the co-ordinates of the "moment" (or integration mix).

Existential Definition: (1) a definition that views the realness of a given phenomenon with respect to what happened on the physical universe level; (2) an observational phenomenon that views the nature of an occurrence from outside of that occurrence based on how that occurrence is perceived to have happened.

Existential Observation: (1) observation with respect to "how" something seems to be—as separate from the spiritual context of that something; (2) observation with respect to what appears to be happening (in terms of the physicality of that something—and how it "is"—in terms of its "movement" or "low system"), but not in terms of the composite all spiritual nature of that "something."

Existentialism: (1) the phenomenon and state of being that arises when spiritualism is subjected to logical analysis without respect for its proper affinity adjustments, which results in despiritualism and emphasis instead on the "particulars" of a physical universe occurrence—with the understanding being that "something that happens is really what has happened" as opposed to "something that happens is an expression of ... greater forces."

Expansion Condition: (1) a concept that has to do with how change is solidified in cultural terms; (2) having to do with the reality of intentions surrounding how change is perceived and moved towards.

Expansion Condition (1): the reality and concept of expansion as it relates to composite focus (that being humanity and all spiritualism).

Expansion Condition (2): the reality and dynamics of expansion as it relates to the individual desiring that expansion.

Expansion Dictates: (1) the reality of procedure as it involves expansion; (2) the infra-structure particulars—in their correct order—underlying expansion dynamics (in a given context).

Expansion Dynamics: (1) a term that has to do with the conceptual or vibrational factors that are related to a particular point or kind of expansion. In other words, a given approach or area of expansionism carries its own vibrational or actual implications.

Expansion Information Basis: (1) the phenomenon of increasing the idea spectrum of a given information line as a means to better understand the multi-complexual realness of principle information; (2) the attempt of increasing the affinity dynamic postulates related to what a given information line really means or could mean; (3) the solidification of an idea platform that has relevance to all of the people in its culture, and in doing so, having the dynamics related to what this phenomenon poses to information dictates.

Expansionism: (1) the phenomenon of growing in a given period of time, or the inherent additives that result from a "solidification" in a given time; (2) the move to encompass more territories and/or information without regard for whether or not the inhabitants of those said territories are in agreement with that encompassing; (3) the conscious move to increase the territories or "stuff" of a given culture as a means to "grow"—or support a "growth" that has already occurred.

Extended Dynamics: (1) the uncovering of more information or vibrational possibilities as that phenomenon relates to the reality of investigation; (2) the solidification of more insight about the reality of participation and/or living as that insight relates to a given discipline's meta-secrets or methodological possibilities.

Extended Functionalism: (1) a discipline that provides more insight as to the spiritual and actual particulars underlying what is normally perceived to be "real"; (2) a discipline whose infra-structure and/or particulars are related to, and gives insight into, the dynamics of positive transformation; (3) a discipline whose utilization can provide greater affinity insight as well as composite positive assistance for bringing about positive insight and change; (4) the act of advancing a given discipline to where its meta-reality can begin to provide some of these attributes.

Extension: (1) to move deeper into or towards; (2) coming into, closer to.

Form: (1) how something is; (2) the structure concerning how something seems to be or how something happens; (3) the context, and its related laws, that house a given phenomenon; (4) the spiritual platform that houses a given phenomenon; (5) the physical universe materialization of a vibrational ritual—that being, the context of a participation as well as what that participation means.

Fundamental Dynamics: (1) the focus particulars related to what a given discipline is, or could be in its optimum state; (2) the spiritual and "actual" possibilities that are related to a given "law," or discipline's reality.

Fundamental Particulars: (1) a principle focus or aspect of a given discipline's dictates; (2) the reality of a given discipline's separate parts.

Gradualism: (1) the phenomenon of re-defining information and/or particulars to have that information be viewed in accordance to the intent of its re-definers; (2) the phenomenon of changing information or contributions by groups or nations as a means to have that information or achievement perceived (or re-documented) as coming from the culture of those who changed the information; (3) the act of claiming ownership of concepts and/or achievements done by others as a means either to claim superiority or to claim historical "right of" or "linkage to."

High Purpose: (1) participation with respect to what is most positive for humanity; (2) participation with respect to what is perceived to be "most positive" for humanity; (3) spiritual participation that is done for what is most real for the greater forces; (4) cosmic phenomena that are about cosmic phenomena.

Improvisation: (1) a discipline that involves the science of creative postulation as it unfolds in "actual" time; (2) a discipline that utilizes the dynamics of moment postulation in both the context of individual postulation and its related affinity dynamics, as well as cultural vibrational transference; (3) the science and multi-discipline of existing—having to do with the appearance of "moments" and making life choices (either with respect to "particulars" or spiritual growth) and the gradual awareness of how best to proceed with that information in "rapid-moment-decision contexts."

Individual Dynamic Reality: (1) that being those "particulars" of the greatest positive attributes in a given individual's physical universe reality; (2) a concept that accents the realness of the individual and what that individual's vibrational spectrum could be in its most positive sense, as related to the particulars of his or her physical universe reality.

Individual Dynamics: that being, the "natural" or "particular" vibrational properties that each individual has—and is born with (or can acquire, depending on the situation)—having to do with the areas that individual is attracted to, the areas that individual can excel at, the information that individual can relate to (and later contribute to as well). Having to do with "what is most" or "can be most" about a given individual in his or her most positive state.

Individual Tendencies: (1) having to do with what region of principle information a given individual is continually drawn to, and functions from (in his or her natural feeling and "postulation" nature); (2) a concept which observes that given individuals vibrate to different areas of the same information because every information continuum is related to its particular "nature spectrum"—and this phenomenon also corresponds to the different types (or so-called types) of people.

Information Affinity Basis: (1) that being, the vibrational particulars which determine what a given idea structure is to really mean. My viewpoint is that the dynamics of vibrational postulates come before the actual idea or concept interpretation; (2) the affinity or vibrational nature that determines what aspect is to be affirmed of a given principle information line.

Information Alignment: the reality of a given idea or concept as it connects to principle information, and also the reality of a given interpretation as it affirms its vibrational basis.

Information Compression: (1) same as affinity compression but also involves the physical universe removal (or put-down) of given areas of information which are not in the interest of those who choose to do the compression; (2) the blockage of information.

Information Convergence: (1) the coming together of different continuums of information—either involving principle information dynamics or particulars; (2) the phenomenon of information expansion and/or affinity linkage.

Information Degrees: my term for information tenets. I have chosen this term because it moves to involve the reality of spiritualism more than the word "tenet." By "degree" I am saying that each aspect of a given information line moves to both substantiate the reality of its principle focus as well as its spiritual designation. I view the term "tenet" as more related to intellectual dynamics—having to do with the dynamics which support a given focus's particulars but not its affinity basis.

Information Dissemination: (1) the phenomenon concerning how given ideas and concepts are spread on the physical universe level; (2) the phenomenon that underlines how given practices are transmitted to the greater culture or through a sustained time cycle; (3) the spread of information.

Information Documentation: (1) the recording of knowledge—whatever the context or focus—as a means to have it taught or later re-examined; (2) having to do with the reality of recorded concepts and ideas and how it is passed on through different time cycles.

Information Focus: (1) the particular emphasis on a given aspect of principle information; (2) the point of a given intention as manifested in actual terms; (3) the reality underlying how a given principle information line is perceived in actual terms (that being, the reality concerning what factors and affinities underlie how a given information line is repeatedly perceived and practiced).

Information Focus Distortion: (1) that being, the particular point in a given information tenet structure that is consciously or not consciously distorted as a means to have an understanding that corresponds to what one wants to believe, rather than what that information seems to be saying; (2) the point in a given information complex that is misused or not understood, or not viewed correctly.

Information Forum: (1) the reality of what information is available in a given context; (2) the solidification of what information is to be made available in a given context—and in what terms; (3) a platform for information—or given information—that can or cannot be experienced by the greater public.

Information Integration: (1) solidifying given areas of information—regardless of thrust alignment or affinity nature; (2) bringing given continuums of information together.

Information Interpretation: the reality of attempting to deduce what a given idea or concept means—with respect to both that concept's principle information greater context, as well as its particular degrees.

Information Order: (1) the reality structure that underlies a given area of information; (2) the focus ingredient that establishes a given area of information; (3) "how" a given type of information is, and "how" it should be in its most correct alignment.

Information Projection: (1) this term refers to the actualness of a given viewpoint and what that viewpoint poses for its greater information multi-complex. In other words, a projection in this context is indicative of "one particular" manifestation of a given principle information complex; (2) that being, an actual example or particular of a principle information multi-complex.

Information Reality: (1) viewing the actualness of a given information concept with respect to its physical universe realness; (2) an informational example in concrete physical universe terms; (3) that being, "how a given information is" in the physical universe context of its existence.

Information Solidification: (1) bringing all aspects of a given focus (or set) of information particulars together; (2) completing the infrastructure of a given information continuum as a means to make it (the information) real—or correct; (3) the same as information integration (but in a more progressional sense).

Information Transference: the changing of information—either from person to person (whether vibrational or actual) or culture to culture.

Infra-Spirituality: (1) that being, the reality of spirituality as it involves the particulars of a given discipline; (2) how a given part of a particular discipline also has spiritual connotations; (3) finding the "god" of a given discipline or point of activism.

Infra-Structure Dynamics: (1) that being, the possibilities related to the particulars of a given system in terms of what the procedure of that discipline implies for other focus spectrums; (2) having to do with the ritual implications of a given participation—that being, every aspect of a given structure carries a physical universe and vibrational multi-implication.

Intellectualism: (1) having to do with the reality of ideas and the dynamics of inter-relationship seeded by the vibrational concern (or attraction) to what is perceived to be "interesting" or logically true, as opposed to what is spiritually true; (2) the reality of ideas without regard for its spiritual context; (3) the dynamics of concepts and isolated information focus with the intent to understand as separate from spiritual insight.

Intention: having to do with the reality of a given motive.

Interpretation: (1) having to do with extracting the meaning of a given phenomenon or information line; (2) the reality of providing the context and tools to receive insight into the state of a given phenomenon; (3) having to do with viewing what a given principle information line means or could mean for the beings in a given affinity focus—or spectrum; (4) having to do with providing insight into how a given spiritual and vibrational actualness can be solidified—and understood—on the physical universe level, and practiced.

Investigation Dictates: (1) the reality of correct observation as it relates to a particular focus; (2) the reality of perception dynamics as this concept involves establishing correct criteria for examination; (3) investigation with respect to the tenets of what is being investigated; (4) the reality of proper investigation as it involves procedure.

Isolated Activism: (1) participation with respect to the particulars of a given focus; (2) participation with respect to one or "whatever is defined" area of interest or focus, for the purpose of achieving a desired result; (3) participation that is practiced without respect for the composite physical or vibrational universe situation but instead is directed to deal with the immediacy of a particular (or particular set of) focus or focuses.

Isolated Focus: (1) that being, to view the "particulars" of a given phenomenon rather than the composite picture; (2) to focus on only certain aspects of a given phenomenon as a means to deal or not deal with that aspect.

Isolated Focus Activism: (1) that being, participation with respect to the interest of particular sectors or people, rather than the composite sector; (2) participation that is undertaken from the reality of a particular focus rather than a composite focus.

Isolated Focus Dictates: (1) the pedagogical structure underlying a given focus; (2) the reality of fundamental information that supports a given focus; (3) taking into account—in the perception of a given focus—its underlying information tenets; (4) the reality underlying how a given focus must be observed with respect to its fundamental support systems.

Isolated Particulars: (1) having to do with separating a given idea or focus from its principle information multi-focus as a basis to only deal with a given independent idea; (2) that being, a particular focus that is separated and viewed with respect to whatever the intentions of the viewer are.

Isolated Systematic Alignment: (1) that being, the independent logic systems which are solidified as a basis to view the particulars of a given focus—as opposed to an all-encompassing logic system; (2) the reality of linkage as it involves different isolated idea focuses (as made or viewed separately from its vibrational foundation).

Journalism Dynamics: the possibilities inherent in the reality of present-day journalism—involving its interpretation dynamics, its focus (or not focus) dynamics, its semantical dynamics, and its ability to profoundly affect the greater culture (both positively and negatively—especially negatively).

Language: (1) the reality of symbols as a basis to codify particulars; (2) the reality of symbols as a basis to transmit intention; (3) the reality of procedure as a basis to convey information.

Language Dynamics: (1) that being, the inherent possibilities that are related to the particulars of a given functionalism (or set of symbols) in terms of what can be successfully communicated through its particular use; (2) having to do with what the use of a given language poses for dynamic postulation as well as spiritual insight; (3) having to do with how a given communication discipline can also affect and determine the option-spread possibilities of the person or culture utilizing the discipline.

Linkage Implications: (1) the possibilities related to the coupling or inter-relationship of two phenomena and/or focuses; (2) the reality of possibilities as it relates to the coupling and/or inter-relationship of two different phenomena and/or focuses.

Logical Dissolution: (1) that being, the rational result of; (2) that being, the rational consequences of—as a result of using a particular technique and/or discipline or act; (3) in accordance to the context that has been defined—or dissolution in accordance to the context that has been defined.

Manipulation: (1) having to do with controlling the meaning of—or use of—how a given phenomenon is viewed or utilized; (2) having to do with the intention to utilize a given phenomenon in a way to achieve a desired result that is not necessarily related to what that same phenomenon would achieve if utilized differently; (3) the conscious use of materials and things as a means to solidify and/or establish a given result or results.

Media Dynamics: (1) the reality and vibrational dynamics related to how the media works; (2) how the media is, and how it can be; (3) the inherent possibilities related to the reality of accelerated information transference and its established institutions.

Meta-Implications: (1) vibrational related possibilities or consequences; (2) cosmic or vibrational relationships (and possibilities).

Meta-Reality: (1) the vibrational or cosmic "living" or "being" context of a given phenomenon; (2) a term that injects cosmic or spiritual being matters as a consideration not separate from what is being discussed; (3) having to do with the spiritual or vibrational weight of a given idea or focus.

Meta-Reality Significance: (1) the vibrational or spiritual meaning of a given postulation or focus; (2) having to do with what a given function or focus will ultimately mean in vibrational or spiritual terms.

Methodology: (1) the reality particulars of a given function or discipline; (2) the science of a given discipline and how to execute a given function; (3) how something is done and the discipline to make it happen again; (4) the spiritual and vibrational procedures necessary to gain insight into the "all motion" realness of the physical and vibrational universe; (5) the reality of doing in its most highest context with the establishment of ritual as the most correct or effective procedure to make a particular "thing" happen.

Mono-Dimensional: (1) the reality of one context or one observation plane; (2) a concept that has to do with viewing a given phenomenon in only one affinity and/or actual context; (3) the reality of a given phenomenon as it is viewed in only one or two (or a limited amount of) contexts—and in doing so moves to limit that phenomenon's affinity and/or actual life options and/or "being" options.

Motivation Dynamics: (1) the reality of intention as it applies to a participation; (2) the spectrum of intentions related to a given participation.

Multi-Dimensional: (1) many dimensions on many different levels; (2) dynamically complex and related to many different factors and/or contexts; (3) means more than only one interpretation and extends into many other areas, and things.

Multi-Information: (1) information that is not only about one particular focus but instead is relevant and meaningful on many different levels; (2) information—ideas and concepts—that have relevance on many different levels and/or focuses.

Multi-Informational Degree Basis: (1) a western information phenomenon that utilizes dynamic information in a way that enables a given word or statement to be utilized and interpreted in as many ways as is necessary for the real purpose to be actualized; (2) a phenomenon that helps to keep the reality of western information dynamics in constant motion.

Multi-Transfer Shift Activity: a concept that observes the different dynamic contexts which dictate the reality of a given discipline's effectiveness.

Multiple Diversification: (1) a term that comments as to the many different possibilities related to a given phenomenon; (2) a term that comments on a given phenomenon's dynamic possibilities as well as the realness that those possibilities are not limited to any one particular level.

Multiple Interpretation: (1) to decipher meaning on several different levels; (2) a term that comments on how a given focus is interpreted and on how many different levels.

Observation: (1) to view something; (2) the reality of viewing a phenomenon as a means to understand it (or some aspect of it).

Option Spread: (1) the opportunities available for a given person on the physical universe level; (2) the life pursuance possibilities of a given individual in terms of his ability to achieve either information, economic gain, cultural recognition, and/or cultural participation.

Participation: (1) the reality of "doing something"; (2) to be a part of and actively functioning; (3) the act of doing something.

Particular Focus: (1) a particular subject; (2) an isolated subject that is being viewed for whatever reason.

Particular Progressionalism: (1) an isolated continuum; (2) having to do with the reality of a given continuum of either information or people (culture) or vibrational "way of doing things."

Perceived Physical Universe Fundamental: that being the perception of a given discipline or focus as indicative of a fundamental or primary law that underlies how the all-motion dynamics of earth—and/or the heavens—are made "real" (or work).

Perception Dynamics: (1) the reality of observation with respect to the variables—and spectrum of possibilities—underlying a given way of looking at "things"; (2) the vibrational and "actual" factors that underlie a given observation context (or platform).

Physical Universe Context: (1) having to do with viewing a given phenomenon with respect to what that phenomenon reveals as it is made real in actual concrete terms; (2) in concrete terms or in "actual" context.

Physical Universe Fundamental: (1) a law that seems to be dynamically and cosmically related to how the actualness of this experience (living and the appearance of things as they seem to be and the realness of vibrations as it seems to be) is made real; (2) a law or discipline that expresses some aspect of how the physical universe is able to be as it is.

Physical Universe Particular: (1) that being, a focus or particular that can be viewed in concrete terms as a basis to participate in that context; (2) a given focus that is concrete with respect to the dimension we refer to as the physical universe.

Political Consciousness: (1) awareness of what is taking place in the reality of politics; (2) the awareness of what politics means—or could mean as an expression of dynamic spiritualism; (3) the awareness of politics and how given realities are solidified and/or maintained.

Political Dynamics: (1) the inherent possibilities that are related to the political context of a given physical universe space; (2) the related possibilities of a given political system as it concerns cultural option dynamics—spiritual dynamics, social dynamics, and particular focus dynamics.

Political Order: (1) the securing of a given political philosophy and reality posture and its actualization on the physical universe level; (2) establishing a given reality context in accordance to a given political system (or philosophy).

Political Policies: (1) involves the reality of what laws are established in a given political state; (2) involves the particulars of a given political system as it relates to what is viewed as correct, positive and beneficial, as opposed to what is labeled negative, not correct and "against the state."

Political Significance: (1) has to do with what a given action poses to the reality of the political arena it takes place in; (2) has to do with what a given postulation poses to the reality of its given political space; (3) has to do with the reality of "meaning" as it relates to political tenets and/or dynamics.

Political State: that being the reality of politics as it shapes the particulars of its culture's actual living.

Postulation: (1) the act of bringing something forth as in expressing an idea or a feeling; (2) the reality of what one aspires to and works towards—that being the creation of an objective and/or focus that did not exist before; (3) the phenomenon of vibrationally expressing the actualness of a given phenomenon from one's own affinity particulars (or culture affinity particulars); (4) the expression of a cosmic and/or vibrational dictate that is manifested and/or made real through dynamic existence—as in "doing" or "movement."

Primary Affinity Tendencies: (1) a concept that views the reality of vibrational postulation with respect to (a) what is called traditionalism, (b) stylism, and (c) restructuralism.

Primary Intention: (1) the basic motivation of; (2) what a given phenomenon really makes happen when utilized and the purpose behind who decides whether it is to be utilized (or explored) or not.

Progressional Continuance: (1) a term that views physical universe reality changes and/or events with respect to sequential time blocks and/or parameters (and/or time cycles); (2) looking at given time periods with respect to blocks of tendencies (and/or variables) as a basis to view the world expansion principle.

Progressional Extended Functionalism: (1) the phenomenon of viewing a given discipline and/or science and how it moves into greater areas of its dynamics; (2) the reality continuance of advanced discipline in its own right (that is, how a given advanced discipline has continued its existence as separate from the composite arena of a given continuum and/or discipline).

Progressional Significance: (1) the meaning and/or value of a given phenomenon as that phenomenon advances different time periods; (2) the reality of change and the reality of a given phenomenon's significance as it advances through change cycles and/or time periods.

Progressional Transfer Cycles: a concept that refers to those periods in time which are conducive to or "about" the interchange of composite information and/or information dynamics.

Projection: (1) a term that is used to comment on information off-shoots as it involves ideas and concept lines from a principle information continuum; (2) a style or isolated information focus continuum; (3) in music, "projection" is my word for style or music type.

Projectional Continuance: (1) the continuation of a given style of idea type focus throughout a given time period or periods; (2) the use or realness of a given projection in the larger context of time or time changes.

Projectional Dynamics: (1) the diversity or possibilities related and/or based from the reality of a given projection; (2) the possibilities connected to a given projection; (3) a term to comment on the spiritual dictates related to the particulars of a given discipline, and what those dictates translate into as actual and/or vibrational terms.

Race: (1) the compilation of a people in a given physical universe space for an extended period in time to the degree that their physical traits and affinity spectrum traits move to affirm a particular identity; (2) the vibrational attraction phenomenon that underlies a given group of people with respect to their affinity dynamic dictates and destiny; (3) an applied precept concerning the reality of isolated particulars as this concept involves the family of humanity and existence; (4) the dynamic realization and/or actualization of affinity dynamics—as made real in human beings and/or all living things (and non-so-called living things) that expresses some or all aspects of the cosmic realness of "it" and/or "is" and/or "this."

Reality Alignment: (1) the physical universe application or view of; (2) the physical universe context and use of; (3) viewing a given phenomenon with respect to what that phenomenon would mean on the physical universe level—if utilized, or as a context to view from.

Reality Dynamics: (1) the possibilities or diverse particulars of a given physical universe situation; (2) the related possibilities of a given physical universe context.

Reality Implications: (1) the related information and/or phenomenon possibilities to a given physical universe situation; (2) what a given physical universe situation poses for extended circumstances.

Reality Initiative Traits: (1) what is most common to the reality of postulation as it concerns a particular physical universe space; (2) the "way of doing things" in a given physical universe space and/or culture.

Reality Options: (1) that being, the opportunities or avenues of participation in a given physical universe space and/or culture; (2) having to do with what living opportunities are available for a person or persons in a given physical universe context.

Recontinuance: (1) the continuance of a given phenomenon that seemingly was not there before; (2) the re-appearance of a given "way of doing things" or "viewpoint"—"law system"—that seemingly was not there before; (3) a cosmic phenomenon that underlies how given areas of information (or "things") are brought into and out of being in accordance to factors that have nothing to do with what we know about.

Redefinitions: (1) giving a definition and new definition; (2) changing the meaning of a given definition and/or focus.

Redocumentation: (1) changing what is documented; (2) either rewriting or correcting what has been documented.

Related Procedure: (1) a term used in the integration schematics to denote that a given combination of terms should be utilized at that point in its solidification; (2) a term to denote the usage of a given set of variables in the information schematic.

Relevant Application: (1) the reality of what is "most real" to a given application; (2) application with respect to the cosmic dictates of positive utilization; (3) application with respect to what is most effective.

Relevant Technology: (1) technology that is solidified in accordance to spiritual and dynamic dictates; (2) the use of technology with respect to what is "most" (for humanity) about that technology; (3) technology that is related to what one professes to be about—or would like to be about (both dynamically and spiritually).

Restructuralism: (1) the reality of realigning how a given system or structure works; (2) changing the surface particulars of a given structure but keeping the fundamentals that gave that structure its laws; (3) changing the particulars of a system as well as its dictates.

Responsibility Ratio: having to do with what extent and/or degree a given person or culture is to be held accountable for the reality and/or particulars of a given focus and/or discipline and/or reality; (2) the spectrum of an individual's responsibility in a given context.

Retrograde Affinity Tendencies: that being, those vibrational urges which, if allowed, would pursue their particulars in focuses that are considered in the past.

Ritual Dynamics: (1) the possibilities and diverse particulars related to the use of a given ritual; (2) the dynamic possibilities that underlie what a given ritual is or does or makes happen.

Scientific Dynamics: (1) the possibilities and/or particular discoveries that are related to a given use or reality of science; (2) the particulars related to a given type of area or science.

Self-Realization: (1) having to do with the individual becoming aware of who he or she really is—as made real through both physical universe particulars and spiritual insight; (2) spiritual discovery.

Social Programs: (1) organizations established to help uplift given aspects of social reality; (2) organizations for bringing about positive changes—and participation—in social reality.

Social Reality: (1) the particulars related to events on the physical universe level; (2) the "way of life" on the physical universe level as it involves living and functioning in a given space.

Social Reality Development: (1) the reality of bringing about positive reforms in social reality; (2) positive participation—or effect—for a given social reality context (or sector).

Social Reality Dynamics: (1) the possibilities and particulars related to a given social reality context and/or physical universe context; (2) the particulars related to what and how a given social reality space is—as far as achievement possibilities and/or postulation possibilities.

Social Reality Interpretation: (1) "meanings" that have solidified in a given social reality context (that have been accepted) for the greater culture; (2) the meanings that are to be accepted in a given social reality context.

Social Reality Particular(s): (1) the actualness of a given focus or focuses that is related to—or draws its ability to be from—its social reality context; (2) that being, the reality of a given focus as that focus is made real from its social reality basis.

Source Initiation: (1) the point and/or reality from which a given initiation solidifies; (2) the reality concerning when a given particular solidifies.

Source Projection: (1) a style or language that has solidified from its historical continuum; (2) an information line that has come into being from its greater information basis; (3) a term that views a given style or focus with respect to its greater continuum position (as related to either principle information or historical point of solidification).

Source Shift: (1) the phenomenon of a given continuum (that being "reality or way of doing things") suddenly realigning its path or "surface nature"; (2) the phenomenon of a projection changing its path and taking the attributes of another continuum; (3) having to do with the phenomenon of two or more continuums entering into a "time or cosmic" cycle whereby either one or all of the continuums will attach it or their self to the "particulars" of the other, and proceed from that point.

Source Transfer: (1) the phenomenon of a given continuum—or documented continuum which is more accurate—adopting tenets and/or particulars from another continuum; (2) the point of a continuum change of information and/or particulars; (3) the phenomenon of a continuum adopting or simply taking the attributes (and way of being) of other continuums.

Spectacle Diversion: (1) a concept involving the rotation of a culture's information dynamics and/or forces as a means to have "people involved" but not involved in "something"; (2) rotating "information dynamics" as a phenomenon to give the impression of either "high culture" or "real involvement."

Spiritual Awareness: (1) the act of having some insight as to the reality of spiritualness and/or spiritual dynamics; (2) understanding something about spiritualism, and what is real "for the person" understanding.

Spiritual Dynamics: (1) the reality of possibilities and/or "things" that are related to or brought about from spiritualism; (2) having to do with what can happen through spirituality.

Spiritual Growth: "becoming" as made real through learning about and "being in" a spiritual state or trying to be in a spiritual state—or "becoming" because of one's relationship to spiritualism.

Spiritual Unification: (1) the bringing together of concrete and abstract information and affinity dynamics as a means to "be" in accordance to "greater forces"—or as a means to solidify the proper platform for real "insight"; (2) the bringing together of all religions as a means to establish a composite "all religion."

Style: (1) the appearance of a projection or "way to be"; (2) the reality of a particular interpretation line as that line is actualized into physicality; (3) the manifestation of a particular information dynamic focus into concrete terms; (4) the reality of "ways to be" as it involves actualizing the particulars of a proven information and/or vibrational continuum.

Technological (or Technology) Dynamics: (1) the reality of possibilities—or variables—related to a given functionalism (or related to composite technology); (2) the vibrational and "actual" dynamics related to a given technology (or to composite technology—with respect to its composite position in "all information").

Terminology: (1) the reality of a definition; (2) the reality of how a given language is made real and for what reason; (3) the reality of a given definition as it is made real from its vibrational and/or spiritual base.

Theoretical Science: (1) the reality of ideas as a focus to dynamic methodology for extended functionalism and/or scientific discipline.

Thrust Affinity Alignment: (1) That being, the reality of a given continuum (vibrational and physical universe) way of being; (2) the dynamics of a particular continuum and how it is constructed.

Thrust Continuance: (1) the time advancement or advancing reality of a composite continuum or vibrational and empirical continuum; (2) the reality of a continuum as it advances through time.

Thrust Continuance Dynamics: (1) the dynamic possibilities related to a given continuum as it moves through time—in terms of that continuum's information order and/or vibrational alignment.

Time Continuance Implications: (1) having to do with what results to a given phenomenon in the course of a particular time cycle and/or progression; (2) the possibilities related to a given phenomenon in a given period of time.

Time Lag: (1) the phenomenon of a given particular and/or focus as viewed past the interpretation dynamics of its allotted or designated time period; (2) the reality of a given phenomenon when viewed after the time cycle that made it real; (3) the effects of a given phenomenon and/or focus when viewed and/or perceived past its actual time parameter.

Time Presence: (1) the phenomenon of participation with respect to and awareness of the reality of "actualness" and what that means with regards to events in time and moment awareness; (2) "doing" with respect to (and awareness of) the vibrational realness of the moments in that "doing"—as that "doing" relates to what we call time and what we call motion; (3) the spiritualness of "doing" and also the related vibrational dynamics of "all motion" (or "actual motion").

Trans-Definition: (1) an interpretation that carries over different time periods and/or so-called culture groups; (2) an interpretation that actualizes cosmic significances and as such cannot be simply ignored or stopped because of physical universe particulars or information dynamics.

Transformation: (1) a concept that involves total physical and vibrational universe change; (2) the close of a given or particular physical and vibrational universe cycle and the beginning of the next.

Trans-Information: (1) information that spans physical universe territories, having to do with the laws of this "state" and the experiencing of this "state"; (2) information that is universal and "all real"—regardless of time or culture; (3) information that is not about a given culture and/or focus but instead is cosmically directed because it is "real."

Transition: (1) the change of a given and/or particular state in terms of its surface information and/or focus dynamics—but not its total "beingness"; (2) the change of some aspects of a given physical universe and/or vibrational universe state.

Underlying Philosophical Basis: (1) the reality of a given phenomenon's idea and focus bases—having to do with viewing the factors which support what a given information interpretation means, or is supposed to mean.

Unification: (1) the affinity solidification of humanity as a means to live in accordance to the dictates of dynamic spiritualism; (2) the actual and/or vibrational bringing together of a given phenomenon; (3) a state of composite intentions.

Utilization: (1) the use of a given terminology mix in the information schematics; (2) in other words, the point in the schematics where the given terms should be utilized.

Value System: (1) the ethical and spiritual weight of a particular focus or participation; (2) the reality of a given focus with respect to whether its implementation advances the particulars of spiritual well-being and positive composite well-being, or not; (3) the reality of a given "state of being" and/or phenomenon as evaluated with respect to its assignment and/or desired assignment.

Vibrational Affinity and/or Attitude: (1) the reality of a vibrational state with respect for how a given attitude colors what can or can't be achieved or completed; (2) the reality of given feelings and what those feelings mean in actual terms—as far as whether or not a given objective can be achieved or understood.

Vibrational Attitude: (1) that being, the real attitude before the "words," or before the particular focus that the attitude is directed on; (2) the "way" of a particular vibrational way of being.

Vibrational Dynamics: (1) the possibilities and diverse focuses related to a given vibrational "way of being" (or way of "not" being).

Vibrational Implications: (1) the related possibilities and "things" connected to a given vibrational state and/or position that aren't necessarily connected to the basic focus or reality "stuff" of what that vibration really is—when viewed in its separate state and/or basic reality tone—but can be activated if that vibrational state is utilized or not utilized correctly.

Vibrational Platform: (1) having to do with utilizing the reality of a particular vibrational position as a basis from which to mount either a participation or a focus; (2) the reality of basing an assumption and/or action from a particular vibrational focus—or focuses.

Vibrational Postulation: (1) the same as affinity postulation but not as "deep"; (2) the same as affinity postulation but semantically having less to do with an individual's vibrational and affinity nature and more to do with the act of postulation as this phenomenon happens with respect to other factors (e.g., like the greater culture).

Vibrational Science: (1) that being, the reality of mystical or high spiritual or vibrational (e.g., music or what is called art) discipline with respect to its law position or moving to understand its law position—as made real through multi-information dynamics and high spiritualism; (2) observation and participation in vibrational discipline as that discipline unfolds some aspect of the dynamic functionalism and/or order of the universe (or what we call the universe); (3) vibrationally doing as a means to cosmically grow and love.

Vibrational Tendencies: (1) the reality of possibilities—or attractions—as related to vibrational dynamics; having to do with postulation or "vibrational reception"; (2) the reality of vibrational tendencies as related to the individual (i.e., see individual vibrational tendencies) or environment—or focus dictates.

Vibrational Universe Particulars: (1) the reality of a given focus that is seeded in vibrational terms; (2) the reality of a given focus as it unfolds some aspect of its vibrational universe dynamics.

World Change: (1) the re-alignment of earth in terms of how people live and how people perceive of living—and the reality of postulation and participation.

World Expansion Principle: (1) the reality of change as it affirms the dynamic particulars underlying composite physical universe change.

World Methodology: (1) the reality of a given procedure when viewed in its greater context; (2) a term to underline that a given focus or particular cannot be viewed as the result of one or two countries but, instead, is the property of or related to composite humanity.

World Unification: (1) bringing people and "things" together—harmony with what the "experience of living could mean" in its most positive state.

www.ingramcontent.com/pod-product-compliance
Lightning Source LLC
Chambersburg PA
CBHW071850290426
44110CB00013B/1088